S0-BFA-424

CLINICAL
AND
SOCIAL
REALITIES

CLINICAL AND SOCIAL REALITIES

by

Donald M. Kaplan, Ph.D.

edited by

Louise J. Kaplan, Ph.D.

JASON ARONSON INC.
Northvale, New Jersey
London

Production Editor: Elaine Lindenblatt

This book was set in 10 point Palacio by TechType of Upper Saddle River, New Jersey, and printed and bound by Book-mart Press of North Bergen, New Jersey.

Copyright © 1995 by Jason Aronson Inc.

10 9 8 7 6 5 4 3 2 1

All rights reserved. Printed in the United States of America. No part of this book may be used or reproduced in any manner whatsoever without written permission from Jason Aronson Inc. except in the case of brief quotations in reviews for inclusion in a magazine, newspaper, or broadcast.

Library of Congress Cataloging-in-Publication Data

Kaplan, Donald M., 1927–1994
  Clinical and social realities / by Donald M. Kaplan ; edited by Louise J. Kaplan.
    p. cm.
  Articles by Donald M. Kaplan reprinted from various sources.
  Includes bibliographical references and index.
  ISBN 1-56821-472-3
  1. Psychoanalysis. 2. Psychoanalysis and culture. I. Kaplan, Louise J. II. Title.
  DNLM: 1. Psychoanalysis–collected works.WM 460 K165c 1995]
RC509.K37 1995
616.89′17–dc20
DNLM/DLC
for Library of Congress   95-1285

Manufactured in the United States of America. Jason Aronson Inc. offers books and cassettes. For information and catalog write to Jason Aronson Inc., 230 Livingston Street, Northvale, New Jersey 07647.

*. . . born of the sun, they travelled a short while toward the sun
and left the vivid air signed with their honour.*

—Stephen Spender

❦

Donald Kaplan's individual mark was on everything he did. In his public presentations, in the papers, in his private conversations there were echoes of the Bronx, extravagant epigrammatic elegance, jokes that were sometimes mischievous and sometimes gave resonant illumination to his ideas and formulations, but at the core a seriousness of discourse that came from his long and intense devotion to the psychoanalytic precincts of the life of the mind. It was the address where he most truly resided.

—Aaron Coleman, M.D.*

*Reprinted from *The International Journal of Psycho-Analysis*, Summer, 1995, and used by permission.

CONTENTS

FOREWORD*

Donald Martin Kaplan was born on May 8, 1927 in the borough of the Bronx in the city of New York. He died at one o'clock on a sunny Tuesday afternoon on September 20, 1994 in Greenwich Village, across the street from his home and office and family. Each was deeply invested with his great passion of mind and heart.

Donald was a lyricist and dramatist. His psychoanalytic mind was sparked by the great dramas of human existence. He loved Shakespeare; and so it is a good place in which to begin to remember him:

And when he shall die
Take him, and cut him out in little stars.
And he will make the face of heaven so fine,
That all the world will be in love with night,
And pay no worship to the garish sun.

Donald was a great light. He was a wonderful friend. He was a prince. The prince spreads his light upon his world. He brings youth, optimism, generosity of spirit and the promise of the reclamation of the kingdom from agedness and narrowed purpose. The double shock of Donald's death comes from his unfailing youthfulness.

Freud's ideas and ethical quest were Donald's passion and his

*The tributes by Mark Grunes and Maynard Solomon that follow were printed in *American Imago*, vol. 52, no. 1, pp. 1–4, copyright © 1995 by The Johns Hopkins University Press. Grunes's remarks were first given at a service on November 20, 1994–"Celebrating, Remembering: A Memorial for Donald M. Kaplan"–at the NYU Postdoctoral Program in Psychotherapy and Psychoanalysis.

love—never his fetish. Like Freud, Donald understood the difference between Krafft-Ebing and Sophocles. Donald's understanding of human motivation was deeply informed by the drama of those great, overarching structures of the mind—ideals and morality, Eros and Thanatos.

The dynamics of the Freudian landscape—the Oedipus complex, family romance, transference, and the unconscious—were the stuff of everyday life for Donald, suffused with realness, continuously alive, and amazingly immune to dilution and repression. He could entrance students with a heart-leaping account of his oedipal love affair, at age five, with a gorgeous maternal aunt.

Donald was a great reader, writer, and speaker. His combination of penetrating intellect and scholarship with wit, elegant style, and autobiographical entertainments could be delightfully absorbing, His productivity, too, was impressive. During his lifetime, in addition to thirty years of continuous psychoanalytic teaching, he made more than fifty professional presentations, published more than forty papers, and wrote more than eighty book reviews and popular articles.

Donald's mind had wings. He suffused our familiar concepts with depth and a sense of infinite thematic variation. He could evoke surprise and pleasure with paradox and juxtaposition. Here in a discussion of narcissism he describes the "narcissistic gratification of meeting obligations of social realities, which originate in the contingencies of early interaction with parental authorities."

His mind could be epigrammatic and dramatic. In describing one of his patients he spoke of "idle tears as passive incontinence."

Donald had a gift for psychoanalytic portraiture. Here he speaks of a patient and her mother and deals evocatively with complex matters of identity, identification, and development of the self. "She [the patient] evinced signs of a whole other life, poignantly suppressed within the mother, but nevertheless available to her child as a basis for the development of yet another self-object scenario."

Here is one of his perspicuous observations upon the pathology of the moral life: ". . . a manifest compliance with the means of the analysis to maintain a buoyant defiance of its possible ends—a monument of defiance wrought in a spirit of virtue."

In one of his early papers Donald wittily described the masochistic function of depression: ". . . the felt suffering in the present is a provisional alternative to the supplies forthcoming in an indefinite future. A depression is a parody of the virtue of passive waiting."

Donald was eminently classical in his work with patients. He was never orthodox. Here he is on the subject of abstinence in a 1967 article in *Harper's* magazine:

> The rule is that abstinence should be no more nor less than the patient can tolerate. The dosing of this abstinence—how little, how much—is a matter of the analyst's humanity and courage. The cruel truth is that there is no certainty about abstinence. Each day is a fresh struggle to reduce the error in the analyst's estimation of what the patient is able to stand. . . . Typical abuses can include answering a question with a question too often. The patient might be sent away in the middle of a sentence, as not a minute longer than the agreed-upon time is conceded. None of the patient's jokes are responded to. A slip of the tongue becomes an occasion for ruthless probing, as though a butterfly is about to be assaulted with a sledgehammer.

On a more personal note, Donald and I first met in 1946 at the City College of New York in a Latin class. We then spent a year together in classes in the Romantic and Victorian poets. Donald in all things was a classicist in the best sense of the word. He had a love of and a gift for leanness and economy. He had no patience with falsification or superfluous bric-a-brac. In all things of mind and person Donald knew the proper fitness and proportion of things. He understood the importance of clear distinctions. On one occasion I must have released some animosity toward someone close to me, and elevated someone we both regarded as much less worthy. Donald instructed me, "Mark, you don't hate your friends and love your enemies. You're supposed to love your friends and hate your enemies."

Donald understood neurosis profoundly partly because he so disliked its waste of life. He loved to think, but he was one of the most unobsessional people I have ever known. He gave those who knew him a great gift of participation in his love of action and activity.

In the summer of 1969 a congress of the International Psychoanalytic Association was being held for the first time in Rome. One spring day Donald suddenly said, "Let's go to Rome. We'll have a great time." So we all went to Rome. It was as if we simply got on the plane and just went. There was no discussion, no deliberation, no rumination. And we did have a great time. And there were lots of great times wherever Donald was.

Donald was a person of extraordinary decency and generosity—to his family, to his friends, to his students and patients. Most of all he gave us and shared the vitality of his spirit and his love of life. His inclusion of others in this spirit was a great part of its delight and vitality. He was a person of great personal authenticity. He was capable of deep sentiment, but he hated sentimentality, as he hated hypocrisy.

There was not a mean bone in Donald's body. He could cut you quickly and deeply if angered or offended. But I never knew him to take any pleasure in inflicting pain or in exacting tribute.

Donald was a man of incredible range—of incredibly many parts. To everything he loved he brought his love of thought, of action, and of play—theater and drama, literature, poetry, jazz and the popular music of the forties and fifties, movies, baseball, poker, tap dancing, joke telling, letter writing, the art of the casual phone call, and conversation.

Donald lived every day of his life to the fullest. He seemed to love and enjoy everything he chose to do. He knew better than anyone I have ever known that the purpose of life was living. He always looked everything full in the face. He knew what was good. He knew what was bad. He knew when to begin, and he knew when to end.

Donald Kaplan was beyond compare. He was a joy and a treasure. There will never be another like him.

Mark Grunes
New York, NY

❦

With the death of Donald M. Kaplan on September 20, 1994, *American Imago* lost a valued and beloved editor, contributor, and friend.

Donald Kaplan was an eloquent advocate of applied psychoanalysis in our time. He burst upon the scene in a series of much-discussed papers on theater which appeared in the pages of *Tulane Drama Review* in the 1960s, throwing open for psychoanalytic inspection such varied issues as stage fright, homosexuality in the American theater, and the symbolic implications of stage architecture. Art and artists were—and remained—at the center of his interests, both as a psychoanalyst in private practice and as a practitioner of Freudian criticism. Walking in the tradition of Lionel Trilling, with whom he had studied at Columbia University, he saw art as a regenerative force, as bearing upon "the restoration of morality"; in "Character and Theatre: Psychoanalytic Notes on Modern Realism," in 1966, he wrote, "art continues to find eloquence for our suffering, heraldry for our strife, lyricism for our passion."

From the fall of 1967 until his death Donald was an Associate Editor of *American Imago*, helping to guide its editorial direction, evaluating manuscripts, and giving freely of his time and knowledge. His contributions illustrated the extraordinary range of his interests, from an erudite and informed discussion of K. R. Eissler's concept of the special communicative functions of art (which Eissler termed the "Doxaletheic Function") to reflections upon the close historical intertwinings of psychoanalysis and surrealism. His affectionate memoirs of two mentors, Theodor Reik and Harry Slochower, published in these pages, are small masterpieces of characterization and anecdotal reportage, showing at their best Donald's gifts as a literary artist in his own right. In papers for *American Imago* and other psychoanalytic journals he also dealt with more abstract and metapsychological issues—the crucial distinctions between creativity and neurosis, the suggestive similarities of art-object and transitional object, analogies between psychological modalities and artistic forms. His final study in applied psychoanalytic theory, "What is Sublimated in Sublimation?," pondered the anomaly that in many psychoanalyses, "the work of art in its own right becomes what might be called a nonsubject," and he came to believe that "an analysis of an artist is largely about rescuing . . . the life of art from the infiltrations of symptoms in the artist's ordinary life." He was well aware of the fragmentary nature of psychoanalytic interpretations of creative works; in a splendid paper entitled "The Psychoanalysis of Art: Some Ends, Some Means," he wrote, "My point is that depending on one's ingenuity and psychoanalytic interest, there are no limits to what can be analogized." But, far from sounding a retreat, this only stimulated Donald to reflect upon the teeming diversity of psychoanalytic models that potentially could illuminate the meanings of art. Despite all difficulties inherent in any analysis that operates beyond the bounds of the basic rule, he insisted on the unique value of psychoanalytic interpretations of art: "Psychoanalysis makes its invaluable contribution to art; it brings to the inevitable act of interpretation a highly special and cunning slant on life as it is lived in its disunities, trivialities, incidentals to which it restores the momentousness lost to defense and compromise."

Donald Kaplan's untimely death has deprived us of a keen mind, a sensitive artist, a gifted psychoanalyst, and a grand colleague—who will be mourned and remembered.

Maynard Solomon
New York, NY

PART I

Clinical Realities

1

The Unfinished Manuscript in the Drawer

I arise in the morning torn between a desire to improve (or save) the world and a desire to enjoy (or savor) the world. This makes it hard to plan the day.

— E. B. White

The individual does actually carry on a twofold existence; one to serve his own purposes and the other as a link in a chain, which he serves against his will, or at least involuntarily. The individual himself regards sexuality as one of his own ends; whereas from another point of view he is an appendage to his germ-plasm, at whose disposal he puts his energies in return for a bonus of pleasure.

— Freud [1914, p. 78]

The observation by E. B. White reminds us of our ordinary susceptibility to experience life on a daily basis as a contention of aims, each with its own appeal. The epigraph from Freud's study of narcissism is a psychoanalytic reflection on such dilemmas. Freud, too, is referring to the pursuit of conflicting ideals—conflicting because ideals can entail pleasure. One ideal has to do with the fulfillment of what one deems purely personal ends, and the other with the narcissistic gratification of meeting the obligations of social realities, which originate in the contingencies of early interactions with parental authority. Thus the concept of narcissism provided understanding of the incentives, over and beyond the threats of authority, for modifying libidinal gratification in deference to the reality principle.

Psychopathology, often in the form of inhibitions and obsessional postponements of particular plans and projects, is a vicissitude of such ordinary dilemmas (Kaplan 1993). However, not all patients presenting apparent work inhibitions fit a single diagnostic category. To treat an inhibition as though it were a symptom can be a costly mistake with certain analysands whose unconscious aims regarding specific projects can lure analytic therapy onto some of its most drawn-out courses. These are patients whose procrastinations about a particular undertaking eventually lead to a conviction that one life is being lived provisionally at the expense of another. Such patients are apt to exploit the clinical situation as an extended reprieve from having to come to a decision about something that has been nagging them for years. I will be presenting a case involving an unfinished literary project that had already consumed fourteen years of the life of a patient in her early forties. One of the hazards with such cases is that the analysis itself can go on to acquire a design analogous to the unfinished project. When an unspoken assumption begins to hold sway to the effect that the analysis must continue as long as it takes the analysand to accomplish some task or other, the analyst may lose sight of the differences between treatment goals and life goals (Ticho 1972).

A few examples of drawn-out undertakings from accounts other than clinical psychoanalysis will suggest how common a state of affairs we shall be looking into. From *The New York Times Book Review*, one story has to do with the author Henry Roth, "as famous for his agonizing case of writer's block as for his legendary novel *Call It Sleep*" (Michaels 1993, p. 3). Roth, at 87, had not yet brought out his second novel, which appeared and then disappeared rather anticlimactically in 1994, over 60 years after his celebrated first novel. *Call It Sleep* was published when he was 28 years old. When the novel was issued in paperback, it sold over a million copies. Roth, who remained committed to literary work, eked out a few inconsequential short publications from among thousands of pages of scribbling. In fact, most of his readers have long thought him dead. (Roth referred to himself as the dead writer.) Among the personal conflicts over writing that he is able to describe, a political crisis figures. As though needing to acquit himself of the personal success of *Call It Sleep*, Roth, then a Communist, wanted to follow this up with a "proletarian novel," which he was unable to write because whatever he thought this entailed, it conflicted with his Jewish literary voice. In the long meantime, he kept himself going in a succession of jobs—factory worker, farmer, hospital attendant. From his present vantage, Roth regrets not having adopted someone like Picasso as an example. In regard to his painting (and much else besides), Picasso had a take-it-or-leave-it attitude. He declared himself sympathetic to the Communist cause, but his style was anything but Socialist Realism. Though the ideological terms of Roth's personal crisis changed over time, he could never find his way out of his meanderings among divided ideals, whatever they were.

In *The Times* story, he describes his whole existence as "tormented," and he is anguished that he lived the wrong life—he should never have been a writer. Here, too, in Roth's literary inhibitions, the psychoanalyst surmises certain psychological advantages, tragic though their outcome is in this instance; for example, if (personal) success is the equivalent of (political) transgression, ongoing bondage to an unattainable ideal—a Great Lost Cause—can keep one's moral accounts interminably balanced.

Ralph Ellison, who is well known for his first and only novel *Invisible Man*, has been at work on a second novel for the past forty-two years—since the early 1950s. Ellison spends his days in a modest apartment overlooking the Hudson River, where he sits down routinely in the late mornings to push on from his previous day's efforts with this manuscript. " 'Very often I'll start in the morning by looking back at the work from the day before and it ain't worth a damn.' When that happens, as it does more frequently than he would like, Ellison will turn away and stare out of the window, watching the river flow" (Remnick 1994, p. 34). Though he reports a piece of very bad luck in the early 1970s when a large number of manuscript pages were burned in a fire in his summer house, this was over twenty years ago. Following a period of five or six years of literary idleness, Ellison has since been unable to recover anything of the book from his original intentions and memories of it. At this writing, Ellison has turned 80 and warns his colleagues that as far as his literary career is concerned, what's done may be done.

Finally, I will mention Henry James's marvelous short story on the subject of stalled undertakings called "The Madonna of the Future" (1873). Briefly, this is a story about the encounter of an American tourist in Florence, Italy and a resident "painter," who tantalizes the tourist with descriptions of a painting of the Madonna he has been working on in his studio for an unspecified extent of time. As the relationship between the two men becomes more familiar, the painter invites the tourist to visit the woman who has been the model for this alleged masterpiece. The tourist is appalled to discover that this woman is no longer the youth the painter has described, and he forces this perception on the painter, who seems to have been completely unaware of the fact. The American, who narrates the story, tells us, "The poor fellow's sense of wasted time, of vanished opportunity, surged in upon his soul in waves of darkness" (p. 195) in the painter's realization that twenty years have passed "like a twelvemonth." The painter vows to complete the painting within the next two weeks. The narrator then visits the painter's studio to look at the progress of the Madonna thus far and is by that point not surprised that the reputed canvas is merely blank and discolored by time. "The whole scene savored horribly of indigence," the narrator tells us (p. 203). The painter is again overcome by further realizations, in the midst of which he exclaims, "I wasted my life in preparation." With a prescient clinical acumen, the narrator counsels him "about his being ill and needing advice and care."

Variations of struggles with consuming but failed projects, such as those of Roth, Ellison, and the painter in James's story, are familiar to psychoanalysts, who are often called upon to modify the course of things long before such catastrophic outcomes. In these cases, settlements of conflicts of object loyalty and aggression are postponed in nerve-wracking passages of time, which acquire the significance of unending devotions to virtue. These are patients who, owing to a certain pathology of the moral life, never seem to get their acts together.

In the clinical account that follows, I will be highlighting the pathogenesis of a stalled literary project and its fate in the course of analytic therapy. I am preparing to single out a few relevant principles for their technical value in such cases. One of these has to do with the matter of time and its implications in a psychopathology of the moral life; the patient's moral masochism is a particular hazard for the analyst, who must be wary of joining a cause that simulates virtue while ravaging the future of the patient. Regarding the history of the patient and its manifestations in the analysis, I will be directing my report to a pathogenesis of identifications with conflicted ideals of the parents and various subversions of these identifications, which figure among the secondary gains of the symptoms.

THE CASE OF MISS A
AND THE UNFINISHED MANUSCRIPT
IN THE DRAWER

Miss A, a widely published writer of topical magazine articles and book reviews, was in her early forties when she entered my practice with a list of complaints that amounted, as she put it, to her having come to the end of her rope. Her principal complaint had to do with an unfinished novel that she had been wrestling with for the past fourteen years. This was to be her second novel; she had already published a novel when she was in her late twenties, a more modest work than the one that preoccupied her.

Miss A was referred by a colleague with whom she had been in analysis for the two previous years, the last four or five months of which had been mired in an impasse that became insurmountable. In connection with the referral, my colleague explained that despite his efforts, the patient remained rigidly obsessed with similarities between himself and certain demoralizing characteristics of her mother. When they agreed on the measure of her getting off the couch and talking face-to-face, they soon found themselves exploring in earnest the plausibility of her continuing her analysis with another analyst. In the two years Miss A had been in therapy, she had made a number of gains, which included considerable relief from a painful and socially limiting erythrophobia. Still, all things considered, my colleague thought it best to refer Miss A, albeit with regrets on both their parts.

Miss A was a strikingly pretty woman, who dressed with great care in a variety of styles from gym clothes to designer dresses. Though she spoke in a soft, plaintive voice, she was able to register a broad range of affect. She was good-humored and good-natured and tried to assume responsibility for much of the adversity she described. She remarked that she was given easily to idle tears and reported weeping at stray scenes in movies and even television commercials. (The idea of these idle tears as a passive incontinence barely crossed my mind, though it could have been an early signal of the defiance and opposition that was being expressed in Miss A's cultivation of the image of a compliant and responsible Good Little Girl.) On the other hand, she could be quite declarative when she wanted something, such as an improvement in her traveling or hotel arrangements or a higher speaking fee or a change in her appointment time. She attributed her recent ability for registering straightforward requests to her previous analytic experience.

Miss A was the one member of her family who pursued a literary career, which was a definite prospect early on in her life in view of her precocious verbal attainments that evoked encouragement from her elementary-school teachers and eventually from her English professors. Part of her cultural ambitions came from her mother, who spoke with some bitterness of having had ambitions to paint, which she abandoned when she married at an early age and began to raise a family. Miss A's mother continued to keep a hand in the art world and traveled from Baltimore to New York City to visit museums and galleries. Otherwise Miss A regarded her mother as a severe realist, who had looked after all of the household details commandingly.

Miss A also noted that it was hard to get any comfort from her mother, because when you went to her with distress of any kind, she always had some bright idea about something you should do to improve matters, a definite plan of action; this only put more weight on your shoulders; therefore it was easier to bear distress alone. Her mother would even burden her in connection with happy events. For example, in her late twenties, Miss A had published a novel, and in the midst of celebrating the first positive reviews, Miss A's mother, at the other end of the phone, complained that the type on the book jacket was too large and insisted that Miss A make a note of this, so that it could be remedied when the paperback edition came out. "It may not be fair, but this was one of the reasons I got into the jam with Dr. C [her first analyst]. He had the same kind of 'yes, but' attitude as my mother."

While a financial success in commercial real estate, Miss A's father always protested that this life was beneath him. Within the family, he was aloof and rather histrionic. As Miss A described him, he exploited the prerogatives of a kind of family arrangement in which the husband-father is left undisturbed to pursue the "higher things" of life; but, as the patient complained, like many cases of such male privilege, her father was no more than a dabbler. These were conclusions Miss A, of course, developed later in her childhood and thereafter, though there was always something in her mother's attitude toward the father—a patronizing and infantilizing forbearance—that could not be missed earlier by an alert and highly socialized child.

As for Mr. A's influence on his daughter's choice of vocation, as far back as she could remember, Mr. A fancied himself a "litterateur" because of an interest in books that was exceptional within his business and social circle. Miss A also described her father as putting on airs, which consisted of swaggering about in blazers, striped ties, and tennis shoes and hinting at occasional affairs with certain unmarried women in the suburb where Miss A's family resided. It was in her relationship to her father and his mythic sex life that Miss A developed a playful, but also driven curiosity that expressed itself in elaborate ruminations about the personal life of virtually everyone she came in contact with.

In view of the unaccountability afforded the patient in the clinical situation, Miss A was able to badger both her analysts with prying questions about their family structures, social comings and goings, cultural activities, and various objects present in their offices. She registered this inquisitiveness with childlike giggles and enjoyed being put off, so that things were always left harmlessly unchanged.

Miss A's brother, four years younger, went on to become a real estate lawyer connected to the father's business and a socially busy bachelor. Her sister, six years younger, followed closely in one set of the mother's footsteps, marrying young and having two children, which delighted Miss A's parents but caused considerable envy in Miss A, who tried out a lot of men over the years but no one she could actually team up with. Bringing me up to date in our early sessions, she said wryly that her brother and sister had their lives already cut out for them; one followed the father's example, the other the mother's, while she, the patient, had to invent something from more ephemeral parental aspirations.

It was around the age of ten that Miss A's father began to burden her with intellectual challenges meant to put her above and apart from her peers. In a playfully teasing spirit intended as entertainment, he soon piled on a precocious indoctrination into his alleged extramarital sex life, which led to a secret ritual of verbal banter between father and daughter, in which Miss A insinuated and her father evaded. As we shall see, this game would figure prominently in Miss A's interactions with her analysts.

Here I will jump ahead chronologically in order to pursue the extraordinary hitch in the patient's vocational life involving her stalled writing project. Years of getting nowhere with this particular project was what eventually led to the psychological plight that brought her into treatment. In her late twenties, Miss A had published a short novel about the coming of age of an adolescent girl during a long summer at a popular seaside resort, a work of extensive psychological internality, which was, nevertheless, turned into a successful television movie. Thereafter, and with good reason, Miss A thought of herself as a novelist. Her mother encouraged her to waste no time and get on to a second book. Her father, in an expansive gesture, paid for an extended trip to London where Miss A promptly got involved in a torrid affair with an older, married professor of literature. Miss A had already had several sexual involvements with older married men and was to lament to her analyst years later how carefree she is in the role of the younger "other woman" and how anxious she gets if she gravitates toward the role of the number one woman in a man's life. (The reverse was true with women. "With women it's best-friends or nothing and no triangulations, if you please.") After several months of high-spirited excitement on that London trip, which included some book reviewing for a London newpaper, Miss A was abruptly turned off when her paramour revealed a sexual perversion he had on his agenda.

She returned to New York charged up to start a second novel, the theme of which had to do with a succession of several generations of owners, managers, and guests of a large hotel in a particular American locality. One of the plans for the book was to have the hotel itself emerge as the central figure, capable of arousing the emotions and sentiments a reader might feel toward an actual, living hero. To keep account of a large cast of human characters in the novel, Miss A plotted a strong story line to enable the reader to keep them in mind, which she constantly fiddled with at odd times along with writing the book itself. Two years went by, writing, rewriting, starting over, and so forth—to no avail.

She began taking increasingly more time out from her daily endeavors with this project to write articles and reviews for magazines and newspapers, which soon led to a lot of traveling and public appearances and eventually to a nonfiction book about a current story in the news. Her social life, which was now intertwined with her vocational life, became a hectic but pleasant enough routine, though Miss A was often puzzled at her inability to connect with a man suitable to become what she called a "real boyfriend." She was attracted to what she described as "gorgeous, sexy, passive-aggressive creeps—an uppity accent completes the deal." Later in her analysis, she would account for this ideal as a composite of what was socially charming about her father—"If you're doomed to fall for your father your whole life, it might as well be for his best features, bad as they are." These were the features Miss A imagined had attracted those mythic other women in her father's life.

Seven years went by. Now in her mid-thirties, she became

deeply troubled by the contradiction between her still thinking of herself as a novelist and her having nothing further to show for it. She began assigning herself actual writing deadlines. These came and went rather breezily. Then following a succession of momentous but not astounding events—the weddings of her brother and then of two close women friends, the thriving family life of her sister, a sudden decline in her father's health—the patient resolved to get down to business on her neglected book. She was now approaching forty and was feeling agitated and desperate. Several close women friends began to take her in hand, and finally convinced her that she was seriously depressed and should consider getting professional help. It was at this point that she began her analysis with my colleague.

At the time she came to me, her spirits were improved over what they had been a few years before, though she recognized that her bouancy was rather delicate. As for the novel, which continued to absorb her thoughts, it was no further along. She described it as a pile of disconnected pages that she kept in a left-hand drawer of her desk. Alone in her apartment, she would often have a strong sense of its presence. She once likened it to some moribund fetus crying out to her. Though she took fewer and fewer occasions to open the drawer, when she did, the very sight of all the scribbling and disarray could evoke a pang in the pit of her stomach. On the verge of panic, she would shut the drawer, and her eyes might then fill with tears.

However, this albatross, which is how Miss A would refer to the project, was not always in the foreground of her complaints. In her social life, she characterized herself as a perfectionistic control freak, whose standards very few survived, least of all the men she dated, who were now becoming fewer and far between. She complained of stomach pains that might follow a particular state of mind in which she sat down to a meal or of body-weight fluctuations or of sensitivity to heat and cold. Her increasingly sporadic sex life she pursued during visits to other cities or when various men from other cities came to New York on business; her avoidance of male residents of New York she knew amounted to a phobia, having something to do with her need to maintain the role of the other woman in order to feel sexual. Withal, Miss A kept up an extraordinary output of magazine and newspaper writing, and derived considerable pleasure being in demand for lectures and seminars.

Though one would have expected otherwise in view of the pressured quality of her comings and goings, Miss A did not present herself as a rapidly moving target in her daily behavior on the couch. She would lie down on the couch with little ado, pause for a moment to get her bearings, and would begin speaking in a low, tentative voice that soon gained its usual volume and composure. Left to her own initiative, her remarks took the following form: She would begin with how she felt at the moment, for example, anxious, distressed, terrible, excited, happy, disappointed. The ostensible reasons for how she felt would follow, for example, whom she had spoken with on the phone the night before, what she had done after the previous day's session, reckonings about whether a man she had met at some party or cultural event would call her, in which case she would ruminate about her appearance, her body weight, her dissatisfaction with her end of a conversation. Often as not, these openings were preambles to dreams she would then report—no week went by without three or four dreams.

Whereupon I might invite her attention to some unremarked upon, passing detail of that day's reported dream—she reacted with delight to my occasionally pointing out double entendres, puns, repetitions of images from previous dreams, and so forth. She would reply to such comments of mine with associations that might lead her into confessions of having avoided embarrassing thoughts and therefore of having created secrets— secrets figured prominently in Miss A's history (with many of the consequences Jacobs [1980] observed in his paper on secrets, alliances, and family fictions). That I would sometimes take the initiative in regard to details in her dreams led her into comparisons of me and her previous analyst. She graded me less strict than my predecessor and therefore more like her father than her mother. Toward this I had, of course, mixed feelings, as she also had. I invited her attention to the triangulation resulting from her sense of procedural differences between her former and present analyst, and we were able to advance some understanding of how her valuing both of us, each according to our differences, corresponded to her experience of pursuing two lives—one of which consisted of her unfinished manuscript, and the other of everything else. It was indicative of a certain flux in her object loyalties and oppositions that Miss A could not determine decisively which of her two analysts represented opposition or approbation of which of her lives.

Several months went by in this manner. Like Miss A, I also had mixed feelings about how our time was passing. While it seemed desirable to me that Miss A experience the analysis as a haven from her otherwise demanding life outside the sessions, there was something unproductively repetitive about what was transpiring.

It was particularly the feeling that I was an accomplice in some sort of pleasant passage of time that often turned my thoughts to Miss A's unfinished manuscript. When I did bring it up, which was hardly an arbitrary matter since it resided almost always as a subtext to whatever Miss A was reflecting upon, she reacted with brief but genuine annoyance, as though I was nagging her about practicalities, and in this I became a killjoy as her mother could be. However, she would quickly revert to what she regarded as my good intentions and then playfully solicit my forgiveness for her flashes of anger. In the next moment she was resurrecting an aspect of her experience with her father, whose high-blown expectations of her were what now corresponded to her analyst's reminding her of the manuscript. She transformed a feeling of being pestered into one of being flattered. This note of warmth could then become the point of departure into coy, childlike probings into my personal life, and constructions of my likes and dislikes and my comings and goings based on humorously flimsy observations of the design of my necktie, the number of hangers in the clothing closet, the brand of soap in the bathroom, and so on.

In connection with such enactments, Miss A began to develop the idea of how the worst possible turn in our relationship would be my yielding to her curiosities and disclosing the facts about whether or not I had affairs. It was not so much the prospects, one way or the other, of the two of us ending up in an actual sexual situation (an idea that she entertained at this point mainly in the form of negation), but merely my spilling the beans about this most salient issue. The banter between us seemed all that mattered, and it would have been this that my replying would have put an end to. Compared to the pursuit of it, the secret itself seemed devoid of excitement.

However, Miss A was realizing her loss of excitement even in the pursuit, and this duplicated something that had since come to pass between her and father. Ever since her father had lost the faculty for verbal horseplay with her, she hadn't the inclination to get into one of those exchanges with him about his extramarital sex life. I was able to convey to the patient that the ritual — stalking but without intent to kill — had been a restraint of her own destructiveness of her father's already shaky authority, which rested precariously on his preservation of sexual secrets.

Rather soberly for her, she went on to a new set of concerns about where she was in her life and what she was doing with it. In one of her sessions toward the end of the first year of her analysis, she pressed her hands to her face and spoke intently of how she was on the wrong side of forty and yet felt herself carrying on emotionally like a twenty-year-old, no, worse, like a five-year-old. She railed against the fact that she had, by all counts, an enviable career, which she treated like a summer job of a college kid. There were tears but not her dainty tears. "You're going to love this. I'm thinking what a spot this must put *you* in and how I can make it up to *you*, as if you think I think this is all your fault, all this kidding around I've done out there, in here." Touching her wet face, she paused in alarm. "What do I do now, I must look terrible! Do I go back to my apartment and start the day over? Screw you, screw them. From now on, what you see is what you get."

She repeated a complaint she had made many times before, but now it included the analysis as an example of how she sizes up what is expected of her and then goes on to participate with playful compliances. This was why it was hard to tell whose analysis this was, hers or mine. In the meantime, what we had all these months was what she called a stand-off.

She was wrought up at the thought that she hadn't the faintest idea of how to go about this in a different way, as if she needed a new set of instructions. I invited her to consider how this state of affairs could be brought to bear on the matter of the unfinished manuscript, which she also spoke about quite often as a stand-off she had no idea how to get on with.

In the weeks that followed, we were able to get to several distressing reconsiderations about a number of things, for which the unwritten novel can serve as a talking point. In regard to this, Miss A began to entertain the possibility that whatever that thing in her desk drawer was, it was no longer simply a novel waiting to be written. Therefore it was preposterous to be still thinking about it as a writing inhibition or a phobia. What we were dealing with was a delirium, and when that went, so might the whole project.

Among the ruminations that followed this momentous idea was that she simply walk away from the project and be done with it. She could then think of it as a miscarriage following a crazy pregnancy, and she could observe the death of the project funerially by making collages out of pieces of the pages of the manuscript, framing them and giving them out to her friends— "The Unfinished Manuscript on the Wall." When she brought up the possibility of chucking the whole thing, she couldn't decide what reactions I would have. On the one hand, I would be angry at her for abandoning something she had come to me to achieve. On the other, I would be glad that she was at last free of a useless burden.

While I understood the plausibility of these notions about my feelings as a therapist, neither choice corresponded to anything that resonated in me. When I invited her to speculate further about my feelings, she began to develop a fantasy prompted by the idea that I was also saddened for purely personal reasons at the possibility of her not writing the novel—deeply saddened, as if some happy chance had entered or reentered my life, only to come to nothing. The fantasy went on to portray me as once having wanted to achieve something spectacular myself, for which I thought I had the talent and the intelligence, but that somewhere along the way, I lost my nerve. For whatever the reason, I abandoned the promise I thought I had and went on to settle for a straightforward profession. My original ambition might have had something to do with philosophy, perhaps even the arts, but the point was that one day a patient came into my life, who soon filled me with hope as I became totally identified with her cause, only to have it all come to grief a second time. This was the cause of my sorrow at hearing her intention not to pursue the manuscript. For reasons I won't go into, this fantasy of Miss A struck a personal chord in me.

"I would like to help you with this one," Miss A said in dramatic tones to indicate that she was quite aware that she was advancing a fantasy, "but I can't—no, I *mustn't*, because I'd just be throwing my life away. As things stand right now, I mustn't write the book, because I'd be doing it for you, not for me. You had your chance way back then, and you blew it, and now you're over the hill. Tough. Deal me out."

I had no doubt that Miss A was bringing up certain notions about her mother's life prior to her marrying Miss A's father, and about her mother's sacrifice of that prior life to family and social responsibilities. However, I interrupted her to clarify a detail. "Over the hill? Tough? Deal me out? You're imitating someone. Who talks like this?"

"You do. Or you could in that New York manner you're sometimes on the verge of. I can definitely imagine you saying, 'Deal me out.' Like someone's on the phone. . . . blah-blah-blah. . . . and I can imagine you saying, 'Oh, yeah, well, deal me out.' [Long pause] You want to know something, also my mother sometimes talks like that." Whereupon Miss A went on to remind me that her mother was born on the outskirts of New York City, and though she lived there only until she was nine or ten, she maintained a little of that regional speech, which she used, now and again, humorously. Miss A enumerated a few of her mother's phrases—"What do you take me for?"—"Nuts to you."—"Get a load of this."—mischievous signs of a whole other life poignantly suppressed by the mother, but nevertheless available to her child as a basis for the development of yet another selfobject scenario.

PATHOGENESIS OF THE UNFINISHED MANUSCRIPT

While Miss A's fantasy of the mother's prior existence began to account for a good deal about the patient's conflicts and the intricacies of contending aims over the project, it, of course, settled nothing one way or the other as far as pursuing or dropping the project was concerned. At this point Miss A was well into her second year of analysis with me, and while there is much that could be reported about her ongoing difficulties with her social life and particularly her growing fears of ending up unmarried and all that that began to mean to her, for the sake of getting on with the matter of the unfinished project, I will branch off into a more restricted account of the symptom itself.

Miss A's encounter with a fantasy about my past rather than hers, and particularly my past as corresponding to a fantasy about her mother's past, was the beginning of a departure into what can be called the prehistory of the patient. By prehistory I do not mean anything exotic or arcane. I simply mean it in some ordinary sense of a construction by a child of a parent's prior existence formed out of a parent's idiosyncractic behaviors, bits and pieces of family stories, reminiscences, photographs, and other artifacts from the parent's life prior to the actual birth and development of the patient.

In an earlier paper (Kaplan 1972), I reported several cases in which prehistory figured especially in the pathogenesis of family romance fantasies, and I am increasingly impressed that notions about a parent's previous existence supply crucial elements of the content of these protean fantasies of unfulfilled destiny. That is, in the well-known fictionalizing of one's past common to family romances, the content of such fiction is often derived from the fictional prehistory of one's parents. Moreover, the plight of the parent redressed by the rescue motif also common to these fantasies is often that of a derailed parental destiny, which the child imagines was painfully interrupted by the parent's marriage and domesticity. Family romances, especially in precocious and talented children (Greenacre 1958), supply the would-be happy endings to oedipal ordeals—how things are supposed to work out (Kaplan 1972). This, in turn, creates a multiplicity of contradictory objects out of a single set of parents and a susceptibility to get caught up in a prolonged experience of a double life.

Thus at that crucial moment in Miss A's life when, in her late twenties, she published a novel, the differing reactions of her parents are in character for each of them only in the social sense that that particular mother at that particular time represented immediate practicality, while the father embodied an ideal of leisure and recreation. However, Miss A's perceptions and evaluations of this dichotomous version of authority constituted merely one outlook on her parents, which in itself cannot account for why this conflict of authority went on to become a pathological division in Miss A's vocational life that would consume years of unproductive ambition and effort. When Miss A took off for London, there could have been as yet no telling what the fate of her intention to do a second novel would be. She was off on a brief holiday, but she was fully prepared to return home and get down to brass tacks. Of course, at that time there was no analyst present in her life to help her investigate the conflicts that would lead to her initial symptomatic procrastinations over her new project.

However, from various reports and events in her analysis years later, it is possible to reconstruct a few things about her psychological situation in her late twenties. For example, a most important point about the symptom itself at that earlier time can be appreciated in my now correcting a temporal sequence I have retained up to this point for the sake of discussion. In referring to the patient's second novel as a "new project," I was speaking behavioristically. As it turned out, Miss A's "Unfinished Manuscript in the Drawer" would have been her second novel only in the sense that its publication, though not necessarily its conception, would come after the publication of the novel she succeeded in finishing.

In the course of her analysis, Miss A brought up the fact that the idea of doing a novel about a hotel—her so-called second novel—began dawning on her in her early twenties out of odds and ends of experiences and memories of the architecture and landscapes of the college she attended and the many novels and poems she had read during her college years, all of which coalesced in her imagination into an imposing architectural structure in some ideal locality. It was a huge literary conception, and what she imagined was required for it to be brought off successfully already troubled her. She was not at all confident that she was up to it and was therefore not entirely sold on the idea. The point is that the novel she went on to write and publish in her late twenties was, from a psychological point of view, her second novel, which was a more modest undertaking than the first, which she was already planning. Thus even before the first became "the unfinished manuscript in the drawer," it was already functioning psychologically in the service of the feasibility of something less than itself. As a respository of higher and therefore more elusive ideals, it was already acquiring secondary gains.

Also, from the sequence of transference events in Miss A's analysis, we can discern some additional gains of her symptom as it incubated in her late twenties. The crisis between Miss A and her first analyst is, to be sure, complicated beyond what I have gone into. The complications were limited at first to a particular version of Miss A's mother and father, which included the idea of the mother as a harsh realist and the father as an unaccomplished dabbler. It was clear at the start of the analysis the admonishing mother was the enemy, though it was not yet clear that another version of the mother was being protected and maintained as an object of identification and love. Thus Miss A's defection from her first analyst had a spirit about it not of matricide, but of a manifestly congenial moratorium on conflict, so that it could be said that if Miss A was eliminating the enemy, she was also sparing the enemy even as she set about finding a version of her father in her second analyst. What we have here is a peculiar absence of psychological bloodshed in a patient driven by high ambition. Indeed, a general inhibition of parricidal inclinations went on to characterize a good deal of Miss A's transference enactments with her second analyst. Recall, for example, her penchant for stalking me but then backing off lest she incur real injury.

Now, there is an abundant psychoanalytic commentary on the role of unconscious parricidal impulses (to murder either or both parents or parental surrogates) in symptomatic restraints on personal ambitions. Freud's observations (1916) of "Those Wrecked by Success" in his study on character types met with in psychoanalysis are an early example. With respect specifically to difficulties with writing projects, Loewald (1979) reminds us that every increment in personal development, such as is embodied in a significant writing project, is an unconscious act of violence against an encouraging and supportive parental imago. Loewald described the temporary but troublesome symptom of one of his patients as a postponement of a further waning of this patient's Oedipus complex, which is the crisis in development that Loewald's paper elaborates.

This makes good sense as far as it goes. When Miss A was in her late twenties and beginning to become embroiled in what might have been called, at that early stage of things, a writer's block or work inhibition, it would have been possible to regard this as an outcome of conflicted identifications and aggressive aims having to do with the developmental crisis suggested by Loewald. In this scheme, Miss A returns from her holiday to take on a task at the very edges of her abilities. By comparison, Miss A's already published novel was, in her estimation, a mere stab at literary accomplishment. This new task (actually, as we have seen, a return to something already held in abeyance) would be for her a total commitment to serious writing and, as such, it constituted a total choice of personal ambition that challenged her mother's whole example of what a woman should choose, in the end, to do with her life. Thus, like Loewald's patient, Miss A's ambition threatens a parent's authority and an ongoing source of support. Moreover, should she succeed, Miss A would emerge as one of those menacing women outside the immediate family whom the father was attracted to. Worse, Miss A imagined these "other women" as unaccomplished "Barbie Dolls," while she was on her way to becoming a brilliant star in the literary firmament. Of course, it is with this fantasized achievement that Miss A lost her bearings among a number of diverging causes she could have been serving, including the causes of prehistory I referred to earlier.

Negative aspects of her oedipal conflicts also figure importantly. For example, poking around ineffectually in her manuscript during those earlier years soon resulted in a lasting sense that she was merely a "dabbler" like her father. In regard to this, I was able to help her to appreciate how she employed this long-standing experience of herself to appease her female friends, who would not be threatened by Miss A's journalistic career, since she, herself, represented this vocational pursuit as a default, a lamentable alternative to her failed literary ambitions; in this way she defended herself against the envy and hatred she projected. This was a strategy she was already familiar with in herself, and she was able to develop its history in her adolescence in connection with certain social and academic successes, which she also represented as alternatives to failed ambitions.

In connection with her relationships to women, Miss A was to become conversant with the possibility that being a "dabbler" derived from a desire to be like her father, because, as a "dabbler," she would be loved and desired by her mother as Miss A's father appeared to have been early in Miss A's childhood, before and shortly after Miss A's siblings arrived. Paradoxically, these negative oedipal strivings contributed to the indelibility in Miss A's personality of her self-image of Daddy's Good Little Girl, a compliance with a desexualized social stereotype that Miss A adopted when her father was prevailed upon to fill in for the mother who was taken up with caring for Miss A's newborn siblings. Such appropriation of the father by a child's continued preoedipal strivings is not an uncommon deferment of the father's oedipal sex difference.

What we have thus far unpacked from the symptom is still merely a prelude to its pathogenesis. The conflicts of object relations derived from various stages of Miss A's development that were embodied in the unwritten manuscript account for just so much. For example, the fact that Miss A was unable to decide whether her project was a triumph or a compliance, a defeat or a rescue, an expression of hate or love with respect to her oedipal mother assigns the ego a considerable task, but not necessarily the consuming task we are observing. As Loewald (1979) reminds us, conflicting versions of oedipal authority and jeopardies of preoedipal supplies are reckonings in all developmental undertakings. In Miss A's case, we must add to this the grandiose ideals of a family romance fantasy that furnished a difficult criterion of how such conflicts and threats should be resolved; this lively fantasy was a source of her high literary ambition, nothing short of which would seem a sufficiently authentic resolution of her destiny. But, again, these matters, crucial as they are, cannot by themselves fully justify the amount of spirit consumed in the pros and cons that characterize the particular symptom Miss A and others in a similar plight present.

Despite the obsessional ruminations and the varieties of hopeless daily rituals with which patients report approaching and avoiding such projects, we are dealing with a symptom that appears to reverse a common observation about symptom formation. While it is true that most neurotic symptoms, including perversions, plague the lives that they are subtracted from, they do leave over a sense of reality about the remainder of that life. That is, symptoms do not put one in constant doubt about which should go and which should be retained—the symptom or the life it troubles.

Miss A's symptom is another matter. "The Unfinished Manuscript in the Drawer" seemed to her a principal constituent of a life she should be living. The life she actually led, while public and gainful and therefore real, was experienced nevertheless as something provisional that took place in the meantime. That her symptom may have rendered the life she led feasible felt to her entirely beside the point. In this connection, recall the remark of the 87-year-old writer Henry Roth that his life of tormenting literary failure turned out to have been the wrong life—somewhere along the line he should have relegated his literary ambition to fantasy, a painful rearrangement of actualities entailing a vast work of mourning.

This brings us to another distinguishing feature of these symptoms, which I have already noted. I am referring to the alarming consumption of time and the patient's constant realization of this. Typical clinical depressions, for example, also entail attenuations of time (Rosner 1962), but, by comparison, the passage of time goes by unconsciously, which is why Lewin (1961) described depressed patients as being asleep at the breast. In cases like Miss A's, on the other hand, the conflicts of historical stages and object relations we have observed dwell in extended passages of time that constitute a major feature of the patient's description of the symptom.

A significant literature on the psychoanalysis of time has accumulated but has not been assimilated into psychoanalytic thinking to the extent it may deserve (e.g., Arlow 1984, 1986,

Fraser 1988, Hartocollis 1983, Kurtz 1988, Loewald 1962, 1972, Maroda 1987, Namnun 1972, Orgel 1965, Waugaman 1992, and much else). One of the reasons for the scattered interest in the problem of time is that temporal phenomena, psychoanalytically considered, are closely related to affects, which, in the clinical situation, make better talking points than a less palpable variant like the perception of time. I do not intend to review the psychoanalytic problem of time. (Morris [1983] gives an excellent review of the problem.) I merely want to suggest that the problem comes into psychoanalytic theory in connection with early developments in the mental life around the exigencies of delay, postponement, and detour, which lead to experiences of waiting, longing, and reminiscence, which, in turn, lead to affective experiences such as anxiety or excitement, depending on the context of fantasy, and eventually to psychic structure— indeed, this was why Loewald (1962) remarked, with reference particularly to the superego, that "psychic structures are temporal in nature" (p. 264).

As is true of all outcomes of development, the sense of time is susceptible to a variety of psychopathologies. Expenditures of time for gratifications of moral masochism are a significant matter in symptoms like Miss A's and in attitudes toward the psychoanalytic situation as a process ultimately without consequence and therefore without end. Reik (1989/1940) has made a most incisive observation about the role of time in perverse masochism, which can be extended to the moral level. In perverse masochism necessity has been transformed into pleasure, and delay, which is a necessary means to the establishment of the reality principle, can become an end in itself. This is why Reik speaks of the end-pleasure in perverse masochism as anticlimactic. In moral masochism the triumph can also be traced to the instinctualization of the processes of delay and attention that lead to socialization and to the accomplishment of work (Jacques 1990). Thus in moral masochism postponement becomes more gratifying in itself than the accomplishment it originally was meant to bring about. In these terms, the "Unfinished Manuscript in the Drawer" is a monument of defiance wrought in a spirit of virtue. Psychoanalysis speaks of such constructions as collusions of id and superego aims.

As we have seen, in cases of unfinished projects extending over years, distinctions must be made between the symptom at one point in time and at another. In his classic paper on primary and secondary gain, Katz (1963) distinguished the initial process of symptom formation—the primary gain—from what he called the "symptomatic state" (p. 32). The symptomatic state is the experience the symptom acquires over time, which experience the ego goes on to incorporate into its organization. This subsequent fate of the symptom is, in large part, its secondary gain. Moral masochistic gratification figures prominently in symptom states such as Miss A's, because unfinished projects luxuriate over time as good intentions toward worthy goals—manifestly virtuous strivings that seem eminently worth preserving in the mental life, even if a symptom is inextricably part of the bargain. To be sure, virtually all symptoms implicate the moral life and succeed in regulating and reducing moral anxiety. However, not all symptoms deliver such a bonus of moral rectitude.

A COMMON FATE OF THE UNFINISHED
MANUSCRIPT

One of the manifestations in the clinical situation of the infantile morality at large in Miss A's symptomatic project was a bland ambivalence that routinized her congenial participation in the analysis. Ambivalence in this sense is a counterpart of moral masochism in that it employs a manifest compliance with the means of the analysis to maintain a defiance of any of its possible ends. For this to go on, the nature and locus of authority in the analysis must not range too widely. The analyst must be kept in place as a benevolent but absolute dictator, well-meaning but morally coercive about the necessities of the analysis. Variations of this particular structure of power could be recognized in Miss A's personal relations outside the analysis.

At the outset of a particular session during her fourth year with me, Miss A reported a telephone conversation with a close female friend regarding a dinner invitation at the apartment of the friend and her husband. Miss A asked about her bringing along the man whom she had been seeing rather seriously for the past several months, an architect in the midwest in the final stages of a divorce from a ten-year marriage. Miss A's friend, who had not yet met this man but had been kept up-to-date on the relationship on a number of previous occasions, was high-spirited about the arrangement and got off the phone without volunteering a word of advice or reservation, which would have been characteristic of this friend's reactions to accounts of Miss A's relationships, especially with men. The other shoe Miss A anticipated in such exchanges with her friend never fell.

Now, this incident marks something crucial because it appeared to be a more common experience with others as well than Miss A had realized at this time. Whatever characterological changes she was now presenting to personal friends, a former "Yes, but" reaction was not as forthcoming from them. Even her mother related to her in a more accepting spirit. Miss A went on to detect in herself a certain disappointment, if not alarm in all this, which had an important bearing on the unwritten novel. While it had been a number of years since her mother had inquired about Miss A's plans and opportunities with respect to her having children—"She must have accepted the fact that I'm over the hill in that department," toward the unfinished novel Miss A's mother still showed an interest in how some particular circumstance or other might affect the project. However, recently Miss A noticed a loss of interest even on her mother's part. Following a rather long, contemplative silence, Miss A reflected, "If my one remaining devotee no longer cares, who am I still holding out on?"

It was this feeling of holding out on someone that restored some traction to the subject of the unwritten book, because it enabled us yet again to get into a parallel between the symptom and the analysis, this time confronting Miss A's buoyantly defiant aims in the analysis. When I inquired where Miss A imagined I stood these days with regard to the book, she formulated the idea that, even prior to her mother, I had long since lost all belief in her ever getting down to the book, which was how she explained these increasingly long silences in the analysis with respect to the book. She explained that recently whenever the subject came up, she felt ashamed to be suggesting that she had remaining hopes about the project. Anticipating a feeling that I would no longer be a party to any conflict she might have about it one way or the other, she had found it harder and harder to talk about the manuscript.

Whereupon she reported a wave of anxiety and accused me of once again putting pressure on her. "What's going on here all of a sudden, sleep faster, we need the pillows?" Then, as though to represent my side, she added sardonically, "What the hell, it's only been fifteen, sixteen, seventeen years. What are you trying to tell me, I'm no longer a spring chicken? I get it, you want me to become one of those Number One Women, marry Charlie, the Architect, and move out west. Thanks a lot. Who are you working for?"

Though much could be pursued about the special problem of simply entertaining the termination of an analysis in which an unfinished project figures, this must go without saying. Regarding the fate of the symptom itself, where we now were in the analysis is a definite place we are likely to arrive at one way or another in all such cases. It is where the analysis, bit by bit, has worn out the last illusion that the symptom is still more than it has long since become and is therefore salvageable as a feasible project. This illusion capitulates to the loss of a prevailing fantasy that something worthwhile in the symptom will survive everything the analysis has brought to light about it, as if the analysis is in earnest only up to the margins of the symptom.

Thus Miss A seemed to be at a place she had been before, when she would wonder, for example, what would happen to her project if certain ideas it embodied were subtracted from it, including, as we saw, what she imagined was my personal stake in it. However, previously she experienced me as a partner going after those matters that seemed extraneous to the project, such as distracting features of its history and its secondary value for other activities in her life. But at this present moment she could hear that I was questioning the project itself in its own right.

In regard to this, I proposed that I was merely catching up to a conclusion she had already come to herself. She did not protest but asked forlornly, "What should we do?"

This question contained a last-ditch effort to rescue what was fast becoming a hopeless cause for both of us. Much as the analyst, who has been dealing with a project such as Miss A's, is intimidated at such crucial moments by the prospect of an eruption on the patient's part of bitterness, agitation, and eventually grief, this is no occasion to hedge or pacify or disingenuously inquire for more feelings and fantasies from the patient; otherwise the chances for conclusiveness and eventual terminability are again postponed. While one does not, of course, want to represent aggression as brutality, hesitations of looking closer at what the analysis itself has brought to light only repeat the patient's own compromises with aggression. "Maybe the jury is already in," I replied to her question. "When was the last time anything permanent was added to the manuscript?" The passive voice here embodies a remnant of my own trepidations.

The point I went on to develop was that the reason the manuscript no longer corresponded to what is meant by a manuscript was that the activity performed on it did not, for many years, qualify as actual writing in any sense of the term. Prepared with the intention that the two of us go back and review the whole history of the manuscript, this in the interest of turning a huge loss to some account, I do not believe my directness came across as an ultimatum, but rather as a support of Miss A's own conclusions. As for the future of the analysis, it now had more degrees of freedom to reckon with where the patient was in the flux of things and where she was going.

None of this is to suggest that what followed was a psychoanalytic pastoral. At first, Miss A registered alarm that like some bad-boy-up-the-block, I had lured her away from virtue and into some wild delinquency. This was a new manifestation in the transference and enabled us to go over some further ground in her adolescent development. We had already made headway with the problem of how perfectionism advances anal scrupulosity in the moral guise of high standards; in this way, perfectionism is ripe for phobic processes involving touching taboos, which can claim the sexual developments at adolescence. Between waves of lightheadedness and despair over the manuscript and the years of emotional investment and frustration it represented, Miss A had to make a serious decision about Charlie, the man she was presently seeing, who seemed to her not like anyone she would have imagined marrying. She came to understand that her idea that there was such a thing as a Mr. Right and therefore a Mr. Wrong represented another of her perfectionistic dichotomies, this one disguising a phobia about marriage itself.

As for the "Unfinished Manuscript in the Drawer," which was no longer a process but now a thing, toward the end of the fourth year of the analysis, Miss A reported at the beginning of a session that the night before she had gathered up the pile of pages that had dwelled in her desk drawer all those years and unceremoniously let them go down the garbage chute of her building. If we recall the psychological context and spirit of Miss A's earlier intentions to destroy the manuscript physically, what we have here is a similar piece of behavior but with a significant change of function. It was a huge relief, to which she associated a number of bodily memories and experiences. However, she saw no danger in keeping the title page, which she had dropped off at the frame store on the way to her session.

REFERENCES

Arlow, J. (1984). Disturbances of the sense of time. *Psychoanalytic Quarterly* 53:13–37.

_____ (1986). Psychoanalysis and time. *Journal of the American Psychoanalytic Association* 34:507–528.

Fraser, J. T. (1988). Time: removing the degeneracies. In *Fantasy, Myth, and Reality*, ed. H. Blum et. al. New York: International Universities Press.

Freud, S. (1914). On narcissism: an introduction. *Standard Edition* 14.

_____ (1916). Some character-types met with in psycho-analytic work. *Standard Edition* 14.

Greenacre, P. (1958). The family romance of the artist. *Psychoanalytic Study of the Child* 13:9–36.

Hartocollis, P. (1983). *Time and Timelessness*. New York: International Universities Press.

Jacobs, T. J. (1980). Secrets, alliances, and family fictions: some psychoanalytic observations. *Journal of the American Psychoanalytic Association* 28:21–42.

Jacques, E. (1990). *Creativity and Work*. New York: International Universities Press.

James, H. (1873). The Madonna of the future. In *Henry James: Representative Selections with Introduction, Bibliography, and Notes*, ed. L. N. Richardson. Urbana, IL and London: University of Illinois Press, 1966.

Kaplan, D. M. (1972). On shyness. *International Journal of Psycho-Analysis* 53:439–454.

_____ (1993). What is sublimated in sublimation? *Journal of the American Psychoanalytic Association* 41:549–570.

Katz, J. (1963). On primary gain and secondary gain. *Psychoanalytic Study of the Child* 18:9–50.

Kurtz, S. A. (1988). The psychoanalysis of time. *Journal of the American Psychoanalytic Association* 36:985–1004.

Lewin, B. (1961). Reflections on depression. *Psychoanalytic Study of the Child* 16:321–331.

Loewald, H. W. (1962). Superego and time. *International Journal of Psycho-Analysis* 43:264–268.

_____ (1972). The experience of time. *Psychoanalytic Study of the Child* 27:401–410.

_____ (1979). The waning of the Oedipus complex. *Journal of the American Psychoanalytic Association* 27:751–776.

Maroda, K. J. (1987). The fate of the narcissistic personality: lost in time. *Psychoanalytic Psychology* 4:279–290.

Michaels, L. (1993). The long comeback of Henry Roth: call it miraculous. *New York Times Book Review*, August 15.

Morris, J. (1983). Time experience and transference. *Journal of the American Psychoanalytic Association* 31:651–675.

Namnun, A. (1972). Time in psychoanalytic technique. *Journal of the American Psychoanalytic Association* 20:736–750.

Orgel, S. (1965). On time and timelessness. *Journal of the American Psychoanalytic Association* 13:102–121.

Reik, T. (1989/1940). The characteristics of masochism. *American Imago* 46:161–196.

Remnick, D. (1994). Visible man. *The New Yorker*, March 14.

Rosner, A. (1962). Mourning before the fact. *Journal of the American Psychoanalytic Association* 10:564–570.

Ticho, E. (1972). Termination of psychoanalysis: treatment goals, life goals. *Psychoanalytic Quarterly* 42:315–333.

Waugaman, R. M. (1992). Analytic time. *Journal of the American Academy of Psychoanalysis* 20:677–688.

2

Gender and Social Reality

Since the social order embodies and authorizes ideals of femininity and masculinity, a psychoanalysis of gender must entail decisions, witting or otherwise, as to how social reality figures in the clinical situation. Though it is true that social reality contributes to development in varied and crucial ways, the following discussion limits the idea of social reality to a constant in the maintenance of neurosis. What such an approach emphasizes about social ideals is their role in a psychopathology of conformity, which constitutes a stage in the development of neurosis. This view corresponds to certain technicalities of the psychoanalytic method, in which all versions of normality are analyzed as aspects of resistance.

The following discussion also extends some lines of thought from a previous collaboration on the problem of gender in psychoanalysis (Grossman and Kaplan 1988). In that study of gender, principally in Freud's writing, Grossman and I distinguished several kinds of commentary on femininity and masculinity on the basis of their varying psychoanalytic technicality.[1] We described how certain ideas of Freud on the subject of gender were nontechnical in the sense that their justification had nothing to do with Freud's version of the psychoanalytic method. His assertions about female and male traits (e.g., in

---

1. An exposition is technical to the extent that its meaning is restricted to specifiable clinical and theoretical principles. This does not mean that exposition lacking such character is for that reason alone not worthwhile. There are always things worth saying that cannot be said within the stringencies of technicality. However, it seems desirable every so often to review and assess an area of psychoanalytic exposition for its level and degree of technicality.

love, women are narcissistic, men anaclitic [Freud 1914]) are examples of this. While it is true that traits and the various ideals they correspond to constitute actual social realities, from a clinical view a trait is a "surface" phenomenon, a point of departure in a particular investigative process.

With respect to gender, a commentary more faithful to the psychoanalytic method, hence more technical, can also be found in Freud, often among his asides and prefatory remarks and in passages not nominatively about gender. This commentary locates the problem of gender among the variabilities of development that include chance events, parental idiosyncrasies, and individual dynamics. Retaining the complexity of any psychoanalytic account of an outcome of conflict and adaptation, this commentary supersedes the dichotomies of static traits as well as the fixed linearity of well-rehearsed narratives of development. The problem of gender in mental life becomes a vicissitude of the very same principles of pathogenesis by which psychoanalysis conceives of symptoms, character, and "libidinal types." In other words, from what we were calling a technical point of view, gender is an outcome of development in the same way as character and neurosis. All are the result of a process of maturation, conflict, and conflict resolution. There is nothing crucial to gender that eludes a general theory of neurosis. What remains critical in this commentary are the technical problems that arise in the encounter of gender issues and the clinical method. As for what is optimal, normal, typical, or ideal femininity and masculinity, these become subjects of applied psychoanalysis (Kaplan 1988) or of those disciplines, such as biology and sociology, with the technical means for addressing something more than a psychopathology of gender.

One thing that is apt to be troubling about such a critique is the restriction it places on how psychoanalysis entertains, and therefore what it can elucidate about, gender. What we have here is an instance of a general controversy having to do with the nature of a psychoanalytic point of view and what is and is not amenable to it. Therefore some remarks on such controversy might be useful so that the argument that follows can also be taken as a case in point for much more than gender itself.

A regular source of contention across any interdisciplinary

boundary as well as among intradisciplinary schools of thought is the loss of complexity of certain of one's cherished concepts as they turn up in another's methodological scheme. Though they are not always explicit, decisions as to what to simplify and what to complicate in a field of interest are inevitable. Such decisions must be made because they are operationally what determine an identifiable subject matter and the very discipline concerned with it. There is no way to talk about something in particular, especially along technical lines, and not indicate in one way or another which variables of a subject are at issue and which are not.

This was a point made by Wallerstein and Smelser (1969) in a classic study of the relations between psychoanalysis and sociology. They described how the subject matter and organizing principles that distinguish various disciplines depend upon what they called "parameters," deliberate simplifications of what are otherwise complex phenomena. In such epistemic decisions variables of one point of view become constants of another. As they put it, "What is . . . often not appreciated, because it is a silent additional 'given,' is that a sharpened focus . . . has been achieved in each discipline by making a variety of simplifying assumptions about the other aspects of the world it has not chosen to study (the content areas of other behavioral sciences)" (p. 695).[2]

Hence across disciplines nominatively shared interests are actually different subjects. This is what makes such difficulty for the unification of knowledge. Should you combine in some integrated fashion the interests and findings of, say, two related disciplines, you do not end up with one discipline because you have digested the two with which you began; you now have three, as happened, for example, when Freud trafficked be-

---

2. In regard to the psychoanalytic process itself, Bleger (1967) wrote of a similar process of juxtaposing variables and constants to enhance the analytic grasp of process. "The [analytic] situation comprises phenomena which constitute a *process* that is studied, analysed, and interpreted; but it also includes a *frame*, that is to say, a 'non-process', in the sense that it is made up of constants within whose bounds the process takes place" (p. 512). See Kaplan (1973) for yet another version of this arrangement of constants and variables and its advantage in advancing clinical understanding.

tween psychiatry and sexology and, not altogether intention-
ally, created psychoanalysis, which went on to develop
alongside of psychiatry and sexology. In the bargain, you have
produced some additional boundaries in connection with your
new approach to things, inasmuch as you will also have
produced a particular set of what Wallerstein and Smelser called
parameters.[3]

And since you have not retained all the complexities achieved
or aspired to by the disciplines you are superseding, you are
open to charges of retreating from their hard-won frontiers of
knowledge. This was an allegation, for example, in respect to
Freud's (1896) early proposals about the origin, function, and
structure of paranoid ideas. Whereas psychiatry saw itself as
steadily advancing on an organic explanation of insanity,
Freud's psychological approach was said to have been a "regrettable back-sliding into popular superstition," a reversion to an
"old-wives psychiatry" (Freud 1985, p. 203, Sulloway 1979, p.
454).

In this we also have an example of how boundaries arise
within one and the same discipline when certain variabilities of
a subject are put on hold, while others are given a prominence
not currently accorded them. Since it is not clear when such
shifts of focus have resulted in a new subject matter, hence a
new discipline, conversation and argument about such developments are apt to be at cross-purposes, for one is not sure if
one is dealing with colleagues, reactionaries, renegades, oppor-
tunists, or prophets. Proprietary and other ideological issues are
bound to figure among critiques of a school of thought because
every school of thought exists at the expense of something
crucial to the conceptual schemes of another school of thought.

There is something inevitable in all this. Reiser (1985) speaks
of the formation of antidisciplines that inevitably split off from
parent disciplines, as psychoanalysis splits off from social science or biology from psychoanalysis. The antidiscipline then
goes on to challenge the precision and claims of the parent
discipline. Reiser limits his observations to the constructive

---

3. This use of the term parameter should be distinguished from its usage
deriving from Eissler (1953) as a variant of ideal psychoanalytic procedure.

dialectical possibilities of the process, the "creative tensions" that arise for the parent discipline (p. 18). However, if this were all there was to it, the development of science would be a wholly congenial story. Of course, it is not. As Grossman (1986) described in the controversies between Horney and the Freudian school, this is a state of affairs rife with the reactive possibilities of a narcissism of difference. Thus crises of infantile perception can also contribute to controversies about theory and practice.

This is worth bearing in mind because the subject of gender, to which these observations are a prelude, is particularly burdened with conflict that is virtually certain to be carried over into discussions of theory. Nevertheless, decisions about how the subject of gender is defined, what is to be included and therefore excluded, have to be made as they have to be made with respect to any subject.

A crucial decision in a psychoanalysis of gender is what to make of social reality; for insofar as gender refers to concordances of sex (male/female) with various social ideals of masculinity and femininity, gender, whatever more it is, is an aspect of social reality. In technical terms, the issue has to do with what the analyst is prepared to make of the patient's involvements with particular social ideals of womanhood and manhood. In the parlance of the problem of boundaries, this is a question of where the variables of social reality are and are not in a psychoanalytic view—or, at least, in one, as compared to some other, psychoanalytic view.

I think it is a misapprehension of the history of psychoanalysis to suppose that this particular problem of social reality has undergone a progressive development. A familiar version of the story is that once upon a time, in the classical epochs of psychoanalysis, social norms and ideals were excluded from the analyst's point of view. Then, with the development of ideals of social reformation and the advance of social science, room was found in the clinical situation for considerations of social factors in neurosis. A certain cool and arrogant indifference to much that mattered to the patient about the social order gave way to a more inclusive and nurturing humanism on the part of the analyst.

Actually, the classic psychoanalytic literature, both theoretical and clinical, is hardly indifferent to social values and ideals. On the contrary, it is loaded with them, and they appeared to have been brought into the clinical situation in significant ways. In regard to female sexuality, analysts had plenty of ideas about proper strivings and conduct, which corresponded to prominent social stereotypes. The curious notion of the vaginal orgasm, for example, was joined to certain long-standing social ideals and prevailed far into the century as a criterion of personal development, therapeutic progress, and even readiness for termination—to the harassment of untold numbers of female analysands. Similarly, there was something smugly diagnostic attributed to women's decisions to marry or not and bear children. Indeed, one almost wishes that the mythic austerity of earlier clinical situations had been more actual.

On the other hand, it may not be an improvement in our reflections on this history to discern the existence of all sorts of social values in prior psychoanalytic thought but to attribute what we do not like about this to the fact that our forebears simply held the wrong values, as if inflicting patients with better values would have amounted to something analytically more desirable. If criteria signifying a scheme of social normality have a questionable technical basis in psychoanalytic thought, it is not good practice to substitute what are deemed better norms for the traditional ones. Nor does it matter how big-hearted we think we are compared to our allegedly stringent forebears.

In the question of social reality, it seems to me more consistent with what has deservedly survived history to regard social reality and other sources of normative strivings as tangential to more salient analytic issues. In this view, the actual variability of social reality is not the technical problem for psychoanalysis, as it is, say, for certain sociologies. What is more in keeping with the interests of the analytic method is the variability of uses to which social reality is put in neurosogenesis. With respect to the problem of gender, this option has far-reaching consequences for what the analyst is and is not expert about.

The distinction I am beginning to make was illustrated in a paper by Hartmann and colleagues (1951) on the relation of culture and psychoanalysis. They were speaking of traits of nationality in patients, but their point was as well made for any social traits, including gender traits. They observed the wide variety of social manners and attitudes that would be presented in the initial contact of, say, a Frenchman, an Englishman, a New Yorker, or a Bostonian with a psychoanalyst. Before long, however, these initial differences in social style inevitably lose interest to the development of transferences, which embody the crucial variables that will go on to distinguish these patients from one another in the psychoanalytic situation. This is because transference is the realm of diagnosis for psychoanalysis. (Nor should we forget that in a psychoanalytic perspective diagnosis and analyzability are synonymous.) This is to say, moreover, that analyzability is independent of social traits in themselves, including gender traits that may appear so prominent in the initial presentations of patients.

As I have admitted, an elucidation along these lines of the fate of certain social facts in the psychoanalytic situation will hardly be congenial to one and all. The culturalist schools of psychoanalysis, for instance, arose in contentions with such a technical point of view and its concomitant minimization of factitious social ideals in the tribulations of the patient. Thereafter, various feminist critics took umbrage at this seeming neglect of social issues, though it is hard to say how their recommendations about social ideals and values would actually fit the overall structure of psychoanalytic thought; for what psychoanalysis is concerned with is not so much which ideals and values are avowed and professed by the patient as how the avowed and professed figure in a scheme of repression.[4]

This was the point of view on social ideals taken in Freud's earliest cases. In the case of Fräulein Elisabeth von R. (Breuer and Freud 1895), for example, we can already see how little attention Freud gave—indeed, he gave virtually none—to the

---

4. This option of regarding all social reality *in the clinical situation* as an advantage in the process of repression is continuous with a whole psychoanalytic literature on normality as a species of neurosis (e.g., Abrams 1979, McDougall 1980, Wolff 1988). Indeed, Wolff attributes the Freudian critique of culture to this particular option and describes the neo-Freudian attempt to dispense with it in favor of frank or subtle endorsements of social norms as "reactionary."

content of the social values that burdened and constrained his suffering and unhappy patient. He wrote movingly of Elisabeth's feelings and the deep sympathy they aroused in him. But he distinguished this aspect of his experience from his passion to help her by discovering the trauma that figured in her symptoms (p. 144). When Freud confronted his patient with her repressed thoughts about her brother-in-law, she protested vehemently about her incapacity for such wickedness. In this episode we have a précis of what about the moral life is emphasized in the psychoanalytic process. Though Elisabeth was soon able to appreciate Freud's evidence for the conclusion—it came, after all, from the details of her own account—Freud tells us, "But it was a long time before my two pieces of consolation—that we are not responsible for our feelings, and that her behaviour, the fact that she had fallen ill in these circumstances, was sufficient evidence of her moral character—it was a long time before these consolations of mine made any impression on her" (p. 157).

What is important to note here is the methodological exclusion of moral prescription in an emphasis on a psychopathology of conflict and defense. Following this interpretive confrontation, the case proceeded along lines of a rudimentary working through, as the analyst went on to search the patient's subsequent daily associations for the additional details of her long-standing repressed inclinations toward her brother-in-law. Freud's theory of therapeutic action had to do with the abreaction of affect strangulated in the repression of trauma, not with any direct reeducation of the content of moral values.

But if there have been significant changes in the social imperatives that once proscribed even a fleeting idea of desire for the husband of one's sister, has not such liberalization of morality of necessity affected the dynamics of neurosis and therefore the principles of their analytic approach? This question shifts our attention to the boundary of psychoanalysis and social history and puts us in mind of those admonitions about the unresponsiveness of analytic thought to the social change in the present century. Thus in the social climate of moral renovation of merely the past several decades, the technical invention I am beginning to identify in the case of Elisabeth von R. has been criticized as an instance of Freud's utter indifference to the social oppression of women, which stamps Freudian thought as irrelevant in the cause of women's liberation. Moreover, the social changes over the past 100 years must put in doubt a psychoanalytic theory whose major outlines were drawn from observations on a population whose social order is no longer a pervasive or compelling reality.

On this occasion, I do not want to examine the specific impact on psychoanalysis of these kinds of criticism.[5] Suffice it to say, they have not fallen on deaf ears and have led to valuable reconsiderations of a variety of concepts. Grossman and Stewart's paper on penis envy (1976), for example, was a response to certain well-taken criticisms that an infantile fantasy had become confused by analysts themselves for an anatomical "fact" (castration) requiring resignation and acceptance on the patient's part. Recently, to give another example, there has been a notable amount of reflection on psychoanalytic therapy with homosexual men and women (Panel 1986, 1987) reaffirming the long-standing psychoanalytic principle that object choice in itself is never a sufficient criterion for diagnosis and therefore for analyzability. The appearance of such discussions in the context of a gay liberation social movement cannot be accidental. Further on in this discussion I will be referring to the masculinization and femininization of the psychoanalytic dialogue, which is a descriptive strategy responsive to a whole development of contemporary interest in certain hidden predicates of texts and discourse.

But this is merely to acknowledge a significant, ongoing interaction between psychoanalytic thought and its social and cultural context. What I want to proceed with at the moment is how it might be, on the other hand, that issues that seem urgent for various social and political theories can, in fact, make virtually no claims on the theory of psychoanalysis.

Since psychoanalytic thought and the social order are dis-

---

5. A good beginning for a pursuit of the problem of the impact of social change on psychoanalytic theory is Steven Marcus's *Freud and the Culture of Psychoanalysis* (1987), especially the chapters "Psychoanalytic Theory and Cultural Change" and "Freud and Biography."

tinctly different organizations, changes in one may not necessarily entail changes in the other. Lively as its transformations
may seem in the social order, social reality may still be kept as a
parameter or constant in psychoanalytic practice and thought.

This can be shown in the case of a woman of contemporary
bearing, who presents for analytic therapy a subtle depression
and several recent bouts of self-destructive behavior. The patient is a 33-year-old corporate executive, attractive, alert, articulate. She is unmarried and has enjoyed the freedom of
behavior, including sexual behavior, this has afforded her. In
therapy, she is verbally forthcoming about sexual matters and
speaks openly about her desires and experiences. Lately, she
has been giving serious thought to "settling down."

Clearly, from a sociological point of view, she is an altogether
different social type than Elisabeth von R. This includes a
difference in another respect that is most pertinent to the point
I mean to develop. Unlike Elisabeth von R., this is a woman who
seems not to be put off by the fact that many of the men to
whom she is attracted and whom she often wins over sexually
are socially attached to other women. Now and again these
other women will be acquaintances, if not friends, of the
patient, in which instances the patient expresses moral consternation and wonders about something perhaps compulsively
transgressive in her conduct. Otherwise, as she is pleased to
report, she doesn't go through life as though it were a moral
obstacle course.

In the past year this patient was seriously considering marriage to a man who had been entertaining a divorce before the
patient came into the picture. In fact, her hopes reached the
planning stage, whereupon her conflicted lover chose to remain
with his wife. Presently, she is in another hopeful relationship
with a man she met at a party, who had shown up with a
woman the patient did not know. The patient has also been
engaged for a number of years in an affair with a married
business associate in a distant city, whom the patient sees
several times a year when she goes out West on business for her
firm—her practice is to give this man a couple of weeks' notice of
her arrival so that he can arrange to spend some time with her
at her hotel.

I focus on merely these aspects of the patient's report in order to establish this patient's relationship to a whole other social code than existed in Western society at the turn of the century. Earlier in our century, even women of the elite classes could not avail themselves of the vocational and sexual options our present patient takes for granted. From one or another socio-logical point of view, this contemporary woman is likely to seem less repressed than her social ancestors because in a nontech-nical sense of the term *repressed* she seems less constrained behaviorally in virtually all spheres of life. We should not be surprised if some analysts also were to come to a similar conclusion in a belief that this patient's more facilitating social reality has already accomplished what analysis had to accom-plish in former times. In such a perspective of social history, she might be regarded as someone, for example, already in posses-sion of a personal power that previously belonged to an op-posing and oppressive social structure, so that now the therapeutic task would have to do with improvement in the deployment of personal power rather than its liberation from a bondage to repression. Thus her story might prescribe a new ratio of analytic to educational responses on the part of the analyst, leading to an emphasis on cognitive matters.

On the other hand, should one still wonder what sexual impulses this present patient could be repressing in her com-paratively active sex life at a cost to her development, this would not be to minimize the actualities of social change. (*Plus ça change, plus c'est la même chose* is not the message.) The point is rather that such change does not excuse us from continuing to reckon with ordinary principles of pathogenesis. In the clinical comparison I am making between two patients at two ends of the century, it is hard to see how social change could render less compelling the principle that conflict and repression figure in pathogenesis, despite changes in the way these things are expressed in behavior, character, symptom, and so on.

In theory, it is not an astonishing idea that the presence of other women in so many of this contemporary patient's sexual involvements speaks, as an exaggeration of an opposite, to a particular liveliness of ordinary unconscious homosexual striv-ings in the patient's mental life. I raise this plausible conjecture

because it illustrates a repression of impulses in a patient's
manifest heterosexual behavior, both of which—the repression
and the behavior—could, in fact, be facilitated by changes in the
social order. Moreover, while it is true that present convention
also allows this patient an easier time to talk directly about sex
than Elisabeth von R. had, there is nothing in any convention
that enables a patient to speak more directly of the repressed.
The relation of manifest to latent content is not a problem that
transformations of social convention can solve. Social convention can modify the content of the patient's report, but this
remains a matter of social behavior. Hence the clinical problem
for the analyst of this contemporary patient is still (as it was in
the case of Elisabeth von R.) the recovery of a sexual fantasy that
is repressed in the midst of her heterosexual behavior, a fantasy
entailing, in some way or other, an absent woman, whose
presence in the life of the patient's sexual partners is highly
motivating in her choice of these partners.

Nor is this problem of repression easier to work out than the
one Freud faced in the case of Elisabeth von R. Like Freud's
patient, my patient has available to her attributes of personal
reality with which to resist an interpretation of her repressed
homosexual strivings. Her actual conduct not only shows that
such an interpretation is preposterous, but, even were she to
grant it some provisional merit based on the facts of her report,
it eventually founders on the patient's moral code, which
distinguishes between preferences and proscriptions—the patient's heterosexuality is asserted as a preference, not a proscrip-
tion on some other type of sexual behavior. Thus she uses what
are called "opposing ideas" (Jacobson 1971, p. 122), contradictions between the ego and the id—in this instance, heterosexu-
ality/homosexuality—that are expressed in a repetitive scenario
of seduction, triumph, and abandonment. Like Elisabeth von R.
on the basis of a different morality, this patient also protests that
her compliance to her moral code contradicts the idea of sexual
repression.

To put it another way, this patient's conformity to a certain
moral code insures a subjective experience of normality, which
supports a resistance in the form of a disinclination to entertain
further meanings of her sexual behavior. Thus social change

does not lessen the problem of resistance; it merely provides other ideals of normality, against which the patient can measure herself. Such ideals, which specify normality as a social fact, are always implicated in repression. Fraser (1970) summarized the problem this way:

> It would be correct to say . . . that all ideas of what is normal are put to use by the unconscious portion of the ego only for their permutation potential. . . . The ego tries to offset the . . . demands of the id by means of a nimble employment of everything inside and outside itself which is mutable. . . . The resistances are conspicuous for their ingenious variability, drawing into their service all manner of details, including culturally determined ones. . . . We cannot fail to notice that, in contrast to the mutability of the norms in the unconscious portion of the ego, the definitions of normal in everyday life are strongly defended and made to appear unchanging. We may speculate, guided by certain clinical impressions, that the tenacious urge to define normal in a final way is based upon unconscious super-ego demands. [p. 110f]

One should add that the ego uses *all* aspects of external reality defensively, because such reality can serve so well as a respite from the sometimes more difficult responsibilities of psychic reality. Paranoia is a model of this in its use of one reality (perception) against another (apperception). We also see this commonly in the clinical situation when the patient insists upon some fact or statistic in order to justify a trivialization (repression) of personal experience, as if factuality in and of itself usurps the significance of anything experiential. In this way, reality and analysis are often put into a competing order of importance.

A patient, late for the first time to his analytic hour, assured the analyst that the subway train sat for nearly 20 minutes between stations. Whereupon the patient, in a spirit of returning to business-as-usual, proceeded to recount a dream he had been remembering from the night before. At a later point in the session, the analyst invited the patient to give some further thought to the lateness. At this the patient felt that his report about the stalled train was under suspicion, and he somewhat testily insisted on its veracity, adding that he therefore couldn't imagine what more one could say about it. As it turned out, this persecutory reaction to the analyst's inquiry embodied an en- actment of an issue the patient had wanted to avoid for several weeks. On the delayed train, the patient had had the impatient sense of being deprived of his huge enjoyment of the analysis. When he thought of having to report this positive feeling about the analysis to the analyst, he drifted into the fantasy that the analyst would do something to change the atmosphere of the sessions because one was not supposed to enjoy one's experi- ence in psychoanalysis. The immutable factor in the patient's lateness—the stalled train—lent itself to a warding off, a "fore- closure" of the idea of having to confess a pleasure construed as prohibited and a concomitant persecutory expectation in the transference.

Similarly, gender stereotypes or roles, insofar as they have come to correspond to actual bits and pieces of customary social reality, are eminently suited to justify repudiations of psycho- logical issues in the clinical situation.[6] Like the uses of a stalled subway train and depending on the urgency of defense, a patient's conformity to a particular gender stereotype allows just so much and nothing more to be pursued of a particular set of psychological issues. For example, a male patient, who equates masculinity with an anti-intellectualism and therefore idealizes what he deems to be "practical" knowledge, could become impatient and incompetent with those matters of inconclusive- ness in the clinical situation whose relevance to practical action is not immediately apparent. "Genitalization" of discourse is a common problem for analysis. It contributes to the narcissistic gain of various cognitive shortcomings by an idealization of an intellectual (or psychomotor) limitation into a positive gender characteristic.

Thus a female patient, who regards intuitive modes of

---

6. I emphasize the matter of stereotypes or roles to limit the meaning of gender to socially ideal concordances between sex (male/female) and various notions of masculinity and femininity. My discussion does not require a complement of technical definitions of such terms as "gender identity," "sexual identity," and so on, for which see Meyer (1982).

perception stereotypically feminine, may have trouble feeling understood by a male analyst. She might activate an unconscious sadomasochistic scenario by regarding intuition by a male as oppressive divination and so feel found out and caught rather than understood. On the other hand, such a patient in the care of a female analyst might have trouble attaining the changes attendant on insight, because interpretation, which is instrumental to insight and decision, might be, to this patient, a masculine capacity and therefore not credible in a female analyst. Empathy, which is the basis for appreciating, and therefore perhaps supporting, the inevitable, is more expectable, so that what is empathic in the stages of interpretation may be profoundly felt to the exclusion of what is clarifying of choice and decision. It would be as if a male analyst, simply by virtue of being male, is impatient for change, while a female analyst, simply by virtue of being female, appreciates the inevitability of the patient's plight, hence its plausibility. *Any* stereotype, not merely those that offend us, is always poised for use in defense and could impose limitations on the analytic process.

A corollary of this worth specifying at this social moment is that, from an analytic point of view, there is nothing extensively practical, much less theoretical, to go on about from the fact that an analyst is female or male. The mere fact of the sex of the analyst does not predict anything crucial about a specific, individual psychoanalysis. For one thing, within-group differences among female and male analysts are likely to be as significant as any between-group differences that could conceivably affect the conduct of an analysis. For another, just as there is no such thing as a standard psychoanalyst, there is no such thing as a standard female or male psychoanalyst.

Indeed, the literature is beginning to confirm the idea that much may escape notice in the clinical situation because of manipulations and other concessions to the reality of the actual sex of the analyst (Raphling and Chused 1988, Roth 1988). In the mental life, femininity and masculinity are always subject to "debasement" (Freud 1912), to being caught up in multiple conflicting meanings. In this view, once the analyst assents to a notion of ideal sex-gender concordance—women are this way, men that way—whether for temporary expedience or because of a lapse into a role of mediator of social values, to that extent she or he has surrendered an analytic point of view and has made an epistemic move to a boundary of psychoanalysis where the variabilities of a trait psychology take on technical value.[7]

We should note that stereotypes in themselves are not what create the clinical problem. The problem is in the nature of the patient's *conformity* to stereotypes, a problem that can be designated the *psychopathology of conformity*. From the social point of view, conformity is, of course, a fact of life by virtue merely of the existence of social ideals. But it does not follow that particular ideals, as they are embodied in gender mythologies and social prescriptions, also particularize universals of social experience, as if the identification of an ideal predicted something absolute in the way of conformity.[8] From a psychoanalytic point of view, conformity is a process of considerable variability. Freud (1914) spoke about the importance of distinguishing the mere adoption of ideals from how they figure as actual motives in behavior. One can be arrested by and enslaved to the most lofty ideal. Or an ideal can be "sublimated" in the cause of personal development. "It is precisely in neurotics" Freud wrote, "that we find the highest differences of potential between the development of their ego ideal and the amount of sublimation of their primitive libidinal instincts; and in general it is far harder to convince an idealist of the inexpedient location of his libido than a plain [person] whose pretentions have remained more moderate" (p. 95).

In consideration of this, a psychoanalysis of gender becomes an account of its attainment in development and its functions in

---

7. Grossman and I (1988) reported some indications of controversy in academic circles (e.g., Deaux 1984) about restricting gender traits to mere essences rather than fluctuating motives in broader mental processes. This is spreading to studies in personality in general where there has been a lamentable "practice of treating personality concepts as unchanging essences that transcend all assessment contexts" (Kagan 1988).

8. In the course of their astute review of many of these issues, Barglow and Schaefer (1976) offered a sound word of caution, "We must be careful before we decide just what or whose kind of reality the myth reflects, or just what relation it bears to social behavior" (p. 314).

neurosis. Freud (1933) spoke to this point in a famous statement on female sexuality: "In conformity with its peculiar nature, psycho-analysis does not try to describe what a woman is—that would be a task it could scarcely perform—but sets about enquiring how she comes into being, how a woman develops out of a child with a bisexual disposition" (p. 116).

Normative matters of gender are left to other disciplines, such as functionalist sociology, whose spokesmen were right to observe how unsystematic a vocabulary psychoanalysis offered for a taxonomy of normal behavior traits and types (Inkeles 1966, Levine and Scotch 1968). A few things about the encounter of development and social reality suggest why psychoanalysis cannot grasp very much in the way of a set of purified social ideals. For one, social standards of any kind, particularly of masculinity and femininity, are never precisely mirrored in the development of any individual, because they are always subject to interpretation in accordance with the individual's immediate interests and capacities for understanding. This is the case if for no other reason than that a distinction between primitive authority and social codes is never clear-cut or firm. No matter what the seeming merits of any particular social code, it never speaks for itself in development, but must be conveyed at its outset by primitive authority. This is a fundamental principle in a psychoanalysis of socialization (Kaplan 1984). The acquisition of social standards always occurs in an emotional climate of struggles between children and parents, among other authorities, so that social standards are never simply abstract cognitive representations but are issues in conflicts among pleasure, object relations, and narcissism.

Moreover, parenthood, indeed, mentorship in general are developmental stages (Benedek 1959, Erikson 1964). If it is an emotional problem for the disciple to acquire social standards, it is also an emotional problem for the authority to become reinvolved with these standards in the socializing process. Therefore, no authority brings to the disciple what we casually call a set of social codes; for example, girls are this way, boys that way. The authority brings as well his or her own conflicts with social codes. Hence social codes are conveyed idiosyncratically; for they embody the authority's own personal history of their acquisition. In this respect, authorities always transmit merely a *version* of social reality.

Then there is the problem of transformation of the meaning of ideals at different stages in development, which complicates and personalizes the outward appearances of socialization in one's approximations to conventional aspects of social roles and morality. Consider a common and expectable strategy of the child to employ resolutions achieved at one stage of development to solve problems arising at another. In the anal stage, for example, the child acquires a sense of cleanliness, wholesomeness, self-regulation. The alternatives to be avoided have to do with being dirty and uncontrolled, hence bad and rebellious. Disgust is a prominent affect developed in the anal stage toward previously pleasurable fecal experience. These developments become interpretive possibilities—the states of mind—brought to the subsequent oedipal stage where genital impulses become prominent issues between the child and the environment. The child's genital sensations and impulses evoke social prohibitions, which are then interpreted by the child in anal terms. A genital impulse can acquire a disgust reaction that developed appropriately at the anal stage, since this affect has already come to signify prohibition. When disgust arises in connection with genital impulses, their repression involves anal qualities: sex is dirty; the penis is a fecal stick; the vagina is a dirty hole, and so on. In this way, genital prohibitions are established on the basis of self-control leading to a sense of cleanliness. Whereas from the social point of view, conformity to genital prohibitions indicates socialization, from the psychoanalytic point of view, such conformity may become interesting as a vicissitude of the anal and genital components of the sexual instinct.

Such developmental events signify both manifold causality and multiple function within the general concept of overdetermination. Indeed, in his best commentary, one of the things Freud regarded of significant interest about female psychology was a set of issues arising in the encounter of early pregender ordeals of the little girl and certain later childhood exposures to ideals of femininity. It was his sense, for example, that much distress that relates ostensibly to female sexuality, for example, the genital difference, genital prohibitions, and other social constraints on the female role, are displacements of the earlier pain of all that had to perish between the female child and her preoedipal mother; Freud (1931a) spoke of "rationalizations devised later to account for the uncomprehended change in feeling" between daughter and mother (p. 234). This does not mean that Freud deemed the oppressions of the sex difference purely figments of an imagination repressing more primary events. He meant that the story of development is always more complex and less conclusive than it may at first appear. Jacqueline Rose (1986) put all this cogently (and with significant implications for feminist politics):

> If psychoanalysis can give an account of how women experience the path to femininity, it also insists, through the concept of the unconscious, that femininity is neither simply achieved nor is it ever complete. The political case for psychoanalysis rests on these two insights together—otherwise it would be indistinguishable from a functionalist account of the internalisation of norms. In fact the argument from a biological pre-given and the argument from sociological role have in common the image of utter passivity they produce; the woman receives her natural destiny or else is marked over by an equally ineluctable social role. [p. 7]

Development is not restricted to early childhood. It is an unending process, in which vibrations of gender are never still (L. Kaplan 1984). Thus beginning, say, at adolescence, a variety of gender stereotypes become available to the individual from the social order that further socialize earlier developmental events. Since stereotypes reside finally in institutions and mythologies of the social and cultural order, psychoanalysis takes them for granted. But this is not to say that they are entirely of no interest; for they do vary, and in their variations the analyst can glimpse something of a choice the patient has made or is trying to make. The Good Clean American Boy, for example, is a stereotype an adolescent encounters in the schoolyard, conformity to which can normalize the anal resolutions of genitality I described. In this way, a selection of stereotypes residing in the social order provides subsequent opportunities for previous shortcomings in development to pass as normal to oneself and others. The Lone Ranger stereotype, with its assignment of the adolescent to the periphery of the peer group and its exciting rescue fantasies, can compensate, libidinally and narcissistically, for certain exaggerated primal scene mortifications in development.

A common social stereotype for women, particularly in the southern United States, which Greenacre (1947) wrote about many years ago, consisted of an attractiveness that accrued to a large-eyed innocence and an immature helplessness and impracticality. Women conforming to this social ideal were chatterboxes, who proudly knew nothing about such matters as money or arithmetic, though they might have had a flair for clothes and household decoration. They were often called "Honeychile" and never seemed to mature over the years, but only to fade away into a shell of eccentricities. Greenacre (1947) called them Eternal Child Wives and described a particular oedipal conflict that was provisionally normalized by conformity to this stereotype.

This social type was, in turn, immensely appealing to a man whose developmental conflicts made a heterosexual peer relationship impossibly difficult. In such instances, the man's conformity to a stereotype of the Infallible Husband Authority was supported by a marriage to an Eternal Child Wife, this to the narcissistic enhancement of all concerned.

Thus the social order is stocked with ideals that enable much of the outcome of individual development to transcend social deviance. However, from a psychoanalytic point of view, social conformity and repression go hand-in-hand, so that in the clinical situation, as I observed earlier, social conformity appears as a resistance to the analytic process.

There is a further complication in the psychoanalysis of conformity. Though often represented by the patient as a univocal stability, social reality also entails perceptions and fantasies of conflicting alternatives, which lead to comparative judgments of difference. As Freud (1931b) observed about "libidinal types," an aspiration toward one social ideal is a repudiation of another. The point is that a psychopathology of conformity is also a psychopathology of difference, which always figures as a factor in analyzability. This was one of the meanings of Freud's remark (1914) that the nature of the patient's narcissistic attitude toward difference constituted one of the limits to the patient's "susceptibility to influence" (p. 73).[9]

The valuation that development imparts to a set of social norms is coupled with a devaluation of an alternative set of ideals. One of the phrases Freud used to speak about such categorization was the "narcissism of minor difference" (Freud 1918, p. 199, 1921, p. 101, 1930, p. 104). By this he meant an exaggeration of a minor difference selected from a larger similarity for the sake of maintaining identity. In connection with this, Freud mentioned the enmity between the Southern and Northern German, the Spanish and Portuguese, the Aryan and Semite, the Caucasian and so-called colored races. In *Gulliver's Travels*, Swift provided an example of the "narcissism of minor difference" in the episode of the voyage to Lilliput, where a kingdom is divided in war because of a difference over which end of the egg is to be broken for eating, the larger or smaller.

A similar process can take place, of course, in connection with major difference. In the oedipal stage, the difference between the sexes becomes a major difference. The narcissism of the difference pertaining to the sexes becomes a later edition of such infantile dichotomies as strong/weak, clean/dirty, good/bad, and so on. At the oedipal level these are transformed into subject/object, active/passive, sadistic/masochistic, and so forth. These infantile and childhood paired opposite dichotomies also acquire dichotomous values along infantile lines, for example, clean/dirty, good/bad.

Psychoanalysis reveals that transformations of infantile narcissism are universally incomplete. In respect to gender, this is evident in the fact that masculinity and femininity are generally thought of and discussed dichotomously as consisting of paired opposite traits, which is indicative of the infantile origin of the

---

9. Berenstein (1987) spoke of one of the criteria of termination as "a reduction in the narcissistic cathexis which blurs differences" (p. 33). The defensive minimization of difference, for example, between past and present, is a way of avoiding a conflict of alternatives.

classification. This being so, value judgment is inevitably assigned to the classification. In the cradle of narcissism, perception and value judgment are closely linked; to a child, two
persons of average but different physical height are likely to be
categorized as big and little. Infantile perception is never entirely free from preoccupations with value. Nor is adulthood
ever entirely free from infantilisms.

Freud (1921) gave an explanation of the enmity arising in
difference, which can also be taken as an explanation of the
Battle of the Sexes. He wrote, "In the undisguised antipathies
and aversions which people feel towards strangers with whom
they have to do we may recognize the expression of self-love—
of narcissism. This self-love works for the preservation of the
individual, who behaves as though the occurrence of any
divergence from his own particular lines of development involved a criticism of them and a demand for their alteration" (p.
102). In other words, the perception of difference in another is
experienced as a mockery of the repression of impulse that
shapes the "libidinal type" one has become. Envy of the other,
who appears less repressed in those respects in which the other
is different, is also present among one's suspicions. In the
fantasy of the other being less repressed in certain ways, one
concludes that the other is also less ideal, less ethical, less
civilized, and one's hostility can then take the form of socially
sanctioned, hence righteous, indignation and denigration.

So in the clinical situation, the sheer fact of social reality is an
item in the dynamics and economics of narcissism. Nor will
radical manipulations of difference—women analyzing women,
men analyzing men—relieve much of the problem of resistance.
For the narcissism of similarity is merely the other side of the
coin. Besides, in the clinical situation, sex difference is only one
instance of the struggle with the narcissism of difference. The
divided roles of the analysand and analyst, which are noninter-
changeable, are the fundamental circumstance leading to transference, which is a technical term that signifies a defensive
minimization of difference, that is the difference between a
libidinal object of the past and the psychoanalyst of the present.
Indeed, it may be worth wondering how much of the conflict

around this particular fundamental division of labor we mistakenly lay at the doorstep of the sex difference between the analysand and analyst.

This is not to deny that the sex of the analysand and analyst is a matter of importance in every analysis. But does this require special technical accommodations different from those matters entailing other differences and similarities, factual or fancied, with respect to analysand and analyst, such as ethnic, cultural, generational? I have been arguing that such a question is begged by wholesale appropriations of the findings of boundary fields, such as sociology, social history, biology, and evolutionary theory, to the problem of sex and gender in the psychoanalytic situation.

There may well be a sense, for example, in which the comparative moral lives of women and men, taken as separate social groups, can be said to be at variance in certain specifiable ways (Gilligan 1982). However, this does not mitigate the problem for psychoanalysis of discerning a psychopathology of conformity to such normative differences in moral aims. What is a finding in a sociology of moral development is reflected upon by psychoanalysis as a case in point in a general theory of the superego. And if the analyst is not to repeat a mistake of Freud, who sometimes regarded the conscientiousness and scrupulosity of the obsessive-compulsive as well-developed virtues (attained more favorably by males), the analyst will be prepared to analyze all affects and attitudes of narcissistic rectitude resulting from conformity as persisting infantilisms, despite the fact that such conformity may be to what a boundary science of moral development tells us are the virtues of authentic womanhood and manhood.

The Oedipus complex is not a pastoral. It does not lead to completely deinstinctualized moral attainments in anyone, let alone in an entire population of experimental subjects. What psychoanalysis can begin to add to the findings of a sociology of moral outcome, such as Gilligan's (1982), is its unique psychological understanding of the very idea of morality itself. This includes an understanding of the *vicissitudes* of the moral life— how, for example, infantile sexuality infiltrates virtue, as when anal scrupulosity is disguised as honesty, sadism as justice, masochism as mercy, and how states of narcissistic rectitude acquire the meaning in the mental life of virtue itself.

A concluding proviso: despite the difficulties and hazards, interdisciplinary commerce has been indispensable to the development of psychoanalytic thought. As I have suggested, psychoanalysis itself emerged from the very boundaries between sexology and psychiatry, and it went on to thrive upon interests in art, social anthropology, history, biology, neuroscience. My aim has not been to stifle influence from such quarters by erecting impossible standards for intellectual exchange. I have merely been insisting that every so often, as on this occasion, some stock be taken of ordinary standards of technicality, so that differences in points of view and disagreements in conclusions can be well conceived. Toward this end, I have tried to indicate a few things worth keeping in mind in regard to the problem of gender in psychoanalysis. Principally, I have been emphasizing certain psychoanalytic technicalities that should be reckoned with in connection with gender as an aspect of social reality.

REFERENCES

Abrams, S. (1979). The psychoanalytic normalities. *Journal of the American Psychoanalytic Association* 27:821–836.

Barglow, P., and Schaefer, M. (1976). A new female psychology? *Journal of the American Psychoanalytic Association* 24(suppl.):305–350.

Benedek, T. (1959). Parenthood as a developmental phase. *Journal of the American Psychoanalytic Association* 7:389–417.

Berenstein, I. (1987). Analysis terminable and interminable, fifty years on. *International Journal of Psycho-Analysis* 68:21–36.

Bleger, J. (1967). Psycho-analysis of the psycho-analytic frame. *International Journal of Psycho-Analysis* 48:511–519.

Breuer, J., and Freud, S. (1895). Studies on hysteria. *Standard Edition* 2.

Deaux, K. (1984). From individual differences to social categories. *American Psychologist* 39:105–116.

Eissler, K. R. (1953). The effect of the structure of the ego on psychoanalytic technique. *Journal of the American Psychoanalytic Association* 1:104–143.

Erikson, E. H. (1964). *Insight and Responsibility*. New York: Norton.

Fraser, A. W. (1970). Concepts of normal behavior in the light of psycho-analysis. In *Man and His Culture*, ed. W. Muensterberger, pp. 101–111. New York: Taplinger.

Freud, S. (1896). Further remarks on the neuro-psychoses of defence. *Standard Edition* 3.

———— (1912). On the universal tendency to debasement in the sphere of love. *Standard Edition* 11.

———— (1914). On narcissism. *Standard Edition* 14.

———— (1918). The taboo of virginity. *Standard Edition* 11.

———— (1921). Group psychology and the analysis of the ego. *Standard Edition* 18.

———— (1930). Civilization and its discontents. *Standard Edition* 21.

———— (1931a). Female sexuality. *Standard Edition* 21.

———— (1931b). Libidinal types. *Standard Edition* 21.

———— (1933). New introductory lectures on psycho-analysis. *Standard Edition* 22.

———— (1985). *The Complete Letters of Sigmund Freud to Wilhelm Fliess*, tr. and ed. J. M. Masson. Cambridge, MA: Harvard University Press.

Gilligan, C. (1982). *In a Different Voice*. Cambridge, MA: Harvard University Press.

Greenacre, P. (1947). Child wife as ideal. In *Emotional Growth* 1:3–8. New York: International Universities Press, 1971.

Grossman, W. I. (1986). Freud and Horney. In *Psychoanalysis: The Science of Mental Conflict*, ed. A. D. Richards and M. Willick. Hillsdale, NJ: Analytic Press, pp. 65–88.

Grossman, W. I., and Kaplan, D. M. (1988). Three commentaries on gender in Freud's thought. In *Fantasy, Myth, and Reality*, ed. H. Blum, Y. Kramer, A. Richards, and A. D. Richards. New York: International Universities Press, pp. 339–370.

Grossman, W. I., and Stewart, W. A. (1976). Penis envy. *Journal of the American Psychoanalytic Association* 24(suppl.):193–212.

Hartmann, H., Kris, E., and Loewenstein, R. M. (1951). Some psychoanalytic comments on "culture and personality." In *Psychoanalysis and Culture*, ed. G. B. Wilbur and W. Muensterberger. New York: International Universities Press, pp. 3–31.

Inkeles, A. (1966). Freudian theory and sociological research. *International Journal of Psychiatry* 2:550–555.

Jacobson, E. (1971). *Depression*. New York: International Universities Press.

Kagan, J. (1988). The meaning of personality predicates. *American Psychologist* 43:614–620.

Kaplan, D. M. (1973). A technical device in psychoanalysis and its implications for a scientific psychotherapy. In *Psychoanalysis and Contemporary Science* 2:25–41. New York: Macmillan.

———— (1984). "Thoughts for the times on war and death." *International Review of Psycho-Analysis* 11:131–141.

_____ (1988). The psychoanalysis of art. *Journal of the American Psychoanalytic Association* 36:259–294.

Kaplan, L. (1984). *Adolescence*. New York: Simon & Schuster.

Levine, S., and Scotch, N. (1968). The impact of psychoanalysis on sociology and anthropology. In *Modern Psychoanalysis*, ed. J. Marmor. New York: Basic Books, pp. 598–625.

Marcus, S. (1987). *Freud and the Culture of Psychoanalysis*. New York: Norton.

McDougall, J. (1980). *Plea for a Measure of Abnormality*. New York: International Universities Press.

Meyer, J. K. (1982). The theory of gender identity disorders. *Journal of the American Psychoanalytic Association* 30:381–418.

Panel (1986). Toward a further understanding of homosexual men, reporter R. C. Friedman. *Journal of the American Psychoanalytic Association* 34:193–206.

_____ (1987). Toward the further understanding of homosexual women, reporter A. Wolfson. *Journal of the American Psychoanalytic Association* 35:165–174.

Raphling, D., and Chused, J. (1988). Transference across gender lines. *Journal of the American Psychoanalytic Association* 36:77–104.

Reiser, M. (1985). Converging sectors of psychoanalysis and neurobiology. *Journal of the American Psychoanalytic Association* 33:11–34.

Rose, J. (1986). *Sexuality in the Field of Vision*. London: Verso.

Roth, S. (1988). A woman's homosexual transference with a male analyst. *Psychoanalytic Quarterly* 57:28–55.

Sulloway, F. (1979). *Freud, Biologist of the Mind*. New York: Basic Books.

Wallerstein, R. S., and Smelser, N. J. (1969). Psychoanalysis and sociology. *Internal Journal of Psycho-Analysis* 50:693–710.

Wolff, P. H. (1988). The real and the reconstructed past. *Psychoanalysis & Contemporary Thought* 11:379–414.

3

The Place of the Dream

Long-standing and well-reasoned technical admonitions warn the analyst that dream material should be evaluated in the same spirit as any other material introduced by the patient in the course of analysis (Freud 1911, 1923, Waldhorn 1967, 1971). Nevertheless, in actual clinical experience, the dream continues to assume an exceptional place in the psychoanalytic situation; that is, the dream continues to constitute an exceptional trial for the analyst beyond what is entailed in all other clinical exchanges. One aspect of the problem relates to the analyst's professional claim of a trained competence in dream interpretation. Since this fact has a history that has not been entirely left in the past, I begin on a historical note because something in the history of dream interpretation seems to recur whenever the analyst is presented with a dream in the course of therapy.[1]

HISTORICAL BACKGROUND

Early in the development of psychoanalysis as a profession, Freud's (1900) "Interpretation of Dreams" was a crucial text for any would-be psychoanalytic practitioner, not only because it represented virtually all the interests and theoretical principles of the psychoanalytic viewpoint, including a technique for interpreting the latent content of manifest revelations, but also

---

1. See Blum (1976) for a less restrictive and more academic version of the history of the dream in psychoanalysis, including the relationship of the dream to the evolution of practice.

because the interpretation of dreams seemed to Freud himself to be the most compelling demonstration of the value and incisiveness of the psychoanalytic approach to certain problems of the human spirit. "During the long years in which I have been working at the problems of the neuroses," Freud wrote in the preface to the dream book, "I have often been in doubt and sometimes been shaken in my convictions. At such times it has always been the "Interpretation of Dreams" that has given me back my certainty" (p. xxvi).

Years later, in his Clark University Lectures (1910), following an extensive psychoanalytic explanation of hysterical symptoms, Freud confessed that he had intended all along during those lectures to give a detailed account of dream interpretation but hesitated to do so because such an interest of psychoanalysis might have struck his audience as "indecent" in a series of purportedly scientific lectures. Yet he insisted then that if "you can accept the solutions of the problems of dream-life, the novelties with which psychoanalysis confronts your minds will offer you no further difficulties" (p. 33). He added that the dream is not only "the royal road to a knowledge of the unconscious" (by which he meant the theory of unconscious process), but it is also the road to becoming a psychoanalytic practitioner. "If I am asked how one can become a psychoanalyst, I reply: 'By studying one's own dreams' " (p. 33). He noted, moreover, that every opponent of psychoanalysis directs an intellectual hostility against "The Interpretation of Dreams" above all.[2]

Given this initial priority of dreams, both as a demonstration of psychoanalytic principles and as a proof of the analyst's practical comprehension of those principles, it is easy to see why the early epoch of psychoanalytic professionalization entailed a preoccupation with dreams among would-be analysts that extended to the clinical situation itself. Like Freud, our professional forebears faced an incredulous public that included the

---

2. In this connection, William James (Hardwick 1980), who was present at the Clark Lectures and came away with mixed reactions, documented his reservations in a letter to Theodore Flournoy with the complaint, "I can make nothing in my own case with his [Freud's] dream theories" (p. 256), his only substantive comment on Freud's lectures in this letter.

patients who came for analysis. These burgeoning analysts were also ambitious to prove themselves as analytic clinicians to their teachers and supervisors, and treatment and training were imbued with a didactic zeal for which work with dreams was a principal activity of proof. "The Interpretation of Dreams" took on the characteristics of a practical manual for conduct. In fact, common analytic wisdom once regarded a session in which the patient brought no dream as an occasion of exceptionally high resistance, and a session in which the dream yielded to a less-than-satisfactory interpretation as a failure.

From his supervisory experience, Freud soon caught on to the misapprehensions of his students about the dream in clinical practice, and he expressed his views in "The Handling of Dream-Interpretation in Psycho-Analysis" (1911). In it, he distinguished the technique of dream interpretation as it appeared in the dream book from dream interpretation in the psychoanalytic treatment of patients. "Anyone coming from dream-interpretation to analytic practice," he wrote, "will retain his interest in the content of dreams, and his inclination will be to interpret as fully as possible every dream related by the patient" (p. 91). He then summarized certain elementary principles of psychoanalytic technique, including the principle that the initiative for beginning the analytic hour should be left as much as possible to the patient and that the analyst should engage without prejudice whatever material arises. There is no place among such principles for the analyst's preference to hear a dream or even to interpret one. "I submit, therefore, that dream-interpretation should not be pursued in analytic treatment as an art for its own sake, but that its handling should be subject to those technical rules that govern the conduct of the treatment as a whole" (p. 94). In other words, the interpretation of dreams as a demonstration for a theory of mind is something quite different from the interpretation of dreams in a psychoanalytic process, to which the dream surrenders its special status among the patient's varied means of communication.

Freud (1923) later reiterated this point in counseling against a disarming intimidation from the "mysterious unconscious." "It is only too easy," he wrote, "to forget that the dream is as a rule merely a thought like any other" (p. 112). This statement is true only up to a point, and I will address its limitations later.

Other references also show that Freud was actually of two minds about the special status of the dream in clinical practice. One of his most ambitious case studies (1918), for example, turns crucially on a patient's dream of some wolves in a tree. In any case, Freud's attempts to redress the early exaggeration of the dream in clinical practice have had wide exposure. In the 1960s, a Kris Study Group on the place of the dream in clinical psychoanalysis (Waldhorn 1967) concluded that from a clinical point of view, the dream (1) conveys neither more nor less than any other source, (2) does not give access to material otherwise unavailable, (3) is neither more nor less useful for analytic understanding than any other material, and (4) is not particularly salient for the recovery of repressed childhood memories (summarized by Greenson 1970).[3] Although Freud might not have concurred with such conclusions, he nevertheless lent a certain authority to them.

Greenson (1970), in his Brill lecture on the exceptional place of the dream in psychoanalysis, disputed the findings of the Kris Study Group. He noted—persuasively in my view—that the dream occurs in a unique psychological state, which in itself imparts an exceptional character to the dream as a mental outcome and as a report to the analyst. Although the psychoanalytic principles of dream formation are the same as for other clinical phenomena (e.g., symptoms, transference), in dream

---

3. Arlow and Brenner (1988) made some similar recommendations with respect to the dream in psychoanalytic training. They observed that the psychoanalytic curriculum overemphasized dream interpretation, even though most analysts are "by now convinced . . . that dreams are not the high road to the unconscious mental life that Freud first thought them to be" (p. 7)—as if a loss of something exclusive in the way of unconscious signification deprives the dream entirely of its value for incisive instruction in unconscious processes. Therefore, as a teaching text, "The Interpretation of Dreams" is "superannuated." This view is consistent with Arlow and Brenner's general sense that psychoanalytic thought has long since achieved a stage of development that enables it to be taught topically rather than historically as a limited number of updated subjects, for example, drive, defense, affect, compromise, and structure. As a special subject, dreams would disappear within such superordinate considerations.

formation these principles operate in an exceptional topographic circumstance.[4] This circumstance invites a mentality in the analyst that differs somewhat from that required for other kinds of patient reports. Greenson's emphasis on the dream did not imply restoration of its misapprehended prominence in clinical practice. He simply meant that even in the clinical situation the dream is always a communication of some peculiarity, whether or not the clinical moment is suitable for entertaining it. Freud himself made it clear that he did not regard the dream as "merely a thought like any other." He (1900) quoted Fechner: "The scene of action of dreams is different from that of waking ideational life" (p. 536), referring to this remark as the only sensible one he had found in the literature on dreams.

CLINICAL PROBLEMS WITH THE EMPHASIS ON THE DREAM

The clinical problem concerns not only the capacity to become receptive to the dream's peculiarities, but also our various attitudes toward being expected to possess the capacity and to exercise it in an expert manner. Greenson (1970) noted that much of the controversy over the special value of dreams in the clinical situation is a function of the variability of this capacity among analysts. Those who are less endowed with, or less inclined to marshal, this capacity will underplay the exceptional character of the dream, rationalizing their position as a deference to the theory of technique, which assigns equal weight to all material in the analyst's "evenly hovering attention."

One problem with Greenson's statement is its suggestion that the capacity to interpret dreams is a more or less fixed functional trait that distinguishes populations of therapists. If there is a sense in which this notion might be true, it is no less necessary

---

4. Shevrin (1986) has devised a simple and yet most incisive scheme to account for the particular quality of consciousness that characterizes a dream. He speaks of the confounding of ordinary frames of reference, of perception, of memory, and of judgment, and the relationship or lack thereof in consciousness of the source of dream states and awareness of such states.

to wonder if the capacity fluctuates greatly in individual therapists at different stages of their careers, at different stages of
particular cases, and with different patients. However, Greenson's salient idea was that a concept of the capacity to interpret
dreams actually influences our attitudes toward the dream's role
in clinical practice. To the extent that we imagine a special
capacity for understanding dreams, we will be at odds with our
intent of impartiality toward whatever the patient brings to us.
If we listen to the patient's dream material in order to interpret
it, the interpretation will echo something of the history of the
dream's role in psychoanalytic practice.

In fact, our expertise tends to revert clinical practice to the
early years when dream interpretation was proof of a distinctive
professionalization. We may disabuse our clientele of all sorts of
premises about our other capacities. The analysand's idea, for
example, that the analyst is curative in a certain medical sense
may challenge us, but we deal with it with a conviction that the
idea is the patient's contrivance of metaphor, analogy, and
fantasy elaborated from the immediate likeness of the clinical
situation to the doctor–patient relationships the analysand has
submitted to since childhood. On the other hand, when an
analysand expects us to possess an expertness in understanding
the meaning of dreams, whatever else is at issue, the expectation rests on an unassailable fact.

This fact, moreover, differs from those of our age, gender, or
ethnic background, which theoretically have no functional
counterparts in the matter of technique. But the undeniable fact,
however socially received by the patient, that we have a special
point of view on dreams does have a functional counterpart.
Quite apart from the patient's fantasies, the psychoanalytic
clinician confronts dreams from the perspective of a special
competence in dream interpretation.

This expectation of performance cannot be entirely eliminated
by analysis. Now and again analysts must undertake dream
interpretation, and although they strive to enhance a full
psychoanalytic reflection on the patient's mental life, it is
impossible for them to avoid varying degrees of performance
anxiety and narcissistic apprehension. Freud attempted to mitigate these fears by his assurance that a self-consciousness about

dream interpretation could be laid to rest among the general principles of analytic technique. However, dream interpretation is in part a performance that exposes the analyst to admiration or disappointment in a way that nothing else in the clinical situation quite does. Thus it creates conflict in our attitude toward dreams and alters the frame of mind with which we approach them.

THE DREAM IN THE INITIAL PHASE OF ANALYSIS

This enigma is particularly evident in the opening phase of an analysis. The therapist strives to establish rapport, to facilitate the patient's attachment to therapy, and to educate the patient about the division of roles in the clinical situation. The patient inevitably seeks answers to often unspoken questions: Is this procedure best for what troubles me? Will anything really significant happen here? Is this the best pace for me? Is this person experienced enough? Or, if obviously experienced, is this person jaded and bored by too much experience? Although there are no direct reassurances, we address such questions by bringing them to light, by inviting our patients to elaborate their concerns, and by demonstrating that we are alert and in charge of our role. We employ our skills to assure our patients that we do try to make the most of the sessions and that we can become helpfully concerned with what troubles them in their own terms. If the patient brings a dream into the midst of these endeavors, we face an issue that cannot be ordinary, insofar as anything is ordinary in the clinical situation. First, a whole new morale arises that surpasses the demoralizing communication of symptoms. Also, the patient risks a new experience with a further aspect of the analyst's professional calling. The communication of the dream can, of course, become useful to the patient's resistance, and we anticipate the possibility by avoiding exceptional reactions.

But the fact remains that the analytic therapist is expected to interpret dreams. Moreover, interpretation of the patient's first dream in particular can be among the most starkly impressive acts the analyst can perform. In light of this tempting possibility to employ the dream to substantiate analytic competence and power (reminiscent of the early years of the professionalization of psychoanalysis), it is no wonder that our approach to the first dream has acquired a mystique of great restraint. Indeed, the lore of doing analysis once mandated (and likely still does) that we should let the first dream go by on such grounds as the transparency of the dream and the premature defensiveness any interpretation of it would arouse. I am no longer sure of the validity of such grounds. But I suggest that the reason for such counsel has as much to do with regulating narcissistic impulses in the analyst as with the alleged characteristics of the first dream. When in doubt about your affective state, do nothing is the wisdom here.

Our axiomatic restraint toward first and early dreams is unfortunate because such dreams present valuable early opportunities to convey certain concerns and assumptions of the analytic situation. No other material lends itself so economically and with such conviction to these uses. I shall avail myself of the psychoanalytic tradition of using one's own dreams to make a point because I want to address the firsthand experience of the patient, particularly the experience of a difference between analysis and the immediacy of therapeutics.

Although it was nearly 30 years ago, I still vividly recall the first dream I presented in my personal analysis and how meaningful I found my analyst's interpretive comments about the nature of wishes and conflicts and how influential I found his observations on the extraordinary role of the analysis in my entire life. I want to emphasize that there is always a difference between the technical intent of an interpretation and the full experience of it by the patient. This point helps us to understand why, having once been patients ourselves, we go on to idealize dream interpretation in our fantasies of how our colleagues do better with dreams than we do or shall ever do.

My dream occurred toward the end of my second week of analysis. In the dream, I was lying on an examination table with my shirt sleeve rolled up to expose a bruised forearm. A lean and bespectacled man in a suit and tie was sitting on a stool next to the table, and when he saw the bruise, he turned away in disgust. I was astonished at the dream's clear resemblance to an event that occurred the night it took place. I had gone to a hospital with my father where a friend of my family was ill and required blood transfusions. My father and I went to donate blood. While on an examination table at the hospital, I did roll up my shirt sleeve, and the resident, who was seated on a stool beside the table, noticed a small skin flap on my forearm and moved his face closer to study it for a few moments out of curiosity. He then tied my arm with rubber tubing and proceeded to take some blood. From my reading and cursory reflections on my dreams, I knew that dreams are formed in part from day residues. But in an actual clinical situation, this idea suddenly acquired the lasting impact of an awesome piece of firsthand knowledge. Part of my initial delight in disclosing the dream in connection with one of its day residues must have come from my relief that a concept—the day residue—had been verified in my actual experience. So if it was analysis I wanted, I must have come to the right place.

Evident, yet unexamined, as this reaction was, my analyst let it go by at this early stage. But he did pursue the dream's alteration of the day residue—the man in the dream had replaced the resident, and his reaction of offense had reversed the resident's benign curiosity. I could infer just enough from these inquiries to suggest that the man in the dream was my analyst and that I was emphasizing his characteristic as a stranger in contrast to my father, the hospitalized family friend, and my family physician. As for my analyst's reaction in the dream, I was puzzled. Did I fear that he couldn't handle my case? No doubt there was something to this. When I had come to a pause in my ruminations over these matters, my analyst said quite simply and straightforwardly, "So if you show me what hurts you, and I turn away in disgust, you will be free to continue in the ways of your father."

This was no huge insight into my feelings about the analysis. A prominent theme in my initial revelations in the analysis was my fear that it constituted a betrayal of my parents, my first versions of whom were most benevolent. In fact, I attributed virtues that I liked in myself to the good fortune of having had such parents. I had the common fear that analysis led to a corruption of the values one cherishes. Thus the interpretation of the dream went no further than a restatement of something I was already anxiously conscious of. It could be said that all my analyst had done was to point out that a conscious concern had turned up in my dream life. Nevertheless this simple demonstration of the transposition of a waking thought into a dream thought stands out as one of the more auspicious moments of my life.

EXCEPTIONAL ASPECTS OF DREAM
INTERPRETATION

Why was that moment in my analysis so stirring? Aside from the latent contents of the dream, which were to become extended themes of the analysis itself, I believe the answer involves specific realizations by the patient that the dream is particularly suited to provide. When issues in a dream can be related to both a day residue and a current theme in the analysis, the patient has the experience of being a patient between sessions and around the clock; that is, the patient has the experience of a synthesizing mental activity that implicates the analysis in everyday life. Later in the analysis, such experiences contribute to the crucial working-through process. Interpretation of nondream material also enables such experience — the interpretation of acting out, for example, as a relationship between something imminent in the transference and a manifest action in everyday life. However, in the dream life, the experience is less conflicted and hence more convincing, all things being equal, because dreams, unlike acting out, are once removed from the experience of personal agency and so their telling and understanding are less harassed by the distressing affects of the moral life. De Monchaux (1978) referred to the dream as a benign form of dissociation in which "an unbearable truth [is] both told and denied by locating it for the time being in the context of an unveridical thought form which is commonly not taken too seriously" (p. 452).

Also, the dream is an access to how wishful aspects of the patient's life have acquired the form of adversity. "So if you show me what hurts you, and I turn away in disgust, you will be free to continue in the ways of your father." This interpretation suggests that a bad state of affairs is preferred to a worse one. In my dream, suffering entailed a wish because disloyalty would have been worse. Suffering was proof of moral integrity. This understanding exemplifies Freud's concept that all dreams are dreams of convenience. Although such a formulation was not spelled out to me, I was relieved at that moment to realize there was something to be questioned in the way I had compromised myself between the issues of accepting psychoanalytic care and obeying parental law. It was in no formulation of my analyst but only in his relocating the plausibilities of my actual strivings to the realm of my own imagination that I encountered myself rather than circumstance as the author of my own plight. Hence I could glimpse the possibility of revising the compromises I had struck in life. This insight is an enormous enhancement of the value of analysis to matters in the patient's life apart from symptoms.[5]

Yet another advantage is worth stressing in connection with the special value of dreams in the clinical situation. De Monchaux (1978) described the dream as a reduction of dimensions in comparison to waking experience. She did not mean that waking experience is not selective, but rather that descriptively the dream is usually composed of fewer selections than is ordinary perception. Such reduction of dimensions gives the dream its focal advantages for the clinical process. Although

---

5. Years after my dream experience, Calef (1972) described "dissolution of object loyalty" as a typical conflict in the opening of analyses and used a patient's first dream to demonstrate this phenomenon. This conflict (or apparent lack of it) could be an indication of the initial problem of analyzability, inasmuch as "object loyalty" interferes with a collaborative relationship to the analyst-as-stranger. Although I cannot always define the process in a clinically helpful manner, I suspect that first dreams invariably warn of the patient's conflicts among analysis, "object loyalty," and unconscious fears about the consequences of disrupting defenses and symptom formations. Apart from this contribution, I doubt that first dreams have any incisive diagnostic value because content fails to reveal its function in the patient's mental life, knowledge of which is crucial to diagnosis.

focus may not be an advantage in certain stages of that process, particularly as psychotherapy becomes more analytic, it is sometimes warranted and is, in fact, an outcome of any inquiry or interpretation. Focusing on something is one prerogative of the analyst's role. But to do so in connection with a dream can be the least arbitrary exercise of focus because the dream represents a focus determined by the patient's own mental activity. In the instance of my own dream, I can think of nothing more convincing of the immediate order of business of my rationalized reservations about patienthood than the focus contrived by my own nocturnal solipsism.

Lévi-Strauss (1962) made some observations about art that pertain to an exceptional impulse in the analyst to interpret dream material. He described art as "miniaturization," in the sense that art is a transposition of life involving a sacrifice of dimension. I do not suggest that dreams are art. (I have explored some of the differences in Kaplan [1988].) No dream requires the talent and conceptual skill necessary to compose a Pindaric ode. However, Lévi-Strauss's observations apply to dreams because of the aspect of miniaturization. He pointed out that any encounter with an experiment in scale invites an impulse to interpret. Indeed, mere contemplation of anything so reduced is synonymous with interpretation. Without pursuing the reasons, I want simply to note that the analyst's very act of listening to a dream initiates an interpretive response, whether or not that response is shared with the patient. No other material in the clinical situation works quite this way. Moreover, patients suspect this fact, which is why they single out the dream as the only material they seem to be expected to remember. A patient regrets no other lapse of memory as much as forgetting a dream or one or more of its salient details.

Other advantages of dreams in the clinical situation, which, if not exclusive to dreams, are certainly facilitated by them include: the conviction dreams convey about the psychoanalytic perspective on the nature of wishes and compromises; the omnipresence of the analysis, as evidenced by dreams, in the life of the patient once an analytic process has been established; and the focus dreams give to various occurrences in the great flux of ordinary experience. Merely the recovery of day residues is a valuable step toward restoring significance to those moments of the patient's life that defense has trivialized.

STEREOTYPICAL ATTITUDES
ABOUT DREAM INTERPRETATION

I do not want to pursue the concept of resistance in depth, but we should be mindful that any advantage of the clinical process can also serve expectable resistances to the process. Too much of a good thing soon becomes something else. Too much focus becomes exclusionary. Too much communication of dreams becomes the gratification of the exercise of secondary elaboration that simply aims to restore the reduced dimensions to the dream by bringing it nearer to waking experience.

However, the relationship between states of resistance and the opacity of dreams bears on my earlier observation about the fluctuations of the capacity to interpret dreams at different moments in an analysis. At those moments when our capacity is undermined by a state of resistance, we detect in ourselves a letdown, a sense of demoralization and futility (even before the patient concludes the telling of a dream). We are awakened more rudely than usual to the universal fantasy among clinicians trained in dream interpretation that there is an ideal population of analysts who do enviably better with dreams than we shall ever do.

This fantasy[6] is not simply a variation of a general fantasy that there are more ideal interventions; now and again we all have fantasies about our shortcomings and how we can improve, should we only resolve to do so. That is, we can exhort ourselves, self-deceptively or not, to pay more attention to the transference or to become more witting about abstinence. But such personal resolve with respect to improving our responses to dreams seems implausible. There is something about dream interpretation that differs from other kinds of interventions. We imagine the aptitude for dream interpretation as something

---

6. Abend (1986) discussed such a general fantasy among analysts as a response to certain ordinary stresses in the analyst's life.

innate, and it never seems sufficient. In his Brill lecture, Greenson (1970) lent substance to this fantasy when he spoke about the capacity to interpret dreams as a talent or a gift. Whether or not it entails a gift—and I see no reason why it shouldn't—is beside the point.

As far as analysis is concerned, a flair for making statements of warranted assertability about dream material may or may not be clinically helpful in an actual analysis. But our resulting fantasies about the capacity and the idealization of hypothetical others are concrete problems in their own right, problems related to the performance anxiety I spoke of earlier in connection with the expectation, both the patient's and the analyst's, that as an analytic practitioner the analyst should be able to interpret dreams.

In the instance of my own dream, I have no way of knowing how my analyst's intention corresponded to the effects of his remark on me. However, I was bound to learn, as we all do, that there are inevitable differences between the analyst's intentions and their effects in the psychoanalytic process, and that the analyst will discover that what was meant to be merely a prompting observation has struck the patient as a resounding insight born of ideal wisdom. From the patient's point of view, I believed at the time of this early occurrence in my analytic work that whatever I was experiencing, my analyst meant for me to experience. Patients commonly believe that whatever happens in analysis is a response to the analyst's grand design that predicts all that happens. If a patient is in clinical training, as I was, such a notion becomes an indelible standard for how analysts will command interventions in their own practices. Although the analyst may not immediately disabuse the patient of such a notion by protestations of modesty, the idea eventually succumbs to a succession of depressing insights about the actual powers of the analyst. But this realization does not mean that the notion is ever completely laid to rest, which is why I described it as indelible. Before it becomes an illusion, it is a real experience, and too happy an experience not to be remembered as a standard of how things should proceed. Thus one source of the fantasy of the ideally perspicacious dream interpreter is the analyst's personal analysis, even though the moments when one's own analyst seemed dramatically keen and shrewd were kept optimally rare.

Supervisors may contribute to the fantasy of the ideal dream interpreter not only because of their extensive experience, but also because they hear dream material from their students in a setting once removed from the transference–countertransference structure in which the dreams are reported. If states of resistance correspond to the opacity of dream material, the supervisors, who are once removed from the effects of such states on their perceptions, are always in a better position than their students to see a bit more. I make it a point to share this fact with students who are astonished by my insight regarding a difficult dream. But I am not sure how effective this explanation is because the students have had actual experiences with me of an incisive moment with a dream.

Yet another source of the fantasy, the last I shall mention, is a notion deeply ingrained in the profession that the capacity to interpret dreams is a measure of cultural attainment. Because dreams share with art, literature, and mythology the primal themes of human plight in civilization and something of their symbolic devices, we view dream interpretation as the hallmark that characterizes us as more than philistine middle-class professionals. Although this idea is not nearly as rampant as it once was, it still strikes a few sparks. Thus we are not only incompetents for not being facile with dreams, but we are also Babbitts.

Some version of this intimidating fantasy awakens in us when we begin to entertain a dream. We may revert to the position of Freud's early disciples, who saw the dream as an opportunity for professional self-justification. We may attempt to exercise competence with the dream too far in advance of the patient's participation; that is, the patient's immediate associations to the dream do not inform the therapist's remarks about the dream, as if its interpretation were an independent function of the analyst. One of Freud's (1911) first admonitions was that the art of dream interpretation for its own sake makes the therapy too much a property of the therapist. Greenson (1970) found this tendency in the writings of Kleinians where the manifest content of dreams was interpreted according to the analyst's theoretical convictions. However, this tendency is certainly not limited to Kleinians. (See Reed [1987] for an excellent study of "allegorical" interpretation of manifest content using self psychology as a talking point.)

Another manifestation of the fantasy is some form of trivialization of dreams. The fantasy of the ideal dream interpreter is finessed by the fantasy that one need be only an ordinary member of the species "Compleat Analyst." The Compleat Analyst is in command of an overriding point of view that homogenizes all material in a single set of principles. To such an analyst nothing is trivial, nothing is exceptional with respect to anything else. As regards the dream, the Compleat Analyst scrupulously avoids rising to the occasion so as to prevent any possibility of suggesting that the dream matters or figures differently from anything else the patient brings in—a technical principle of obvious merit, but, like any principle, suitable for purposes of defense. In this stance, the challenge of dream interpretation and its narcissistic issues are merely transformed into a pervasive complacency that conveys its own spirit of superiority. Greenson (1970) cited an example of this attitude in his review of the Kris Study Group report. A patient had presented a dream with a rather painful content involving medical treatment:

> After the patient reported the . . . dream and a few innocuous associations, the analyst asked: "About your dream. What do you associate to the business about the doctor?" To me, the way the question was put gives the impression the analyst is either defensive and hostile or even contemptuous, otherwise he would not use a phrase like "what about the business about the doctor." Furthermore, it is all too intellectual. Words like "what do you associate" push the patient in the direction of intellectual compliance. [p. 529]

Therapists who defend against the fantasy of ideal dream interpretation by exaggerating the inherent problem of understanding dreams and conveying this attitude to their patients are less arrogant but no less affected in their approach to dreams. This device undermines the patient's fantasy of a competent therapist who takes charge of things with certainty and insight. This therapist is always wondering out loud ("I wonder why you . . .," etc.) and confesses to being puzzled by the patient, emphasizing the obscurity of dreams as a good example of why the patient should never expect to get to the bottom of anything. This analyst construes a kind of frank and self-congratulating mousiness as a triumph over an imagined hot-shot with dreams who does not distinguish between a literary and a clinical point of view. If you are too good with dreams, it follows that you had the wrong training (like Freud's early students).

These illustrations, of course, portray stereotypes and stereotypical interferences with the clinical cause of dream interpretation. I have singled out only a few of many attitudes that seem to me wrong-headed—the unilateral usurpation of the dream by the therapist, the minimization of the uniqueness of the dream as a psychological phenomenon, the disparagement of insight as a function of theatricality. But objectifying these attitudes does not exempt us from them; I regard the fantasy as virtually universal throughout the profession. However, we can detect such tendencies toward the dream in all of us—to what extent depends on our styles of rationalization and other defenses.

Nor is the fantasy with respect to the dream simply a variation of the same problem one could attach to any number of issues in the clinical situation. For example, transference and resistance are the hallmarks of any psychoanalytic therapy. But although our attitudes toward the clinical phenomena relating to these concepts betray variations in our sense of professional identity, we live with this problem more easily than we do with the problem of dream interpretation, which is also a hallmark of analytic therapy. How we handle transference and resistance is a problem in the background of our ongoing experience, a problem that our efforts of professional good faith and continuing education will increasingly resolve. Even though we expect to do better with transference at some future time, we can rest assured that we at least do good by it in the present. No such assurance is afforded by our daily confrontation with dreams. Dream problems are incessantly in the foreground of our experience because we are naggingly conscious with each dream of a wealth of content that eludes our understanding. Such consciousness is inherent in claiming the ability to interpret the dreams of another.

CONCLUSION

The exceptional place of the dream in the clinical situation finally accrues to this: With all due regard to the idea that in the clinical situation we are always in the midst of both too little and too much data for purposes of optimal understanding, this ordinary problem is inevitably exaggerated in connection with the presentation of a dream. What we otherwise put aside of this problem returns with the dream because, in a manner different from anything else the patient conveys, the dream is also a celebration of the mysterious and the obscure. Technical principles counsel against distress over this fact, but they cannot tame the fact into a complete submission to a purified clinical atmosphere. Nor should we desire this submission because analysis does not intend to deprive the patient of the ambiguities inherent in a particular mode of thought. Dreams speak for the demonic that is still our grace to concede to the human spirit. They are not simply thoughts like any other, tactical as this view would seem.

Thus, if there is still substance to the argument that the dream continues to occupy an exceptional place in the clinical situation, and if there is something undeniable about our expected competence with this exceptional phenomenon, we are bound to be challenged by the dream in a way that concerns a special aspect of our professional ideals. This being so, there is nothing to be done for the ideal itself. It is as it must be. But we must remind ourselves that the trouble with an ideal is not the ideal itself, but the psychopathology of our conformity to the ideal—our anxieties and shame in connection with our discrepancies in ideal attainment, and our rigidities in both pursuing and opposing the ideal. Dreams are burdens because of all they signify of such a plight each time one appears in the clinical situation. However, in the case of this particular burden, we bear it best with our ingenuities, our open-mindedness, and, not least, our completely undivided attention to the patient's entire presentation. In this regard, it can be said at last that dreams demand nothing exceptional from the analyst.

REFERENCES

Abend, S. M. (1986). Countertransference, empathy, and the analytic ideal: the impact of life stresses on analytic capability. *Psychoanalytic Quarterly* 55:563–575.

Arlow, J. A., and Brenner, C. (1988). The future of psychoanalysis. *Psychoanalytic Quarterly* 57:1–14.

Blum, H. P. (1976). The changing use of dreams in psychoanalytic practice: dreams and free association. *International Journal of Psycho-Analysis* 57:315–324.

Calef, V. (1972). A theoretical note on the ego in the therapeutic process. In *Moral Values and the Superego Concept in Psychoanalysis* ed. S. Post, pp. 144–166. New York: International Universities Press.

De Monchaux, C. (1978). Dreaming and the organizing function of the ego. *International Journal of Psycho-Analysis* 59:443–453.

Freud, S. (1900). The interpretation of dreams. *Standard Edition* 4–5.

———— (1910). Five lectures on psycho-analysis. *Standard Edition* 11.

———— (1911). *Standard Edition* 12.

———— (1918). From the history of an infantile neurosis. *Standard Edition* 17.

———— (1923). Remarks on the theory and practice of dream-interpretation. *Standard Edition* 19.

Greenson, R. R. (1970). The exceptional position of the dream in psychoanalytic practice. *Psychoanalytic Quarterly* 39:519–549.

Hardwick, E., ed. (1980). *The Selected Letters of William James.* Boston: David R. Godine.

Kaplan, D. M. (1988). The psychoanalysis of art: some ends, some means. *Journal of the American Psychoanalytic Association* 36:259–293.

Lévi-Strauss, C. (1962). *The Savage Mind.* Chicago, IL: University of Chicago Press.

Reed, G. S. (1987). Rules of clinical understanding in classical psychoanalysis and in self psychology: a comparison. *Journal of the American Psychoanalytic Association* 35:421–446.

Shevrin, H. (1986). *A Proposed Function of Consciousness Relevant to Theory and Practice.* Paper presented at the meeting of the American Psychological Association, Washington, DC, August.

Waldhorn, H. F., ed. (1967). *The Place of the Dream in Clinical Psychoanalysis.* Monograph II of the Kris Study Group of the New York Psychoanalytic Institute. New York: International Universities Press.

Waldhorn, H. F. (1971). Dreams, technique, and insight. In *Currents in Psychoanalysis,* ed. I. M. Marcus, pp. 167–186. New York: International Universities Press.

4

The Psychopathology
of Fate

Although I have in mind to pursue a few aspects of the errant psychoanalytic concept of personal fate, I begin on something of a literary note, inasmuch as I shall be dwelling throughout on Helene Deutsch's 1930 paper, "Hysterical Fate Neurosis," a paper that warrants comment as a species of historical contribution.

Deutsch's paper is one of those in the annals of psychoanalysis that might be called a classic in the sense that its sustained consideration of a particular subject achieved an originality that has not been superseded. In this sense a classic is a standard with respect to which further advancements of its conceptual issues are oriented. In the bargain, Deutsch's paper enjoys a certain historical distinction, in that the case around which the paper is constructed was the first psychoanalysis presented in a continuous case seminar for candidates of the Vienna Psychoanalytic Institute in the 1928–1929 academic year. The paper acquires a further interest in connection with the fact that Deutsch went on to report a follow-up of its case in a 1959 number of the *Journal of the American Psychoanalytic Association*, a report quite striking for the continuities between the concerns of the original analysis and the course of the patient's life over the ensuing twenty-five years.

None of this insured much in the way of a lively future for the original paper. However, in noting that it is an unread classic, I am not preparing to admonish an oversight of scholarship or to register misgivings about the uses to which the development of

psychoanalytic thought has come to put its published past. On
the contrary, both the theme and the style of Deutsch's paper
strike us as quaint from our present vantage. The theme is fate,
which is sustained in the paper through a case of its psychopathology. Yet the idea of a psychopathology of fate or what had
come to be called a fate neurosis has failed to retain a clear and
definite place in the structure of psychoanalytic thought. Whatever fate used to signify from a psychoanalytic point of view, the
concept has long since been assimilated by more systematic
concepts, so that we no longer find it urgent to hold any
opinions on the subject of fate. Thus, as a theme in a publication
of a former epoch, it seems to us a curiosity, a provisional
construct that was bound to succumb to a process of conceptual
reorganization.

Deutsch's paper is certain to strike us as quaint also because,
like so much of the psychoanalytic literature around 1930,
including much of Freud's own writing of that period, it
employs a style that Thomas Kuhn (1962) has called totally
normal discourse. Normal discourse occurs at a stage in the
development of a discipline when its practitioners are joined in
the belief that basic assumptions and principles are well established, that the meanings of all the crucial organizing concepts
are at last clear, and that the methodology has been so perfected
that all parties properly initiated into the discipline can be
trusted to be conducting a common practice without having to
justify that they are. Much about such a state of affairs, of
course, will turn out to have been matters of shared illusions of
a professional community at one or another moment in the
evolution of its thought. Indeed, it is inevitable with any
passage of time that things prove not to have been as simple and
straightforward as our intellectual forebears thought. When we,
in our perusals, encounter a publication rendered entirely in the
normal discourse of its period, undisturbed by any consciousness of complacency, we feel we are in the presence of something starkly historical. Our pleasure then goes in the direction
not of enlightenment about current problems but of historical
musings and the gratitude we experience toward those in our
past whose efforts have made our present simply possible.
Complacent, unassuming, even naïve, Deutsch's paper on hys-

terical fate neurosis, to the extent that it is read at all, is most likely read for this experience of history.

A further point should be made, however, about this matter of normal discourse. While it is true that normal discourse represents a moratorium on epistemological reflection, it has the advantage of liberating those who are parties to it to examine straightforwardly otherwise arcane phenomena in some detail and thus to advance the interests and concerns of a professional community without the distractions of questioning first principles. Much that we have become skeptical about yet continue to puzzle over is still what was singled out in the past as meriting our attention. This is not to say that the past embodies an unimpeachable authority, for we know also that it is a vast realm of nonsense. Nevertheless, it is often instructive to revisit an idea that has fallen by the wayside in the course of things because certain ideas corresponded to crucial observations in the empirical domain of psychoanalysis, observations that our present complement of ideas may no longer urge so strongly upon our attention. Fate and its psychopathology was an idea corresponding to the larger outlines of the patient's strivings, surpassing the more limited repetitions of symptomatic acts and the day-to-day trials that character structure creates in the patient's psychological commerce with the social order. In our present epoch, rightly or wrongly, we think virtually nothing of the idea of fate, although to Deutsch and doubtless to most of her colleagues in 1930 the idea of fate was current, ordinary, and plausible, even though it was not often placed at the center of a sustained examination. Indeed, Deutsch's paper on hysterical fate neurosis seems to be the only sustained clinical study of the idea in the literature.

I have mentioned that the case presented in Deutsch's paper was one she treated in the late 1920s and wrote up in 1930. It appeared in English in 1932 as the nucleus of the second chapter of her primer, *Psychoanalysis of the Neuroses*, a work that was reissued in the United States in 1965 as the first part of an enlarged text called *Neuroses and Character Types*. One of the strategies of Deutsch's book entailed the long-standing psycho-analytic principle that what psychoanalysis differentiates diag-nostically are vicissitudes of ordinary processes operative in a

general conception of mind. While the successive chapters of
Deutsch's book constitute a taxonomy of symptoms, what she
was at pains to demonstrate were not separate etiologies but
rather continuities among clinical phenomena owing to factors
of variation within an underlying set of genetic, structural, and
economic principles. This explanatory point of view was explicit
as early as 1894 in Freud's "Neuro-Psychoses of Defence," in
which he explained conversions, phobias, obsessions, and even
hallucinations as variations of a return of the repressed in a
process of defense against trauma. This explanatory approach
went on to assimilate increasingly attitudes, experiences, and
behavior previously outside the scope of clinical concern. In
fact, when Freud observed that in his early years of psychoanalytic practice he did not know when an analysis was finished,
one of his meanings was that he had not been sure what was
and what was not clinically his business. He had not yet realized
how far into the human spirit his method was to reach, or that
a full psychoanalytic reflection on every neurosis would eventually involve a psychopathology of development, character,
social life, ideals, morality—even personal destiny, which he
later impelled to clinical interest in his 1916 study, "Some
Character-Types Met with in Psycho-Analytic Work." In short,
the complete realization of the psychoanalytic method exempts
nothing in individual existence from conflict; hence the psychoanalytic principle that the abnormal is a vicissitude of the
normal. By 1930 this version of the scope of psychoanalysis was
commonly held by psychoanalysts in varying degrees of com-
prehensiveness, and Deutsch's book, *Psychoanalysis of the Neuroses*, can be read as an exercise of its versatility.

Thus it is that Deutsch introduced her case of hysterical fate
neurosis with the statement: "We shall be able to show that the
patient, who was without symptoms and as unsuspicious as her
friends and relatives of the pathological element in her fate, was
nevertheless subject to the same difficulties and pathological
fixations in her mental life as other people who suffer from
severe hysterical symptoms" (p. 16). Whereupon Deutsch presented as much of the case as would "illustrate the typical
features of a 'fate neurosis' " (p. 17).

The patient, we are told, was a young woman in her mid-twenties, quite beautiful and versed in the manners of wealth. She had made a long overseas journey to Vienna not only for treatment but also for respite from her actual surroundings in which she had recently experienced some rather dramatic turmoil. Shortly before her departure she had made an attempt at suicide with a revolver in a small hotel in her hometown. A scarcely visible scar on her temple was all that remained of the incident. By the time she presented herself to Dr. Deutsch, the emotionality of the suicide attempt and the events that led up to it had subsided, and in her first interview she appeared calm, self-possessed, and at a loss to say what she needed treatment for. As the interview drew on she began to detect something vaguely morbid in the larger story she told of her life but nothing so definite or acute as to account for the crisis she had recently brought about. And so the analysis began with this puzzling contradiction.

Although the patient's attempt at suicide was a culmination of a succession of events in her love life, all that she could repeat about it was that it occurred in the midst of preparations to marry a man she regarded with great respect and with whom she felt fulfilled, amorous, high spirited. Early on in the analysis she could recall an apprehension about the marriage; if there was anything to despair about, she made a distinction between the person she was about to marry, whom she exempted from her concern, and the act of marrying itself, which seemed to her hasty and demanding of capacities beyond her and therefore doomed. What was intolerable to her about the prospect of a marital failure was the idea that she would be forced to resume her material dependence on her father. For years she had tried to win independence from her father by embarking on several careers, but despite her obvious intelligence and talents, all her efforts had come to grief.

In connection with this she began to single out in the analysis a clear and long-standing complaint about her life. In an otherwise subjectively uneventful childhood and adolescence, she was increasingly troubled by the fact that vague inner difficulties prevented her from fulfilling her intellectual ambi-

tions to enter a university and pursue a profession. Her academic interests were in the physical sciences. Yet she had not
been able to finish high school.

The patient's love life began to reveal correspondences to this
academic problem. While failing in high school, she became
engaged to marry a young man, a distant relative, with whom
she had a tender love relationship for several years. This was
not altogether satisfying, however, because her fiancé related
exclusively to the "woman" in her, ignoring her intellectual
ambitions. Consistent with this, the patient elaborated, he was
something of a womanizer, although she denied any jealousy.
During this relationship, on one of her travels, the patient
gravitated into a friendship with a man significantly older than
she was, a man of appreciable intellectual attainments in an
important diplomatic position. The man's first wife had died,
and his second marriage seemed at first to the patient a happy
one. But as their friendship deepened, he confessed to the
patient that his second marriage never compensated him for the
loss of his first wife, whom he had loved adoringly, and this
intimate information inspired a sudden mutual erotic infatuation. The patient recalled the exciting prospect of being loved as
passionately as the deceased wife. She broke off her engagement, her new lover separated from his second wife, and a
period of great happiness was launched for the patient. In
contrast to her previous relationship, this one was entirely
satisfying, owing to the high regard her new lover, himself so
gifted, placed on the patient's intellectual life.

Here the patient's story was beclouded by what Deutsch called
a strange incident. By what measure, we might ask, is an incident
in a patient's life strange in the view of an analyst, who expects,
after all, that no incident in life speaks wholly for itself and that
all incidents under the aspect of analysis are symptomatic? What
affects us as strange is not the incident in itself so much as the
manner in which it is related. A deed may be wasteful, stupid,
self-defeating, even out of character, but it becomes strange
when the telling cannot include a design of personal agency, an
account of motivation accruing to the functions or even malfunc-
tions of ordinary ego processes, an account, in other words, of

how reality testing, good or bad, was being maintained in and by the deed. Whereas Deutsch's patient could give an account, however truncated, of why her second lover seemed preferable to her first, in the following incident, which involved an impulsive sexual encounter, she could not say what cause of life she was advancing—curiosity, vanity, doubt, challenge. While this quality of self-presentation is seen in varying degrees now and again in the narratives of all patients (indeed, the total repression of motive was one of the first processes Freud used to account for symptom formation and for a patient's experience of the strangeness of symptoms), it figured prominently in the presentations of what had come to be called a neurosis of fate. In such cases it occurred in connection with actions larger and more sequential, hence more consuming and consequential, than what we ordinarily call symptomatic acts.

The incident was this. The patient's lover was called away to the sickbed of his estranged wife. The patient looked upon his departure as an ordinary act of civility, which aroused no protest in her, and she took the occasion to go on a short pleasure trip. While away, she ran across a man of slight acquaintance and disinterestedly went to bed with him. She became pregnant, and an immediate marriage was decided upon. However, in short order, she changed her mind, aborted the pregnancy, and returned to her lover full of remorse. He forgave her. Their relationship became as fulfilling as before, he went on to divorce his wife, and a marriage date was set.

The narrative continued. It was during this happy period that the patient began to go through nights of torment from feelings of inadequacy and inferiority, as she converted her fiancé's admiration of her intellectual potential into demands she felt she could not possibly meet. As the wedding drew near, the patient made her suicide attempt, and this put an end to her relationship with her fiancé. She was convinced that they would never meet again. The suicide attempt, which closed a chapter on the patient's life, was as inexplicable to the patient as to others in her life—Deutsch used the term "unmotivated."

Perplexed only at what now had receded to memory, but increasingly calm and self-possessed, this no longer beleaguered young woman decided on the trip to Vienna for psychoanalytic treatment.

Now it was mainly on the basis of this story, which predated the patient's actual treatment, that Deutsch presented us with the idea of a fate neurosis. As I have noted, such an idea enjoyed ordinary currency in 1930, dating back to Freud's 1916 paper, "Some Character-Types Met with in Psycho-Analytic Work," the second section of which described "those wrecked by success." The story Deutsch's patient told corresponds precisely to what Freud described. In fact, the first case with which Freud opened his own discussion involved a young woman, well brought up, whose adventurousness led her on long travels from home. During one of these she made the acquaintance of an artist who could appreciate not only her feminine charms, as Freud put it, but the finer qualities she possessed as well. They began to live together, and it seemed to her that all she needed to achieve complete happiness was a marriage to this man. After some years, her lover succeeded in winning his family's approval of her, and they went on to prepare for the wedding. At that moment she began to go to pieces. She became obstreperous and delusionally jealous of her fiancé. She felt persecuted by his family and involved herself in what Freud called an incurable mental illness.

Freud gave another case in point in Ibsen's character, Rebecca West, who won the man she loved in a cunning triumph over his wife but who then threatened suicide on the occasion of her lover's proposing marriage.

Reflecting on the seeming contradiction between those onsets of neurosis in which a long-cherished wish is about to come to actual fulfillment and the psychoanalytic finding that an increase in frustration is one of the essentials in the onset of neurosis, Freud went on to resolve the contradiction by reminding us that it is never frustration alone that is pathogenic. A fuller explanation of pathogenesis entails the addition of guilt arising from an increase in an effort to alter the economy of frustration. Freud (1916) wrote:

> In those exceptional cases in which people are made ill by success, the internal frustration has operated by itself; indeed it

has only made its appearance after an external frustration has been replaced by fulfillment of a wish. At first sight there is something strange about this; but on closer consideration we shall reflect that it is not at all unusual for the ego to tolerate a wish as harmless so long as it exists in phantasy alone and seems remote from fulfillment, whereas the ego will defend itself hotly against such a wish as soon as it approaches fulfilment and threatens to become a reality.[1] The distinction between this and familiar situations in neurosis-formation is merely that ordinarily it is internal intensifications of the libidinal cathexis that turn the phantasy, which has hitherto been thought little of and tolerated, into a dreaded opponent; while in these cases of ours [those wrecked by success] the signal for the outbreak of conflict is given by a real external change. [pp. 317–318]

Freud added that the signal is the distressing affect of guilt, which he attributed to transgressions of incest derived from oedipal strivings.

Deutsch's case not only resembles quite closely this view of things, including, as we shall see, an oedipal pathogenesis revealed by the analysis but its presentation is also informed by subsequent ideas of Freud regarding the psychopathology of fate, namely, ill-fated actions as repetitions of traumas, that is, of issues preliminary to guilt in its association with the imminence of forbidden pleasure. In *Beyond the Pleasure Principle* Freud (1920) would attribute to certain actions the function of producing a distressing affect that the ego had failed to develop as a regulatory signal anticipating trauma. Simply put, his thesis was that the repetition of certain actions, limited merely to the experience of distress and its cessation, mimicked the mastery of trauma achieved by the ego in its development of complex defensive processes. This subsequent idea, spelled out in *Beyond the Pleasure Principle*, was already implied in the passage I have quoted in which Freud spoke of the outbreak of the affective signal of conflict as something "given by a real external change."

---

1. A bearing on Freud's observation here will turn up further on in my discussion in regard to Boesky's (1982) idea that imminent actualizations of unconscious fantasies in the transference are warded off by the patient through acting out. I might add that the concept of acting out is one of those into which the idea of a psychopathology of fate has been assimilated.

His implication was that in what he called neurosis-formation a signal by the ego is sufficiently anticipatory to restrict the consequence of drive arousal to the formation of a restricted (and restricting) symptom. In the fate neurosis, on the other hand, the signal—the motive for defense—is not readily produced by the ego, so that a more extensive approach to a situation of danger takes place in the form of a large, comparatively unrestricted action. While such massive collusion with psychic danger is facilitated by an impairment of distressing affect, the "real external change" that is brought about by the patient goes on to produce its own distress and ultimately the inhibition otherwise missing in the ego's response to danger, as if the patient created by actual circumstance what could not be created in an affect-laden fantasy. In this regard such massive actions leading to "real external change" represent impoverishments of thought, which is clinically evident in Deutsch's case in the patient's difficulty in furnishing even a feeble rationalization for her suicide attempt. This is what Deutsch meant when she referred to the patient's suicide attempt as "unmotivated."

But, then, so do symptomatic acts and perversions represent impoverishments of thought, insofar as the patient can give no account of their motives. Also, they retain in their repetitions a traumatic quality in their being experienced as subjectively alien. Moreover, it is not easy to distinguish in the performance of symptomatic acts and perversions the aroused aspect and the anticipatory aspect of the distressing affect involved. If Deutsch followed Freud in his distinguishing a "neurosis-formation" from a fate neurosis, she also followed him in regarding the two as manifest contents related to similar genetic and dynamic principles. (Freud [1923] began later to subsume the difference between symptoms and large symptomatic actions under the unifying concept of the unconscious need for punishment.) Thus Deutsch described the patient as "without symptoms," yet "nevertheless subject to the same difficulties and pathological fixations in her mental life as other people who suffer from severe hysterical symptoms" (p. 16). Nor is the aim with respect to reality different in the two neuroses. In Freud's (1924) "The Loss of Reality in Neurosis and Psychosis" he recalled a patient he had treated many years before (doubtless Elisabeth von R.), who repressed sexual impulses toward her brother-in-law and fell ill with a hysterical paralysis when her sister died and she pushed away the thought, "Now I can marry him." Although the patient's symptom, unlike a fate neurosis, curtailed further contact with the reality at issue, as Freud observed, in this curtailment it achieved the same end as a fate neurosis, albeit in a preservation of larger aspects of the patient's life. The point is that part of the therapeutic endeavor with both Freud's patient and Deutsch's was the restoration of a capacity to engage the environment actively and directly, a capacity from which both neuroses took significant tolls. This is a point in Deutsch's case I shall return to further on.

As for the analysis of Deutsch's patient, it reconstructed a particular and rather straightforward oedipal scenario, as Freud suggested about the fate neurosis and as had become customary in 1930. The patient perceived her father as an efficient, opinionated, and intimidating authority and her mother as stupid, uneducated, and slavishly devoted to the patient's father. Beautiful and talented as a child, the patient recalled the experience of being her father's favorite and of despising her mother. Early on she was already negativistic, hostile, full of protest, and, we might surmise, imperiously so—in later life she was to break off three marriage engagements in rather short order with no evidence of remorse or sympathy for the jilted fiancés. These tendencies were exacerbated by the birth of a brother when the patient was 4. At first she denied in play and in fantasy that it was her mother who had had this child by her father. But not only did this denial fail, the brother also began to endanger the patient's position as the father's favorite. Still worse for the patient, the brother was to go on to impressive academic success up to the point of his death when the patient was 24 and long since an academic casualty. The patient's childhood culminated in "vindictive tendencies toward the unfaithful father, the despised mother and the little rival" (p. 20). The patient's vindictiveness, jealousy, and divisive impulses were not settled by a reaction-formation but by a supervalent conscious rebelliousness that repudiated the mother as a model for feminine strivings—"I refuse to play the part my mother played." Deutsch tells us, not to our surprise, that such vehemence "against the mother's masochistic attitude was, it proved, really a protest against her own masochistic fixation" (p. 21). This protest, limited to the mother, also preserved the father for the patient's unconscious subjection. Deutsch gave several specific details from the patient's early years, including an accident that figures in the form the patient's suicide attempt later took. But merely Deutsch's adumbration of the patient's positive Oedipus complex is sufficient to represent a conflict soluble in the future only by compromise. In this case the compromise at issue is synonymous with neurosis. For only in neurosis will a masochistically submissive aim play itself out in a successful seduction and fantasied triumph, which prove to be merely the prizes poised to be sacrificed in a massive episode of self-defeat.

Deutsch reported that from early adolescence on the patient gravitated toward any male figure perceived as bereft owing to having lost a beloved wife. When the patient was 12, for example, she was drawn into a mortifying incident involving an 18-year-old youth who played upon the patient's susceptibility with a story about his unabated passion for a deceased wife. He set up a liaison with the patient later in the day, but the address he gave her proved to be a hoax, and she never saw him again. Again, while in treatment with Deutsch (and away from home), the patient came into contact with a man who was deeply depressed over the recent loss of his wife; the patient was aroused to rescue him in a brief affair.

But none of this is yet what Deutsch would call a fate neurosis. What she was describing was simply a repetition of libidinal object choices that were made on the basis of the patient's version of her oedipal triangle. Deutsch was quick to assure us that there is nothing pathological in this. "The fact that our patient made her object choice on the model of the father was not in itself neurotic, nor even her preference for widowers. All we can say is that a peculiar repetition tendency could be clearly traced in the course her life had taken" (p. 26).

Nor is repeated disappointment a criterion of a neurosis of fate. Deutsch reminded us that "disappointment is the normal fate of *every* love relationship" (p. 24), by which she meant that the narcissistic basis on which one falls in love will sooner or later give way in varying degrees to a perception of difference between actuality and the ideal. This is a source of the ordinary frustration, experienced as disappointment and unhappiness, which the ego tolerates in its development. Deutsch rejected the idea that "whoever is unhappy is therefore neurotic" (p. 27). In this she removed the problem of diagnosis from judgments of behavior or what she called the "method of social valuation" (p. 26).

The diagnostic problem, then, does not have to do with the infantile origins of ambition or with the missions and designs we pursue as the ongoing and plausible causes of our individual existence, that is, with what I begin here to call our fate. Nor does it have to do with our grief at the perception that our fate is never precisely realized in any achievement, inasmuch as reality testing includes a differentiation of past and present. The diagnostic problem is rather a commentary on the origin of disappointment in fixation and regression, in what Deutsch referred to as an anachronistic relation to the present version of the object and to present circumstance. And the extent to which this anachronism insists that approximations of fate are psychologically exact correspondences to the past is the extent to which discontent must be elaborated into symptoms or, short of that, into a pitch of doom. This idea is not unlike Freud's early point of view on a goal of therapy as a transformation of hysterical misery into common unhappiness, a reply he made to the protest of a hypothetical patient complaining that he could do nothing to change her fate (Breuer and Freud, 1893–1895).

Deutsch demonstrated such protest in her patient against the approximations of the present with an example of regressed ego function. The patient's attraction was to men whose love belonged to another woman, a situation in which the patient's oedipal rivalry came into play. The fact that the other woman was already dead had the advantage of relieving the patient of the necessity of bringing her aggressive impulses into full play. But, then, Deutsch tells us, the patient unconsciously protested "the real facts in the matter of her predecessor's death" (p. 25) and assigned a personally referential meaning to this indifferent event in the present, assuming the guilt for her rival's removal, as if the patient herself had murdered her by wish fulfillment.

The subsequent disposition of guilt becomes a crux of the fate neurosis, in Deutsch's phrase, a "criterion of morbidity" (p. 27). In symptom neurosis guilt motivates the ego to create a symptom that distracts the patient from some critical engagement with the external possibilities of fate; one's fate is played out restrictively in the symptom. In a fate neurosis the guilt becomes regulatory only after one's fate has been advanced to the brink of an anachronistic realization in large external circumstance. This was the outcome Deutsch's patient presented at the beginning of the analysis.

In a passing remark Deutsch made another observation that is crucial to an appreciation of fate neurosis. She attributed the patient's crisis of fate also to "a provocative compulsive acting out" and thus distinguished acting out as an ego mode or function from fate as a content of libidinal and aggressive striving. Actually, she tossed off the distinction as if it were common lore of that time, but I single it out because the recent literature seems to find no occasion to reckon with such a distinction, although it remains important to certain clinical considerations of a broad and general nature. We have seen that the idea of fate is of seemingly only academic interest until it appears as an issue of psychopathology. Such psychopathology is in turn merely descriptive until it is accounted for by a psychopathology of function—here the psychic deployments of distressing affects, the regressions of ego functions, the subversion of thought and judgment by regressions to action. Since these are the concerns of our present literature, the fate neurosis appears to us as a clinical glimpse that quickly succumbs to a longer look at a psychopathology of functions. If acting out seemed to Deutsch a good handle for grasping the fate neurosis as a clinical category, this was because the assumptions about acting out as a distinct and abiding characteristic of certain patients were not challenged by sustained clinical observation.

How much this has changed is evident in Boesky's (1982) recent reconsideration of the concept of acting out. Boesky's study has the merit of returning now and again to observable differences in patients with respect to acting out. Speaking of "the ubiquitous shifts during analysis from intrapsychic, introspective experiencing [a capacity rather lacking in Deutsch's patient at the outset of her analysis] to action, behaviour and reality," Boesky noted:

> Obvious and profound differences separate those patients who cross this boundary rarely from those whose bustling traffic at this frontier is a source of bewilderment and even danger. We want to know why certain patients can't tolerate average levels of frustration and we assume that the patient's intolerance of painful affects is crucial in determining the shift to behaviour. [p. 51]

However, Boesky went on to caution that while there are important differences among patients in this regard, "it may be wise not to segregate prematurely the major [acting out] and minor [symptomatic] categories," because potential, concealed similarities may provide an understanding of the underlying reciprocities between the manifest categories of functioning (p. 51).

One point here is that all patients act out. Such ubiquity is particularly observable in psychoanalytic therapy in which the transference forces confrontations with fate in the form of what Boesky described as imminent actualizations of unconscious fantasies. Boesky's formulation is that action opposes actualization by preventing a conscious realization of the aroused infantile fantasy—action is the antithesis of thought. In acting out, the distressing affects of actualization are warded off. Although Boesky nowhere mentioned the idea of a fate neurosis, this drift of his thinking suggests how the concept has been assimilated in the present literature. Where Boesky spoke, for example, of the bustling traffic at the frontier of action as a source of bewilderment and even danger, we encounter the ghost of the idea of a fate neurosis in the language of description and magnitude.

Another point Boesky made is that the value of a hard and fast separation of the neuroses of action and of symptom may not survive clinical scrutiny. The issue here is not only that a general theory of neurosis accounts for both types but that a separation of these particular types may be a function simply of the moment in time at which the patient is being observed.

But, then, Deutsch herself told us as much in a conclusion to her paper that is rather forward looking in its surrendering the specific clinical phenomenon she had singled out to a superordinate view of neurosis. If one reads Deutsch generously, a fate neurosis is a phase of a process of a larger neurotic structure and therefore cannot always be distinguished from symptoms and from what Deutsch called the "diffuse disharmonies" of character. Indeed, Deutsch's patient revealed a long history of discomfort with her external world that contrasted with the clear and specific critical disharmony of her fate neurosis. This history entailed the same determinations of character that enabled the patient to exploit so high-handedly the various persons in her story for the purposes of her eventual life crisis. Nor was the patient significantly free of neurotic inhibition, specifically a demoralizing intellectual inhibition, this despite her propensity for acting out, an ego mode that in the end does not guarantee a permanent involvement in a category of neurosis that Freud and Deutsch distinguished from "neurosis-formation." Thus the fate neurosis is a diagnostic state of affairs only at a point of clinical observation when its prominence is the issue in an otherwise fuller consideration of a more complex and extensive neurotic process. This accords with one of the meanings of the term given by Laplanche and Pontalis (1973). They noted that the fate neuroses "constitute a sequence of events which may imply a lengthy temporal evolution" (p. 161). Had Deutsch's patient come for analysis some years earlier, it is doubtful that she would have suited so well Deutsch's purpose in this particular paper.

In the end Deutsch has it that diagnosis from a psychoanalytic point of view is a function of analyzability. Whether a patient presents a neurosis of character, symptom, or fate is prognostically insignificant compared to the patient's analyzability. Deutsch concluded that a fate neurosis is eminently treatable "because the blows of fate are . . . conditioned by the same inner motives as neurotic symptoms. Indeed the suffering of the individual will be accessible to analytic therapy in so far as he himself recognizes it to be morbid" (p. 28).

In 1959 Deutsch published a follow-up of the patient whose crisis she had described thirty years earlier. The subsequent report was based on a chance meeting with the patient when the patient was nearly 50. It offers an instructive epilogue to the problems of the patient's fate as it was liberated by analysis from the total arrest the patient presented when she was in her mid-twenties. Deutsch did not raise any questions of analytic technique either in the original paper or in the follow-up, which is just as well, since they would be digressive from the point I mean to pursue.

Deutsch stated flatly in her 1959 report that the patient's analysis "ended in complete success" (p. 451). Deutsch also remarked that the woman she encountered was as strikingly beautiful as ever and quite alert and energetic. By a complete analytic success she meant this: at termination the patient returned to the man she was about to marry when she attempted suicide. As an object choice, he was still modeled after her oedipal relationship to her father but, in Deutsch's phrase, "the anachronistic effect of the previous taboo" had lost its hold on the patient. The patient's wish for a child, originally acted out and then retracted destructively, could now be realized—though not so soon. Also at termination, after Deutsch's active encouragement all along, the patient completed high school and entered college coincidental with her marriage. Her fiancé's divorced wife had died in the meantime, which precluded certain complications, although it is unlikely that the patient would not have proceeded with the marriage had the second wife lived. After years of what the patient described as a fulfilling marriage, she gave birth to a boy, a wonderful and adored child. However, what seemed to the patient most important was her intellectual achievement over the 25 years, which began with high honors in college and proceeded to a most distinguished career in physics. Her husband, who had also achieved fame in a different profession, was extremely proud of her on this score. When Deutsch inquired why she had waited so long to have a child—the patient must have been around 40 when she became a mother—she replied hesitantly that she had wanted to establish a career first.

"Toward me," Deutsch observed, "she showed a certain condescending benevolence, as to a good, old aunt" (p. 452). When Deutsch remarked how successful the analysis seemed to have been, the patient might have let bygones be bygones—it

was, after all, 25 years later, and Deutsch was an aging presence—but she could not transcend her imperious inclinations.
She said, "You have helped me a great deal, but analysis gave
me nothing. I don't believe in analysis at all—it is a hoax—all
bunk—purely constructions of your own mind" (p. 452). This
ungracious impulse toward Deutsch was, in fact, present early
in the analysis itself. When the patient's father had retracted his
offer to pay for the analysis, Deutsch continued the treatment
without a fee. The incident had informed a dream in which
Deutsch appeared thinly disguised as a loathsome and tactless
woman who was coming between the patient and her father. In
the follow-up we are told that it was now the patient's husband
who was not favorably disposed toward psychoanalysis. Moreover, the persistence of the patient's narcissistic sensitivities
would have made any reminder of her neurotic past a sore point
and cause for reactive hostility. Deutsch also assumed that the
old hostility and devaluing attitude toward the mother were
lively in the patient's comment about analysis, this despite
considerable analysis of the negative transference. "She expresses this devaluation by displacement from my role as
woman and mother into the sphere in which she herself feels
secure: in the professional life where she achieved so much (as
physicist) and I so little ('Nothing') (as analyst)" (p. 453). And
insofar as the patient's neurosis included conflicts with her
brother, her remark is compensatory for a long-standing phallic
narcissistic injury. "I speculate," Deutsch went on, "that her
declaration, 'Analysis gave me *nothing*,' expresses her unconscious dictum that analysis did not change the biological fact"
(p. 454). Nor did Deutsch fail to detect what she called a
"residual of acting out" in the patient's follow-up story, although she did not supply an example of this.

So it was not that analysis contravened the issues of the
patient's fate but rather that it transformed her ego so that her
fate could be worked out over the course of an eventful,
gratifying, and, at times, trying life. What did analysis do for
this patient, Deutsch asked. Through a better deployment of
guilt feelings toward her brother and a more realistic sense of
her own powers, the patient achieved a career. Also, she could
allow herself to marry a man chosen under the influence of her

Oedipus complex, perceiving the death of her rival as something independent from her unconscious matricidal strivings,
and she was able to realize her wish for a child. That her fate
could be pursued in some chronologically linear fashion rather
than in the disorganized manner that brought her to catastrophe
years earlier might say something for her capacity to delay and
to tolerate frustration. Much that remained characterologically
headstrong could be said to have been diverted to the service of
her ego aims.

But all this had to be on her own terms. "To her," Deutsch
wrote, "femininity was and is the degradation to the passive,
slavish role of her mother. She can accept the reality of her
marriage and her motherhood . . . by opposing defensively her
femininity with work and intellectual life" (p. 454). The postponement of motherhood was not, if indeed it ever is, a
logistical matter but emphatically a psychological one.

When Deutsch concluded that this was an eminently successful analysis, she explicitly referred to a message in Freud's
"Analysis Terminable and Interminable" (1937) to the effect that
analysis has accomplished its task when it secures for the ego
the best conditions for solving the problems that individual fate
has already assigned. Thus Deutsch stated at the end of her
follow-up: "What we conquer are only parts of psychogenesis:
expressions of conflict, developmental failures. We do not
eliminate the original sources of neurosis" (p. 458).

Here I am about to draw this review of Deutsch's case and
commentary to a particular conclusion. I begin by admitting an
uneasiness with certain limitations in Deutsch's psychoanalytic
interests. Her exclusive emphasis, for example, on her patient's
reconciliations with personal destiny, portrayed largely in terms
of active attainments, obscures considerations of the patient's
intrapsychic experiences and processes, modifications of which
also figure in the goals and outcomes of analysis. In this and
other things she makes too little of too much. However, I note
this merely to acknowledge that there are enough questions
about Deutsch's psychoanalytic sense of things so that, had one
a mind to, one could go on to some ending in a critical vein for
whatever lessons might come of this. However, the lessons I
foresee in this direction are too well known to merit the effort.

What I would rather pursue is that aspect of my uneasiness having to do with Deutsch's remarkable tolerance and acceptance of her patient's destiny. In her follow-up Deutsch displayed pride in her own knowledge of the enduring unconscious significance of her patient's major sexual and vocational lines of development over the many years since the termination of the analysis, and she was quite pleased with her patient's engagements with these motives. In this point of view, Deutsch was implying a distinction between the unconscious as a source of motives and as a source of conflicts. Having resolved her patient's crucial conflicts, Deutsch seemed entirely at ease with the knowledge she retained of her patient's unconscious motives. This attitude in Deutsch may have been expressed on this occasion too complacently for our own comfort, but we might also regard this attitude as an expression of neutrality. In one of its meanings, neutrality refers to the analyst's capacity to accept the patient's reclamations of various pieces of his existence following resolutions of repression and conflict.[2] This safeguard of objectivity is a most difficult one to maintain, especially at termination when, knowing better, we are still disturbed by the fact that the unconscious survives the analysis and eternalizes the patient's fate and that the patient is about to depart in the midst of actions on behalf of personal causes still traceable to unconscious history. In fact, termination itself is an enormous and vastly consequential action. We speak of object loss and object removal and the psychic structures that develop in these processes, but at termination we wonder at the quantitative status of such things, particularly when regressions

---

2. One of the points made by Sedler (1983) in his paper on the concept of working through, which appeared after the completion of this present discussion, is that the recollection of the past in the analytic situation presents decisions to the patient about what in the past might remain continuous with the present and what might become discontinuous, that is, relegated to the realm of ideas (memory) rather than active strivings. Sedler went on to emphasize that such decisions belong to the analytic process, not to analytic technique. This was why Freud regarded working through as the patient's contribution and a "trial of patience" for the analyst, who does not suggest the decisions the patient should make regarding the past but who accepts such decisions made in a present analytic context of improved ego conditions.

occur at the eleventh hour. Ticho (1972) in his paper, "Termination of Psychoanalysis: Treatment Goals, Life Goals," referred to "research anxiety" that arises when analysts are interviewed about the outcomes of even well-terminated cases. Something of such defensiveness may have to do with the analyst's distress in an avoidable passive-receptive position toward the irrepressible survival of much of the patient's personal fate, albeit lived out now under more—even greatly more—favorable psychological auspices.

In the last chapter of his book, *Aspects of Internalization*, Schafer (1968b) wrote about "The Fates of the Immortal Object," exploring the proposition that "in psychic reality the object is immortal" (p. 220). His discussion is more sophisticated than Deutsch's but his point is continuous with hers. Schafer spoke of the object's losing or gaining importance, disappearing and reappearing. "It is broken apart and put together again; . . . it is replaced by a substitute and may later replace its replacement; it is either swallowed up by or swallows up the subjective self, or both" (p. 221) and so on. However, while "the object of primary process does change in these ways, it nevertheless appears to retain a fundamental sameness; and this sameness reflects the subject's unchanging fundamental wishful tie to the object" (p. 221). Fate might be a term for the survival of the object in psychic life.

Further on in this chapter, Schafer took up the problem of dealing with the object in its guise in external actuality and posed this as an antithesis to internalization. While both modes of reckoning with the object complement development and adaptation, Schafer did not let us forget that "experience that includes significant, lasting and realistic external objects is psychically more mature and satisfying than one that involves primarily desperate internalizations in the passive mode" (p. 236).

This is interesting in light of the encouragements to action that Deutsch's commentary suggests, despite the fact that her patient presented at the outset a gross psychopathology of action. But, then, paradoxically, a fate neurosis, like any neurosis, becomes an inhibition of what Schafer called experience with realistic external objects. When Deutsch's patient presented herself for analysis, she was arrested from action in every area of life except for the analysis. A great part of the success of her analysis consisted in the patient's renewed capacity for what Schafer also called the alloplastic mode of engaging the immortal object. The extent to which· this persistence of the immortal, hence unconquerable, object arouses trepidation in the analyst, as though the unconscious itself was not a fact but a defiance of improved development and adaptation, is the extent to which we would also react uneasily to the taking of action by our patients. Whatever shortcomings we surmise in Deutsch's presentation, this is not among them. Rangell (1968) has referred to such uneasiness as an "anachronistic persistence of a moralistic attitude . . . toward 'acting' on the part of an analytic patient" (p. 200). His remarks are worth having (and not incidentally they contain an explicit comment to Deutsch on precisely this issue):

> The goal of normal life, and of psychoanalysis, is an optimum blend between thought, feeling, and action, suited of course to the particular constitution, life situation, and idiosyncratic development and character of the individual. I believe that an examination of clinical experience will show that the limitation of actions, imposed for good reason during the analytic process, is, in a certain number of cases, allowed to proceed to a generalized and more permanent inhibition of action which outlives the analysis and may go on to a long-lasting deleterious effect. I have seen a wrongly moralistic, anti-action attitude which creeps into some analyses fortify the patient's own phobic avoidance of action and lead in some cases to almost a paralysis of the latter and a taboo against even the necessary actions of life. Such analyses may hit a snag somewhere after midpoint where a marked indecisiveness eventuates at the necessity to convert long-standing insights into effective action. Deutsch . . . has similarly remarked, in discussing the acting out of a patient with 'fate neurosis', on the necessity to be equally alert to the patient's serious tendency to inhibition of action. [p. 200]

Rangell was not wrong in his observation of such a tendency in the analyst's point of view. Are we not instantly familiar with this statement of Freud (1914)? "One best protects the patient from injuries brought about through carrying out one of his impulses by making him promise not to take any important decisions affecting his life during the time of his treatment . . ." (p. 153). Yet we are less familiar with the sentence that immediately follows: "At the same time one willingly leaves untouched as much of the patient's personal freedom as is compatible with these restrictions, nor does one hinder him from carrying out unimportant intentions, even if they are foolish; one does not forget that it is in fact only through his own experience and mishaps that a person learns sense." This, in turn, is followed by a sentence reminiscent of Deutsch's conclusion about the analyzability of a fate neurosis: "There are also some people whom one cannot restrain from plunging into some quite undesirable project during the treatment and who only afterwards become ready for, and accessible to, analysis."

I might add here that Erikson (1964) spoke about this very problem of action as a matter of therapeutic urgency much in the vein of Rangell:

> Some mixture of *"acting out"* and of *age-specific action* is to be expected of any patient of whatever age, and all patients reach a point in treatment when the recovering ego may need to test its untrained or long-inhibited wings of action. In the analysis of children, we honor this to some extent, but in some excessively prolonged treatments of patients of all ages, we sometimes miss that critical moment while remaining adamant in our pursuit of totally cleansing the patient of all "resistance to reality." Is it not possible that such habitual persistence obscures from us much of the ego's actuality, and this under the very conditions which would make observation possible on clinical background? [p. 174]

In this same paper Erikson assures us that "Luther sang, Gandhi waltzed, and Kierkegaard drank—all for brief and disastrous periods" (p. 203).

Kafka somewhere said, "In the battle between you and the world, back the world." This is a diabolical aphorism on the failure of thought to find a dialectical relationship to action, in which failure is the failure of personal destiny. We surpass the limitation lamented by Kafka when we find correspondences between our fate and certain causes in the world which we then take up actively as our own. Then in backing the world, we are also backing ourselves.

This is a lesson Deutsch exemplified in her emphasis on the restitution of her patient's capacity for active engagement of a world embodying her personal fate. And in this regard her patient was unwittingly describing something as it should be in her manifestly disparaging remark that analysis gave her nothing.

REFERENCES

Boesky, D. (1982). Acting out: a reconsideration of the concept. *International Journal of Psycho-Analysis* 63:39–55.

Breuer, J., and Freud, S. (1893–1895). Studies on hysteria. *Standard Edition* 2.

Deutsch, H. (1930). Hysterical fate neurosis. In *Neuroses and Character Types Clinical Psychoanalytic Studies*, pp. 14–28. New York: International Universities Press, 1965.

_____ (1959). Psychoanalytic therapy in the light of follow-up. *Journal of the American Psychoanalytic Association* 7:445–458.

Erikson, E. H. (1964). *Insight and Responsibility: Lectures on the Ethical Implications of Psychoanalytic Insight*. New York: Norton.

Freud, S. (1894). The neuro-psychoses of defence. *Standard Edition* 3.

_____ (1914). Remembering, repeating and working-through (further recommendations on the technique of psycho-analysis II). *Standard Edition* 12.

_____ (1916). Some character-types met with in psycho-analytic work. *Standard Edition* 14.

_____ (1920). Beyond the pleasure principle. *Standard Edition* 18.

_____ (1923). The ego and the id. *Standard Edition* 19.

_____ (1924). The loss of reality in neurosis and psychosis. *Standard Edition* 19.

_____ (1937). Analysis terminable and interminable. *Standard Edition* 23.

Kuhn, T. S. (1962). *The Structure of Scientific Revolutions*, 2nd ed. Chicago IL: University of Chicago Press, 1970.

Laplanche, J., and Pontalis, J.-B. (1973). *The Language of Psycho-Analysis*. New York: Norton.

Rangell, L. (1968). A point of view on acting out. *International Journal of Psycho-Analysis* 49:195–201.

Schafer, R. (1968). *Aspects of Internalization*. New York: International Universities Press.

Sedler, M. J. (1983). Freud's concept of working through. *Psychoanalytic Quarterly* 52:73–98.

Ticho, E. A. (1972). Termination of psychoanalysis: treatment goals, life goals. *Psychoanalytic Quarterly* 41:315–333.

5

The Actual Neurosis

At first blush the idea of the actual neurosis seems to have expired as a burning issue in the developments of psychoanalytic thought. It has become, one might say, a ghost of its former self, a haunting rather than palpable concern about which it no longer seems necessary to have views.

However, in Gediman's (1984) paper "Actual Neurosis and Psychoneurosis" we have a corrective to such notions. For her paper demonstrates, among other things, that, wittingly or not, we do take views on those manifest and virtual mental states for which the term *Aktual* is still useful. Moreover, such views become decisive in one's version of psychoanalytic practice.

Gediman's paper (1984) also brings up to date a history of the idea of the actual neurosis, including a valuable account of its shifting meanings over the long years since Freud (1894) first distinguished, provisionally as it turned out, the actual neuroses and the psychoneuroses. Thus my own remarks on the subject can dispense with a great deal that would otherwise have had to have been brought in by way of reminding the reader of many details of the status of the problem in psychoanalytic literature. This leaves me free to use the idea of the actual neurosis as a talking point for several problems of a more general nature. I shall be addressing the actual neurosis as an issue of nomenclature, as an infantile core of complex neurotic structures, and as certain observable states in the current clinical situation. Finally, I shall have something to say on the relationship in psychoanalysis between analyzability and diagnosis and the hazard of overtechnologizing the psychoanalytic situation.

The idea of the actual neurosis is one of those in psychoanalytic thought that began in certainty but went on to become elusive to observation and something of a trial for theory. By 1908 Freud (Abraham and Freud 1965) already remarked in a letter to Abraham, "I see that pure cases of anxiety neurosis are great rarities and perhaps once again only abstractions" (p. 26). (The "once again" probably refers to Freud's increasing dissatisfaction with reifications of diagnostic nomenclature, a point I shall be returning to further on.) But such transformation of definition by ongoing clinical observation cannot be a critical reason that the idea of the actual neurosis eventually lost an established place among the crucial concerns of psychoanalytic thought. Most psychoanalytic concepts have undergone no less transformation of meaning in the course of clinical history. In commenting on her experience with the concept of the transference neurosis, for example, Marjorie Harley (1971) was not sharing a problem unique to herself when she noted, "Now I must own that for many years, whenever I attempted to observe clinically what appear to be the more general theoretical views regarding the definition of transference neurosis, I repeatedly found myself missing the center and losing my way" (p. 27). Yet the idea of the transference neurosis has lost none of its urgency for psychoanalytic consideration.

Entertaining such terminological problems, Anna Freud (1968) once observed several trends in the historical disposition of various kinds of psychoanalytic terms. Certain terms that began as loose generalities went on to become narrower in their applications. She gave the term "complexes" as an example of such a trend. Terms such as character, narcissism, and self, are other examples of terms whose histories resulted in more restricted technical meanings. Still other analytic terms evolved in an opposite direction from highly restricted meanings to such general application that their meanings continue to be useful only in connection with a gloss or the tradition of a school of thought. As examples of this Anna Freud gave transference and countertransference. Yet another development she exemplified by the term acting out, in which a concept loses its moorings from the particular stage of technical evolution in which it was conceived and thereafter leads an uneasy existence among other concepts that answer to similar observables. Indeed, Calef, who summarized the symposium on acting out, to which these remarks of Anna Freud were addressed, noted at one point: "We could not agree on the clinical description of the entity under discussion and therefore it remained unclear just what the metapsychological formulations were intended to encompass and explain" (Quoted in Boesky 1982, p. 40). This is not unlike Harley's statement of her problem with the concept of the transference neurosis.

Yet we continue to reckon with the issues of the transference neurosis and acting out as a matter of course because these concepts belong to a synoptic version of psychoanalysis in a way that the idea of actual neurosis does not. In Calef's observation about acting out the problem is not whether the concept can be entertained within a general theory of psychoanalysis. The concept refers to a representation in action of an unconscious fantasy that would otherwise be actualized in thought. From a theoretical point of view the process is clear. However, precisely the same process accounts for other concepts as well. Working through, for example, entails representations in action of unconscious fantasy and, like acting out, is also a vicissitude of transference states. The problem with the concept of acting out, then, is not so much theoretical as diagnostic in the sense that the process does not readily signify its function. That is, acting out and working through bring into play similar theoretical matters, but we distinguish the concepts on the basis of the functions of actions at one or another moment in the analytic process, and it is not always easy to say when certain actions of the patient are at the service of resistance in acting out or of advancement of analysis in working through. This is a point explored by Boesky (1982) in his paper "Acting Out: a Reconsideration of the Concept." Thus acting out and working through are continuities of a superordinate conceptual state of affairs, vicissitudes distinguished for the necessity of assessing states of analytic process.

Even a more difficult term like narcissism draws its meanings in a continuity with a general theory, once its several usages are distinguished. For example, narcissism refers to a perversion, which is a particular outcome of a theory of neurosogenesis. Narcissism also refers to an inevitable feature of a theory of development, and inasmuch as development is an aspect of the theory of neurosogenesis, narcissism also figures in how we understand the process of neurosogenesis. In yet another meaning narcissism describes a quality of tránsference, and in this sense becomes a continuity with fantasies about certain issues in the psychoanalytic situation and begins to bear relevance to such ideas as acting out and working through. The point is that the difficulty with the term narcissism does not discourage our ongoing considerations of what it purportedly refers to because the term in its various issues has functions within the structures of psychoanalytic thought.

With the actual neurosis, on the other hand, things are different. The difficulty resides in something equivocal in the relationship of the actual neurosis to the structure of thought that brings these other concepts into a continuity. The problem of the actual neurosis is what to make of a discontinuity. As we shall see, this is no less a technical than a theoretical problem.

I continue with some remarks of Waelder on the actual neurosis because they demonstrate a typical disposition of the concept itself. Waelder was not one to make less of things than they warranted. Yet when he arrived at the problem of the actual neurosis, as he was bound to in his 1967 retrospect of Freud's "Inhibitions, Symptoms and Anxiety," he had merely this to say:

> Freud maintained that this type of neurosis [i.e., actual neurosis] of which he had seen many examples in his earlier professional life did, in fact, exist. Few of his disciples followed him on this point; most of them held that the cases diagnosed as *Aktualneurose* in the early days would reveal themselves as genuine psychoneuroses if looked at with the more experienced diagnostic eye of a later day. [p. 23]

Waelder himself went on in this passage to leave the issue he drew between Freud and those colleagues Waelder had in mind moot, proceeding with the phrase "In any case . . ." as if a decision in the diagnostic controversy was not imperative or even interesting for Waelder's ensuing discussion of Freud's two theories of anxiety.

Now Waelder's depiction of this diagnostic controversy is a mixture of truth and inaccuracy blended by a methodological point of view. The inaccuracy is historical owing in part to a terminological issue. The methodological point of view has to do with the principles by which the problem of the actual neurosis lost its urgency in this passage of Waelder. While there are three meanings of actual neurosis—certain syndromes, certain infantile events instituting neurotic process, and certain current phenomena reactive to trauma but not integral to neurotic process—Waelder doubtless had in mind the first meaning: certain syndromes. Since an endeavour of the psychoanalytic method has been to claim for metapsychological comprehension, hence for the designation psychoneurosis, those clinical phenomena that provided substance to Freud's original designation *Aktualneurose*, Waelder's dismissal of the existence of an actual neurosis *qua* neurosis is not without plausibility. With respect to this first meaning of actual neurosis, subtractions from the very value of the concept have been a measure of a development of psychoanalytic thought. Waelder's view is rather prevalent, and it is what I had in mind when I said at the outset that at first blush the idea of the actual neurosis seems to have expired as a burning issue in the developments of psychoanalytic thought.

However, if only for the historical record, I should note the fact that however much was diagnostically wrested over the years from the syndromes Freud originally called actual neurosis, Ferenczi, Abraham, Jones, and later Nunberg and Fenichel, to mention only a few, continued to deal with the diagnosis in this first meaning and often with the technical precepts that seemed to follow from Freud's original etiological notions about the specific pathogenic practices leading to one or another form of actual neurosis. As late as 1920 Ernest Jones, for example, in his manual *Treatment of the Neuroses*, still singled out neurasthenia as a distinct entity, the therapy for which was advice and guidance having radical and palliative aims. The former was intended to wean the patient away from masturbation, the latter to install a regimen of rest, relaxation, agreeable interests. Even hydrotherapy was recommended for its soothing effects.

I might add in this connection that the diagnostic controversy

Waelder left moot has continued to attract parties to it from widely scattered quarters. In 1952 Abram Blau produced a paper "In Support of Freud's Syndrome of Actual Anxiety Neurosis," which is still cited as the most ambitious effort to resurrect the diagnosis and certain aspects of Freud's etiological ideas. Nor should Max Schur's (1955) "Comments on the Meta-Psychology of Somatization" escape mention while one is recalling significant efforts to preserve the actual neurosis in its original meaning. Turning as it does on the problem of regression in chronic and acute "actual" phenomena, Schur's paper still retains technical remnants of what we see in earlier treatments of the subject like those of Jones. Though much further along in etiological, hence technical, sophistication, Schur's recommendations are still a bit jarring in the sense of their being distinctly discontinuous with his version of classic psychoanalytic technique. Schur presents an analysis of a case in which an actual-neurotic symptom—a generalized atopic eczema conceived by Schur as a resomatization of an anxiety response—figured prominently in the clinical picture. Yet among his conclusions, he recommends for such patient populations varieties of psychotherapy, such as group therapy, whereby regression can be arrested in favour of intellectualization. I do not mean to suggest that Schur's prescription here is without merit, but only that while numerous clinical phenomena of the actual neurosis have been metabolized, as it were, in the developments of psychoanalytic thought, several have not.

In fact, Rangell (1968) complained in a paper some years subsequent to the Waelder paper that Waelder had cited Rangell disparagingly as "one of the very few analysts who still actually believes in the existence of *Aktualneurose*," to which Rangell rejoined, "I would ask whether there is any analyst who does *not* believe in the existence of this psychic traumatic state?" (p. 379). But with this the diagnostic controversy moves on to a terminological one. Waelder's remarks did not refer to fleeting symptomatic states but to neurosis as an extensive and prevailing organization. On the other hand, he should have known that Rangell's interest, in his paper on poise (1954), for example, was in various acute anxiety states, not in structured neurotic organization.

Faltering as it does on the historical record, Waelder's statement is still worth reflecting upon because it so well represents a general loss of urgency for the whole problem of differential diagnosis in a particular sense in which psychoanalysis inherited the problem from late nineteenth-century neuropsychiatry and sexology. Early on and thereafter the development of psychoanalytic thought was more enlightening for its discoveries of continuities among manifestly different phenomena than for its accounts of their differences. In this respect, Waelder's rather casual attitude toward the diagnostic issue reminds us of a decisive psychoanalytic point of view that has it that what psychoanalysis differentiates diagnostically are vicissitudes of ordinary processes operative in a generalized conception of mind. The original symptoms, syndromes, and nosology that psychiatry assigned to Freud were matters of historical chance. Having accepted the assignment and having applied himself provisionally to the very classifications themselves—it was Freud, after all, who differentiated anxiety neurosis from neurasthenia—what Freud went on to create was a program—a methodology—embodying its own necessities, which included the relating of all manner of disparate manifest phenomena by means of an organization of certain genetic, structural, and economic principles. From the outset, Freud began to emphasize the continuities among differentiated clinical phenomena, continuities accruing to the fact of mere variation with respect to underlying psychological processes. In his first paper on defense and symptom formation (1894), for example, he concluded about phobias, conversions, and obsessions:

> These three forms of illness . . . may be combined in the same person. The simultaneous appearance of phobias and hysterical symptoms which is so often observed in practice is one of the factors which render it difficult to separate hysteria clearly from other neuroses and which make it necessary to set up the category of "mixed neuroses." It is true that hallucinatory confusion is not often compatible with a persistence of hysteria, nor, as a rule, of obsessions. On the other hand, it is not rare for a psychosis of defence episodically to break through the course of a hysterical or mixed neurosis. [p. 60]

In this paper the problem of differential diagnosis gave way to the singular problem of defense and the return of the repressed.

Another example: at the beginning of the "Three Essays" Freud (1905) addressed the then extant classification of homosexuality—*absolute*, *amphigenic*, and *contingent*—for which sexologists alleged separate etiologies. While not disputing the phenomenal distinctions, he did bring to bear upon them clinical observations that drew lines of continuity among the classifications and went on with the momentous statement that "we are driven to conclude that we are dealing with a connected series" (pp. 136–138). The ensuing monograph then becomes the theory of development connecting not only these varieties of homosexuality, but the perversions and neuroses as well, not to mention so-called normal outcomes; for Freud insisted in the "Three Essays" that it was no less important to understand how a person develops heterosexuality than to understand how he develops homosexuality, and in so far as psychoanalytic principles of development are concerned, we do not expect to find exceptional principles for any outcome, only variations.

Though it is true that developmental variation is a crucial factor in the evolution of mental structures, including neurotic formations. Freud maintained that yet another factor was involved in a full psychoanalytic reflection on diagnosis. This was the quantitative factor; in the course of comparing delusional paranoia and hysteria and remarking upon certain observations common to both, Freud (1922) wrote:

> It seems to me that we have here an important discovery— namely, that the qualitative factor, the presence of certain neurotic formations, has less practical significance than the quantitative factor, the degree of attention or, more correctly, the amount of cathexis that these structures are able to attract to themselves

and he adds further on, "Thus as our knowledge grows we are increasingly impelled to bring the economic point of view into the foreground" (p. 228), by which Freud implied in this context the dynamic point of view as well—conflict in one or another state of vitality. He will repeat this virtually in the same language in "Analysis Terminable and Interminable" (1937) in the course of discussing the contribution of drive-arousal to pathogenesis and analyzability (p. 226ff.).

These principles and their extensions not only embody certain organizing objectives and interests of the psychoanalytic method, they also transform the whole problem of diagnosis from a taxonomy of symptoms and etiologies to issues of the analyzability of neurosis. And since the extents and limits of analyzability came to be conceived as functions of the transference, so the transference became the realm of diagnosis for psychoanalysis. Was it not Freud's analyses of the kinds of transference that occurred in patients he claimed he could not treat that led him to much of the knowledge he gathered about the so-called narcissistic neuroses? In fact, when Freud counseled great care in making a diagnosis, as he did for its prognostic value in his paper on beginning treatment (1913), he suggested that the diagnosis be made by a trial analysis. "No other kind of preliminary examination but this procedure is at our disposal; the most lengthy discussions and questionings in ordinary consultations would offer no substitute" (p. 124). Whatever diagnostic procedures have been developed for psychoanalytic purposes since these remarks of Freud, such procedures are ultimately assessments of analyzability by other means.

The point is that the diagnostic terminology of psychoanalysis signifies psychological process primarily and outcome only secondarily. This is nowhere as clear as where Freud (1926) took up the various neuroses in "Inhibitions, Symptoms and Anxiety," describing them throughout simply as vicissitudes of the process of repression. When he spoke of obsessional symptoms, for example, he spoke entirely in terms of undoing and isolation, referring to both as "surrogates of repression," and he went on to describe how these defenses appear in the conduct of free association (p. 119ff.). Since hysteria is the outcome of repression and all other neuroses the outcomes of "surrogates" of the very same process, Freud (1924) was able to declare: "Hysteria is the prototype of the whole species neurosis" (p. 191). Thus differential diagnosis in the sense of naming an outcome from its presenting appearance loses its urgency. Worse, it can also be misleading because a differential diagnosis at any moment of observation is always a partial conception in an inquiry where a fuller diagnostic conception occurs only among the developing problems of a therapeutic process set in motion. In a passage dealing with the problem of presenting symptoms, Freud (1913) speaks of the "over-estimation of the selective power of analysis," insisting that no matter how much the analyst can do in supervising the process he sets in motion, a neurosis as a categorical state cannot be foreseen.

> A neurosis . . . has the character of an organism. Its component manifestations are not independent of one another; they condition one another and give one another mutual support. A person suffers from one neurosis only, never from several which have accidentally met together in a single individual. [p. 130]

It is along this line of psychoanalytic thought, where diagnosis becomes a problem primarily of observations of clinical process and only secondarily a problem of classificatory nomenclature, that the issue of the actual neurosis *qua* neurosis has surrendered much of its original interest. This is why Freud in the letter to Abraham I quoted from earlier denied the prevalence of what he called pure cases of anxiety neurosis, shrugging off the idea of its classification as an obfuscating abstraction. However, this point of view on the actual neurosis does not exhaust its interest for psychoanalysis but only deploys it to other considerations. After all, the observations that correspond to the idea of the actual neurosis were observations of something, and if they did not survive as outcomes of neurosogenesis continuous with a developing conception of neurosis, they might still figure somewhere in the problem of neurosis. This brings us to what I am calling the second meaning of actual neurosis, its infantile aspect. Here yet another controversy having to do with clinical expectations joins a point of consensus about the actual neurosis.

By the infantile aspect I mean what is sometimes called the "actual" core of the psychoneurosis. Freud formulated this as follows: "The psychogenic symptom has an actual-neurotic core, like a grain of sand which is the stimulating agent for the formation of a pearl" (Reich 1951, p. 82). This is an aphoristic statement of a whole principle of symptom formation in which an actual immediate experience is of such a nature as to produce the distressing affect that becomes the motive for an assimilation of the experience in the mental life as an issue of repression. The conversion symptom is sometimes used as the model of the psychoneurosis conceived with its actual-core because the conversion symptom arises as the simplest vicissitude of the actual experience. Hartmann, for example, employed the idea of the conversion symptom this way (Reich 1951). The conversion symptom rests squarely on the idea of the traumatic event but advances an account of the event a step further to include the actual response to the trauma in the way of a perception, thought, inhibition that is then the basis for a symptomatic elaboration. Freud (1926) spoke of conversion symptoms this way, and it is clear from the following passage that actual-core — the as yet "unpsychologized" experience — was present in his thoughts:

> Analysis can show what the disturbed excitatory process is which the symptoms replace. It usually turns out that they themselves have a share in that process . . . For instance, it will be found that the pains from which a patient suffers were present in the situation in which the repression occurred; or that his hallucination was, at that time, a perception; or that his motor paralysis is a defence against an action which should have been performed in that situation but was inhibited . . . or that his convulsions are the expression of an outburst of affect which has been withdrawn from the normal control of the ego. [p. 111]

It is with respect to this matter of a real childhood event in the etiology of symptoms that this new controversy about another meaning of actual phenomena I mentioned comes in. Though we understand what Freud is saying in this passage about a real event as a component in the process of symptom formation — the infantile "actual" event leading to drive arousal, its mental representation, its meaning, and final transformation by compromise into a symptom — there is a question about what is therapeutically tractable in the component of the event. That is, what can analysis recover differentially of this component? This is the controversy between those like Greenacre who emphasize the possibility in analysis of recovering and working through the original actual event as distinguished from its vicissitudes in fantasy and further affective elaboration and those like Freud (1926) who found the problem of reconstructing this component "so obscure a thing" as to "afford us a good reason for quitting such an unproductive field of inquiry without delay" (p. 112). (Freud's position on this matter varied considerably. Compare Laplanche and Pontalis 1967.) Coltrera (1981) has summarized this issue of reconstruction cogently, and I am inclined to agree with his conclusion that the controversy is not as deep going in practice as it appears in published exposition:

> Greenacre seems closest to Freud's original position, holding that the reconstruction of critical childhood events, especially traumatic ones, is intrinsic to the basic genetic premise of psychoanalysis. Where Freud was undecided in the matter, Greenacre believes that the real trauma has greater psychopathological effect on development than does fantasy, and that the working through process often turns on the reconstruction and recovery of the specific traumatic event. To Greenacre, the greatest aid to working through is the consistency of interpretation and the accuracy of reconstruction . . . Ernst Kris and, to a lesser extent, Anna Freud are not as sanguine as to the efficacy, let alone the possibility, of an accurate reconstruction. Kris maintains that the complex modifications and elaborations to which the genetic experiences are subjected would preclude any possibility of an accurate reconstruction. To Kris, the basic dynamic of resistance is to break the connections between past and present, and so, the less important is repression in any constellation of defences, the less important reconstruction would be in the analysis . . . .
>
> Both Ernst Kris and Anna Freud appear to regard the interpretation in its historical function to be the facilitation of a recognition through regressive recall within the conditions of the transference, whereas Phyllis Greenacre seems to be going against "the rise of transference" in recent psychoanalytic thought, returning to the older idea of recovery through working through an abreactive remembrance of a critical *real event*. I feel that these differences may be more apparent than real, representing the oppositions of a polarizing exposition rather than any real operational difference over the genetic premise of interpretation. [pp. 100–101]

Coltrera's last point in this passage is worth stressing. A difference in views on a clinical issue does not necessarily lead to operational differences in clinical conduct, or, at least, to a radicalization of operational differences. But disagreement without consequential differences in the theory of practice is only possible where there is a consensus about most matters short of those that have to do with the limitations of actual practice. The parties to controversy in Coltrera's observations are not in dispute about a theory of pathogenesis but only about what to expect as a rule of the psychoanalytic process, which may be largely a personal matter of one's being better at certain things than at others.

Here, I turn to the actual neurosis in the sense of current states in the clinical situation discontinuous with what I referred to near the outset as concepts belonging to a synoptic version of psychoanalysis. It is in this sense in which I believe a problem with the actual neurosis continues to be lively and significant. Much of the controversy over technique involving such ideas as the therapeutic alliance, the working alliance, the so-called real as distinguished from the transference relationship—ideas that are analogously discontinuous with a synoptic version of the psychoanalytic method—reflects a difficulty about "actual" phenomena in the clinical situation. Indeed, ideas like the therapeutic alliance, on the one hand, and "actual" phenomena, on the other, do not refer to what are called "vicissitudes" in the psychoanalytic sense. Blocking is not a vicissitude of repression; a temper tantrum is not a vicissitude of anger; palpatation and tremor are not vicissitudes of anxiety. Nor are expressions in the clinical situation of distress, discomfort, irritability, lethargy, or apprehension necessarily vicissitudes of fantasies of the analyst as a libidinal object. To the extent that one speaks of the analyst's reciprocities in these reactions with a special terminology, for example, working alliance, one is speaking of social variables that are discontinuous with a classical theory of practice. Extending the magnitude of a variable is not, as we shall see, the only option with variables that arise in the psychoanalytic process.

If actual phenomena are not vicissitudes of defensive and

affective processes, then they are usurpations of such processes. This is a sense in which we speak of ego deficiencies. Nor is the idea of a usurpation of process strange to psychoanalysis and limited only to actual phenomena. Freud (1900) and Jones (1916) at one or another point raised the problem of the analyzability of certain symbols that are imported, as it were, directly into the dream unrevised from culture, thus usurping the dream work through which analysis of dreams proceeds. Perhaps to a greater extent than we care to believe dreams are the junk yards of burnt-out metaphors, representing responses to the conflicts of day-residues by something other than the outcomes of the problem-solving processes of dream work. Analogously, actual phenomena are the unanalyzable elements that sometimes occupy the transference. This is not an unusual idea. If the transference has so much in common with dreaming, there cannot be elements, in this instance, unanalyzable ones, peculiar to dreams but precluded from the transference.

However, this is as far as I would carry the similarity between dreams and transference with respect to the problem of unanalyzable elements because the differences go on to become more crucial by virtue of the technical consequences of encountering such elements in dreams, on the one hand, and in the transference, on the other. Unanalyzable elements in dreams do not pose the possibility of radical technical options. But actual phenomena are usurpations of the transference inasmuch as they are usurpations of psychological process, and as such they invite special technical interventions. The most common option has been simply to manage actual phenomena by advice, reassurance, and so on as adjunctive to getting on with analysis proper. The analytic literature is laced with this approach since Freud's first distinctions between what should be managed, for example, anxiety neurosis, and what should be analyzed, for example, anxiety hysteria. Blau, whom I cited previously, used the term control for dealing with the actual neurosis. Schur mentioned intellectualization as a way of controlling actual phenomena by avoiding regression. Current concepts, such as the therapeutic alliance, owe something of their histories to this option, though actual phenomena may not be mentioned specifically in connection with the value alleged for such technical constructs.

On the other hand, such options of the analyst are often criticized because they evade rather than advance the analytic process. Indeed, one of the earliest examples of such criticism comes from Freud (1910). In his paper on "wild" psychoanalysis he admonished a physician who appeared to have followed Freud's own advice of a decade earlier in recommending certain sexual practices to an anxious female patient. Freud complained that the advice left "no room for psychoanalysis . . . And where does analytic treatment come in, the treatment we regard as the main remedy in anxiety states?" (p. 225). (Why Freud diagnosed the patient in question as having anxiety hysteria as opposed to anxiety neuroses he does not say. However, it is plausible that by 1910, as he wrote to Abraham [Abraham and Freud 1965, p. 26], he was disinclined to surmise an actual neurosis particularly without his own hand in the diagnostic process.)

However, to deplore the giving of advice and other more subtle departures from neutrality as a matter purely of the analyst's option is not always fair to clinical experience. Ultimately, the problem is never exclusively the analyst's. For transference as an analyzable element in the psychoanalytic situation accrues no less to the ego capacities of the patient than to the determinations of the analyst to perform analytically. This was a major point of Eissler's (1953) crucial paper on technical parameters. In other words, the patient may usurp the analytic situation in accordance with certain urgent needs that are not as yet differentiated from desires and wishes. This is how we might understand Bird's (1972) use of the term "reality" and its impact on the transference. Reality to Bird is anything that "contrasts with the impact the analyst has through his representation in the patient's fantasy life, neurosis and transference" (p. 248). Part of reality in Bird's view is the help—the substantial and easily immense help—the patient gets from the analytic situation whether the analyst means to offer it or not. Here I should note that when Schur spoke of intellectualization as helpful to his patient's skin condition, he did not mean to encourage this; the patient simply usurped the analytic situation to this stabilizing end in the very act of verbalization. Bird refers to such events as one of the most serious problems of analysis, because it is "the worst enemy of the transference," a usurpation surpassing resistance. The point here is that "actual" phenomena, for example, irritability, acute lethargy, blocking, or rage, fit Bird's conception of reality very nicely inasmuch as they replace a readiness for reflection by a demand for help pure and simple. And such phenomena are inevitable in every analysis.

Rather than turning such issues into problems of technical options, Bird prefers to leave them as open challenges, noteworthy as is anything else in the clinical field but unaddressed by special procedural concepts that would bifurcate the field into what should and should not be analyzed. The problem then becomes the nature of the commerce between the analyzable and the real. Technologizing the presentation of the real would interfere with the analysis of such commerce. This is also the view Brenner (1979) takes in his discussion of such concepts as the working alliance, the therapeutic alliance, the real relationship. Brenner does not deny the existence of the phenomena, subtle or catastrophic, that constitute what Bird calls "reality" in the clinical situation or in the patient's ordinary life, for that matter. However, what Brenner questions is the introduction of a reciprocating analytic function for an inevitable variable that has the effect of maximizing the variable simply because it exists. Gill (1982) makes a similar point in his review of this controversy. He questions whether we should be pressed to fashion a "deliberate" response for every category of observation we make in the clinical situation (pp. 96–106).

An important aspect of the technical issue turns on a methodological point. Not all variables that appear in a structured situation must be accorded a maximum emphasis. Certain variables are noted with a view toward reducing their influence upon the functional and observational tasks at hand to an optimal minimum. In the psychoanalytic situation one does this with the varieties of social codes of one's patients by amplifying instead the variables having to do with the nature of the patient's conformity to those codes. Though an analyst is bound to hear a great deal about the sociology of a patient, this is incidental to the clinical issue, which is the psychopathology of the patient's social conformity, a variable that can be entertained only to the extent that the sociological structures embodied by the patient—an aspect of reality in Bird's sense—are not advanced as analytic issues. Conformity has vicissitudes in a psychoanalytic sense: sociological structures do not.

With "actual" phenomena I would argue that we are dealing with issues analogous to the sociological. Distinguished from their secondary gains and from conversions, "actual" phenomena repair to physiological processes and are therefore no less opaque to the psychoanalytic method than sociological ones.[1] In this sense, "actual" Phenomena are boundary problems for psychoanalysis as are the sociological variables that inevitably appear in the clinical field. I would then say that a psychoanalytic reflection on such problems becomes a species of applied psychoanalysis having its own methods, whatever these may be. This is why I would call Fenichel's (1945b) deservedly celebrated paper on the "Nature and Classification of the So-called Psychosomatic Phenomena" an exercise of applied psychoanalysis, a contribution to the problem of how psychological stress and conflict enlist physiology and contribute to the wear and tear of organic structures.

Though it is true that the stress and conflict present themselves economically to the psychoanalytic situation, it does not necessarily follow that these variables require separate technical concepts. The alteration of psychic economy, which Freud sometimes called the taming of instinct, is an outcome of

---

1. Fenichel (1945a) noted the special significance of secondary advantages in certain cases of actual neurosis going so far as to say that such gains "play an even more important role than in the psychoneurosis," adding that such gains may not even have anything to do with the origins of actual-neurotic states (p. 126). A critique of Kohut's (1977) technical idea of "soothing" that figured in this recommendation of the analysis of disturbances of narcissistic equilibrium, viewed by Kohut as "contentless" tension states, must take into account this feature Fenichel observed; for if "soothing" occurs without some systematic reckoning with the secondary gain in traumatic states, then the "soothing" becomes a gratification of the advantage of the neurosis but no advantage to the analysis or to the patient's adaptation outside the clinical situation. Indeed, in the epinosic gain is where I would locate the commerce between the analysis and the reality, which I spoke of earlier.

analysis like marriage, divorce, changes in income, life goals, and sexual objects, not a matter of direct and specific techniques. In this regard, technique and the process it sets in motion and maintains should be distinguished. Inasmuch as one is concerned in the clinical situation not with biological or cultural processes but specifically with the psychological processes by which biology is transformed into culture, it does not advance this concern to introduce technical functions that make more of the boundaries where applied psychoanalysis best takes over.

Leaving the problem of the actual neurosis at this pass, I am aware that I have ended up locating the issue within certain controversies that have always existed for psychoanalysis. One controversy involves boundary problems and what to do with them. For some a boundary is a desirable limit on a field of inquiry, as Kant would put it. But a boundary is also a frontier and as such attractive to another spirit of inquiry.

Another controversy has to do with the problem of humaneness in the psychoanalytic situation, as though this is somehow at odds with the problem of maintaining a psychoanalytic attitude. Actually what is at stake is the ordeal of civility that distinguishes the analytic situation from all other social and therapeutic situations. If I have been inclined toward restraint in accommodating technical theory to "actual" phenomena, it is not in the spirit that a patient's suffering is no business of analysis. It is rather that this has the unavoidable aim of resolvong an ordeal whose very existence is crucial to an analytic process. An ordeal motivates ingenuity. Further technical concepts that address the economics of the actual neurosis in a way separate from the concepts that create the transference — neutrality, abstinence, and so on — reduce the ordeal of the transference as a problem and the need for the ingenuity to solve the problem. Standardization is one of the great cures for the burdens of ingenuity.

Kafka said somewhere: "All human error is impatience." Rather than more technology at this point for the "realities" of the psychoanalytic situation, we might do better to leave them to try our patience.

REFERENCES

Abraham, H., and Freud, E., eds. (1965). *A Psycho-Analytic Dialogue: Letters of Sigmund Freud and Karl Abraham, 1907–1926*. New York: Basic Books.

Bird, B. (1972). Notes on transference: universal phenomenon and hardest part of analysis. *Journal of the American Psychoanalytic Association* 20: 267–301.

Blau, A. (1952). In support of Freud's syndrome of "actual" anxiety neurosis. *International Journal of Psycho-Analysis* 33: 363–372.

Boesky, D. (1982). Acting out: a reconsideration of the concept. *International Journal of Psycho-Analysis* 63: 39–51.

Brenner, C. (1979). Working alliance, therapeutic alliance and transference. *Journal of the American Psychoanalytic Association* 27 (Suppl.): 137–158.

Coltrera, J. (1981). On the nature of interpretation: epistomology as practice. In *Clinical Psychoanalysis*, ed. S. Orgel and B. Fine. New York: Jason Aronson, pp. 83–127.

Eissler, K. (1953). Notes upon the emotionality of a schizophrenic patient and its relation to problems of technique. *Psychoanalytic Study of the Child* 8: 199–251.

Fenichel, O. (1945a). *The Psychoanalytic Theory of Neurosis*. New York: Norton.

_____ (1945b). Nature and classification of the so-called psychosomatic phenomena. *Psychoanalytic Quarterly* 14: 287–312.

Freud, A. (1968). Acting out. *International Journal of Psycho-Analysis* 49: 165–170.

Freud, S. (1894). The neuro-psychoses of defence. *Standard Edition* 3.

_____ (1900). The interpretation of dreams. *Standard Edition* 4/5.

_____ (1905). Three essays on the theory of sexuality. *Standard Edition* 7.

_____ (1910). "Wild" psychoanalysis. *Standard Edition* 11.

_____ (1913). On beginning treatment. (Further recommendations on the technique of psycho-analysis I.) *Standard Edition* 12.

_____ (1922). Some neurotic mechanisms in jealousy, paranoia and homosexuality. *Standard Edition* 18.

_____ (1924). A short account of psycho-analysis. *Standard Edition* 19.

_____ (1926). Inhibitions, symptoms and anxiety. *Standard Edition* 20.

_____ (1937). Analysis terminable and interminable. *Standard Edition* 23.

Gediman, H. (1984). Actual neurosis and psychoneurosis. *International Journal of Psycho-Analysis* 65: 191–202.

Gill, M. (1982). *Analysis of Transference. Volume I*. New York: International Universities Press.

Harley, M. (1971). The current status of transference neurosis in children. *Journal of the American Psychoanalytic Association* 19: 26–40.

Jones, E. (1916). The theory of symbolism. In *Papers on Psycho-Analysis*. Boston: Beacon.

_____ (1920). *Treatment of the Neuroses*. London: Bailliere, Tindall and Cox.

Kohut, H. (1977). *The Restoration of the Self*. New York: International Universities Press.

Laplanche, J., and Pontalis, J.-B. (1967). *The Language of Psycho-Analysis*. New York: Norton, 1973.

Rangell, L. (1954). The psychology of poise, with a special elaboration on the psychic significance of the snout or perioral region. *International Journal of Psycho-Analysis* 35: 313–332.

_____ (1968). A further attempt to resolve the "problem of anxiety." *Journal of the American Psychoanalytic Association* 16: 371–404.

Reich, A. (1951). The discussion of 1912 on masturbation and our present-day views. *Psychoanalytic Study of the Child* 6: 80–94.

Schur, M. (1955). Comments on the meta-psychology of somatization. *Psychoanalytic Study of the Child* 10:119–164.

Waelder, R. (1967). Inhibitions, symptoms and anxiety: forty years later. *Psychoanalytic Quarterly* 36: 1–36.

6

Shyness

Like depression, envy, boredom, and other symptomatic states, shyness is reported by virtually all patients now and again as part of their varied experience of the psychopathology of everyday life. And in some patients shyness is a prominent symptom. For so ubiquitous an experience there are not many direct studies of it in the psychoanalytic literature. Of note are Kaufman (1941), Lewinsky (1941), Glover (1956), and Sandler and co-workers (1958). Fenichel's references to shyness (1945) are passing; he alluded to it by one of its customary labels "social anxiety." Nominal studies, however, do not exhaust the literature on shyness. The subject is lively, if latent, within a constellation of studies having to do with its obverse, which goes by various names such as poise (Rangell 1954), "confident expectation" (Benedek 1938), and "basic trust" (Erikson 1950). Also, the subject of shyness is latent within certain studies of social self-representation, like Greenacre's on the impostor (1958b), Ross's on the "as if" concept (1967), and Kernberg's on the narcissistic personality (1970). Thus an inquiry into shyness will involve a collation of topics of varying apparent relevance. This will complicate our clinical interest in this common symptom and hopefully our clinical approach to it.

Principally I should like to advance the psychology of shyness by relating its phenomenology to a psychoanalytic perspective. One of the promises of such a perspective is the discovery of more than one derivation for what often passes as one phenomenology. That is, neurotic shyness arises out of a different set of dynamics from shyness in certain schizophrenics and in very young children. Indeed, like depression (Bibring 1953, Rapaport

1959), shyness may be a response to psychic trial at virtually any level of psychosexual development and may represent part of a fundamental "loss complex" susceptible in the normal, neurotic, narcissistic, schizophrenic, and immature personalities.

Also, a psychoanalytic perspective on symptoms often accounts for alternative outcomes of apparently similar conflicts. In regard to shyness, I am thinking of patients whose conflicts resemble those leading to shyness in other patients, yet who are, on the contrary, capable of a seemingly self-assured social presence. Thus we should not be surprised to discover an alternative to shyness as, say, a counterphobia to a phobia, as occurs, for example, in impostors whose social composure belies a defective sense of self-esteem. Poise "ranks high among the various pleasurable states striven for by man" (Rangell 1954, p. 313), and, as such, can acquire neurotic and perverse conditions for its attainment and maintenance.

But let us begin with some of the manifest characteristics of shyness. Among these, the most defining characteristic consists of the fact that the symptom is activated only in social situations. Though the state of shyness can be anticipated in solitude with symptomatic dread, shyness itself, which involves an actual detriment to poise, cannot be experienced in solitude. In this, shyness is distinguished from other anxiety states and from other states of flawed self-esteem, like blushing and a manifest sense of shame, both of which can occur in solitude. Even embarrassment can be felt when one is alone, as a palpable exponent of solitary fantasying.

That shyness is activated by exposure to an actual physical situation classifies shyness as a species of phobia (Kaufman 1941). As is often the case with "situational anxieties," the shy reaction may occur as a completely surprising attack without conscious anticipation, as when shyness figures in the psychopathology of everyday life as an outcome of a displacement and projection regulating a specific transitory economic and dynamic psychic situation preceding the shy reaction—I shall present an instance of acute but transitory shyness further on. However, in morbidly shy persons the social anxiety reaction can usually be anticipated with dread, as is more common of phobias. Then there are those persons whose specific avoidances of certain social situations have been rationalized into ego-syntonic "dislikes," so that their social phobias remain latent; "or instead of full avoidance, there may be a decrease in functions" (Fenichel 1945, p. 169), that is, the hyperinhibition of shyness (Lewinsky 1941) may be warded off by a system of ego-syntonic inhibitions, which is a common fate for phobias (Reich 1930).

Finally, in yet other persons social anxiety may not be best captured by the nosological category of phobia. Certainly in young children we distinguish "stranger anxiety" from subsequent shyness in the sense that "stranger anxiety" emphasizes the idea of an attainment of a level of reality testing involving both ego functions and the libidinal object, the latter in the attained perception of the dichotomy mother/stranger (Spitz 1965a); but the term shyness connotes the loss of reality testing through a regression of both function and object. In the borderline patient social anxiety may involve a regression of ego function but not of object relations, which indeed may be arrested at a dichotomous friend/enemy cognition, advancements of which are only weakly attained. In the neurotic, shyness is experienced with the ongoing conviction that the dreaded other person is not an enemy, or at least does not possess the power he is being idealized as possessing. In certain borderlines any such antecedent convictions vanish in the anxiety. Whether this is due to the kinds of defenses described by Kernberg (1967) and others, for example, splitting or projective identification, which play extraordinary havoc with object representations and thus with the symbolic processes by which we ordinarily understand phobia formation, the point is that there seems to be something different about the social anxiety of borderlines when compared to neurotics, however similar the phenomenology of the symptom during the excruciating moments of its activation.

But, again, let us proceed with the manifest characteristics of the symptom. In shyness, the danger is specifiable. Sandler and colleagues (1958) have identified several salient components of dread on the side of the subject himself. Among these are fear of loss of bodily control, fear of excessive display, of ostentation (exhibitionism), and fear of revelation of personal inferiority (narcissistic mortification).

When the social object is included, the danger goes on to involve the anticipation of rejection through the failure of a particular social dynamic. Foremost in the dread of shy persons is that "dialogues" will not be initiated, or if they are, they will soon be "derailed" (terms of René Spitz that we shall return to before long). The inability to make small talk is a handicap of shy persons. Moreover, there is a loss of confidence in those poise-maintaining mannerisms of everyday life that sustain one through the initial trials of spontaneously originating social "dialogues." A shy person feels at a loss to know what to do with his hands or how to sit or stand, and he is painfully apprehensive that he will not be able to control his facial expressions. This awkwardness and the loss of the capacity to make small talk are the immediate signs by which the attack of shyness is recognized. Along with this is the feeling of being misunderstood and very quickly ignored.

Thereafter a characteristic fantasy prevails, a fantasy of being a stranger to the social occasion. At this point, when shyness has proceeded to this fantasy of being an outsider and an exception, the dread shifts from the imminent, which has already happened, to the possibility of being discovered in one's exceptional standing. The shy person must now bend his efforts to concealing his plight in a semblance of poise. Devices for retaining poise under such conditions are various and involve limitations on social interaction. The most common device is reticence, which passes for composure. Another common device is the assumption of a role, the performance of which makes one's lack of social interaction plausible. Playing host, for example, is sometimes more welcome to a shy person than being a guest; for a host can absorb himself in the extrasocial mechanics of the role.

Thus in shyness we can observe the symptom in two phases: first, the experience of trauma with imminent or manifest anxiety; second, a partial restoration through an ideational conceptualization of the nature of the trauma, which fantasying goes on to determine social inhibitions. Moreover, the depersonalization arising in the first phase with the sudden consciousness of a bodily disharmony (Oberndorf 1950) is lessened but not entirely extinguished by the second phase, inasmuch as the second phase retains a consciousness of estrangement. Where the second phase fails to get established, which is rare, depersonalization phenomena develop vividly. A borderline woman once reported to me a materialization of shyness upon entering a crowded party that was so unregulable that her reaction quickly involved spatial disorientation and loss of color vision, and she finally fainted. In respect of the fantasy characteristic of shyness, this woman's self-description in this episode was cogent: "My uniqueness was unbearable." Somewhere in shyness is a dangerous grandiosity, which we shall also have to account for.

That shyness does indeed have something in common with depersonalization is further evident in some remarks of Edith Jacobson (1959) in her paper on depersonalization. Jacobson observed that transient states of depersonalization are commonplace as "mild, fleeting experiences . . . when persons are suddenly placed into a strange, unfamiliar environment," an environment, furthermore, that need not be unpleasant and that, in fact, can be fascinating and pleasurable. These virtually normal reactions Jacobson describes as vivid feelings of not belonging, and they develop in situations that "invite new identifications which the ego refuses to accept immediately" (p. 605). The experience of not belonging, an aspect of shyness as well as of depersonalization, is not based upon the ego–superego conflict such as would establish a depression with concomitant loss of felt motivation to "belong"; the experience of "not belonging" is, according to Jacobson, based upon "contradictions in the superego, that is, activated "discrepancies between opposing identifications," which result in the detachment of an observing part of the ego (the "hypercathexis of perception") from the observed faulted part. This is typical of the experience of shyness. "Such processes may be induced by traumatic external events or by experiences which for inner reasons have a traumatic effect" (p. 606). Though social events, a *sine qua non* of shyness, are not what Jacobson is alluding to exclusively, social events are those most likely to acquire traumatic qualities because of their inevitable drive-arousal effects, as we shall note in the work of Spitz.[1]

The "inner reasons" that conspire with an external event to produce a traumatic situation may vary. However, we can generalize about the dynamics that lend pathogenic vitality to "inner reasons." Here Freud's earliest conceptions of symptom formation (Freud 1894) will be relevant. In their generality these conceptions subsume all sorts of symptoms. I shall recall Freud's ideas very briefly. Symptoms (like shyness), though consciously discrete experiences, are actually continuities of more extensive psychological processes. The painful interruption to the sense of psychological integrity by a return of the repressed serves a function of minimizing the felt importance of fantasies (wishes) consciously entertained at other moments. Symptoms are fashioned out of affects borrowed from wishes active in the present. Freud went on to add that the repressed wish concealed in a symptom is subjectively undecipherably symbolic of the original wish whose "incompatibility" created the trauma now repeated in the symptom.

Freud's early scheme of symptom formation had not yet included the infantile variable or the concept of regression. Hence the emphasis in this scheme is on the contemporaneous activities of the patient's general functioning. Though this emphasis is retained in current clinical practice, it is very often missing from current clinical theory, as a state of affairs that goes without saying. In so admirable a theoretical study of symptom formation as Arlow's "Conflict, Regression, and Symptom Formation" (1963), for example, the idea is virtually

---

1. Experimental psychology contains an excellent and expanding literature on the effects of the presence of other persons on drive arousal in the individual. The study of such effects has come to be called "the problem of social facilitation" (though flawed performance is more often of interest in this research than facilitation). A central concern of this literature is the measurement of "anxiety" induced by a social event and the fate of the aroused state in its correlations with fantasies about the "audience" arousing the state. Thibaut and Kelley (1959), Cottrell (1968), and Lott and Lott (1968), among others, reveal interesting correspondences with the concerns of any psychoanalytic study of social anxiety. For a brief critique of this area of experimental psychology, see Zajonc (1965).

absent that the fantasy embodied in a symptom has a symbolic correspondence to a fantasy indulged at other times contemporaneously with the symptom itself. Arlow's emphasis is on the function of fantasy in the symptom as a transformation of a preoedipal wish—a phobia for tunnels, Arlow suggests as an example, may result from an infantile wish to impregnate the mother by entering her body; the conflict may arise in connection with the fear of encountering the paternal phallus inside the mother. Yet this infantile wish is bound to find transformed expression in the patient's mental life outside the symptom itself, and this *relatively* nonsymptomatic expression is as much an "inner reason" for the conversion of an external event into a trauma as the more repressed form of the fantasy.

I am singling out Freud's earlier (and uncompleted) version of symptom formation because in shyness the traumatic force of the social event *begins* with a displacement of a "dangerous grandiosity" from elsewhere in the patient's life where it is active in a subjectively more benign form. The torment embodied in the symptom of shyness—the dread of being overlooked, ignored, rejected—is also displaced on to the social event from subjectively more benign expressions of derogation and disdain elsewhere in the patient's life. Indeed, the phenomenology of shyness becomes increasingly vivid as these displacements are relocated in the patient's everyday life.

It is clinically remarkable, for example, that the clinically shy patient has lively impulses of derogation and disdain that arise toward others with intense self-righteousness. In the treatment situation such impulses appear invariably toward the therapist, sooner when shyness does not extend to the therapy situation, later when it has extended to the therapy situation but is finally removed. I recall a young lady patient whose shyness was so pervasive as to have included myself and so consuming as to have precluded her initiating self-reports. In my initial work with her I resorted to direct questions, which she seemed glad to answer. But her perfunctory replies were always accompanied by an uncontrollable tremorous—and embarrassing—raising of her eyebrow, suggesting absolute scorn. When her shyness toward me relented after several months, she entered upon a phase of overt contempt for me, which contempt she went on to recognize as precisely what she expected herself to be the victim of in virtually all social situations. I must hasten to say that nothing that transpired here mitigated this patient's actual shyness in her everyday life. I am merely observing the vicissitudes in a shy patient of an impulse to scorn. However, during the treatment phase when the impulse was ego-syntonic in its overt expression toward me, it diminished in its overt expression toward intimates of the patient, such as those in the patient's immediate family who tolerated the patient's stormy abuse from her earliest years on. I might add that though it is not invariable, an infantilizing, dependent-inducing tolerance of abuse is common in the parents of shy patients. Loud contentious derogation between parent and child fills the histories of many shy patients.

I have also found it clinically remarkable that in solitude morbidly shy persons are inordinately preoccupied with grandiose fantasies that afford enormous pleasure. Indeed, prolonged, vivid daydreaming is an important characteristic of the existence of clinically shy patients. And their fantasies are of a sort having to do with the achievement of a lasting communion with an idealized benefactor. The above patient, for example, found a remarkable solace in a fantasy of marrying a prominent avant-garde painter (whom she had never met), the details of whose career she searched out in periodicals and whose life she tracked down in gossip and dwelled upon in solitude for hours on end. In her fantasy of their life together she planned meals, drew up party lists, selected his clothes, and arranged vacation trips. In this kind of fantasy activity, which is comparatively ego-syntonic despite its usurping all other activities including ordinary interpersonal ones, I submit that we are dealing with the manifest content of the "dangerous grandiosity" that contributes to the traumatic transformation of the social situation in which symptomatic shyness is activated.

Thus the social situation becomes contaminated by displacements and unsuccessful projections of highly egocentric hopes and reactive narcissistic mortifications. Even where it figures in the psychopathology of everyday life, shyness is indeed preceded by a fantasy of grandeur whose displacement idealizes the imminent social situation in which the symptom will arise. A patient with a usually reliable social presence recounted an instance of shyness, which I shall report rather fully because it is not only illustrative but will also further our inquiry.

This 34-year-old man had written a book that had been brought out over a summer during which he had been vacationing at a resort populated by a book-reading public of professionals, media executives, and writers. Inasmuch as their author was vacationing in the community, his publishers thought it a good idea to display a large quantity of the book in the window and on the counter of the local stationery store. My patient described how the prominence of his book filled him with a sense of celebrity (as well it might). Later that day he and his wife received an invitation to a large dinner party. The hostess, who was putting the party together on the spur of the moment, remarked on the telephone that she had seen the book, and she congratulated him. His expectations as to how he would be received and related to by the other guests that evening can easily be imagined. Alas, he arrived that evening to a house full of strangers and detected at once that no one else had any knowledge of the book, or if they did, they did not connect him as the author. His composure suddenly began to leave him, and he was astonished that he had to turn down the offer of a cocktail for fear that his hand would tremble violently. When the subject of his authorship was brought up by the host, the patient was at a loss to hold forth on the nature of his book. He changed the subject, dissembling his shyness by feigning modesty. Moreover, he suspected that an unwitting contempt had been expressed in his waving aside the invitation to speak about his book, that is, he retained the derogatory impulse, though not with conscious intention. Very soon after he recovered from the symptom.

Both his fantasy anticipating recognition and the experience of contempt (which was activated but not projected) are specific elements of a more hazily experienced and disjointed series of psychic events prior to the dinner party. Part of my patient's anecdote of the day's events included his fleeting sense of disappointment that the appearance of his book did not markedly alter his experience of himself within his family. To be sure, his wife and two young children responded joyously to this milestone of his literary project, but how could they not in the end take his virtues for granted? There was no heroic metamorphosis. This inevitable disappointment was clearest to him while he was helping his wife straighten up their kitchen prior to rushing off to the dinner party.

He had the annoying thought that this tedious activity was ridiculously incongruous with his sudden fame. The kitchen, his wife, his children took on an aspect of despised banality.

Alluding to his obvious identificatory confusion, I commented that he had passed the day feeling like both the Prince and the Pauper. He supplemented this observation by likening himself to Cinderella, demeaned in the scullery in anticipation of sublime recognition.

The plight of this patient can be captured in a primal fantasy the psychoanalyst knows as the family romance, a ubiquitous modification of the oedipal situation that contravenes oedipal disappointments by reviving earlier glories in a recovery of lost and noble parents. And I mean to suggest that the themes of the daydreaming of shy patients are variants of the family romance, at least inasmuch as these themes have to do with deliverance from painful mediocrity through participation in the life of some extraordinary, often celebrated, figure, or some idealized occasion. In the chronically shy, this fantasy is obsessional, but the fantasy can be activated in virtually anyone through a conspiracy of circumstances in everyday life, as happened in the patient I have just described.

Though clinicians have reported aspects of the family romance that date from preoedipal periods of patients' lives— Lehrman (1927), for example, reported a piece of the fantasy in a 4-year-old—Greenacre (1958a) is right, I believe, in her general observation that "family romance fantasies of a *well-organized* nature seem to emerge most clearly in the early latency period" (p. 10, my italics). In the normal and neurotic personalities, the fantasy undergoes defensive transformations following its clarifications of residual prelatency conflicts, though regressions do reactivate derivatives of the fantasy. In the schizoid or borderline personalities, the fantasy may take on such a feat of structuralization that it is retained as a "fixation" around which accumulates a "false-self organization"; Khan (1971) describes a type of developmental problem "in which the cumulative traumata disable the child from achieving that internalization of experiences" that lead to an infantile neurosis, and "instead, the whole issue is, as it were, postponed into the future to be later elaborated and given structure" (p. 245). The family romance is very often a significant organizer of such postponed traumata. But either way—activated in a regression or prevalent as a fixation—the displacement of family-romance ideation on to a social situation creates the traumatic context in which shyness appears.

I shall come back to this primal fantasy and its connections with shyness, but we might prepare the way for a further pursuit of these matters by resuming our inquiry into the symptom state of shyness. Here I should like to recall principally several studies of Rangell and Spitz.

In shyness the mastery of anxiety involves the redoubling of efforts to retain the sense of poise, which has been jeopardized and is now failing by the individual's usual methods of maintaining it. Rangell's "The Psychology of Poise" (1954) is one of few studies of the complex state of poise. It carries the subtitle "with a special elaboration on the psychic significance of the snout or perioral region" and locates the traumatic components in states of unpoise at their oral level.

In his description of the state of poise, Rangell notes one of the crucial elements we have singled out about shyness, namely the social element; a loss of poise cannot occur in solitude. He adds that the state of poise rests "on the condition of expectation rather than of action" (p. 318). The pleasure in the state of poise derives from a favorable outcome in the ego's sampling an imminent situation in connection with the ego's capacity to master it. "With poise," Rangell comments, "there exists a confidence of mastery, an ability to neutralize the oncoming encounter" (p. 318). Thus poise is a state of pleasure in the long instant of anticipation. A paradigm of the eventual ego function of anticipation is the infant's confidence that the presentation of the drive object in a state of need will result in satisfaction.

> The breast becomes ready to give and is on its way. The supplies are to be forthcoming, and the action is about to be set off . . . The object and recipient are "poised" for action. Both know their parts, and the subject is in a state of calm satisfaction, secure in his anticipation of the immediate future. [p. 319]

But if poise is initiated in early interactions with the external drive object, it is not, of course, perpetuated there. Among the first developmental steps toward autonomy from the environment in respect to salvation from primal anxiety is hand–mouth exploration and eventual coordination. The hand is the first object in connection with which certain pleasurable experiences of facility with the mother can be reproduced without the mother's collaborating presence (cf. Hoffer 1949). The significance of this for our discussion is that the establishment and maintenance of poise in later life activate the hand significantly. Indeed, in everyday social life the hand is constantly involved in compensating for the disequilibriums in our anticipations of how others will participate in and facilitate social interactions. Rangell adds that as maturation proceeds, the musculo-skeletal system supplements the hand in this regard. All manner of posture is enlisted in establishing and maintaining poise. There is a constant shifting of postural positions, as well as hand movements, in everyday social life. How much we take these everyday poise-retaining movements for granted can be appreciated when we consider the emotional state called "stage fright." I have found, and have reported elsewhere (Kaplan 1969), that among the most terrifying aspects of stage fright is the performer's anticipation prior to appearing on stage of a complete deprivation of his everyday poise-retaining mannerisms, which are about to be supplanted by the gestures of the performance. It is dreadful to realize that you are about to face others without the freedom to make all those habitual and often imperceptible hand gestures and strike all those postural nuances that accompany the state of poise in everyday social life.

If the hand and musculo-skeletal system in general can be thought of as poise-maintaining, what they are enlisted to protect is a visceral sensibility related anatomically to the facial region, which Rangell calls the snout and which he describes as a circle about the mouth "with its centre in the philtrum of the upper lip. . . . Its lateral margins would be the two nasolabial folds; its upper margin, the ventral surface of the nose; its lower margin through the middle of the chin" (p. 320).

In respect of this area, Rangell observes several interesting properties. For one, the snout, from both a phylogenetic and embryological consideration, is "the true rostral tip of the organism," and it is the only anatomical region that must remain in contact with the world for individual life to continue. Moreover, in this region is where the mimetic expressive system is most active, more active than in the eyes, for example, and it is in connection with the snout that we most fear betrayals of our inner emotional states. Since the neurological mechanisms for mimetic expression are mediated in pathways separate from those for voluntary facial activity, the perioral region is susceptible to involuntary revelations of libidinal and aggressive appetites with shame-producing possibilities. Blushing is an example of an involuntary confession of feeling that is experienced as radiating from the perioral region, though it should be emphasized that blushing, unlike shyness, is not experienced as a failure of a regulatory articulation between the perioral region and the musculo-skeletal system; "awkward hands," for example, are not part of the experience of blushing; it is possible to blush within a continuing state of poise.

Such a conception of poise, turning as it does upon the idea of an equilibrium between visceral arousal and executive facilitation and reconstructing the primal situation that it does, is consistent with the more detailed contributions of Spitz, not the least of which is Spitz's cogent vocabulary for the "interpersonal" dynamics of poise and for its maturational, developmental, and eventually stabilizing ingredients.

Thus the exchanges between the needful infant and the supplying mother that lead to the sense of equilibrium that Rangell has singled out, Spitz has named the "primal dialogue" (Spitz 1963, 1965b) and has analyzed microscopically. According to Spitz, a salient characteristic of the primal dialogue is a cyclic unit consisting of an anticipatory-appetitive phase originating in the infant, which phase is linked to a consummatory act in collaboration with the mother. "Action cycle" is the term Spitz uses for this appetitive-consummation reciprocity, and he has gone on to describe a variety of pathologies originating in specific disruptions of the action cycle (Spitz 1964). Delinquency is one such pathology, which further on I shall relate to shyness.

A libidinal enterprise shaping discharge and mastery, the dialogue regulates aggression. The famous studies of Spitz on primal depression (1945a, 1946) have to do with the vicissitudes of aggression unregulated by adequate dialogues. Subsequently

Spitz related such diverse phenomena as "doll anxiety," "stranger anxiety," and "fear of the dead" to a "derailment of dialogue," a traumatization of expectancy in the sudden absence of a collaborative consummatory function in the doll, the stranger, and the corpse (Spitz 1963, 1964, 1965b). Anxiety results from the sudden degradation in the quality of aggression in the psychic apparatus (a loss of neutralization).[2] In these terms, social anxiety (shyness) may be conceptualized as an admixture of a fantasy to the crude aggression released in a failure of a primal dialogue.

The poise-maintaining articulation between the snout and the musculo-skeletal system, which Rangell outlined, Spitz has studied as part of a general maturational and developmental scheme involving two gross anatomical organizations, which Spitz has named the "coenaesthetic" and the "diacritic" (Spitz 1945b). The coenaesthetic organization consists of the smooth-muscle viscera and employs the autonomic nervous system. This organization registers appetite in the broad sense of the term. The diacritic organization includes the musculo-skeletal system and the peripheral sense organs. This organization matures into executive functions, which include perception, consciousness, and motor competence. The snout Spitz conceives as the original bridge between the two systems; for the snout (the oral cavity, as Spitz calls it) is part coenaesthetic, attached as it is to the viscera, and part diacritic in the executive activities of the striped-muscled lips, cheeks, tongue, and throat (Spitz 1965a). The snout contains the nuclear ingredients of poise maintenance in later life. It is interesting that states of unpoise are accompanied often by thirst. The dry mouth and

---

2. The capacity to discern the feasibility of primal dialogues comes to reside in a special sensibility that enables exquisite discrimination between the inanimate and the alive. Spitz has shown that adults can distinguish unfailingly between a doll and a live child of exactly similar size, features, posture, and dress in a black-and-white profile photograph corrected even for skin tone. The early anticipatory equilibrium Rangell reconstructed as a paradigm of poise evolves into a cognitive function that carefully tests whether social conditions are favorable or not for dialogues. This function, like all ego functions, is subject to myriad pathological distortions.

parched throat are invariable complaints of performers who suffer stage fright.

One further point along these lines will restore us to a more psychological realm. These precursors to the sense of poise attain a detectable psychological status quite early in life. So-called eight-month anxiety, which is produced in the child by the presence of strangers, is a clinical observation that leads to the theoretical plausibility of the existence of a libidinal object. In this normal phase of infantile "shyness" at around eight months, the stranger is distinguished from the mother (and other familiar participants in the evolving dialogue), and the child's anxiety reaction more often than not involves covering his face (the snout) in some manner, for example, with the hands, burying it in the mother's skirt, or in the folds of bedclothes.

Following the establishment of the libidinal object and its confirmations in eight-month anxiety, there is a rapid structuralization of personality.

> In the weeks immediately following the first signs of eight-month anxiety, many new behaviour patterns, performances, relations make their first appearance. Foremost and most conspicuous among these is the emergence of new forms of social relations, on a signally higher level of complexity than those present earlier. The understanding of social gestures and their use as a vehicle of reciprocal communication begins. [Spitz 1965a, p. 174]

The capacity for dialogues enlarges to include a variety of persons hitherto strangers. And personal mannerisms in the child become fixed in the service of a personal autonomy that allows increasing emotional and intellectual commerce with a wider social world. Imitation is especially notable in this acute social development, a point I shall want to recall for its significance in pathological states of poise, that is, the pathological absence of shyness.

But here we might begin to distinguish among those later phenomena having behavioristic resemblances to infantile stranger anxiety. We might bear in mind an axiom from Freud: ". . . the form taken by the subsequent illness (the choice of neurosis) will depend on the particular phase of the development of the ego and of the libido in which the dispositional inhibition of development has occurred." (1911a, p. 224).

Psychotoxic events in the first year of life leading to markedly damaged object relations and arrests in the development of "reciprocal communication" often appear in later life as a general interpersonal timidity resembling shyness in neurotics and borderlines but lacking the dynamics of displacement and projection I have suggested earlier. The basic mistrust of many schizophrenics is a mistrust of the possibilities of primal dialogues with anyone not possessing elaborate likenesses to the early maternal object. In the pan-timidity that so limits many schizophrenics in their ordinary social affairs, stranger anxiety has failed to attain consolidation within the personality. For such "shyness" I would propose the distinguishing term bashfulness, which can be thought of as an arrest of a function. The loss of bashfulness in the social interactions of certain schizophrenics is not experienced as a recovery but as an accomplishment.

Although I can point to no such accomplishment in the following case material, the material contains an example of schizophrenic social anxiety. The patient was a 38-year-old man, a long-standing doctoral candidate in linguistics, who complained in the initial interview with me of having failed his dissertation defense several years before, because he had not known what his examining committee expected of him by their questions; he had gone to pieces in the examination, succumbing to blocking and depersonalization. He had forgotten in an instant everything he knew, and attempted to recover by holding forth for half an hour on a theory of the relationship between Semitic and Indo-European languages (a relationship I came to understand to be nonexistent within any accepted linguistic paradigm). Whereupon the committee dismissed him in a bewilderment he shortly thereafter construed as part of a premeditated conspiracy, though at the same time he doubted this paranoid interpretation. What he wanted from me in connection with this disaster was an explanation of what had happened. He explained that he simply did not know in what spirit exactly people convened to have exchanges—he kept missing the point. He had also had a history of dismissals from teaching positions because he could not determine what it was his students were really asking him in the questions they put to him.

A man of mountainous girth, ridden with phobias of dirt and compulsions for order, he lived a life of rumination about the meaning of phrases and gestures of everyone he encountered. To request a telephone repair or other like service consumed days of preliminary speculations. Ordinary conversation drained and exhausted him. Full of social appetite, he suffered excruciating loneliness. The presence of any but the most selected persons evoked near or overt physical trembling.

The damage in this patient's first year of life can be suggested by the fact that twice daily from his birth on his mother had inserted glycerine suppositories into his rectum to guarantee adequate bowel movements—a practice he continued on his own into his adult life. Also, his mother carried him about constantly and fed him continuously because she could not tolerate his merest whimper. These and other patterns deprived him of the opportunity for adequate diacritic integration.

It could be said that his therapy with me came to grief because I could not establish any lasting consummatory patterns in our dialogue; my responses to him were always on the wrong level or beside the point or too soon or too late or gave him too much credit or too little. His tortuous explanations of what was wrong with my responses to him enabled me to sample something of his own experience in the social world. To the degree he survived socially he did so on the basis of intricate but highly stereotyped mannerisms of gesture and speech but without that sense of facility of impostors and other narcissistic characters.

Nor was he a daydreamer in the way I have described the less schizophrenic shy patient. This patient's activity in solitude had to do with compulsive involvements with material belongings—papers, books, receipts, letters, appliances. His ideation consisted of elaborate plans for actions of one sort or another. When he lapsed into daydreaming, his fantasies were erotically sadomasochistic, accompanied by anxiety and agitation. His less manifestly erotic fantasies had a religious cast; in one of them he imagined himself serving God by undoing the linguistic confusions originating with the Tower of Babel.

Sequelae of traumata around the stage of infantile stranger anxiety are quite varied. The patient I have just described had been subjected to an enormous maternal possessiveness. At the other extreme, which is not maternal rejection but maternal blandness, the outcome of this infantile phase is often a striking and morbid absence of shyness. I am thinking of the developmental ego arrest resulting in what is called the "as if" state, where social relations are based upon one of the functions that arises around this infantile phase, namely imitation. In her original paper on this clinical entity, Helene Deutsch (1942) observed that "as if" characters to all outward appearances display social behavior that passes for more than minimal poise. Indeed, such patients rarely complain of shyness and seem even loving and sympathetic. But sooner or later a suspicion arises in those having prolonged contact with the "as if" individual that something is wrong. A lack of genuineness is detected, a shallowness of feeling. In his paper on poise, Rangell noted that too much poise engenders hostility in others, and I believe that the inevitable suspicion about "as if" behavior arises as an epiphenomenon of the unbound aggression that is slightly and unremittingly residual in the "false" dialogue of the "as if" individual.

Now Deutsch conceived of "as if" behavior as a kind of mimicry, a precursor to identification in the eventual oedipal sense of the process. The ego-arresting trauma consists of an affectual impoverishment within the primary family; mothering is adequate up to a point but is so affectually bland that the process of internalization is hobbled by a lack of emotional motivation. The imitativeness of "as if" individuals is a relationship to objects in their external mode.

My clinical experience with "as if" patients has been too limited to characterize their conscious fantasies with confidence. Nor does Ross (1967), who has done a remarkable survey of the literature on the "as if" concept, shed any light on this question. But I would surmise that calculations about and rehearsals of interpersonal activities and life plans constitute a large theme in the conscious daydreams of "as if" characters, but with less distress than schizophrenics experience with similar type daydreams. I have also noted fatalistic and magical—in one patient, numerological—characteristics blended in. "As if" patients do report social panic, but this when a repeated expectation goes haywire, which is a reaction different from shyness. For the most part, their general indifference to motives is misinterpreted by others for a variety of social virtues, like forgiveness and good-naturedness. Incidentally, the consensus of the literature Ross surveyed on the "as if" personality has it that this is a condition of an extremely defective ego whose structures and devices for regulating anxiety remain something of a mystery to a psychoanalytic point of view.

I might mention briefly here other cases where apparent social poise is pathognomonic. The interpersonal facility that Kernberg (1970) remarks upon in certain narcissistic personalities he includes in his picture of their symptomatology. The clinical population Kernberg describes functions by and large at a higher level than the "as if" personality and has evolved a complex structure of grandiose entitlement. Family-romance ideation is already lively in this group but is acted out rather than compromised in symptom formations like shyness. Socially, narcissistic characters employ defensive identification, which is experienced by others as empathetic and flattering; this is also different from the "congenial" impression created by "as if" personalities.

A remarkable freedom from shyness is also characteristic of a population possibly related to, but less delineated than, Kernberg's, a population Greenson (1958) has described as "screen hungry." The social presence of Greenson's population, while intensely sincere (and in this they also differ from "as if" personalities), is counterphobic, that is, they are rambunctiously indiscriminate socially and convey the paradoxical impression of an *im*personal warmth that is irritating and eventually nerveracking. Greenson diagnosed this population as depressive with a hysterical superstructure, which implies a high degree of development. Intensely gregarious—maniacally so—"screen hungry" characters regulate shyness by relating not to persons but stringently to the abstract social occasion, and where this is not possible they fall back on ego-syntonic flights from the social occasion. While they are generally not susceptible to shyness, they are plagued by a symptomatic sense of personal fraudulence.

On the subject of pathognomonic poise, I am reminded of a

paper by Eissler (1963) in which he lamented a dramatic dimi-
nution of social anxiety in a patient who was previously socially
phobic. Eissler contended that this particular patient's sudden
acquisition of social confidence was at the expense of her
continued contact with intrapsychic representations of her conflicts. Thus her recovery arrested her motivation for further
personal development.

The point need not be belabored that the phenomenological
state of affairs we call poise may represent a symptom as well as
a capacity. Poise, as a capacity of relatively good ego integration
and development, is a state that remains subject to jeopardy
now and again. Conversely, shyness might be regarded also as
a capacity and a symptom, both sharing the same dynamics,
though serving different ego purposes in the long run. Nor is
this a strange idea. We have come to regard depression in a
similar way.

Earlier in this discussion I described an episode of shyness in
a patient, a writer, whose expectation of recognition for a recent
public achievement of his had been frustrated. The reaction of
shyness had been preceded by an identificatory confusion
involving an activated family-romance fantasy. We might resume our inquiry into this most common type of shyness with
some observations on the family romance, which I laid such
stress upon.

The oedipal manifestation called the family romance was an
idea Freud first shared with Fliess, limiting the fantasy to
paranoia (Freud 1950). Years later, however, Freud went on to
discover the universality of the fantasy in all children, and he
regarded the fantasy as an effort to regulate the final anxieties of
the dissolution of the Oedipus complex (Freud 1909a). In an
advanced edition (1920) of "Three Essays on the Theory of
Sexuality," Freud again stressed the primal quality of the
fantasy.

The fantasy arises with a conflict over the beckonings of the
social world. It occurs in connection with the child's developing
critical estimation of his parents' actual place in the larger social
world. Anxiety and shame are concomitants of the invidious
comparison between the child's own parents and other parents
and idealized persons, whom the child begins to wish were his

own parents. The family romance embodies the conflict; manifestly the fantasy is about parents other than one's own; unconsciously the fantasy restores a state of affairs prior to the fall of parental esteem when the child enjoyed the advantages of his parents' uncontested power. In the words of Greenacre:

> The germ of the family romance is ubiquitous in the hankering of growing children for a return to the real or fancied conditions at or before the dawn of conscious memory when adults were Olympians and the child shared their special privileges and unconditional love without special efforts being demanded. [1958a, p. 10]

The fantasy itself is an elaboration of the nuclear idea of being a foundling reared by foster parents who substitute for the absent biological parents. The elaboration is usually that the absent parents are of a higher cultural station than the foster parents, and therefore the fantasyer is living an existence in a fallen state. His destiny is to rejoin his real parents and recover his rightful privileges. In the meantime, he is an unacknowledged aristocrat in an ordinary world. There is sometimes the added theme of pardoning the foster parents for ill-treatments, lapses in their realization that the child on their hands was really of exceptional birth. Frosch, in his discussion of the family romance (1959), makes note of Rank's added elaboration of a "rescue" motif. The fantasy is truly protean, far more so than its infrequent appearance in psychoanalytic literature would suggest.

The wishes given structure by this fantasy should be noted. The emphasis in the fantasy is not upon transgression so much as upon the recovery of a threatened and receding infantile position. This is not a fantasy of crime and punishment, corresponding to the myth of, say, Oedipus, which begins with family-romance features but goes on to correspond to later oedipal inevitabilities. This is a fantasy of restoration with its finality in the happy ending. Think, for example, of the story of Cinderella, which I have mentioned earlier, or of Oscar Wilde's *The Importance of Being Earnest*.

Thus shame more than guilt is the affectual exponent of the

family-romance fantasy. Objects related to the ego-ideal are hypercathected; objects related to the superego are hypocathected. Moreover, the fantasy contends with oral-narcissistic rather than with phallic-narcissistic issues. In profoundly morbid manifestations of family-romance wishes—actual imposturousness, for example—the ego's pursuit of oral-narcissistic supplies—love in the form of confirmation rather than a more phallic supply in the form of admiration—is abundantly evident. "For the typical impostor," Greenacre writes in a paper relating the family-romance fantasy and the impostor (1958b), an audience is absolutely essential. It is from the confirming reaction of his audience that the impostor gets a "realistic" sense of self, a value greater than anything else he can otherwise achieve (p. 367).

The phallic-exhibitionistic component of imposturous performances is minimized by the fact that the audience to the imposture is in the dark. Again, it is confirmation more than admiration that the impostor is after.

In shyness confirmation is also an eminent pursuit. But in shyness confirmations of grandeur are inhibited by a retained superego admonition, which is not operative in the impostor whose flawed sense of identity allows, if not encourages, impulsive action. In shyness there is a conflict between the ego-ideal and the superego; there are lively "contradictions within the superego," to repeat Jacobson's phrase about feelings in depersonalization of not belonging.

This last point is decisive in the analytic therapy of neurotic shyness, and in pursuing this point I shall be moving our discussion to a conclusion.

The distinction I am alluding to here between the ego-ideal and the superego proper, a distinction that corresponds at another level to libidinal and aggressive aspects of the superego, is the subject of a long and recently increasing literature (whose recent phase might be dated by Piers and Singer's monograph, *Shame and Guilt* [1953]).[3] Lampl-de Groot's remarks on these

---

3. This, to be sure, is a literature of many moot questions, as Sandler and colleagues (1963) brought to light in their excellent survey of previous and then current contributions to the ego-ideal concept. But if the concept of an ego-ideal is a doubtful theoretical accretion, the clinical distinctions that promote the

distinctions are rather typical. In her paper "Ego Ideal and Superego" (1962), she clarifies the distinctions between these agencies of the superego by regarding the ego-ideal as a wish-fulfilling agency motivating a restoration of grandeur and the superego as a renunciatory agency related to experiences of unpleasure and regulating oedipal compliances that lead to wider social relationships.

Psychopathology has often been related to this theoretical area, and this has given rise to an intrasystemic version of certain symptoms. Lampl-de Groot (1962) has described delinquency in terms of a "discordance of the superego and ego-ideal development." She writes: "In many of these offenders we find a poorly developed ego ideal clinging to very primitive fantasies of grandeur. These pleasurable fantasies are retained in order to compensate for the pain experienced in the clash with the environment" (p. 104).

Thus delinquency and imposturousness, which is a variant of delinquency, are symptoms sharing certain dynamics with shyness. In shyness, however, fantasies of grandeur are less primitive.

This correspondence of shyness with delinquency and imposturousness explains a frequent clinical observation about morbidly shy patients. When the economics underlying an extensive degree of shyness shift unfavorably, the regression often results in sociopathic and/or perverse manifestations as against, say, obsessional or depressive manifestations. The history of several female patients of mine who complained of painful shyness contained bizarre and harrowing escapades of promiscuity. Rangell (1952), in a study of a doll phobia, suggested that acting out is usual in the history of phobics. I might add, incidentally, that such cases contain notable borderline features.

---

concept are widely agreed upon. Thus Schafer (1960) underplays the differentiation of an ego-ideal within the superego, but he does distinguish libidinal and aggressive aspects of superego functioning, following Freud's original formulation that inferiority feelings are the erotic complement to the sense of guilt (Freud 1933, p. 93). For a later and less typical account of the complexities of the ego-ideal concept, see Schafer (1967). A notable and complex discussion of these matters can be found in Jacobson (1964).

The relative freedom from depression among those patients who typically complain of shyness is yet another frequent clinical observation. This is consistent with the narcissistic persuasions of the morbidly shy. In a discussion of the general problem of compensatory narcissism, Annie Reich (1960) observed that the sadistic intolerance of the superego predominant in depressions is absent in cases of oscillating self-esteem, because of the pre-eminence of regulations by the ego ideal.

> The phase of lowered self-esteem is characterized predominantly by anxiety and feelings of annihilation (e.g., social anxiety), not by guilt feelings. Thus it is not the dissolution of an overstrict superego that brings about the positive phase, but a compensatory narcissistic fantasy of restitution via fusion with an archaic ego ideal. [p. 231]

Jacobson also dichotomizes anxiety-annihilation reactions and depressions, attributing the former to "drive intrusions into the ego ideal" and the latter to the usual role of the superego (1959, p. 608).

Greenson (1959) is very concrete on the subject. He writes:

> I believe I can divide my practice into two large groups, the anxiety-ridden patients and the depressives . . . The phobic patients are avoiders, distance-makers, projectors; the depressives are always seeking to get close . . . The anxious patient avoids objects, except for a special few; the depressives relate even too quickly to objects . . . The anxious patient is prone to react with hostility to objects; the depressive is essentially libidinal although sadomasochistic. [p. 671]

But if the superego of the neurotically shy is sufficiently developed to preclude primitive symptoms of grandiosity, like delinquency and imposturousness, what are its nondepressing vicissitudes of guilt? Greenson's clinical finding about hostility to objects in the nondepressive patient is pertinent here. Shy patients are of this group. Toward intimates they are extrapunitive; they assign blame to others. It is rare that they offer apologies. They tend to be dictatorial, tyrannical, and short-tempered. They project guilt. In a paper on shame and guilt,

Levin (1967) describes the metapsychology of supporting narcissistic equilibriums by externalizing blame.

Such externalization of aggression does not entirely eliminate the affect of guilt from the lives of such patients. The guilt is experienced vicariously in the recipient of the externalization. It is another clinical generality that shy patients stabilize relationships with obsessional intropunitive partners in whom guilt is easily provoked. In this there is a resemblance to an observation I made earlier about the infantilizing tolerance for abuse among the parents of shy patients. The repudiation of blame by an intimate can be momentous to the narcissistic equilibrium of the shy patient. It can lead either to further development or to regression destructive to the relationship.

The analytic therapy of neurotic shyness is directed to an alteration of the narcissistic equilibrium. Crucial to such an alteration is the taming of aggression, a transition toward an internalization of guilt and toward depressive affects. While this resembles the therapeutic scheme detailed by Kernberg (1970) for narcissistic disorders in general, the prognosis where shyness is clinically central is enhanced by the compensatory gratification of exhibitionistic drives that are under stringent inhibition in shy persons. Nor does such gratification lead in turn to further clinical complications. For when shy persons begin to achieve, their achievements are not experienced subjectively as spurious and fraudulent. If anything, shy persons tend to be scrupulous about their actual productions; unlike more facile narcissistic personalities, they tend to underrate their achievements, not modestly but apprehensively.

In the clinical situation this transition toward depressive affectivity correlates with a loss in the relationship to the therapist of "playful" tactics, such as coyness, teasing, and derision of the therapeutic situation, tactics that often lapse into painfully hostile impulses toward the therapist. In this there are also painful revisions of incorporative emulations of the therapist; the patient's achievements advance separation rather than fusion. A depressed sobriety becomes an important measure of therapeutic progress.

I should add that this is distinctly not the course of events with shyness in schizophrenics where depression is prognostically negative. In these cases interpretation of extrapunitive impulses is not therapeutically instrumental. Nor are family-romance fantasies available for interpretation in the organized form that they occur in neurotic and borderline patients; though the fantasy is not unlikely in schizophrenia, more likely than not it presents itself in a delusional form (Frosch 1959).

One further observation on the etiology of neurotic shyness as the symptom relates to the family romance: I have found it usual that the mother of both male and female patients presented herself to her child as a more exciting libidinal object than she allowed the father to know, as if a former existence of romantic possibilities came to an end with the mother's marriage to the father. In such intimations from the mother, it is not that the father is represented in a demeaned or impaired manner. On the contrary, the mother concedes his virtues, but they are insufficient in respect to some secret calling in the mother. This, at any rate, is the patient's construction of some early state of affairs.

Such a construction is similar to a variant of oedipal fantasy described by Freud (1910a). In this variant the child imagines the mother in a secret love affair that excludes the father. Repressed is the similarity between the mother's lover's characteristics and the fantasyer's, "or more accurately, of his own idealized personality, grown up and so raised to a level with his father" (p. 171). Freud adds that the "family romance comprises the manifold ramifications of this imaginative activity" (p. 172).

Near the outset of this discussion I mentioned a patient, a woman of borderline features, who on one occasion actually fainted from shyness and who described her feeling at that moment with the statement, "My uniqueness was unbearable." This patient's history furnishes an example of how the oedipal susceptibility Freud described may be highlighted and fixed into a manifestly nonsexual family-romance experience of self and object.

This is a woman, 30 years old, given to periods of sumptuous self-assurance followed by panicky dread. Her periods of self-assurance rest precariously on feelings of aloofness, disdain, intellectual power. The merit to these feelings she derives from the fact that she is quite lovely in appearance and quite intelligent. Moreover, her father, now deceased, taught law at Cambridge, England, before emigrating to New York City, and her mother, a refugee from the Russian Revolution, has continued to maintain her upper-class manners (which appear as pretences in view of the family's eventual entrapment into bourgeois poverty). In addition to this, the family carries the name of a world-famous psychoanalytic pioneer to whom the father was a distant relative.

The patient is the last of four children. She was born into the family after the family had settled in New York and had come upon bad times. The father kept his study intact but was in a depression much of the time, reclusive and unable to pursue his former career. The family lived from hand to mouth on the benevolence of well-to-do relatives. The father died when the patient was 9.

To the patient, as to no other sibling, the mother glorified the father's former professional achievements, lamenting that the patient never knew him as the man he once was and complained cryptically at the same time about his sexual impotence. When the patient was 12, the mother began to come out openly about the father's impotence.

With the other children grown and out of the house, the patient and her mother moved into a large but shabby apartment and took in boarders to relieve expenses. Weekends the mother figure-skated in Rockefeller Center in finery that the patient characterized as ridiculous. Weekdays the mother worked at a clerical job for the Welfare Department. The patient has been a "student" her entire life. Nothing symbolizes for me the plight of this patient with maternal pretence and its traumatic effacement so much as the fact that the French phrases she was plied with by her mother she later discovered were nothing more than a personal patois.

The palpability of actual experience has given to the family romance of this patient an enormous claim to her behavior. More than a daydreamer with painful bouts of shyness, she can actually represent herself socially in an aristocratic spirit. Her existence is as near to Cinderella's as I have ever encountered.

One further example is a 27-year-old English professor, a personable but sometimes boorishly thoughtless man, who complains of a lack of intimacy in his life. Socially he can function in groups but inevitable dyadic relationships incapacitate him, and he avoids them phobically. This is reflected in his professional life; he is thought well of as a classroom teacher but he is very uneasy about private consultations with students; he takes advantage of his social isolation by writing and publishing a good deal. Early in his analysis he dreamed of himself several times as the Lone Ranger.

He was an only child born to a school-teacher mother and school-superintendent father in rural America. At the time of his birth, his mother was 35, his father 37. Pertinent to my present thesis about the family romance is the fact that his mother had been in show business long before the patient was born. A startling incident, which he recalled in his initial interview, was his discovery in his preschool years of his mother's old publicity photographs, which she kept in the attic. These glamorous photographs, which so contrasted with his mother's present life style, bewildered him, and he sneaked up to the attic repeatedly thereafter.

His analysis revealed how the mother's prior existence was conveyed to the patient as a young child, so that a conception of the mother's "other life" grew, while the father, in the patient's eyes, was denied access to it. For example, always in the father's absence, the mother played the piano and sang to her young son; but whereas in public life she played church music and sang in the church choir, on these occasions, alone with her son, she played and sang popular songs—Irving Berlin, Cole Porter, and so on. Also, alone with her son in the family car, the mother became a reckless speed demon, in contrast to her conservative style of driving when anyone else was present.

Later in the patient's life, she sneaked money to the patient in addition to the adequate allowance given weekly by the father. Such inculcations of this mother's yearnings, pointedly secreted from the father, created extremely lively family-romance ideations that were far-reaching in this patient's existence. Even after he had moved to New York and began his teaching career, the mother continued to send money, now large sums drawn from a secret account of hers, which the patient began using for gambling junkets to London and Puerto Rico with fantasies of a great killing and a life of scholarly leisure.

I might add that the crude aggression so typical of the shy patient is not characteristic of this patient. His shyness has more a characterological than symptomatic quality.

These cases are, of course, convenient. More typical cases, which would require inordinate length, would reveal how seemingly fortuitous events conspire to produce a conception in the child of a libidinal vitality in the mother unknown to the father, a conception I am inclined to believe contributes significantly to the psychopathology of neurotic shyness.

CONCLUSIONS

Doubtless there are processes to describe and account for the varying phenomena we call shyness in addition to those I have singled out to emphasize. I am aware, for example, of not having dwelled upon the exhibitionistic-voyeuristic aspects of shyness that the psychoanalytically minded reader would anticipate in a reaction so social as shyness. Also, I have chosen not to discuss the vicissitudes of self and object representations in the shy reaction, the loss of self and object boundaries, for example. Nor have I ventured into group psychology, as Freud opened this area in "Totem and Taboo" (1913); shyness does relate to the loosening of libidinal ties to the primal horde, as Stephen Appelbaum suggested in his discussion of an earlier version of this paper. However, it need not be belabored that the structure of psychoanalytic thought is such that the throwing of a switch to light up one or another corner of the structure lights up all. Our options have to do with which corners to dwell in. My options were to emphasize the following:

1. Neurotic shyness is a species of phobia, specifically social, having phenomenological and dynamic resemblances to depersonalization.
2. The symptom is a continuity of a vivid fantasy activity retained at other moments in the patient's life. (For experimental studies of the relationship between fantasies [dreams in this instance] of vivid quality and subsequent depersonalization reactions, see Levitan 1970. Levitan's bibliography contains references to his ongoing research on dreams and depersonalization.) In neurotic shyness, a primal family-romance fantasy is specifically pathogenic.

3. The regression in shyness from oedipal conflict is to an oral phase of primal anxiety that undoes consolidations of 8-month "stranger anxiety."

4. The loss of the state of poise can be described as a "derailment of dialogue." The concepts of Spitz have been emphasized. In unpoise there is also a regression in the functioning of poise-maintaining diacritic mannerisms.

5. Though neurotic shyness resembles the bashfulness of schizophrenics phenomenologically, the dynamics differ.

6. The pathological absence of shyness in pathological states of poise is cited and described, as this occurs in the impostor, the "as if" character, and narcissistic personalities. The point is also stressed that susceptibilities to shyness can serve ego development.

7. Among the clinical generalities drawn from studies of shy patients are their enormously preoccupying conscious daydreaming, their extrapunitive impulses—their tendency to externalize blame, their warded-off guilt, and depressive affects.

8. Etiologically there is commonly a former overt infantilizing contentiousness between parent and child. There is also a construction by the child of a secret maternal libidinal existence intimated by the mother that excludes the father—a variant of oedipal fantasy described by Freud (1910).

REFERENCES

Arlow, J. A. (1963). Conflict, regression, and symptom formation. *International Journal of Psycho-Analysis*:12–22.

Benedek, T. (1938). Adaptation to reality in early infancy. *Psychoanalytic Quarterly* 7:200–215.

Bibring, E. (1953). The mechanism of depression. In *Affective Disorders*, ed. P. Greenacre. New York: International Universities Press.

Cottrell, N. B. (1968). Performance in the presence of other human beings: mere presence, audience and affiliation. In *Social Facilitation and Imitative Behavior*, ed. E. C. Simmel, R. A. Hoppe, and G. A. Milton. Boston: Allyn & Bacon.

Deutsch, H. (1942). Some forms of emotional disturbance and their relationship to schizophrenia. *Psychoanalytic Quarterly* 11:301–321.

Eissler, K. R. (1963). Notes on the psychoanalytic concept of cure. *Psychoanalytic Study of the Child* 18.

Erikson, E. H. (1950). *Childhood and Society*. New York: Norton.

Fenichel, O. (1945). *The Psychoanalytic Theory of Neurosis*. New York: Norton.

Freud, S. (1894). The neuro-psychoses of defence. *Standard Edition* 3.

_____ (1905). Three essays on the theory of sexuality. *Standard Edition* 7.

_____ (1909). Family romances. *Standard Edition* 9.

_____ (1910). A special type of choice of object made by men: contributions to the psychology of love I. *Standard Edition* 11.

_____ (1911). Formulations on the two principles of mental functioning. *Standard Edition* 12.

_____ (1913). Totem and taboo. *Standard Edition* 13.

_____ (1933). New introductory lectures on psycho-analysis. *Standard Edition* 22.

_____ (1950). *The Origins of Psychoanalysis*. New York: Basic Books.

Frosch, J. (1959). Transference derivatives of the family romance. *Journal of the American Psychoanalytic Association* 7:503–522.

Glover, E. (1956). Sublimation, substitution and social anxiety. In *On the Early Development of Mind*. New York: International Universities Press.

Greenacre, P. (1958a). The family romance of the artist. *Psychoanalytic Study of the Child* 13 .

_____ (1958b). The relation of the impostor to the artist. *Psychoanalytic Study of the Child* 13.

Greenson, R. R. (1958). On screen defences, screen hunger and screen identity. *Journal of the American Psychoanalytic Association* 6:242–262.

_____ (1959). Phobia, anxiety, and depression. *Journal of the American Psychoanalytic Association* 7:663–674.

Hoffer, W. (1949). Mouth, hand and ego-integration. *Psychoanalytic Study of the Child* 3–4.

Jacobson, E. (1959). Depersonalization. *Journal of the American Psychoanalytic Association* 7:581–610.

_____ (1964). *The Self and the Object World*. New York: International Universities Press.

Kaplan, D. M. (1969). On stage fright. *The Drama Review* 14:60–83.

Kaufman, R. M. (1941). A clinical note on social anxiety. *The Psychoanalytic Review* 28:72–77.

Kernberg, O. (1967). Borderline personality organization. *Journal of the American Psychoanalytic Association* 15:641–685.

_____ (1970). Factors in the psychoanalytic treatment of narcissistic personalities. *Journal of the American Psychoanalytic Association* 18:51–85.

Khan, M. M. R. (1971). Infantile neurosis as a false-self organization. *Psychoanalytic Quarterly* 40:245–263.

Lampl-de Groot, J. (1962). Ego ideal and super-ego. *Psychoanalytic Study of the Child* 17.

Lehrman, P. R. (1927). The fantasy of not belonging to one's family. *Archives of Neurological Psychiatry* 18:1015–1023.

Levin, S. (1967). Some metapsychological considerations on the differentiation between shame and guilt. *International Journal of Psycho-Analysis* 48:267–276.

Levitan, H. L. (1970). The depersonalization process: the sense of reality and unreality. *Psychoanalytic Quarterly* 39:449–470.

Lewinsky, H. (1941). The nature of shyness. *British Journal of Psychology* 32:105–113.

Lott, A. J., and Lott, B. E. (1968). A learning theory approach to interpersonal attitudes. In *Psychological Foundations of Attitudes*, ed. T. C. Brock and T. M. Ostrom. New York: Academic Press.

Oberndorf, C. P. (1950). The role of anxiety in depersonalization. *International Journal of Psycho-Analysis* 31:1–5.

Piers, G, and Singer, M. B. (1953). *Shame and Guilt*. Springfield, IL: Thomas.

Rangell, L. (1952). The analysis of a doll phobia. *International Journal of Psycho-Analysis* 33:43–53.

————— (1954). The psychology of poise. *International Journal of Psycho-Analysis* 35:313–332.

Rapaport, D. (1959). Edward Bibring's theory of depression. In *The Collected Papers of David Rapaport*. New York: Basic Books, 1967.

Reich, A. (1960). Pathologic forms of self-esteem regulation. *Psychoanalytic Study of the Child* 15.

Reich, W. (1930). Character formation and the phobias of childhood. In *The Psychoanalytic Reader*, ed. R. Fliess. New York: Basic Books, 1950.

Ross, N. (1967). The 'as if' concept. *The Journal of the American Psychoanalytic Association* 16:59–82.

Sandler, J., De Monchaux, C., and Dixon, J. J. (1958). Patterns of anxiety: the correlates of social anxiety. *British Journal of Medical Psychology* 31:24–31.

Sandler, J., Holder, A., and Meers, D. (1963). The ego ideal and the ideal self. *Psychoanalytic Study of the Child* 18.

Schafer, R. (1960). The loving and beloved super-ego in Freud's structural theory. *Psychoanalytic Study of the Child* 15.

Schafer, R. (1967). Ideals, the ego ideal and the ideal world. In *Motives and Thought: Psychoanalytic Essays in Honor of David Rapaport* ed. R. R. Holt. New York: International Universities Press.

Spitz, R. A. (1945a) Hospitalism: an inquiry into the genesis of psychiatric conditions in early childhood. *Psychoanalytic Study of the Child* 1.

————— (1945b). Diacritic and coenaesthetic organizations. *The Psychoanalytic Review* 32:146–162.

————— (1946). Anaclitic depression: an inquiry into the genesis of psychiatric conditions in early childhood. II. *Psychoanalytic Study of the Child* 2.

————— (1955). The primal cavity: a contribution to the genesis of perception and its role for psychoanalytic theory. *Psychoanalytic Study of the Child* 10.

_____ (1963). Life and the dialogue. In *Counterpoint*, ed. H. Gaskill. New York: International Universities Press.

_____ (1964). The derailment of dialogue: stimulus overload, action cycles, and the completion gradient. *Journal of the American Psychoanalytic Association* 12:752–775.

_____ (1965a). *The First Year of Life*. New York: International Universities Press.

_____ (1965b). The evolution of dialogue. In *Drives, Affects, Behavior*, vol. 2, ed. M. Schur. New York: International Universities Press.

Thibaut, J. W., and Kelley, H. H. (1959). *The Social Psychology of Groups*. New York: Wiley.

Zajonc, R. B. (1965). Social facilitation. *Science, New York* 149:269–274.

7

Transference-Love and Generativity

The title of my remarks—"Transference-Love and Generativity"—suggests that I plan to say some things about love as it occurs in the clinical situation. One of the concepts in my title has to do with love as it is expressed by the patient; that is, transference-love, a concept originated and explicated by Freud (1915). The other concept—generativity—comes from Erik Erikson (1953), and it might be thought of in the clinical situation as a therapeutic form of love in the therapist that reciprocates the transference-love of the patient. Since I shall not be developing any concepts new to you, nor even teasing out meanings lurking in familiar concepts, I expect I shall be much more discursive than didactic. Indeed, since today is Sunday, I may even take the liberty of a little sermonizing.

My thesis is simple: In the clinical situation, transference-love is to generativity as a dependent variable to an independent variable. In other words, transference-love is advanced in complexity and is thus made available to modification only to the degree that generativity operates in the therapist. Here, of course, I acknowledge a bias, which is that transference-love is something to be modified.

Let me begin with some brief observations on transference-love. You will undoubtedly remember that Freud demonstrated the concept in one of his papers on technique with the example of the female patient who falls passionately in love with her male doctor. The technical principles Freud counseled for this extreme situation of romantic love he meant as applicable for all lesser degrees of transference-love. And you will recall that he counseled the therapist to reciprocate the patient's transference-love with prompt interpretation, rather than reactive passion as I suspect he dreaded certain adventurers in his midst (possibly Ferenczi) were toying with, or reactive rejection, as Josef Breuer had done in an earlier era of the psychoanalytic movement. To Freud, the clinical situation granted no privilege or exemption to any human experience, however reputedly pious. Thus transference-love was no less an instance of the return of the repressed than less lofty obsessional symptoms. In fact, at one point in his remarks on transference-love, Freud characterized the patient's emotionality as quite genuine, but he went on to add that if it seemed also "lacking in normality, this is sufficiently explained by the fact that being in love in ordinary life, outside analysis, is also more similar to abnormal than to normal mental phenomena." Mind you, he was speaking of romantic love, which is one particular variety of human love. And he said further that what is essential to romantic love is an indifference to reality, a lack of concern with consequences, a failure of sensibility, and ultimately a disregard for the identity of the loved person. Surely, if we are employed to help someone, transference-love is an experience that should arouse our protective impulses. It is an urgent madness, which should be taken no less seriously for its being so, but it should certainly not be taken on its immediate apparent merits.

A small-minded, misanthropic position? Hardly. For if you regard Freud's essay as a literary document (Freud, after all, did win the Goethe Prize for literature), Freud's observations on transference-love can be located in one of two long-standing cultural traditions on the subject of love. I have in mind a tradition, on the one hand, exemplified by the Elizabethan courtly circles, by the sonnets of Elizabeth Browning, by the poetry of young Lord Byron, and a tradition, on the other hand, exemplified by the Metaphysical Poets, by Pope and Dryden, by the poetry of the matured Lord Byron. The former tradition takes love at its face value and is the tradition of sentimentality appealing to the adolescent mentality. When well wrought, we continue to admire the literature of this tradition, though beyond a certain age in life and after the cultivation of literary judgment and taste, we can never again admire it with the nonreflective enthusiasm with which we first encountered it in our youth. Indeed, like Byron, Freud did make a contribution to this cultural tradition with his touching and effusive letters to Martha Bernays in the early 1880s, a production at a moment in Freud's career analogous to the moment in Byron's when he produced "Childe Harold."

However, with the essay on transference-love, Freud had long since attained an inevitable view of romantic love, a view informed by the wit, the irony, the wisdom that are properties solely of the mature mind. How like Kierkegaard's was Freud's view. Kierkegaard observed: "Perfect love means to love the one through whom one became unhappy." Or like Proust's: "There is nothing like romantic desire for preventing the things we say from having any resemblance to the things in our minds." Or like Sebastien Chamfort's: "Once love is purged of vanity, it resembles a feeble convalescent, hardly able to drag itself about."

Hear my vow before I go
Zoë mus sas agapo.

It is only the generation gap that accounts for a first-rate poet's writing in his tender youth that inane ditty and a third-rate poet's writing a far wittier and superior couplet from the vantage point of adulthood:

Let the love-lorn lover cure insomnia
By murmuring Amor vincit omnia.

(The later Byron might have composed the latter. Actually, it was Ogden Nash.)

Now, it is a pity that Freud had no better word than abstinence for the wit, irony, and wisdom he implored us in his essay to adopt toward the urgencies of transference-love. The term abstinence connotes a retentiveness and stringency Freud never meant. However, the professional literature does contain a vocabulary that makes explicit what might have been implied in Freud's very compressed term. I want to single out one

concept of comparatively recent vintage that illuminates the
spirit of reaction to transference-love—the concept of *generativity*.

In the psychotherapy situation, regardless of the chronological ages of the persons involved, we are dealing really with a generation gap, in which the patient plays the role of disciple to the therapist's role of mentor. This is a way of putting it that subsumes the more common idea that the patient and therapist are, in some special sense, as child and parent. The incestuous possibilities of such a state of affairs, incidentally, is the origin of transference-love. Generativity has to do, among other things, with the maintenance of mentorship, which is the responsibility exclusively of the therapist. "True mentorship," Erikson (1962) writes, "far from being a showy form of emotional sympathy, is always part of a discipline of outlook and method. No good therapist or teacher need protest 'human' respect, personal friendship or parental love." Thus the disciple expects of the mentor not a reassuring protest that the mentor has identical emotional capacities as the disciple—quite literally this qualification in the mentor goes without saying—but that the mentor has a vigorous and experienced ingenuity—"a discipline of outlook and method." If Freud's idea of abstinence has an equivalence to Erikson's idea of mentorship, abstinence is not restraint so much as an engaging counterassertion of a task exceeding what transference-love bargains for. Abstinence is the new bargain for the two birds in the bush, as against the one in the patient's hand.

Generativity, without which mentorship is impossible, Erikson ascribes to the adult phase of the life cycle around the fourth decade, and it serves the mentor's maturing wish for some form of leadership in respect to a younger generation. "The principal thing to realize," Erikson (1962) observes about generativity, "is that this is a stage of growth of the healthy personality and that where such enrichment fails altogether, regression from generativity to an obsessive need for pseudo intimacy takes place." He adds that pseudo intimacy is consistent with treating oneself as a self-absorbed, spoiled child.

We know that regression, like other defenses, is motivated by anxiety. I submit that a therapist's regression from generativity in the clinical situation is motivated by the anxiety of the therapist's envy and jealousy of the patient's prerogative to surrender to a youthful, if not infantile, emotionality for the sake of reparation. The sense of flattery, which Freud observed in the therapist who is the object of transference-love, is a derivative of the therapist's unconscious rivalry. Thus the therapist's experience of flattery is a comic effect, a conversion of deprivation into triumph, and impulses acted out upon it are comical, as lechery is bound to be.

Care is an aspect of generativity that Erikson (1964) has defined as "the widening concern for what has been generated by love, necessity or accident; it overcomes the ambivalence adhering to irreversible obligation." If I understand him rightly, Erikson is also suggesting that care is for something more than the other person in his own right. Though it includes this, it is for something that has arisen between a disciple and a mentor. Care addresses itself to a developmental task accruing as much to what the disciple needs, which he may not be aware of, as to what he wants. Thus care is distinguished from possessiveness. Lacking generativity, therapists are apt to treat their patients with narcissistic possessiveness, like house pets.

Erikson speaks of "irreversible obligation." These are bad times for a phrase like "irreversible obligation" and for the idea of overcoming the ambivalence adhering to it—which overcoming means, I suppose, a submission to duty, an unquestioning subscription to ethics. When I suggest that these are bad times for such ideas, I am not thinking of the youth, whose radicalism wants nothing so much as a restoration of the possibility of "irreversible obligation." I am thinking of our generation and particularly of those of us whose professional calling has always caused us to look with suspicion—and rightly, I think—upon such an idea as "irreversible obligation," ambivalent or not. As students of human behavior we strive for the virtue of open-mindedness and are wary of absolutes.

But what a pity if in liberating ourselves from the fetters of obligation, we detached ourselves as well from the sense of duty. What a pity if the idea that Freud struggled so mightily to establish, the idea that there is no utterance forbiddingly sacred between patient and therapist, should be construed to mean that there is nothing sacred in the clinical situation, nothing to be counted upon, no absolute guides to what is and is not transgression (to use an unfashionable, if not grisly, term), to what is and is not a breach of fidelity between therapist and patient.

Yet, in the crisis of liberal pluralism that typifies this historic moment in the burgeoning mental health movement, it is increasingly difficult to identify the separate attitudes and behaviors that clearly divide the roles of patient and therapist. As the traditional trappings of our professional enterprise fall away in many quarters, including of late our very clothing, alas, it is difficult to determine precisely who is supposed to help whom in the clinical situation. Many of our latter-day therapists appear to crave as much interaction with the patient as the patient craves with the therapist—and of the same sort. And where such a question arises about the degradation of role differences, a reciprocal question arises, it seems to me, about the degradation of the psychotherapeutic enterprise. The enterprise deteriorates into a species of—to be charitable—recreation.

So you see that the controversies that beset us professionally are, in an important sense, no different from what they were when Freud felt compelled to declare his views on transference-love and to implore us to remember that power bestowed upon the loved one is a sacred trust.

But lest you are troubled by the rhetorical quality of some of my terminology, such as "sacred trust," I should like to suggest that there is a growing body of literature in our scientific mode on the subject of postadolescent development that is as relevant to the therapist's personal growth as to the patient's and that provides a rational basis for the ethic of divided roles in the clinical situation. Though most eminent, Erikson is by no means the only investigator of the possibilities of ongoing psychic structuralization throughout the life cycle. More than a decade ago Therese Benedek (1959), for example, did an excellent study of the psychic structuralization that takes place in the *parent* during child rearing. More recently Rubin and Gertrude Blanck produced a remarkable book called *Marriage and Personal Development* (1968), in which a continuing growth process in the adult is identified within the vicissitudes of the marital relationship. Then, of course, we have all experienced the possibility of amalgamating with old identifications newer and more functional identifications in the course of our personal professionalization. The point is that the sacred trust I referred to can be thought of as a postadolescent opportunity for personal growth in the therapist. The therapist who searches for responses in himself that transform the sentimentality of transference-love does this partly in a commitment to his own development. In exercising a "discipline of outlook and method," the therapist provides more than therapy for the patient (as if this were not enough incentive). He enhances his own psychological strength, which is an aspect of sacred trust he owes to himself.

Let me leave you to think of it this way: Transference-love is like a dream. It is fashioned out of neutralized and crude energies. It has a manifest and latent content and involves repudiated wishes, the acceptance or rejection of which cannot be decided until they are brought to light by a "discipline of outlook and method." What advantage is there to the patient if we choose not to take the patient's hand in collaboration with the dream-like scenario of transference-love, but choose instead to arouse the dreamer, which is to arouse as well the angry resistance of one who would cling to that blessed state of sleep? The poet Yeats tells us that "In dreams begins responsibility." The advantage, I would argue, is to liberate from the compulsion to love only oneself in others the capacity to love others for themselves. This is to transform neurotic narcissism into generativity, which is a transition into adult responsibility.

But to leave this choice with the patient is an abandonment— worse, a corruption—of the power that transference-love gives over to us. This choice is the therapist's only and always. And the making of the choice he owes as much to himself as to his patient.

REFERENCES

Benedek, T. (1959). Parenthood as a developmental phase. *Journal of American Psychoanalytic Association* 7: 389–417.

Blanck, R, and G. Blanck (1968). *Marriage and Personal Development*. New York: Columbia University Press.

Erikson, E. (1953). Growth and crisis of the "healthy personality." In *Personality in Nature, Society and Culture,* 2nd ed., trans. C. Kluckhohn and H. Murray, pp. 185–225. New York: Knopf.

———— (1962). Reality and actuality. *Journal of American Psychoanalytic Association* 10:451–473.

———— (1964). Human strength and the cycle of generations. In *Insight and Responsibility,* pp. 109–158. New York: Norton.

Freud, S. (1915). Observations on transference-love. *Standard Edition* 12.

8

Depression and Jealousy

Screen phenomena are conscious presentiments that both embody and repress infantile experience. This idea was first specified by Freud in connection with memories, where the recollection of certain early memories served the repression of later memories and their derivatives (Freud 1899). Shortly thereafter, Freud (1901) added displacements forward and "contiguous" screen memories to the possibilities of their chronological deception.

> Here the essential thing with which the memory is occupied *precedes* the screen memory in time. Finally, we find yet a third possibility, in which the screen memory is connected with the impression that it screens not only by its content but also by contiguity in time: these are *contemporary* or *contiguous* screen memories. [p. 44]

And in a still subsequent work, Freud finally acknowledged his suspicion that *all* memories are screen memories, that is, all memories both retain and distort personal history (Freud 1914a).

Actually, in this final formulation Freud was saying no more than what psychoanalysis always maintains: namely that *every psychological event consists of manifest and latent qualities*. It is only convenience that prompts us to distinguish categorically among psychological events, as, for example, when we distinguish between the forgetting of proper names and the recollection of a screen memory, as Freud does in Chapter 4 of "The Psychopathology of Everyday Life" (1901), or between a dream and a neurotic symptom, as Freud does in the last chapter of "The Interpretation of Dreams" (1900). But what Freud always hoped to reveal about the events he often distinguished was that the laws that describe the articulation of manifest and latent qualities are singular and unvarying—they have a "sameness in essence," to use Lewin's phrase (1961b)—regardless of the category of event under consideration.

Thus Fenichel (1927) found it plausible to compare the function of screen memories to the function of perversions, "where repression of the oedipus complex is achieved . . . by the retention in consciousness of prohibited pregenital impulses." He went on to state that "a hunger for screen-experiences" occurs in connection with conflict-laden percepts that have already attained a vivid clarity difficult for the ego to undo. "If in such a situation a substitute object, as it were, for the percept can be found which unites similarity to the objectionable percept with [relative] unobnoxiousness, then the struggle is decided in favor of repression" (p. 114).

Substitute objects for purposes of screening threatening percepts can originate in regressions, progressions, and contiguous displacements. Here substitute objects may be less threatening aspects of an otherwise unified, complex object image. Siegman (1967) has discussed this process, especially at the service of prestructured defenses like denial. He makes the point that "where one id impulse is described as being used against another," we might observe this through object images "to determine whether one object image is not being used to screen another one, resulting in a shift of id impulses." Siegman counsels against categorizing split object images into "good" and "bad," which is apt to oversimplify the fact that "object images refer to specific historical events, amnesias, and genetic periods . . . What may superficially appear to be a 'bad' object image may actually be linked with less threatening id strivings" (p. 227).

He rightly reminds us that screen images are available for observation, among other places, in rigid, circumscribed transference positions.

Like object images, affect states are also mnemic equivalents and thus can perform screening functions. Freud (1926) spoke of anxiety as "an affect state in accordance with an already existing mnemic image." He added that affective states in general are "incorporated in the mind as precipitates of primaeval traumatic experiences, and when a similar situation occurs they are revived like mnemic symbols" (p. 93). Thus like memories, perversions, and object images, affect states can reveal and repress personal history. Jones (1929a), in his study of the hierarchic relationship among fear, guilt, and hate, spoke of the similarities and differences among these affect states, such that the ego's arousal of one state as a felt affect embodies, yet represses, another, and this in accordance with personal historical circumstance. There is a vast literature on these ideas.

Moreover, clinicians are familiar with the participation of numerous affect states in defensive activities of the ego. Rapaport (1953) concluded that all affects are motives for defense (though he left it moot as to whether it is the affect itself that is the motive or the drive activity underlying the affect). Clinically affects and ego defenses are observed as reciprocities, often in predictably specific ways. When, for example, denial contravenes introjection, one of the observed affectual outcomes is a shift from depression to elation. (There is also a change in the affectual exponent of the transference, often from a circumspect irritability to a breezy indifference.)

In this immediate example of depression and elation does it advance understanding to speak of elation as a screen for depression? "The extensity of the concept of the screen is open to serious question," Reider (1960) has commented, "especially if such looseness is utilized so that almost anything can be used as a screen for something else" (p. 84). But the fact is, as Reider went on to cite, that many things seemingly more disparate than two affect states can have screening relationships to each other. He mentions Freud's reference to taste (in one instance that of bread) as a screen against mnemic recall. Moreover, Lewin (1961a) has referred to the elation sometimes occurring in the course of analytic therapy as a "screen affect." ("Technical elation" is what Lewin calls this, a term I shall return to before long.)

It is, of course, true that affects may be accurately reproduced in analysis, but equally obviously, whatever moods emerge then may not duplicate the original childhood feelings but some that

came later [a regressive displacement]. They might, to stretch an
analogy, be called *screen affects*, in that they present themselves to
hide others. [p. 72]

Like screen memories, Lewin states, screen affects deceive as to
chronology.

Thus on the question of the ubiquity of the screen concept, I
would argue that ubiquity does not inevitably lead to looseness,
if the niché in which the concept functions remains clear. And I
would locate this niche for screen phenomena at the region
where manifest and latent qualities of psychological events
articulate. Here the screen concept operates closer to a descriptive than explanatory level and focuses interest on the simulta-
neities of expression and repression in the patient.

This brings me to a principal concern of the following
presentation. Two affects that have impressed me at times as
having a decided screening relationship to each other are
depression and jealousy, and I should like to make some
observations about instances when the former screens the latter
and about some of the technical problems that arise. Indeed,
depression as a screen affect in respect of jealousy complies
eminently with several ideas I have already cited. For one thing,
depression unites a similarity to the objectionable percepts of
jealousy but with crucial differences; for example, like jealousy,
depression is a reaction to the threat of object loss but excludes
a conscious fantasy of the third person otherwise present in
jealousy. Also, in the kind of depressive manifestation I want to
report, there is a chronological deception: a pregenital conflict is
hypercathected, an oedipal conflict hypocathected—a regressive
displacement. Furthermore, in these depressions an oral object
image is elicited from a more complex object image and then is
employed by the ego to screen the remainder, a process described by Siegman (1967). But while the drive object is altered,
the ambivalence pathogenic for jealousy (Jones 1929b) is retained by the depression, which also involves a high degree of
ambivalence (Freud 1917).

This state of affairs is evident importantly in the patient's
resistance against associating oedipal derivatives, which resistance expresses itself through a prevailing depressive affect with

a typical transference exponent that I shall try to describe. And I might interject here that I shall be describing merely a special instance of what Friedman (1953) observed about numerous patients, namely an initial oedipal presentation quickly dissolved in a protracted presentation of oedipally tinged preoedipal conflicts.

> Frequently in the first few hours of analysis we see unmistakable evidence of the oedipus complex in the behaviour of our patients, in their clearly oedipal dreams, in their associations; and just as frequently, after a relatively short time, we find all this material vanishes and the picture is represented much more in the light of pre-oedipal conflicts. (pp. 311–312)

These remarks of Friedman have a relevance to the cases I have in mind to present shortly. (Alexander [1956] described a case where it took 2 years for the analysis to recover the oedipal material from which the patient had retreated "after the first week.")

One further point among these preliminaries: I have cited Lewin's term "technical elation," by which he meant an elated affect aroused by the therapeutic process itself, rather than by circumstances in the patient's everyday life. Now the observation that the therapeutic process elicits discrete affects as well as behavior not typical in the patient's everyday life is common wisdom among clinicians. The playfulness, for example, of certain very disturbed patients during sessions may contrast markedly with the cautious reticence with which such patients endure their everyday lives. Another example of treatment-specific behavior is the impulsive hostility toward the therapist of certain otherwise morbidly shy individuals. Lewin's adjective "technical" for treatment-specific phenomena is felicitous and reminds us that the mental and behavioral vicissitudes of the patient *qua* patient are not identical with the patient's everyday manifest functioning. One of the distinguishing objectives of the analytic process is its structuring of something other than a "slice of life." The process is like a prism through which the patient's everyday life is broken up into component technical phenomena. And this prismatic effect may even precede the formal therapy situation, when the resolve itself to apply for therapy produces a technical affect that becomes part of the patient's presenting picture. Surely the anxiety states commonly seen in initial interviews are, in this sense, technical. However, there are more complex states aroused by the resolve to enter therapy. So-called flights into health are sometimes marshaled temporarily by the prospect of therapy. And certain depressions also belong to this category.

Here I should like to introduce several clinical abstracts that will enable a further discussion of the problem of a technical depression screening oedipal jealousy.[1]

CLINICAL ABSTRACTS

A 30-year-old woman requested psychotherapy in connection with an increasing experience of marital unhappiness. Since depressive features are of interest, I should note that she revealed at the outset more "a depressive component of neurosis than a typical depressed state" (Levin 1965). Though an attractive woman, she seemed faded and forsaken. But despite a lugubrious aura, she was alert and responsive to inquiries and was not without a sense of humor. Her responses, however, trailed off into vagueness, so that it was not possible initially to grasp much clarity in her complaints about her marriage especially. When she reported, for example, that her husband was annoyed with her for being a leech, she could not specify what

---

1. Mindful of Greenson's classic paper on screen defenses (1958), I must interject that none of the patients I am about to present appear to belong to the kind of population Greenson was describing. His sample exemplified what could be called a "glamour syndrome." "They appear ready and eager to make contact and communicate," Greenson writes. "They seem warm and giving in pouring forth their life history . . . since they keenly need to feel understood. Although they are quite successful in their work, they belittle their accomplishments and have little faith in their genuine merits . . . They become easily enthusiastic and sentimental . . . optimistic . . . They are impressionable, suggestible . . . They tend to exaggerate and have a touch of the swindler about them," and so on (p. 243). None of the following patients have this kind of façade.

he was referring to in her behavior and ultimately even what he meant by the accusation. The initial obscurity she conveyed in trying to illuminate her relationship to her husband—indeed to other human relationships she brought in as well—was the sort of obscurity encountered in patients with "as if" personality trends. Yet, unlike patients with extensive and pronounced "as if" characteristics, whose physical appearance virtually never varies, this patient's appearance fluctuated notably from one visit to the next, from being comparatively unkempt to carefully well groomed.

She had been married for the past eight years to a musician. Before becoming a housewife, the patient herself had been a band vocalist. The marriage was childless, and the patient spent the years inching her way toward a college degree, but deferring a decision about electing a major subject. Her academic ambitions wavered between biological science and fine art. Her husband, 2 years her senior, she described as considerate, easygoing, often lovable, but peculiarly passive in his commitment to things. Though he earned a steady income from year to year, within each year his income was sporadic, and their financial survival often devolved upon the patient, who periodically took on freelance editorial work, which she was highly skilled at but had no enthusiasm for. She complained about her husband's lack of participation in decisions, especially in her wish to have a child, which he discouraged with a peremptory, "What for?" She had the feeling that they both seemed to be drifting with circumstances.

In their sexual life the patient was disturbed by the fact that they functioned only if she aroused her husband by putting on scanty underwear, stockings, and high-heeled shoes and going through erotic dances, which invariably culminated in oral-genital sex. "I've been doing this for years, but it's really not my style. I don't know who I am when I go through that routine."

The patient's initial version of her parents' interaction was strikingly similar to her version of her own marriage. A typical memory of her father was his reclining in an easy chair absorbed for hours on end listening to classical music with his eyes closed, oblivious to activities going on around him. This was a source of exasperation to the patient's mother, who complained of having to make all the decisions alone. Moreover, the patient's mother sometimes worked as a secretary in order to supplement the father's seasonal income. The patient remembered her father as complacent, vain about his attire, and a terrible tease, which seemed to be his only way of giving affection. He would scare the wits out of the patient with horror stories and then would sweep her up with peals of laughter to still her hysterical tears. It was the only animation she initially recalled in her father. Pertinent to the patient's anaclitic tendencies were two hospitalizations of the mother for surgery, once when the patient was 2 years old and again when the patient was nearly 6. In the patient's first 6 years, she sustained additionally the mother's giving birth to two male siblings.

Memories of the mother's latter surgery and the recollection that her father's horror stories were based largely on physical mutilations were to enable the patient to gain a very profound insight into the meaning of her exhibitionistic sexual pattern with her husband and also into her original choice of career as a singer, both having to do with gaining a sense of phallic integrity. An identification with her father through teasing also determined this behavior. Thus her initial account of her history contains, among other things, oral, phallic, and oedipal features, the last very markedly in the similarities between her perceptions of her own marriage and that of her parents.

The extent to which oedipal rivalry figured in the patient's initial presentation can be gleaned from her first reported dream, and not merely from its manifest content but from her peculiar manner of handling it. The dream temporarily impaired the patient's synthesizing capacity, indicating an unconscious conflict of great vitality.

This dream occurred after five weeks of therapy. The dream was that she was witnessing her husband in bed with another woman, someone French or Spanish. Parenthetically the patient stressed that her husband was not making love to this other woman (a comment of secondary revision serving a negation and also an affirmation that the other woman was making love to her husband; that is, the other woman was the aggressor).

Now note the strangeness, not of her associations to the dream, but of her evaluation of them: in response to my asking the patient what actual incident could have supplied the dream with any of its content, she replied that she had recently answered a telephone call from an unknown woman, who wanted to speak with the patient's husband. The patient told the caller that her husband was not in and pressed the woman for her name. When the patient identified herself as the wife, the other woman hung up abruptly. With evident pleasure at happening upon the connection, the patient added that the telephone caller spoke in a Spanish accent. Also, this reminded the patient that several months before, she had noticed among her husband's belongings on a dressertop a slip of paper on which was written a woman's name, definitely Spanish, and a telephone number. To the idea that the woman in the dream could have been French, as well as Spanish, the patient associated the thoughts "sexy" and "sexually experienced." That her own dream confirmed a piece of her academic sense of the psychology of dreams astonished and delighted her.

However, the dream and her associations went on to evoke no overt emotion or conscious fantasy in the patient regarding the situation between herself and her husband. This contraction in her associations was compounded with a very feeble, if not bizarre, rationalization. She told me that four or five years ago she had found a woman's pouch of makeup in the glove compartment of her husband's and her car. She called it to her husband's attention, and he simply laughed it off, not feeling a necessity to offer an explanation. The next day the patient made a point of examining the glove compartment. The pouch was gone. I could not understand what she meant to explain by this incident or how she thought she was relating the incident to the dream. Our dialogue at this very moment became quite odd. It was one of those moments early in therapy when a patient is rocked by a dawning realization that analytic therapy is an earnest and formidable enterprise beyond anything that could have been predicted previously.

Thereupon the dream and these associations were dropped in a passing manner, inspiring in myself a suspiciousness in such contrast to the patient's lack of interest in the possibility of her husband's unfaithfulness that I felt paranoid and decided, therefore, to postpone the issues raised by the dream.

Thereafter the patient went into a hypomanic phase lasting several months, which she mistook for a therapeutic gain. She announced a succession of good intentions regarding school, her neglected social life, her moving back to the city, and her solving her ongoing financial bind by organizing an editorial service or perhaps reviving her singing career. She soon saw how empty these intentions were. She felt stymied, though not yet morbid.

It was when I began to note that her husband had all but evaporated from her remarks that her spirits dimmed very low. She went into a depression that consumed the better part of two years. (Recall Friedman's remarks.) Her physical well-being deteriorated markedly; she became victim to colds, backaches, nausea, all of which provoked by turns her husband's commiseration and annoyance. Again with a significant lack of interest, she reported from time to time that her husband was absenting himself more than usual. The theme of her initial dream of the other woman simply did not engage her, which is not without paradox, for the onimous vitality of this theme was what brought her into treatment in the first place.

I do not wish to imply that therapy grinds to a halt against this protracted depression, which, as I shall discuss in a later section, warded off oedipal (and sibling) conflicts. However, any attempts of mine to interpret vestiges of oedipal material in her reports were countered by the patient with bitter, derisive protests that I was misunderstanding her and misjudging her whole situation. On several of these occasions, which were months apart, the sudden contrast between her now distinct depressive self-presentation and her enraged word-twisting assaults gave me the impression that she was warning me of the possibility of ideational disorder.

When I found the opportunity (which consisted also of the courage) to point this out to her and convince her that a depression was no advantage over any crazy ideas she was harboring, her depression began to yield to a paranoid reaction. Her physical well-being returned. For the first time with conviction she faced the bitterness she felt toward her younger brothers. Also hitherto repressed versions of her father became available to her. She was able to recall, for example, that her father had taken a tender interest in her physical appearance and had once waltzed with her at a banquet, when she was 7, to the delight of everyone present, who had cleared the dance floor. The applause had thrilled her. She recalled her shame and anger at her mother's ostentatious masochism.

Among the classic formulations regarding depression (Freud 1917) is the idea of regulating aggression against an object by punishing the self with those hostile accusations displaced from the object. In a depression the object's malevolent traits are experienced subjectively through a vicissitude of an identificatory process. This patient's depression retained elements of her mother's characterologic masochism and ill health. It also retained self-recriminations about occupying a station in life lower than what the patient felt destined for, which was yet another perception of her mother's plight.

But the oedipal tinge to this depression is evident by the circumstances of its acute onset, a regression in a life situation symbolizing an oedipal contest, the denial against which the treatment situation quickly undermined. (Indeed, the patient was subsequently able to perceive and confirm the fact that her husband had been involved in a succession of affairs, which perception, incidentally, coincided with her husband's entering psychotherapy himself.) Moreover, the depression served the preservation of an oedipal illusion and regulated aggression related to oedipal supplies, this exemplified by a pivotal moment in which the patient extricated herself from an exasperated tirade against her husband's past unfaithfulness long enough to inform me in a tone of cynical disenchantment that when it came to her father and her, "mother didn't stand a ghost of a chance."

This patient is still in treatment currently. At this writing, she has been having difficulty with her emerging receptivity to unintended communications from those around her—a paranoid symptom.

The following is a very brief abstract of the analytic therapy of a 40-year-old man, married and the father of three children, who had a relatively successful analysis in his early thirties with an analyst who had since died. The patient requested additional therapy for a writer's block of several months' duration. An

established freelance script-writer, the patient had been
working on a screenplay, and the work block began with a
string of days of merely staring at manuscript paper, then
several days of fitful starts. He became panicky. There were
several further days of intermittent anxiety attacks, quite unlike
him, and over the span of a month the thought of re-entering
therapy grew into a determination to do so. Whereupon he
went into a depression reminiscent of the presenting symptom
that had instigated his original analysis.

Like the anxiety states that preceded it, the depression was
intermittent. He described it as a mixture of imposturous
feelings and a sense of futility about realizing any further
projects. His previous achievements seemed third-rate, if not
worthless. Involutional concerns also contributed to this depressive pall. He felt emotionally resigned from his family and social
group.

These complaints he related to his tendency to derive oral and
anal fantasies from the act of writing. Recapitulating the substance of his previous analysis, he informed me how his mother
had inspired enormous ambitions in him and extracted great
productivity. Though fond of his father, he described his father
as a bystander in the family. The patient's imposturous feelings
he related to a long-standing susceptibility to liken himself to
Cinderella, confined to the indignities of an ordinary and banal
existence with expectations of being restored to an aristocratic
milieu. Nor was he unaware of the feminine experience that
accrued to this fantasy. And he was also conversant with the
technical term "family romance."

But not to let the impression stand that the patient was a
naive intellectualizer, I should add that he was quite aware that
the most crucial question was what he was entirely in the dark
about. Why precisely at this moment in his life should he have
succumbed so entirely to these infantile susceptibilities he could
not answer, and he understood that a fresh inquiry began with
this matter.

To be sure, the symptom picture he presented was no
exception to the principle of overdetermination. However, I
want to stress the contingency of the patient's wife having come
through a decade at this point of rearing three children. She was

now liberated from certain aspects of a maternal role that had absorbed her with an exclusiveness reminiscent of the patient's own mother. But now she had taken off a good deal of weight, which restored her figure, and she paid renewed attention to her appearance. The patient enjoyed this and encouraged it. Moreover, it did not escape him that other men not only began noticing his wife but noticed the patient in connection with his wife. (From his reports I received the impression that his wife was something of a flirt.) Thus in the person of his wife the patient was losing one set of characteristics while pursuing another. These characteristics corresponded respectively to preoedipal and oedipal strivings in the patient.

Of interest to the present discussion was the reinstated depression that beclouded both positive and negative oedipal anxieties. For the better part of a year, oral and anal conflicts dominated the patient's attention. Among the many incidents in the clinical situation that lent conviction to the importance of the oedipal conflict was the contrast between the patient's rather breezy manner of reporting derivatives of coprophagia and his gingerly manner of reporting associations to homosexuality-tinged dreams and fantasies. Tarachow (1966) reminds us of the typicality of withholding for years the specifics of eliminating, handling, fingering, and eating bodily secretions and pickings. Yet, this patient brought up an extensive array of highly personal coprophagic activities, with defensive aplomb, to be sure, but he brought them up nevertheless. Even he was surprised at the comparative diffidence with which he approached homoerotic ruminations. Also surprising was his distress at his wife's flirtatiousness, which he had never before taken particular note of.

A final abstract involves an unmarried woman attorney in her middle thirties, who had been for several years the mistress of a prominent actor. Though she had agreed that the affair should not curtail one another's sexual freedom with other partners, the patient remained faithful in the affair, while knowing that her lover slept around quite a bit. The relationship she described with her lover resembled Annie Reich's description of a narcissistic object choice in women (Reich 1953), where an extreme submissiveness prevails, punctuated by ecstatic sexual experi-

ences. The patient's interest revolved around her lover's career;
she doted on his public appearances, press notices, his private
doubts, ambitions, and future plans; but she shared with him
none of her own career problems; she suffered hours waiting for
him for appointments, for which he was invariably late and
sometimes failed to show up altogether; hoping for his call, she
was sometimes unable to move out of earshot of one or another
of her telephones. However, her sexual experiences with this
man were intensely gratifying in every way—"screaming" was
one of her adjectives.[2]

The patient's presenting symptom was a depression with
agitated features, relating to this love affair and to her decision
to seek professional help in connection with it, a decision that
embittered and mortified her. She complained of being in the
throes of an "adolescent infatuation" and berated herself for
"emotional stupidity" and "shallow greed" (labels she was
several years later to apply to her lover when their relationship

---

2. I might say in passing that Annie Reich (1953) suggests that the orgasmic
ecstasy in such submissive women restores self-esteem by affording a tangible
confirmation of possessing an idealized body part belonging to the male partner.
According to Reich, this confirmation, the grandiosity of the orgasm, and the
momentary fusion with a disparately more powerful object indicate a relationship of pronounced oral characteristics.

This patient's repetitive situation of separation, passive waiting, and renewed
contact is a frequent feature in the relationships of women who establish this
kind of object choice. This series of loss, anticipation, and regained contact
reminds us, of course, of Freud's formulations regarding the mastery of anxiety
and the conversion of pain into pleasure in the peek-a-boo games of young
children (Freud 1920). Recently, Kleeman (1967) has published a detailed and
valuable study on the peek-a-boo game, in which he distinguishes between
active and passive peek-a-boo "playing" in the infant and raises an as yet
unanswered question as to whether the passive variety—the infant's watching
an adult play the game—is a preimitative stage preparatory to the active variety,
which then becomes imitative. I bring this up because this patient began to
extricate herself from her passive victimization not by actively demanding
reliability from her lover, but by becoming unreliable herself where he was
concerned, that is, she moved into an active peek-a-boo phase, which I
understood at the time as an identification with the aggressor—originally her
mother. This was an important part of the beginning of the end of the affair. The
anxious responses that the patient's unreliability elicited in her lover supplied
the process of deidealizing him and abetted her perceiving him more "realisti-
cally."

was nearing its end). Pathognomonic of her depression was a sleep disorder; she suffered bouts of insomnia, and after finally falling off to sleep, she would awake unable to fall back to sleep. Her concomitant involvement with barbiturates frightened her. Also, her appetite waned, and she lost an appreciable amount of weight. Though these latter symptoms—her sleeping problem and the weight loss—were what finally brought her into therapy, it is not clear whether her growing resolve to enter therapy provoked the symptoms or the other way around.

A psychogenic history of this patient would include an early relationship with a narcissistic mother who combined the affection of maternal attentiveness with the rejection of harping criticism. As a child, the patient was constantly scrutinized by the mother and drilled about physical appearances. The mother had been a fashion model and sometime actress whose self-esteem depended greatly on a glamorous appearance. ("A vain woman, forever dieting, yet inexplicably faithful to my father—inexplicably because she was a type you'd never expect fidelity from.") Academically, the patient took after her father, a book publisher, a large part of whose life went on, the patient recalled, in his book-lined office. The patient was quite successful academically all through school. However, when she got to law school, her leading difficulty for a time was acute fatigue. She would drop off to sleep in classrooms, the library, and other places, a symptom often consistent in late adolescence and young adulthood with identity diffusion. Primal-scene phenomena figured conspicuously in the patient's early history. The patient had also been exposed significantly to heated verbal quarrels between her parents, and she recalled that she eventually sided with her father, to whom she was to draw quite close when her mother gave birth to the patient's sister in the patient's sixth year. Thereafter she remained close to her father and grew very dependent upon him. I should add that the patient's first sexual intercourse was with a law professor whose student she was at the time and that her sexual behavior for the next half dozen years could be called promiscuous, usually with men markedly older than herself. At various times she consumed notable quantities of alcohol, amphetamines, and other drugs.

On the basis of even the little I have presented of this patient, we would be right to suspect that her depression is more malignant than the two previous cases.

On the other hand, the exclusiveness of the presentation of depression in the therapy situation was not altogether consistent with the numerous areas of ego autonomy attained by this woman. She continued to function as a successful lawyer in a legal specialty where being a woman was still a significant disadvantage. In many important situations she was a reliable judge of character and had a high degree of faith in her decisions, which usually proved quite adequate. She was also very charming and conscious of being so. Only in the clinical situation was she unremittingly anguished, forlorn, deprived, and helpless. However, she often brought in with her several opening moments of vivaciousness from her outside life before collapsing, frequently into tears. At these times I dealt with her exhibitionism, which she was able to work with.

But I found it next to impossible to implore even an intellectual interest in the meaning to her of her lover's unfaithfulness, a topic around which she installed a rigid taboo, despite the frequency with which she herself alluded to it. She once reported having had dinner with her lover who had brought along unexpectedly another woman. When this other woman excused herself to go to the ladies' room, the patient's lover turned to the patient and whispered that he was having an affair with the woman. When I called attention to the patient's blandness in reporting the incident, I was berated for being tendentious.

On another occasion—there were many—the session grew stormy with accusations that I was departing from my impartiality because I had invited the patient to return to a slip of the tongue she had made in recounting her having come across yet another of her rivals at a dinner party. The "latent" interpretations of such inquiries produced the disruption Freud (1937) once described: "The patient now regards the analyst as no more than a stranger who is making disagreeable demands upon him, and he behaves towards him exactly like a child who does not like the stranger and does not believe anything he says" (p. 239).

However, only the pursuit of the latent jealousy produced this temporary loss of a working alliance.

For the most part of the first 2 years of therapy the patient assumed a dependent emotional attitude toward the therapist following her initial relief that he was not given to keeping her waiting, altering her schedule, or prone to unpredictable moods of capricious verbalizations. Indeed, her initial attempts to alter these properties of the therapeutic situation were feeble and short-lived, as such attempts go. The constancy and reliability she wanted to be able to take for granted in the therapy situation contrasted notably with the harassing interpersonal situation she had brought into therapy and which she also seemed to take for granted, however much it distressed her. It was as if she was establishing a second type of object choice alongside the first, an anaclitic alongside a narcissistic (Freud 1914a).

The maintenance here of a rather singular affectual position that contrasted with her affectual output elsewhere in the patient's life suggests the "technical" quality I spoke of in my opening remarks. Even her intellectual power faded during her sessions, as such power might be conceived by the richness of information conveyed through vocabulary and language structure. Only in her periodic contentions with me would she marshal her full conceptual power to represent herself, which provided yet another contrast between the "technical" position she gravitated toward and how she must have functioned elsewhere in her life, especially in her vocation. "If you explained yourself out there the way you sometimes do in here," I once pointed out to her not without humor, "you'd be out of business, if not disbarred." To which she ruminated quite earnestly about her peculiar reluctance to sustain an experience with me that involved a sense of her fullest capacities. I inquired what she thought she was protecting. "Our situation, you, myself," was as far as she could take the matter at that particular moment. Thus she articulated one of the dimly felt components of her ongoing transference position brought briefly to consciousness, that the plausibility of her demands upon my conduct in various issues with her was not wholly self-evident but that her demands served a purpose.

"I wish you would understand," she commented nearly a

year later, "that I am not here to *do* anything. I just want to tell
you how I feel," a reference to her complaint that her mother
could never bear the patient's routine unhappiness as a child
without "going into immediate mitigating action," that is,
without holding the child accountable for her feelings, this
prematurely inasmuch as mastery was not amply achieved.
While this remark, with the early issues it alludes to, is another
example of this patient's effort to structure the therapeutic
situation as an opportunity for belated mastery of preoedipal
experiences, it has an important bearing as well on her oedipal
conflicts, which can be said to have been on the agenda, albeit
as a later item of business. This patient's depression in the
therapy situation and the acting out outside the therapy represent an autoplastic imbalance, an attempt to preserve the
environment at the expense of self-victimization. "I am not here
to *do* anything," while manifestly preoedipal in its being derived
from a two-person, mother–child situation, has the latent oedipal significance of a dread of power to achieve forbidden
oedipal wishes directly. This power the patient misconstrued in
several phases of her life, two of which I have already mentioned, the first when she drew close to her father on the
occasion of the birth of her sister and then again much later in
her affair with her law professor and its aftermath of several
years of promiscuity with older men. Thereafter she retreated
into preoedipal versions of her sexual relationships. An apt
description of such versions is Greenacre's: "The wish is to
reclaim the mother as a nurturing but degraded accession and to
rob the father of the genital for the completion of the narcissistic
body needs, sometimes also thereby to impress the mother"
(1960, p. 718). But even this preoedipal scheme retains oedipal
vestiges.

It was to require two and a half years, which included an
interruption of several months, before this patient could explore
fantasies constructed out of consciously recognizable oedipal
object images. Though painful, the jealous affectivity she then
consciously registered was mitigated by her growing capacity to
deidealize the contemporary persons she involved herself with.
In the treatment situation the counterpart of these transitions
has been a loss of desperation over how the hours should be and

a greater tolerance for the unexpected – the patient's associative capacity has enlarged, which includes a tolerance for periods of anxious silence, alternatives to her former active self-deprecatory presentations. Paradoxically, her previous assertion that she is not in treatment to *do* anything has begun to acquire a new meaning.

Among the issues I want to go on to discuss will be the incident I reported in this case of interruption of treatment.

DISCUSSION

Among the clinical factors favoring psychotherapeutic results, Freud (1937) included one where "the patient's ego had not been noticeably altered and the aetiology of his disturbance had been essentially traumatic . . . Only when a case is a predominantly traumatic one will analysis succeed in doing what it is so superlatively able to do" (p. 220). The clinical experience informing this statement is a familiar one. If the transference fails to include a neurotic element (a transference neurosis) and maintains an exclusive pleasure-deriving repetition, analytic therapy bogs down; for the transference then represents an alliance devoid of a task, which task includes the successful belated mastery of trauma.

There is implied in Freud's comment an idea that a workable quantity of unregulated anxiety must be volunteered to the treatment situation, and where, for example, a predominant character disorder is presented instead, analytic therapy faces an impasse. This idea was consistent with Freud's view that in connection with analytic therapy, the psychoneurosis had the most favorable prognosis. While Freud's view may still be true, his idea of a voluntary presentation of a favorable transference situation has been supplemented by the technical possibilities of soliciting a favorable transference situation by making an otherwise quiescent trauma manifest.

Moreover, the distinction Freud makes here between "structured" and "traumatized" ego development is limited to manifest ego performance. A less restricted view (which Freud himself also held) has it that trauma, affect, and defense are inseparable ingredients of a dynamic concept of ego (Rangell 1968a; Schur 1953) and that even so-called successful defenses retain components of the specific trauma and effect they regulate (Schafer 1968a).

A conscientious reactivation of trauma in the treatment situation seems called for when the transference acquires a sustained dichotomous quality, when the affectual transference exponent does not fluctuate but is either repetitively dependent (so-called positive) or repetitively palpable, that is, experientially oppressive, combative, or accusatory (so-called negative). This is when there appears to be an alliance without a task or a task that disrupts the alliance, so that some kind of "management" on the part of the therapist seems appropriate.

Greenson (1967) reminds us of the dangers of actively "managing" the therapeutic relationship by noninterpretative measures, such as suggestion and manipulation, measures, he concedes, that are sometimes unavoidable, though not necessarily of lasting detriment to the ultimate instrumentality, which is interpretation. The "art" of technique, he adds, is in keeping such measures at the service of the analytic point of view (pp. 49–51). Partial and simplistic misapprehensions of clinical phenomena invariably subvert the analytic point of view. "Art" then becomes merely artifactual.

One misapprehension sometimes arising in connection with the kind of clinical material I have presented is that the chronological depth of a regression has a positive relationship to its pathogenesis. That is, a pregenital derivative, like a depression, has a higher clinical priority than an oedipal derivative. Fenichel (1941), Hartmann (1951), Alexander (1956), and others have cautioned against the notion (which reached an extreme in the writings of Wilhelm Reich) that the transference "deepens" according to a chronological schedule. Another possible misapprehension is that a similarity in the dynamics of all depressions indicates a similarity in their regulatory activity. However, some depressions represent an increase in neutralization, others a decrease, and this difference requires different management.

In the clinical episodes I have presented, particularly of the two cases involving female patients, the affectual transference exponent became stridently palpable as I directed the patients' attention to the three-person (oedipal) fantasies that were latent in the reports of their dreams and everyday life. Indeed, in the third presentation (the female attorney), my endeavours threatened such injury to our working relationships that long intervals passed during which I complied with her avoidance of the material, but I could not succeed in mitigating the disorganization represented by her interruption of therapy. This interruption was comparable diagnostically to the defensive decompensation represented in the first patient by an acute ideational disorder, which also coincided with the perceptual undertaking of oedipal material.

By comparison, the second case—the male writer—revealed no decompensation when oedipal material arose. This patient was capable of sustaining a metaphorical sense of our relationship in both preoedipal and oedipal phases of the transference. Though a marked transference palpability was evident when I abstained from conceding an importance equivalent to the patient's regarding his depression, he was capable of an initial marshaling of ego defenses adequate to the task of sampling jealous affect.

With depressions less directly involved in screening jealousy, their loss of clinical centrality, either by "spontaneous remission" or psychotherapeutic effectuality, creates a different state of affairs in the clinical situation. The transference becomes less palpable and defensive activity less driven, and there is no sense of an entrenched affectual position. It is as if reparation has been achieved rather than postponed. The reparation is appropriately preoedipal. With depressions screening jealousy, on the other hand, the reparative task is at an oedipal level, and the defensive decompensation that often (but not always) emerges in connection with the task is not a reliable invitation to restore and maintain the dependent transference position consistent with such depressions. I shall have more to say about this further on.

But what advantage over jealousy does a depression promise in these cases? What are the gains in the symptom? Phenomenologically the patient seems to be choosing a painful affect over an ideational distress. To the patient, a depression is *prima facie* a mood; its conscious fantasy components are dilute, often merely inferential. Jealousy is more than a painful mood. It is complicated by a vivid fantasy component. In jealousy, the patient has the experience of being "crazy" in addition to a painful feeling of dejection. This is not to say that a depression is "objectless," but rather that the experience of a self–other type of conflict is less focalized than it is in jealousy and the issues of conflict are less finely drawn.

Moreover, the two-person paradigm of the depressive state ensures the possibility of future contact with a benevolent fate. The felt suffering in the present is a provisional alternative to the supplies forthcoming in the future. A depression is a parody of the virtue of passive waiting. In a depression there is no fantasy of action. Indeed, the attentuation of time in a depression (Rosner 1962) is always a prominent feature in the therapy of defensive depressions. Years can slip by in a depression, and this is periodically a most nerve-racking realization by the patient, a form of superego injunction: "a command to awaken . . . which is heard but not heeded. [For] as long as the depressed patient is thus admonished, he is evidently secretly or unconsciously still maintaining his regressive place at the breast (Lewin 1961b, p. 330).

The dynamics of this phenomenology have to do with the vicissitudes of aggression. Jacobson (1957) tells us that grief is uppermost in connection with loss only if the libidinous investment can be maintained in the object world, while the aggression is directed to the self. In the cases of my two female patients, the very idea of aggressive action to guarantee narcissistic supplies was for a long time appalling. It would have jeopardized not only the source of the supplies but their nature as well. In jealousy the aggression has a coercive, rivalrous, vengeful homocidal aim toward a phallic-oedipal object. In depression its aim is suicidal in connection with an oral object.

Thus when a three-person paradigm of jealousy threatens to materialize, a depressive response can preserve the grief and screen the object-representations of phallic envy and rivalry. An ideational state is postponed, and an oral object is rescued from aggression. I will not dwell on the psychology of jealousy. Very little has actually been added to the well-known classic studies on the subject by Freud (1922), Jones (1929b), and Fenichel (1935).

In the therapy of the kind of depressive affect I have been describing, the postponed ideational state is a crucial eventuality, and I now want to mention several things about that. Technically, the problem is the therapy of a transitional paranoid phase, to which jealousy is always related, as depression is related to mourning. This inevitable step that the patient must take often falters on the therapist's failure to recognize that a kind of misperception (projection) is often a progression from a kind of nonperception (denial and introjection) (Kaplan 1962). If the patient's fear of an ideational phase finds a confirmation in the therapist's shifting to supportive and instrumental techniques when ideational disorganization is introduced, especially aggressive ideation, the patient will revert to the depression. This painful transition from a technical depression to jealous ideation is one of those rare phases of therapy when, in my opinion, it is better to allow the patient to break off treatment than to "manage" the transference with infantilizing emotion supplies. Though it is generally agreed that disruption of therapy is not in the best interests of the patient, there is some controversy as to the methods of dealing with it when it arises as an issue. The question of interruption has been reviewed in a panel report by Weinshel (1966). I might say that in those instances that I am presently discussing I hold with those who advise against instrumental acts like rescheduling appointments, conversing on the telephone, prolonging sessions, taking a "strong stand" on "acting out"—to mention but a few of the more typical temptations. When a disruption is in the cards, the gentle avoidance of instrumental acts virtually guarantees that the patient will subsequently resume therapy. Furthermore, if dispatch (as distinguished from haste) is of value, the disruption, when inevitable, will occur sooner than later.[3]

---

3. Erikson (1964) discusses a most famous instance of treatment interruption, Freud's Dora case (1905b). With characteristic eloquence, Erikson makes the point that sometimes a profound need in a patient to share a personal historical truth with an analyst may be a need surpassing what we narrowly understand

In the cases I have been alluding to, the transition I have been describing is not like the eruptions of paranoia sometimes seen in the severe manic-depressive states, described so ably by Helene Deutsch (1933). "Strange metamorphosis" is Deutsch's term for those desperate paranoic projections of the melancholic introject in manic-depression, and she speaks of paranoia in such conditions as a defensive reaction against the ultimate dangers of depression, an attempt by the ego to neutralize aggression. Where depression screens jealousy in the psychoneurosis, there are, to be sure, significant quantitative differences from those processes Deutsch described. However, there is also the difference that when a screening depression gives way to jealous ideation, a position of greater neutralization shifts to one of lesser neutralization, like what Klauber (1967) suggests about the patient's bringing a dream into the treatment situation. Klauber writes that "when the patient reports a dream . . . crude energies are being allied with neutralized energies."

Indeed, new ideational material should be approached much as is the presentation of a dream, albeit in these instances a transitional waking dream. Klauber's comments on the presentation of dreams to the therapist are precisely to the point. He says that "the arousal of interest indicates that a new pathway

---

by "acting out." Also, what Dora sought upon her return to Freud was as significant as what she sought in leaving him. Dora returned not only for forgiveness for her infantile revenge, as Freud clearly perceived, but also for reassurance that Freud's vision was professional, that he maintained, to use Erikson's word, his "mentorship." Whether one resumes therapy of a patient who returns after an interruption, as Erikson suggests he would have with Dora, or does not, as Freud did not, the therapist's action should be free of pettiness. One feature of the situation that is often perilous in this respect is the analyst's schedule. That his schedule is very tight goes without saying. Admonitions to this effect when a patient is clearly determined to cancel his appointments may well be intended to apprise the patient of the consequences of the particular action, but such admonitions are also bound to convey the sense of a counterthreat. When a patient asks to resume therapy, expressions by the therapist, especially apologetic ones, of the difficulty in arranging hours possess a retaliatory quality. What actually goes on to happen in a clinical crisis is sometimes less important than what the individual therapist has had to do to safeguard the therapeutic principle. Within bounds, of course, different actions of different therapists can be at the service of one and the same principle.

has been opened up for the cathexis of objects by the id . . . On the whole, the affect of the dreamer and of the listener to a dream, especially if the listener is a psychoanalyst, is one of hope" (p. 429).

The contrast he goes on to make between the presentation of a dream and a symptom is one that, in the instances I have been describing, I should discourage. Klauber says: "By contrast, a patient has to overcome a sense of shame in order to communicate a symptom, and in this case [symptom presentation] the affect of the outside world is suffused with fear, and that of the psychoanalyst with concern and disquiet" (p. 429). Klauber's implication is that it is easier to work with the unconscious in dream-formation than in symptom-formation, and naturally he is correct in this. However, I think we can do no better than to heed Pascal, who once warned against the wish to have in one way what can only be had in another.

A metaphor like "ego priming" has seemed to me apt for what usually goes on to happen clinically when the patient begins to establish some of the ideation screened by a depression. A fresh interest in treatment arises. Saved-up grudges against the therapist come out with temporary cathartic discharge. Though initially the depression is never distant, regressions to it are briefer and responsive to interpretation, since periodicity affords the opportunity to inquire into onset, whereas a chronic depression has no readily demonstrable onset and remission. This helps to enliven the patient's interest in his psychological processes.

Several concluding observations: Nowhere have I meant to imply any normative propositions about jealousy. By itself, a patient's presentation of one or another psychic element is no index of ego development. Diagnosis in its best sense begins with considerations of how various psychic elements articulate, especially how elements derived from preoedipal periods articulate with elements from the oedipal period. The goal of therapy consistent with this is a facilitation of such articulation. This chapter has attempted to identify a common instance of an imminent yet restricted articulation between two phases of development.

Finally, a word on the psychogenesis of a screen depression.

This, of course, is another subject in itself and, like that of all complex symptoms, would involve us in a painstaking account. However, for the moment let me say this much. One important aspect of the problem of psychogenesis is the effect of trauma during the early formative years. Among our interests is whether a trauma tends to reinforce the libidinization of a phase or reinstate a previously developed phase, and this is contingent upon, among other factors, how mature or immature the activated phase is (Greenacre 1953). In screen depressions, the trauma has affected the transition from infancy to childhood, the boundary between preoedipal and oedipal phases, and it is usual that the oedipal phase was potentially more sufficient than the preoedipal phase during which the traumatic effects accumulated. There was no massive deprivation of oedipal opportunity but rather a lack of wherewithal to use the opportunity for further normal development, as the child entered the oedipal phase with certain precocities. Among these I have found that envy was outstanding, usually aroused by the mother's attentions to a sibling following a period of conscientious attention to the patient. Moreover, the original attentiveness suddenly withdrawn possessed a quality of hostile, if not vengeful, worry. Thus compared to depressions related to traumatic neglect, violence, or abandonment, in screen depressions "over-protection" figures prominently.

REFERENCES

Alexander, F. (1956). Two forms of regression and their therapeutic implications. *Psychoanalytic Quarterly* 25:178–196.

Deutsch, H. (1933). The psychology of manic-depressive states, with particular reference to chronic hypomania. *Neurosis and Character Types*. New York: International Universities Press, 1965.

Erikson, E. H. (1964). Psychological reality and historical actuality. *Insight and Responsibility*. New York: Norton.

Fenichel, O. (1927). The economic function of screen memories. *Collected Papers*, 1st series. New York: Norton, 1953.

———— (1935). A contribution to the psychology of jealousy. *Collected Papers*, 1st series. New York: Norton, 1953.

———— (1941). *Problems of Psychoanalytic Technique*. Albany, NY: Psychoanalytic Quarterly.

Freud, S. (1899). Screen memories. *Standard Edition* 3.

_____ (1900). The interpretation of dreams. *Standard Edition* 4–5.

_____ (1901). The psychopathology of everyday life. *Standard Edition* 6.

_____ (1905). Fragment of an analysis of a case of hysteria. *Standard Edition* 7.

_____ (1914a). Remembering, repeating and working-through. *Standard Edition* 12.

_____ (1914b). On narcissism: an introduction. *Standard Edition* 14.

_____ (1917). Mourning and melancholia. *Standard Edition* 14.

_____ (1920). Beyond the pleasure principle. *Standard Edition* 18.

_____ (1922). Some neurotic mechanisms in jealousy, paranoia and homosexuality. *Standard Edition* 18.

_____ (1926). Inhibitions, symptoms and anxiety. *Standard Edition* 20.

_____ (1937). Analysis terminable and interminable. *Standard Edition* 23.

Friedman, L. J. (1953). Defensive aspects of orality. *International Journal of Psycho-Analysis* 34:304–312.

Greenacre, P. (1953). Some factors producing different types of genital and pregenital organization. *Trauma, Growth and Personality*. London: Hogarth.

_____ (1960). Regression and fixation: considerations concerning the development of the ego. *Journal of the American Psychoanalytic Association* 8:703–723.

Greenson, R. R. (1958). Screen defences, screen hunger and screen identity. *Journal of the American Psychoanalytic Association* 6:242–262.

_____ (1967). *The Technique and Practice of Psychoanalysis*, vol. 1. New York: International Universities Press.

Hartmann, H. (1951). Technical implications of ego psychology. *Essays on Ego Psychology*. New York: International Universities Press, 1964.

Jacobson, E. (1957). On normal and pathological moods: their nature and functions. *The Psychoanalytic Study of the Child* 12.

Jones, E. (1929a). Fear, hate and guilt. *Papers on Psychoanalysis*. Boston: Beacon, 1961.

_____ (1929b). Jealousy. *Papers on Psychoanalysis*. Boston: Beacon, 1961.

Kaplan, D. M. (1962). The emergence of projection in a series of dreams. *The Psychoanalytic Review* 49:37–52.

Klauber, J. (1967). On the significance of reporting dreams in psychoanalysis. *International Journal Psycho-Analysis* 48:424–432.

Kleeman, J. A. (1967). The peek-a-boo game. I. Its origins, meanings, and related phenomena in the first year. *The Psychoanalytic Study of the Child* 22.

Levin, S. (1965). Some suggestions for treating the depressed patient. *Psychoanalytic Quarterly* 34:37–65.

Lewin, B. D. (1961a). *The Psychoanalysis of Elation*. New York: Norton.

_____ (1961b). Reflections on depression. *The Psychoanalytic Study of the Child* 16.

Rangell, L. (1968). A further attempt to resolve the "problem of anxiety." *Journal of the American Psychonalytic Association* 16:371–404.

Rapaport, D. (1953). On the psychoanalytic theory of affects. *International Journal of Psycho-Analysis* 34:177–198.

Reich, A. (1953). Narcissistic object choice in women. *Journal of the American Psychoanalytic Association* 1:22–44.

Reider, N. (1960). Percept as a screen: economic and structural aspects. *Journal of the American Psychoanalytic Association* 8:82–99.

Rosner, A. A. (1962). Mourning before the fact. *Journal of the American Psychoanalytic Association* 10:564–570.

Schafer, R. (1968). The mechanisms of defence. *International Journal of Psycho-Analysis* 49:49–62.

Schur, M. (1953). The ego in anxiety. In *Drives, Affects, Behavior*, vol. 1. ed. R. M. Loewenstein et al. New York: International Universities Press.

Siegman, A. J. (1967). Denial and screening of object images. *Journal of the American Psychonalytic Association* 15:261–280.

Tarachow, S. (1966). Coprophagia and allied phenomena. *Journal of the American Psychoanalytic Association* 14:685–699.

Weinshel, E. M. (1966). Panel report: Severe regressive states during analysis. *Journal of the American Psychoanalytic Association* 14:538–568.

9

Dialogue in Classical Psychoanalysis

All human error is impatience, a premature renunciation of method.
— Franz Kafka

I shall never be tired of repeating that we are bound to accept whatever our procedure brings to light.
— Sigmund Freud

Chapter 7 of "The Interpretation of Dreams" (Freud 1900) was a pinnacle of more than 10 years of the clinical observation and intellectual struggle of a genius who was to impart to our present century a significant piece of its modernity. In that famous chapter, Freud arrived at a psychological theory that encompassed not only his observations of dreams, but also of other states and activities of mind ranging from the uncommon to the most ordinary. The scope of Chapter 7, with its elegantly conceived relationships among perception, memory, affect, attention, consciousness, and action, amounts to nothing less than an innovated image of man. Thus the adoption of the model of mind that Freud constructed in that chapter signifies, really, an agreement with a particular point of view about the nature and trials of human existence.

Since interpretation is the most significant instrumentality in that clinical technique deriving directly from Freudian psychol-

ogy, the very act of interpretation—which includes the intentions, goals, and preparations behind the act—presupposes
certain strong partialities in the analyst. Moreover, it presupposes, in that aspect of the public willing to become analysands,
a capacity to be educated into and to work with the analyst's
partialities. Whatever the parametrical necessities may be in a
particular case, a normative concept of "analyzability" is never
entirely absent from the analyst's procedural judgments. The
neutrality that the analyst strives for toward his patient's conflict
resolutions does not extend to his choice of technical measures.
To the analyst, the outcome of a conflict—that is, whether the
ego ultimately accepts or rejects an instinctual demand—is a
matter of indifference, but the matter in which the conflict is
conceived and examined in the clinical situation is anything but
arbitrary (Freud 1940).

I am reminded of a paper by Kurt Eissler (1963) in which
Eissler describes a severely neurotic patient he treated for three
years. The patient left treatment to go on to achieve in her life all
that she had wished for upon entering treatment—marriage,
motherhood, position in the community, even the remission of
a painful erythrophobia. Yet, despite this stupendous clinical
success, Eissler reviews the case with misgivings, berating
himself for a technical error that sabotaged a successful treatment. Eissler remains unimpressed with a behavioral outcome
that would immensely gratify most therapists. According to
Eissler, this particular patient "adhered to what psychoanalysis
offers at a social level—a therapy," and responded to treatment
with the principle, "I would rather act sanely than face the truth
about myself."

To nonanalytic clinicians the psychoanalytic dialogue has
always seemed a bit of much ado about nothing, so much in the
dialogue does a particular concept of mind pale all else—the
traditional healing function of the therapist, our common sense
of the time factor in these matters, not to mention economics,
even questions of action—what the patient actually should do at
one point or another in the course of things. The psychoanalytic
dialogue seems to revise the rank order of what is important in
life. A patient, whom I intend to return to further on, came to a
session one day and reported at the outset that, during her walk

to my office some moments before, she had passed a brownstone whose charm had caught her gaze. She went on to say that approaching it she was conscious of a wish to know the technical name for the doorway's distinctive architectural shape. We were to spend several sessions on this incident. But the point here is that the patient happened to be at this moment in her life in the throes of a serious vocational crisis (and I must add that she is not an architect).

Of course, to maintain that such revisions of seeming import as take place in the analytic situation are the result simply of the unqualified primacy of mind in psychoanalysis would be cavalier, not to say foolish. Granted the centrality of mind, why shouldn't the investigation of the patient's mind proceed by means of issues strongly attractive to the patient's attention in his everyday life, such as financial worries, sexual adversities, interpersonal antagonisms? To be sure, the patient will begin with such issues. But why should he not be encouraged to proceed with them exclusively?

Considering the well-reputed fact that psychoanalytic therapy makes a great deal of the patient's early history, the answer consists of a rather surprising paradox: The patient's chronologically most recent, and subjectively most trivial, thoughts are the harbingers potentially of his most profound self-explanations. I should add that among the reasons for the comparatively frequent sessions in psychoanalysis and the priority of the relationship to the analyst is the insurance of recent and experientially trivial topics in the patient's monologic self-reporting.

Let me quote a bit of Freud (1900) from Chapter 7 (pp. 563–564):

> The reason why these recent and indifferent elements so frequently find their way into dreams as substitutes for the most ancient of all the dream-thoughts is that they have least to fear from the censorship imposed by resistance. But while the fact that *trivial* elements are preferred is explained by their freedom from censorship, the fact that *recent* elements occur with such regularity points to the existence of a need for transference [between the mental systems]. Both groups of impressions satisfy the demand of the repressed for material that is still clear of

associations—the indifferent ones because they have given no
occasion for the formation of many ties, and the recent ones
because they have not yet had time to form them.

Though Freud is here speaking of the formation of dreams
out of day-residues, what he says has to do also with processes
of mind in general: The perceptual attention that imbues experience with felt importance reduces, at the same time, the
likelihood of alterations within the psychic apparatus. To put it
another way, the stronger the feeling about a perception, the
less chance there is to discover alternative solutions to the
conflicts in which the perception participates. And I am relieved
to be able to say that psychoanalytic therapy is concerned with
solving conflicts.

One of the advantages of using Freud's writing for a discussion such as this is that, Freudian or not, we all know Freud in
some detail. I shall unravel a final string of reminders about his
theory: Freud came to conceive of the psychic apparatus as a
compound instrument. The compounding of the apparatus is an
adaptive expedient, for the operation of a neonatal (wish-
fulfilling) mentality alone cannot guarantee supplies appropriate to needs. A fantasy of food has no nutritional value. A
fantasy of warmth does not regulate room temperature. Hence,
in addition to wishing, a second mental activity must come into
the service of the organism, an activity that will address itself to
the actual localities of the wished-for supplies. While wishes are
experienced as internal, the localities for their fulfilling supplies
are soon perceived as external, and the psychic apparatus
begins to negotiate its wishes in accordance with perceptions of
external circumstance. The infant's first perceptions that many
of its wishes are being fulfilled through the cooperation of an
agent separate from himself—an external mother—is an extraordinary event in the maturation of his psychic apparatus. At this
point, we begin to speak of the infant's acquisition of a sense of
reality, and we go on to distinguish two mental processes in
reciprocating relationship, to which Freud assigned the names
"primary" and "secondary" processes. He spelled out the
energic economics obtaining between these two processes and
outlined a theory of psychopathology based upon the articula-

tion of the processes (rather than upon the interaction, say, between a patient and his social environment, which is also a legitimate basis for a theory of psychopathology). The theory of psychopathology, however, is merely a special instance of a general theory of mind.

Now what does all this suggest for a technique? I have mentioned the possibility of recent and trivial thoughts reaching across intrapsychic topographies otherwise closed to thoughts carrying higher degrees of "habit" and import. I have also suggested that these topographies of mind are shaped by a developmental distinction between wish and circumstance. Psychopathology is a special instance of failure of the apparatus to acquire a facility with circumstance sufficient to fulfill (through activity) crucial amounts of specific wishes in accordance with the modalities of secondary process. In psychopathology, the primary process has gained direct access to action, but the fulfillment in this action is in conflict with circumstance, now in the form of present reality, or the superego, or both. The fulfillment creates the intractability in the pathologic process, while the conflict creates the suffering. The psychoanalysis of such a state of affairs demands a current circumstance with an explicit and enduring identity against which the original circumstance can be compared. This current circumstance is the set of arrangements about the time and duration of appointments, the fees, and the functions of the analyst. The analytic situation is an experimental circumstance.

As for the wishes, if they are to come under the regulation of the secondary process, they must be deprived of their most powerful sponsor—direct action and, through direct action, direct gratification. They must suffer a provisional loss of importance. In the analytic situation there are numerous opportunities for action. The most eminent involves the person of the analyst.

The activity of the analyst is restricted to the preservation of the analytic circumstance and to the encouragement of the patient to report recent and trivial thoughts. The analyst's explanatory verbal allusions to all unsolicited modifications by the patient of both the analytic circumstance and the analytic task are called interpretations of resistance. In view of the common, erroneous assertion that "resistance analysis" is synon-omous with psychoanalysis, it should be stressed that the term "resistance" is literally gibberish in a therapeutic situation in which no rule of free association—the reporting of recent and trivial thoughts—is being enforced. The term "resistance" only acquires meaning in connection with an effort to alter conditions between primary and secondary processes through a method involving free association. Where the resistance takes the form of an interaction with the analyst, the analyst's verbal allusion to it goes by the name "transference interpretation." The entire labor is to maximize thought by minimizing action.

It is clear that the analytic endeavor is quite different from the kind of therapeutic endeavor aimed at discovering what the patient wants and then going on to prescribe strategies with which the patient can get what he wants. It is also different from those endeavors that provoke vitalities in the patient deemed absent but worthwhile by a chemotherapist, active therapist, or sexologist.

Although an analysis can be conducted in a variety of human styles and temperaments, it cannot be conducted by a clinician whose personality simply cannot tolerate being in a room with another human being without affectual interaction. A clinician who cannot abstain from an opportunity for verbal and emo-tional give and take cannot conduct an analysis. Anything spectacular in the analytic situation is a sure sign that something has gone wrong. An older colleague of mine, who is now deceased, was fond of relating an incident in which he had gotten into a physical brawl with a patient in the midst of a session. He had subdued the patient finally through great physical effort and was proud to describe how he converted the incident into therapeutic gains for the patient. It was out of affection for this colleague—and respect, for he was not a fool—that I never shared my thoughts with him on the matter. If an analysis was taking place, the incident could not have hap-pened. Things could never have gotten that far in an analytic situation.

On several occasions, Freud (1914a, 1914b, 1937a) counseled wariness against an emotional overloading of the therapist–pa-tient relationship. He advised interpreting derivatives of hatred before a negative affect gained the momentum to sweep away the analysis. He gave the same advice in regard to derivatives of love, for too much love can also freeze the dialogue by destroying the patient's perceptual flexibility. Optimally, the dialogue is contemplative and unhurried. Passion invests the task, not the persons collaborating in the task.

The psychic apparatus has a strong propensity for imparting sense and meaning to experience. The secondary revision in dream recall is an example of such propensity. We revise dreams in their telling because our resistance to leaving experience meaningless is aroused. In reporting a dream, the patient says, "It was a men's room, so I couldn't have been urinating in a toilet. I must have been standing at a urinal." Here the patient discards a fleeting notion and replaces it by something that makes more sense. Only in cooperation with a second person, such as an analyst whose training has created in him an interest in such things, can an individual be held to an examination of fleeting notions, the sense and meaning of which are not yet apparent.

> Not long ago, I moved from an office I had been using for a number of years. The move was anticipated about 7 months in advance. I was aware of the significance of the move (more accurately, I couldn't see how the move would not be filled with significance), so I was prepared to watch for psychological eventualities. They began almost immediately, including an incapacitating lumbosacral sprain. But I was not to understand these eventualities, including the sprain, until a month after I had established myself in my current office, and the understanding began only in my effort—an extraordinary effort, indeed—not to ignore my dialing a particular phone number incorrectly twice in succession. A review of the past 8 months brought into connection a series of unconnected events, each one having possessed at the time it occurred a meaning and justification quite irrelevant to any meaning my office move consciously had for me.
>
> For example, an argument with the agent of the building in which my new office was to be situated was entirely plausible to me at the time it happened, though in retrospect I recognized how I had provoked it. I am certain that, had I been in a formal analytic situation, I would have been held by my analyst to examine innumerable subjective irrelevancies at the outset of the period of

the office move and would thereby have gained a comprehension of the situation in a matter of weeks, rather than the 8 months it took on my own. I have good reason to believe that my sprained back would also have been averted. (I wonder whether we don't overlook among the benefits of psychotherapy the question of what would have happened to the patient without it. The prophylactic value of therapy may be quite as important as its ameliorative value.)

I have been emphasizing the prominence of thought as against action in the psychoanalytic situation. I have been speaking of turning the patient's consciousness away from the perceptual and motor end of the psychic apparatus, where it mainly resides, toward the preconscious system, that psychic zone in which the primary and secondary processes interact. I want to return to the patient I referred to earlier and show how the analytic dialogue nevertheless leads to the possibility of spontaneous actions, actions informed by thought but, in my opinion, free of the intellectualized quality of action-oriented psychotherapies.

I mentioned that the patient was preoccupied with a vocational crisis. The patient was a 30-year-old woman, a biochemist who had entered therapy in connection with a long-standing but painful love affair with a married man much older than herself. After two years of treatment, she extricated herself from the affair and then a year later married a man more consistent with her age and interests.

Throughout all this, her career created persistent dissatisfactions that were never altogether clear. She was respected for her knowledge and competence, but no amount of advancement and study would rid her of the apprehension that she was a novice and a fraud. From time to time, these feelings dissolved in excruciating boredom.

An unexpected shake-up in the hierarchy of the pharmaceutical company at which she worked thrust her into a rather high position. This precipitated an anxiety reaction. Anxiety and derivatives of it preoccupied her for months, especially paranoid derivatives having to do with the incompetence of her colleagues. It was in the midst of this that I suggested to her, at the end of a session, that she had drifted into this repetitive preoccupation because there was something she was afraid to tell me. This was not a shot in the dark: There had been two dreams to which she had had, for her, remarkably weak associations, and both dreams had been stridently sexual. She agreed that there was something she had been keeping from me.

She returned for her next appointment to tell me, with difficulty, that of late she had been performing fellatio on her husband. Yet, she had no idea why it was so difficult to tell me. Nor could she say why she had used precisely her job anxieties in connection with suppressing the information about the turn in her sexual life.

I have already mentioned the incident of her wanting to know the architectural term for the doorway of the building she admired during her walk to my office. Following her telling me about this, she was silent for some time and then said parenthetically and with a trace of sheepish humor that she knew from reading a psychology text that a building symbolized the human body, and that therefore the doorway would represent probably the female genital; whereupon she was again silent, as though waiting for permission to proceed with what felt to her an obvious intellectual train of thought—or permission not to proceed. I told her that she hesitated because she was embarrassed at stealing my thunder. She went on to report a memory of her father's slamming the bedroom door against her when she had happened upon him dressing, a memory she had brought up several times previously. She then spoke of the time she had approached her mother with a question about the mechanics of conception and pregnancy, though already fully informed by clandestine reading in various medical books. Initially, her mother put her off awkwardly, but then went into a rage at the question.

I reminded the patient of her persistent feelings of possessing knowledge without permission and authority. Now the connection between her anxieties at being promoted at work and her withholding her sexual activities from me could be made. For several weeks thereafter, a phase of the transference underwent clarification.

But the action arising from this piece of analytic work was unpredictable and, thus, beyond what any coercive technique could have accomplished. You can't manipulate behavior in a prescribed direction, if the behavior falls outside the realm of specification. This patient's principal professional responsibility involved a kind of trouble-shooting examination and modification of experiments conceived and proposed by others, a function the patient executed with such resourcefulness that it was never an issue of psychopathology. Her professional performance was a network of virtues created out of the necessities of infantile circumstance. An important by-product of this phase of the analysis was that additional functions came into existence with additional gratifications. For example, the patient has since published two papers on original work of her own. However, none of the changes were spectacular. Their subtlety protected them from intellectualization. By-products of the analytic process rather than definite goals, these changes were in every sense of the word spontaneous.

Let me give another example of spontaneity of action. A female patient in treatment for a number of years for an obsessive-compulsive psychoneurosis reported a repetitive sexual fantasy she would have during sexual relations with her husband. The fantasy involved her being sexually molested by a horde of truck drivers on the floor of a commercial garage. The sexual fantasy (I shall pass over the analytic steps) was the manifest content of a latent fantasy containing the wish for a private sexual experience with a particular sibling. The patient had been the only girl in a family of five brothers and had participated in the years of her growing up in a great deal of group sexual play. The fantasy accompanying her sexual relations with her husband served to assuage her guilt at the fact that she was having sex with only one person, rather than with several persons. The lack of privacy in the manifest fantasy had reference as well to her ritual of carefully locking up prior to going to bed, a ritual involving a fantasy of sexual invasion and its prohibition.

While the ritual continued to be a painful compulsion, a behavioral outcome of the analysis of these matters was her ridding her rather large apartment of what sounded to me like tons of old, useless furniture and paraphernalia, thus providing a luxury of living space. Again, this action was not previously stipulated by the patient, nor was the condition of her apartment a conspicuous complaint in her remarks. She went on to refurnish the apartment. I suspect these actions of the patient in respect to her apartment would not have been taken into account in a before-and-after experimental design investigating the effectiveness of treatment; yet, in retrospect, I count these actions as having far-reaching effects upon this patient's sense of herself. Though behaviorally unspectacular, they were among the most courageous actions of her adult life.

These examples also illustrate the evocative character of the analytic dialogue.[1] Provocativeness is alien to the spirit of the undertaking, much as a sledge hammer would be the wrong sort of probe for a pocket watch.

Psychoanalysis regards consciousness as a series of mental events, fugitive and incomplete, yet all that the patient has to go by (Freud 1937b). The analytic situation does not aim to deprive the patient of consciousness, as, say, a hypnotic situation does. It aims rather to degrade the syntactic, logical, rhetorical, and other formal properties of language through which consciousness is conventionally reported to a listener. Free association possesses less formal properties than does conventional speech, but it is not less conscious. However, free association resembles more closely the actual nature of consciousness, and it is something about the patient's consciousness that the analyst wishes to interpret.

Interpretation can be thought of as mending the incompleteness of a portion of a conscious series of mental events. But not only must the analyst locate the disconnections in the fabric of consciousness, he must also go on to mend them with material of like substance. Alien material won't do. Interpretations must be made from data evoked in the patient by the process. (With due regard to this business of "listening with the third ear," what is evoked in the analyst—his feelings, fantasies, and associations—are at most clues to a larger meaning in what the patient is reporting. Clues, however, are not equivalent to solutions.)

---

1. For a discussion of the concept of evocativeness, though in a somewhat different sense, see Applebaum (1966).

To listen, to wait, to gather data, and to inhibit active interventions until a solution is achieved regarding a segment of observation are not easy tasks. Harold F. Searles (Scarizza 1965, p. 14) has commended this stance even in the therapy of deeply regressed patients:

> I have some comments on the therapist's responsibility. It seems to me that this is where Freud made one of his very great contributions, with the free association method, which calls for the patient to take part in therapy. Even a schizophrenic patient can do well to follow this procedure, even if he is not able to talk. If we leave in the patient's hands a comparably high degree of responsibility for setting the tone of what happens between himself and the doctor, for bringing up his ideation—whether by verbal or nonverbal means—it is this kind of setting which promotes the patient's exercising of the degree of responsible initiative which needs to remain in his own hands. I have frequently found myself trying, or have found my colleagues trying, to actively rescue the patient from the illness. It seemed to me that the patient never did open up and make moves toward the therapist, and toward the world of reality, until the therapist finally had tried everything active that he knew, and eventually had given up, had sat back, and thus had given the patient room to reach out.

Elsewhere, Searles (1964) takes exception to John N. Rosen's therapeutic stance, pinpointing the difference between psychoanalysis and therapies based upon substantive preconceptions. Rosen approaches all patients with expectations that the therapeutic relationship will duplicate a specific pathogenic infantile relationship. Hence Rosen can begin "interpretations" immediately, since he carries with him bottled truths about every patient's pathology. Every patient is virtually the same; the patient need not generate the substance of the dialogue; no transference need evolve. Searles scores this as indoctrination. Rosen's is not "an investigative approach in which patient and doctor are engaged in a mutual exploration of what is transpiring in the patient. . . . His approach is, by contrast, a message-carrying approach, a forcing-into-a-preconceivedmould approach, in which the initiative rests not primarily in the patient's hands, as is the case in truly psychoanalytic investigation, but, obviously, in the hands of the therapist" (p. 600).

I like Rudolf Ekstein's comparing the psychoanalytic undertaking to a Pirandello situation (1965): "We might say that the patient . . . is in search of a plot. . . . [In] order to find the plot, he goes to a psychotherapist whom he mistakes in the transference for an author" (p. 163). The therapist's interpretations are ultimately the plot describing the patient's past. Psychoanalysis is thus concerned with producing a script that the analyst ghostwrites, to be sure, but only from what the patient tells him. That a script is to be fashioned is determined by the analyst's theoretical commitment, but the content resides entirely in the patient.

At those fortuitous moments in the dialogue when a verbal relationship is made among the patient's interactional effort with the analyst, a piece of current triviality, and a memory, we speak of analytic insight (Kris 1952). Under analytic auspices it is more usual, however, for insight, like action, to occur as an experientially elusive process, identified in retrospect. The notion of a profoundly felt confrontation of the patient with a fragment of personal truth is much more a lingering social mythology about psychoanalysis than an actuality. Such possibilities of cathartic experience tended to disappear from the analytic situation before the turn of the century, with Freud's technical recommendations in the final chapter of *Studies on Hysteria* (Breuer and Freud 1955). Like the patient who wonders about the status of his analysis because he has not yet burst into tears, as he imagines other patients doing, a therapist may also be the victim of notions about cathartic events in the practice of his colleagues and may provoke such events in hopes of confirming the legitimacy of the therapy. With such attempts to keep up with the Joneses we might compare psychoanalysis with certain current social and professional trends.

In a publication of a large community mental-health clinic, there is an article by a famous psychotherapist-hypnotist (Greenwald 1966), who reports that he is using hypnosis to simulate the hallucinogenic effects of LSD. He hypnotizes the patient and suggests that the patient is under the sway of LSD.

I quote a typical result of this technical procedure. The patient in question was an overt homosexual. "The results in his case were dramatic. Within a period of three months, from having been a lifelong homosexual, he became exclusively heterosexual and, at the age of fifty, reported that he was having full pleasurable intercourse with his wife, six and seven times a day" (p. 47).

In the context of my previous discussion, what is notable about this report is the unscripted quality of both the therapy and the outcome, and also the direct connection between the presenting diagnosis of the patient and his post-treatment behavior. I do not think the author would be inclined to dispute my conclusion that the patient got precisely what he (the patient) thought he wanted in the quickest way possible with the least exposure to what could be called an investigation of his thought processes. Although the author would probably maintain that a complex explanation of what had happened could be furnished with some amount of retrospective thought on his part, I have every reason to believe that he would consider the request for such an explanation a sign of professional anachronism in the asker, if not a sign of pathologic intellectualism.

Anyone who has kept abreast of the proliferating literature on psychotherapy must recognize that this author could go just about anywhere in America at this moment and find himself entirely at home professionally. Unscripted, interactional psychotherapy is not the vision of the future, as Philip Rieff sees it in *The Triumph of the Therapeutic* (1966). It is presently the largest movement among us.

My sense is that this state of affairs in psychotherapy is in rapport with the most prevalent modes of thought in the community. The hypnotic conversion of the homosexual patient is an example of a socialization of both therapist and patient. I quote from an item in *The New Republic* (1966):

> The day before the elections, November 7, the Voice of America began using a brighter, faster broadcasting technique aimed primarily at the world's speakers of English, who now number more than a billion. Announcing this as "the new sound," the director of the government's overseas broadcasting agency, John Chancellor, explained . . . our broadcasts . . . must sound Amer-

ican and reflect the current image of the United States as an interesting, dynamic, and up-tempo place. Giving examples of the "new sound," Chancellor said that the longest single item in the first hour of the day's revised programming was an interview with Secretary of State Dean Rusk that lasted only 4 minutes 38 seconds. . . . Richard Krolick [Chancellor's chief consultant] declared that the "new motto" of the Voice of America is "think short."

This new Voice-of-America technique is in full accord with Marshal McLuhan's now famous dictum, "The medium is the message," the corollary to which is the motto of a mushrooming theater and mass media of happenings and events: "Art is anything you can get away with." In this view of process and outcome, the concept of error virtually disappears, and with it the concept of responsibility. I am reminded of the psychotherapist who told of his having been in a patient's neighborhood in the dark hours of the morning and his yielding to an impulse to drop in on her. "I decided to do it because I'm a doctor and therefore anything I do is therapeutic."

Bell (1965) cites the "eclipse of distance" as the underlying reality of contemporary society, "an effort to annihilate the contemplative mode of experience by emphasizing immediacy, impact, simultaneity, and sensation" (p. 220). The eclipse of distance, Bell suggests, originates in such facts as overpopulation and increased interpersonal interaction due to urbanization. The mass media enhance our interactions symbolically. Individuals today know of countless other individuals. We know not only what others possess and achieve, but also what others seem to experience, for the mass media penetrate traditional barriers of privacy. It is no longer enough to compete with the other fellow's acquisitions and achievements; we must also feel what we think the other fellow feels. Our self-esteem seems to reside at the frontiers of our personal sensual capacities.

Bell's eclipse of distance finds a psychoanalytic counterpart in Spitz's "derailment of dialogue" (1964), an ego-disrupting consequence of overpopulation and urbanization. Spitz, like Bell, observes the widespread lack of privacy and contemplative activity in contemporary society and relates this to a growing inability among the population to complete "action cycles." Mothering that is constantly interrupted by social interactions tends to produce a child unfit for partnership in any kind of dialogue. "With the derailment of dialogue," Spitz adds, "the appetitive branch of the action cycle comes to replace the consummatory one." (I wonder whether our psychedelic hypnotist had not redirected his patient's appetitive impulses, while leaving untouched his consummatory abilities.)

Ellul (1965) regards propaganda as our present environment of instant information, a solvent of ideology, morality, art, and individuality. The fantasies in the poetry of the French Symbolists are at the service of art partly because of the contemplative quality of the creative labor. The fantasies reported by "hippies" are like disposable novelties; they supply the environment with propaganda.

Any psychotherapy that emphasizes immediacy, impact, simultaneity, and sensation is consistent with the most prevalent current processes of socialization. The medium of every such therapy is social propaganda. No matter how uplifting the jargon, the participants in such therapies are attempting to replace the responsibilities of individuality by the advantages of adjustment to the social moment. The painful ambiguities and dialectics of the social role-personal identity dichotomy are mercifully postponed.

I am sure I need not belabor my opinion as to where psychoanalysis stands among such matters, and where the analyst stands in relation to our present society when he maintains that the individual can be regarded intrapsychically — that is, in terms of that elemental system of mind distinguishing each of us from the family we come out of and the society we enter into, that small station of mind where individuality resides.

There is a current idea that psychoanalysis no longer suits our present patient population. But this has always been the charge. From the beginning, if psychoanalysis was not outright nonsense, it was impractical. Riesman (1954) has referred to Freud as a " 'rate buster' — a person who violated 'production norms' as to how much sympathy and time were to be given to patients" (p. 271). Riesman counts among Freud's greatest contributions

Freud's "willingness to spend years if necessary with patients who were neither fatally ill nor important people. . . . Today, it is just this luxury aspect of psychoanalysis—its prolonged concern with individuals as such, and for their own sake—that is sometimes under attack" (p. 272).

Psychoanalysis has always distinguished between what the public wants and what the public needs. Since needs are not as capricious as wants, psychoanalysis, in addressing itself to needs, has enjoyed an eventful but not at all frenetic evolution as an intellectual movement. Its insulation against transitory social fads and against the opportunism that comes into play when a doctrine seeks widespread approval has insured psychoanalysis the orderly development that many condemn as parochial, rigid, or outmoded—the pejoratives vary with the values of those who apply them.

REFERENCES

Applebaum, S. A. (1966). Speaking with the second voice: evocativeness. *Journal of the American Psychoanalytic Association* 14:462–477.

Bell, D. (1965). The disjunction of culture and social structure. *Daedalus*, Winter: 208–222.

Breuer, J., and Freud, S. (1895). Studies on hysteria. *Standard Edition* 2.

Eissler, K. (1963). Notes on the psychoanalytic concept of cure. *Psychoanalytic Study of the Child* 18:424–463.

Ekstein, R. (1965). General treatment philosophy of acting out. In *Acting out: Theoretical and Clinical Aspects*, ed. L. E. Abt and S. L. Weissman, pp. 162–172. New York: Grune & Stratton.

Ellul, J. (1965). *Propaganda: the Formation of Men's Attitudes.* New York: Knopf.

Freud, S. (1900). The interpretation of dreams. *Standard Edition* 5.

_____ (1914a). Remembering, repeating and working through. *Standard Edition* 12.

_____ (1914b). Observations on transference love. *Standard Edition* 12.

_____ (1937a). Analysis terminable and interminable. *Standard Edition* 23.

_____ (1937b). Constructions in analysis. *Standard Edition* 23.

_____ (1940). An outline of psychoanalysis. *Standard Edition* 23.

Greenwald, H. (1966). Hypnosis and hallucinogenic drugs. *Journal of the Long Island Consultation Center* 4:46–51.

Kris, E. (1952). On preconscious mental processes. In *Psychoanalytic Explorations in Art*, pp. 303–318. New York: International Universities Press.

Rieff, P. (1966). *The Triumph of the Therapeutic: Uses of Faith after Freud.* New York:

Harper & Row.

Riesman, D. (1954). The themes of heroism and weakness in the structure of Freud's thought. In *Individualism Reconsidered*, pp. 246–275. New York: Anchor.

Scarizza, S. (1965). *Proceedings of the First International Congress of Direct Psychoanalysis*. Doylestown, PA: Doylestown Foundation.

Searles, H. F. (1964). Book review of direct psychoanalytic psychiatry. *International Journal of Psycho-Analysis* 45:597–602.

Shakow, D., and Rapaport, D. (1964). *The Influence of Freud on American Psychology* (Psychological Issues 13). New York: International Universities Press.

Spitz, R. A. (1955). The primal cavity: a contribution to the genesis of perception and its role for psychoanalytic theory. *The Psychoanalytic Study of the Child* 10:215–240.

_____ (1959). *A Genetic Field Theory of Ego Formation*. New York: International Universities Press.

_____ (1964). The derailment of dialogue: stimulus overload, action cycles, and completion gradient. *Journal of the American Psychoanalytic Association* 12:752–775.

Szasz, T. S. (1967). Behavior therapy and psychoanalysis. *Medical Opinion Review* 2:24–29.

The New Republic. (1966). November 19, p. 3.

Wallerstein, R. S. (1966). The current state of psychotherapy: theory, practice, research. *Journal of the American Psychoanalytic Association* 14:183–225.

10

Freud and
His Own Patients

When Sigmund Freud was in his middle thirties, his medical career began to take an alarming turn. This was in the early 1890s, years before his thinking attained that conceptual shape we call psychoanalysis. A gifted neuropsychiatrist of increasing reputation, Freud was becoming alienated from the professional community of Vienna. The personal advantages his brilliance had already achieved were beginning to slip away, at first into indifference, then derision. For a man approaching middle age and shouldering responsibility not only for his wife and children, but for his parents and sisters as well, the financial jeopardy was nerve-racking. That his professional plight was not the result of something suddenly bizarre or iconoclastic in his assertions about mental illness compounded his frustrations. Iconoclastic opinions were to damage his career much later, and when they did, he readily accepted it. At this point, his was a case of exasperating an establishment not yet prepared for reformation.

For example, Freud's early proposals about the sexual factor in the psychoneuroses were not sensational novelties. They were quite consistent with prevalent opinion. A relationship between the sexual life of patients and their nervous disorders was a suspicion widespread among medical practitioners of the time. Freud credited Charcot, one of his most esteemed teachers, with the remark referring to mental patients, *"Mais, dans des cas pareils c'est toujours la chose génitale, toujours, toujours, toujours"* — with such patients, it is always a matter of sex, always,

always, always. It was Josef Breuer, physician to many luminaries of Viennese society, who said to Freud about a neurotic patient, "These things are always *secrets d'alcôve"*—questions involving the marriage bed. Another indelible reference to sex came from Professor Rudolf Chrobak, the most eminent gynecologist of Vienna. In connection with a woman he sent to Freud for treatment, he recommended with cynical despair: *"Rx. Penis normalis dosim repetatur"*—the best medicine would be an ordinary penis, repeatedly.

Thus when Freud initially codified these ideas into a scientific position, it was not his originality that scandalized his colleagues. What was disturbing was something about Freud's character. As he commented years later, those notions that his colleagues casually flirted with, he married—and took the consequences. Indeed, genius without character is hopeless; for it is character that dares to carry ideas beyond the judgment of a given time and place, into the more risky tribunals of Destiny.

Naturally Freud's character—his almost naïve earnestness—found expression in his daily clinical practice, in his actual conduct with patients. In his therapeutic activities, which flash with character, there are awesome glimpses of his great purpose that have remained comparatively neglected in the dissemination of his thought.

Vienna abounded in so-called classically hysterical women, patients free of physical lesions but nevertheless given to fainting spells, shortness of breath, ill-temper, depression, amnesia, nausea, delusions, migraines, paralyses—the list could be extended to a full page. The male neurotics tended toward elaborate and incapacitating obsessions and compulsions. Theories about the psychoneuroses were far in advance of therapeutic techniques, not unlike the situation today with, say, cancer. To the Vienna medical society (which was one of the best in the world), hobbled as it was by an ignorance as to how to treat the psychoneuroses, neurotic patients were regarded as annoyances, malingerers, pests. Treatment consisted of talking, suggesting, and commanding the neurotic out of his symptoms. This failing, mild electric shock, rest cures, warm baths, and other techniques were called in, largely to emphasize the doctor's determination that the patient get well. The doctor-

patient relationship could be described as one of mutual harassment.

I have mentioned that Freud took quite seriously the business
of sexuality. Another idea—somewhat less common, because it
was more complex—was that neurosis had something to do with
the lengths a patient had to go to avoid unsavory thoughts and
memories of painful events. This Freud also took seriously, and
he pronounced the idea in an italicized maxim in one of his
earliest papers: *"Hysterical patients suffer principally from reminiscences."* For the psychotherapy of neurosis, the consequences of
this idea were extraordinary. It meant that the doctor should
listen to his patient's verbal reports and try to locate the morbid
feeling and ideas his neurotic symptoms replace. With typical
plausibility, this is precisely what Freud did, for hours on end,
day after day. But he not only listened to the nonsense of his
patients; he began to demand that they amplify details that were
obscure and incomplete. Inevitably, Freud was becoming, as
David Riesman once called him, a "rate buster." Where all
around him superficial dispatch prevailed, Freud found it necessary to prolong therapy to unheard of lengths.

Like Philoctetes, Freud now possessed a wound and a bow,
for which he was both shunned and sought. In practicing
psychiatry, this means that you become one of the list of
"extreme measures," and you are referred the most intractable
cases. These days you would have to ransack your directory for
a colleague who would take on the kind of case that routinely
filled Freud's practice at the height of his physical powers. Yet in
all his published accounts of treatment, there is not a breath of
self-pity or self-aggrandizement.

REASON VS. OBSESSION

What was it like to be a patient of such a doctor? It has been said
that Freud was a severe rationalist who reduced human vitalities
to barren mechanics. But this is true only if pettiness is proof of
passion. When a patient consulted Freud, he was in the presence of a man deeply involved in an enterprise larger than the

patient and larger than Freud. It was the absence of personal pettiness in the situation he created that liberated the patient's secrets. There was nothing a patient could tell this man that he couldn't find a proper niche for in the human design. He could walk through nightmares and humanize all demons. He was the passionate enemy of every fear that made freedom of thought less than an absolute principle. Though he staked everything on the power of reason, the scheme that reason served could have occurred only to a man of transcendental sensibilities.

All of this springs to life in the case histories that appear now and again in the long shelf of Freud's writings. The Rat Man case—we shall learn momentarily the reason for this grisly appellation—comes to mind first, because I can't imagine another psychiatrist in practice at that time who, upon hearing the complaints of the Rat Man, would not have come forth promptly with the well-meaning voice of conventional reassurance and thereby blown the case.

The Rat Man (this is his nickname among analysts; "Notes upon a Case of Obsessional Neurosis" is his original name) was a young law student who had recently done military training, and consulted Freud in connection with proliferating obsessions. Their grip upon him could be regulated only by the patient's performing nonsensical acts, which were consuming years of his life. Typical was an irresistible urge to interrupt his studying at a given hour in the evening and retire to a downstairs vestibule where he had to expose his genitals in a mirror while thinking about his deceased father. Many of his compulsions were not so easily carried out, and some demanded exhausting restraint, as when, for example, it occurred to the patient that to remove a jinx from a particular person he was fond of, he would have to slit his own throat with a razor.

Other compulsions existed as far back as the patient could remember, and previous therapy had failed to ameliorate his suffering. What drove the Rat Man into further treatment at the moment was an especially maddening incident involving a fellow army officer. He sought Freud in particular, having chanced upon Freud's just-published *The Psychopathology of Everyday Life*. In the pages of that book he thought he recognized himself. This was shortly after the turn of the century, when

Freud was wholly in disrepute, so that a patient's coming to Freud was a good indication of desperation.

A large part of the notes of the case is given over to the multitudinous details of the army incident that brought the patient to treatment. What was immediately helpful was Freud's unreserved interest in these details. Roughly, the patient had gotten it into his head that he owed a particular army officer a trifling sum of money for the delivery to the patient of a small package. However, the fact was that the patient owed the money to the postal clerk who had received the package and had advanced the COD charges. Though the patient was fully aware of this fact, he could not shake himself free of the compulsion to pay the money to the army officer instead. The package, incidentally, contained eyeglasses, a replacement for a pair the patient had lost on maneuvers. Knowing that the officer would think him crazy for insisting upon paying a debt that was not actually owed, the patient concocted devious plots to get the money into the officer's hands. As if this were not bad enough, these plots had to accommodate all sorts of ridiculous compulsive conditions. One, for example, was that the money had to be paid through a go-between, another officer. I shall forgo a recounting of the patient's final turmoil, which reached its climax on a train speeding back to town. The prospect of even suggesting the patient's agitated ruminations about switching train connections so that he could finally execute his compulsion sets my teeth on edge. Freud marked every detail without contention.

But very soon the patient's recital to Freud struck an obstacle. Before the patient could proceed with the further details of his obsessional debt, he had to bring into his story still another officer. This was the person who had wrongly told the patient which officer had laid out the money for the package. The patient knew the money was really owed to the postal clerk. Why, then, was this person's misinformation so compelling? The patient's attempt to dodge this matter evoked a great instance of Freud's singularity of purpose (but notice the gentility with which Freud exorcised a malignant thought).

On maneuvers, just before losing his eyeglasses, the patient had gotten into conversation with the officer now in question.

This officer, the patient told Freud, began to describe a horrible torture used in the East . . . . Here the patient broke off. He got up from the analytic sofa, unable to continue, and implored the doctor to spare him the report of the details. Freud assured him that the treatment was not designed to torment the patient. The patient roamed about the room, pleading. But the doctor could not grant something that was beyond his power. (The power was now in the idea and no longer in the man who had invented the idea.) "He might just as well ask me to give him the moon," Freud wrote. "I went on to say that I would do all I could, nevertheless, to guess the full meaning of any hints he gave me. Was he perhaps thinking of impalement?" "No, not that—" the patient hesitated—"the criminal was tied up—a pot was turned upside-down on his buttocks—some rats were put into it—and they—bored their way in—." Into his anus, Freud completed the sentence. Whereupon a dam of reserve cracked, and a flood of rat fantasies poured forth, so upsetting that by the end of the session, the patient was calling Freud "Captain."

For months thereafter they sifted the patient's thoughts to try to find out how the idea of rats had acquired its overwhelming effect. They discovered, for example, a forgotten story of the patient's father who had been, during his own army service, a *spielratte*—a gambler—and had lost at cards small sums of money entrusted to him in his duties as a kind of quartermaster. The story mortified the patient, who held his father in impeccable esteem. And they happened upon a memory so vague the patient had to act it out with Freud to gain conviction about it. This memory had to do with his father's physical violence after the patient had (like a rat) bitten someone as a very young child. The patient couldn't reconcile the idea of this beating with the image of his father's gentility, until a point in treatment when the patient found himself moved to rebuke Freud bitterly but unaccountably, for he had grown immensely fond of Freud. What enforced the conviction about the memory was the fact that these verbal attacks on Freud could not be made from the analytic couch. The patient had to leap up and shout his abuse from across the room, thus avoiding the retaliatory thrashing he expected from Freud. Where else but from the example of his otherwise benevolent father could the patient have learned to defend himself against the absurd idea of Freud's punching him in the face? Piece by piece, the rat symbol was dismantled, and what conspired in its symptoms, conspired in other symptoms, which fell away under these auspices.

There is a final footnote, which Freud was moved to furnish for a 1923 printing of the case: "The patient's mental health was restored to him by the analysis which I have reported upon in these pages. Like so many other young men of value and promise, he perished in the Great War."

THE LADY IN THE ALPS

When he treated the Rat Man, Freud was already a mature and seasoned psychoanalytic therapist—the only one in the world. The case of Katharina affords a glimpse of Freud when his intellectual and clinical enthusiasm estranged him professionally from his colleagues. The events took place around 1892.

We know about Katharina from an afternoon's consultation with Freud in a rather surprising setting. It was summer. Freud was on vacation in the Eastern Alps and one day happened into a mountaintop hotel to rest after a strenuous climb. Katharina was the young daughter of the landlady. When she learned from the visitor's book that Freud was a doctor, she approached him and asked for his help. She had "bad nerves." Freud noted that she was a robust, sulky-looking young lady, culturally rural, and that she spoke in a regional dialect. Her politeness and despondency overcame his reluctance to have his holiday intruded upon.

Her complaint, as she described it, was of a sort common in Freud's clinical experience. During the past 2 years, Katharina had suffered periodically from a syndrome of pressure on the chest with suffocating shortness of breath, nausea, and terror at the apparition of an anguished, unrecognizable face, a man's face. She would faint and have to be put to bed for several days. Anxiety hysteria, Freud mentally remarked, was obviously not limited to cosmopolitan society.

Two theories informed Freud's questioning of Katharina as

she sat across from him at a secluded restaurant table. One theory involved the sexual factor, the other, the traumatic event itself. His technique at this time was—to be charitable—naïve: He told her he knew how her attacks had come on 2 years ago. She had seen something embarrassing that she would have preferred not to have seen. Katharina was stunned. It was a perfect hit.

Immediately, Katharina recalled that her first attack occurred 2 years ago, shortly after she happened to see her father in bed with one of the maidservants. She caught the scene through the window of a ground-floor bedroom, but it was too dark to make out exactly what they were doing or whether they were clothed or not. Katharina lost her breath, reeled against the wall, and several days later went to bed with her first full-blown hysterical attack.

A mind less ardent than Freud's might have stopped here, with this gratifying confirmation of his sense of things. But Katharina's reaction really confirmed very little. Why exactly the pressure on her chest? Why not some other symptom? And whose face appeared in the apparitions? Her father's? But, then, why was it anguished, when the scene involved the father in an act of pleasure? Not least, why did the scene have the effect it did? Such reactions as Katharina's are not inevitable.

Direct questioning about these matters got them nowhere, though Katharina was getting caught up in the spirit of the inquiry. At the height of their frustrations, Freud made a grand appeal to a fresh agency—the mind's own lawfulness. "I told her to go on and tell me whatever occurred to her, in the confident expectation that she would think of precisely what I needed to explain the case."

At first Katharina rambled on about her present circumstances but soon gravitated toward several earlier incidents. They were not very remote in time, and they had to do with her father's unsuccessful sexual advances toward her. The first proved very much to the point. It contains every element of her syndrome:

Katharina was 14 when she went on a particular overnight trip with her father. They shared the same room but slept, of course, in different beds. In the middle of night, Katharina awoke suddenly, shocked to find her father in bed with her, his body pressing against her. She rushed to the doorway, nauseous and breathless. "What are you up to!" she remonstrated. "Go on, you silly girl, keep still. You don't know how nice it is." Katharina threatened to take refuge in the hallway, at which her father soured his face and returned to bed. Katharina also returned to bed and slept the night through unmolested.

As for the sight of her father in bed with the maidservant, Freud was able to show her that her reaction was not so much to that but to the memories that the sight stirred up in her. The more recent scene, in short, was charged with her memories.

"She was like someone transformed," Freud observed. "The sulky, unhappy face had grown lively, her eyes were bright, she was lightened and exalted."

Freud left his card in the event that she needed more help. Evidently she never felt the need, for he never saw her again.

I might add that his incident of a single consultation was not an isolated one. Throughout much of his life Freud kept open his noon hour for single consultations. Quite often he gave very significant help in a single hour, without recommending a long course of formal psychoanalysis, which spells the lie to the myth that Freud believed everyone ought to undergo analysis. Indeed, from various accounts we know that Freud treated the conductor Bruno Walter in a single consultation, when Walter became panicky about not being able to conduct with an almost paralyzed arm. Walter recounts in his autobiography how Freud examined his arm and concluded hysteria.

"But I can't move my arm," Walter objected.

"Try it at any rate," Freud urged.

"And what if I should have to stop conducting?"

"You won't have to stop."

"Can I take upon myself the responsibility of possibly upsetting a performance?"

Freud puffed his cigar. "I'll take the responsibility."

Walter conducted beautifully.

Of course, Freud never suggested that such encounters substituted for psychoanalysis. Theodor Reik has a letter from Freud concerning Reik's inquiry about Freud's four-hour consultation with Gustav Mahler in 1910. Mahler apparently benefited immensely, but, as Freud put it in the letter: "It was as if you would dig a single shaft through a mysterious building."

A FAILURE WITH DORA

Did Freud ever mishandle the clinical situation? He was sufficiently secure in the knowledge of his powers to confess his limitations, but even these are full of instruction.

The case of Dora has been a subject of lively dispute. Anticipating future criticism, Freud did attempt to acquit himself in regard to the outcome of the case. But he had obvious doubts. The story is this:

Dora was a mature 18-year-old young lady, bright and vivacious. A hysteric with migraines, nervous coughing, fainting spells, and irritability, she had run through a succession of doctors in a short span of years. Finally she planted a histrionic suicide note on her family that drove them to their wits' end, and they dragged her off to Freud "to talk some sense into her." Her emotional blackmailing and tyranny were evident to Freud almost at once. (She got increasingly better at these things in the course of her long life. She nagged her husband literally to death. Her attending physician at her own deathbed in New York some dozen years ago referred to her as one of the most repulsive individuals he had ever come across.)

However, the story she related to Freud was very poignant. For years, she told Freud, her father had been carrying on an affair with a close friend of the family. Dora's mother, incidentally, was a hausfrau whose days were spent covering and uncovering the furniture in a constant battle against dirt. Her father made no bones about his infidelity. But much worse, when Dora developed into a lovely adolescent of 14, her father began to encourage an affair between Dora and his mistress's husband in the hope of buying off the husband's interference. The husband—I have always thought him a rather decent, though pathetic, fellow—read the father's encouragements gladly and began to ply Dora with gifts and attention. As this charade went on, the husband could contain himself no longer; how much Dora must have provoked this was beyond her awareness. He trapped Dora in a hallway and mauled her passionately. She threw him aside and fled. Shortly thereafter she had her first hysterical attack. And so began her series of high-strung bouts with Viennese psychiatry.

Dora told Freud these things with outraged righteousness and demanded Freud's cooperation in her wish for vengeance. Freud believed the facts of Dora's story. But many hold that he made his first mistake in attempting to analyze her straight off, a doomed undertaking with a patient thoroughly consumed by the merits of her immediate crisis, as Dora was. While she wanted Freud to agree that her symptoms were the appropriate reactions to her father's infamous conduct, Freud wanted her to see how she participated, unwittingly but nevertheless actively, in her own victimization. It was as though Freud took his vehicle for a bulldozer. With Dora, he was driving it right into a mountain.

The "analysis" lasted months. During this time Freud exercised his finest ingenuity in proving to Dora how her symptoms were her self-punitive moral judgments on her own unconscious envy of her father's mistress and on her actual erotic desires for the man who finally forced himself upon her in the hallway. As with her would-be lover, Dora's cooperation with Freud was a setup. She produced astonishing confirmations in her dreams and mental associations, which aroused Freud's therapeutic hopes and theoretical interests. At the peak of his involvement, and at what he deemed the brink of her cure, Dora cut him down. This was the cunning moment her vindictiveness chose for the cool opening remark of what was to be her last session. "Do you know that I am here for the last time today?" Freud recovered in a wink. When had she come to this resolve, was all he asked. She had made up her mind two weeks ago—which drew her thoughts, with Freud's continued collaboration, to a particular incident involving the dismissal of a governess. Like an unwanted servant, Freud had been put on two weeks' notice.

I have suggested one possibility of error, that Dora was

simply in no condition to be analyzed. She may have needed perhaps years of weaning from her narcissism in preparation for analysis.

Another possibility of error was Freud's neglect of the "transference." Dora had succeeded in repeating in the analytic situation what she had done with her aroused pursuer in the hallway. Freud should have known that she was bound to do this and should have taken interpretive steps to prevent it before it got out of hand. Was he too involved at the time in his personal scientific curiosities? Or was he just no good with petulant women?

Erik H. Erikson, among others, has argued that Dora, who was merely 18 at the time of treatment, was entitled to Freud's support and commiseration, that a sense of fidelity is as much an unconditional right of the adolescent as food is of the infant. Was Freud's analytic neutrality too harsh? Freud's own conclusion leaves this question moot:

> Might I perhaps have kept the girl under my treatment if I myself had acted a part? If I had exaggerated the importance to me of her staying on, and had shown a warm personal interest in her . . .? I do not know. . . . In spite of every theoretical interest and every endeavor to be of assistance as a physician, I keep the fact in mind that there must be some limits set to the extent to which psychological influence may be used, and I respect as one of these limits the patient's own will and understanding.

What a discrepancy between this ethic and the hucksterism of some activities of today's psychiatric movement, where the public can find just about anything it wants, so long as the fee can be met. Dora did return to Freud fifteen months later, "to finish her story and ask for help once more." Goodness knows, Freud needed the fee. "But one glance at her face was enough to tell me that she was not in earnest over her request." They talked. She spoke of her gains and setbacks. At the end of her hour Freud sent her on her way. Should he have taken her back? It has been reported that in Dora's subsequent life, first in Paris, then in America, she never missed a chance to aver, with bashful pride, that she was the Dora of Freud's famous "Fragment of an Analysis of a Case of Hysteria." Her 3 months with Freud may have been the only experience with unimpeachable integrity in her long, unhappy life.

Money: The prosperous psychoanalyst is a nepotist. But Freud constantly found it hard to make ends meet. At first there was his falling out of favor, his "splendid isolation," as he called it. Afterwards he was still too busy with the theory and practice of psychoanalysis to make any real money out of his international reputation. In 1924 McCormick's Chicago *Tribune* offered Freud an open price—any amount—to cover the Leopold-Loeb trial in Chicago. Freud turned this down, as he had turned down a similar offer from the Hearst empire, which included a chartered ocean liner all to himself. When Freud's nephew Edward L. Bernays eagerly wrote to him from New York about the possibility of a $5,000 advance and vast sales for a brief autobiography, Freud was appalled, though not without good humor, at the very idea of getting "a hitherto decent man to commit such an outrageous act for $5,000." He added: "Temptation would begin for me at a sum a hundred times as great and even then the offer would be rejected after half an hour."

In renouncing such opportunities, Freud often cited his health, which was very bad during the latter span of his life. But this was never the crucial reason because, despite his physical discomfort—he had cancer—and the wear and tear of advancing years, his output was unflagging. The truth was that he didn't have forever to insure the future of psychoanalysis, and he knew that this would be best accomplished by his technical writing and teaching, activities that kept him respectably poor. For example, he did write a brief autobiography not long after his nephew's overture, but he wrote it for a technical rather than commercial publisher, and received a pittance for it. His own Psychoanalytic Press, whose original editions are now treasures, continued to take every spare dollar. He was once upset for months over a consultation with a renowned oral surgeon who was passing through Vienna, because the fee he paid the man had been earmarked for the Press.

Thus Freud lived mainly from his daily labor with patients. He averaged between seven and ten cases a day, each patient attending six sessions a week. Later the number of sessions was established at five a week to make time for an extra student Freud had inadvertently permitted to come to Vienna, when his schedule was actually full. At the height of his fame in the 1920s, Freud's fees were $20 per session for regular patients and $10 for students undergoing training analyses; in New York, his former students were already getting $25 a session. Royalty and celebrities paid him more, but there were always too many students in his practice for this to make much difference financially. He was forever mortgaging his present for the future. By and large, these students went on to redeem his great sacrifice. A handful survive. In their sixties and seventies, their contributions are worthy of an army of workers.

The mystique that shrouds the analytic fee is not Freud's legacy. Nowhere did he claim that the analytic cure depended upon a painful financial sacrifice by the patient. Freud counseled a straightforward attitude about money, as he did about sex. The fee is the analyst's livelihood. It benefits the analyst, not the patient. As long as the analyst receives his wages from some source, there is no evidence that free treatment is less effective than costly treatment. Karl Menninger has underscored this simplicity. He has written that the best source of money for analysis is a dormant savings account.

What would Freud do with those who came with little means, with those whose "dormant savings accounts" and gainful employment were wiped out by Europe's periodic depressions and political upheavals? His students tell how he was always pestering them to find time for indigent patients. They would have turned down the request of a do-gooder, a sentimental charity-monger. But Freud's character instilled in the merest project a sense of great enterprise.

Indeed, at this writing there is an aged man in Vienna, the only direct representative of Freud in the city that was the birthplace and one-time capital of psychoanalysis, for psychoanalysis perished there with the Nazi occupation. A former patient of Freud's, this man is called the Wolfman because his treatment centered on the analysis of a dream of a tree full of white wolves. The treatment became Freud's masterpiece in clinical exposition, and the Wolfman sometimes grants appointments to analytic students who continue to research his case. The Wolfman earns his bare living as a writer of sorts.

The point is that he was of Russian nobility when he came to Freud. Incapacitated, he settled with his entourage in Vienna to undergo what he now refers to as his "cure with the Professor." After several years, the Bolshevik revolution destroyed his holdings. Overnight he became a destitute refugee. Freud carried him for years thereafter with no hopes of financial repayment. When the Wolfman later required further treatment, Freud thought it better for his case to continue with a woman analyst. He prevailed upon and secured a gifted British analyst for his patient, who was still living from hand to mouth. Until he no longer needed it, the Wolfman continued to receive the very best treatment.

It is no insult either to myself or to my colleagues to observe that our attempts at such gestures, which to Freud had all the grace of lifelong manners, invariably come to grief in anxiety and resentment. The gap between Freud's practices and ours is not cited in order to humiliate, but to reveal the challenges we have still to meet, challenges generated not by his genius so much as by his vision and character.

That we have gone beyond Freud is a figment, unless the windy evangelism of our latter-day psychiatry is an advance on his eagerness to surpass easy solutions to tragic problems. Nor is the adventurism prevalent today what he really meant by versatility in psychotherapy. Beyond Freud? On the contrary. Benjamin Nelson has put it exactly: "Too few years are left in the present century to exhaust the dimensions of his message or to approximate the substance of his hopes."

And that tiresome cliché: "Freud was a brilliant theoretician, but not a very good doctor." Not a very good doctor? Compared to whom?

REFERENCES

Freud, S. (1913). Totem and Taboo. *Standard Edition* 13.

Jones, E. (1953). *The Life and Work of Sigmund Freud.* Vol. 1. New York: Basic Books.

Wiener, L. (1915). *Commentary to the Germanic Laws and Mediaeval Documents.* Cambridge, MA: Harvard University Press.

_____ (1917). *Contributions Toward a History of Arabico-Gothic Culture.* Vol. 1. New York: Neale.

11

The Emergence of
Projection in Dreams

The following is a presentation of a series of dreams illustrating a particular phase in the analytic therapy of a narcissistic female patient. The phase of treatment that will be brought under discussion has to do with the transition in ego behavior from *denial* to *projection*, which seems to be a typical event in the analytic therapy of female patients presenting narcissistic maladjustments. Indeed, the writer hopes to demonstrate that a clinical and psychological evaluation of this specific combination of ego reactions is a significant guide to the therapy and prognosis of narcissistic female patients.

In a discussion of male narcissistic patients, Annie Reich (1960) remarks that while Freud used the term "narcissistic neurosis" to designate psychotic illness exclusively, the last twenty years or so have taught us to "question the usefulness of a too narrowly circumscribed nosology," and she goes on to remind us of the ubiquitous overlapping of developmental phases and to suggest that even marked narcissistic tendencies may not entirely interrupt object cathexes. The narcissistic conditions to which the following presentation addresses itself are those characterized by developmental overlapping with more highly developed structures sufficient enough to preclude a frank, manifest schizophrenic process. Popularly labeled "borderlines" or, even less exact, "ambulatory schizophrenics," narcissistic patients are those who are commonly given to sudden manic-like reactions, acute, severe, though brief, depressive reactions sometimes with suicidal endeavors, promis-

cuous and perverse sexual patterns with significant competence
in anticipating and accommodating sexual patterns and requirements of the partner, homoerotic panic, hypochondriacal involvements, and quite frequently "medicational" addictions of
one sort or another. Further reference to this symptom syndrome will be made later.

That the following presentation will employ only the manifest
content of dreams to the comparative disregard of the latent
meaning might require some additional brief remarks beforehand in the way of reminding the reader of both the value and
danger of focusing attention in some sort of exclusive manner
upon the manifest content of dreams. The manifest content of
the dream is understood to be the final product of the dream-
work, a negotiation among the ego, the superego, and a
forbidden infantile wish. This negotiation represents the efforts
of the ego (albeit, at a regressed level of functioning) and is
interesting for what it tells us about the nature of the ego. Since
ego functioning is a prominent diagnostic criterion, the manifest
content of dreams, especially at the outset of treatment, can be
regarded diagnostically; since treatment can be thought of as an
attempt to alter the patient's presenting diagnosis, subsequent
dream sequences can go on to inform us of how and to what
extent the treatment process is affecting changes in the patient's
psyche. In connection with these issues, the reader's attention is
called to the contributions of Sheppard and Saul (1958),
Erikson (1954), and Lewis (1959) in which attempts are made to
systematize our inquiry into ego function by means of the
manifest dream. This tradition begins with Chapter VII of
Freud's *The Interpretation of Dreams* where Freud's concern with
the dream shifts temporarily from interpretation to the construction of a theory of mind.

The danger here is precisely that danger that sophistication
always holds out to those perceptions that are better made in
innocence. As therapists, the more we learn, the less we are apt
to think we need to be told by our patients. It is, for example, a
common (and often lamented) observation among psychoanalysts that the practice of subjecting dreams to exhaustive analysis has become the exception rather than the rule it once was.
Summarizing a number of reasons for this evolution in practice,

Erikson (1954) included the inevitable fact that "we have learned (or so we think) to find in other sources what in Freud's early days could be garnered only from dreams." The parenthetical aside here is certainly not intended to invite an attitude of pompous humility or affected ignorance, but is rather a caution against our becoming, in our knowledge, overly goal directed and anticipating of the patient's productions, which, in respect to dreams, is bound to lead to an excessive investment of interest in their manifest content.

With these comments in mind, let us turn to the patient whose dreams will be presented.

I

The patient is an intelligent, gifted, energetic, and exceedingly attractive woman who entered treatment at age 33 complaining of severe anxiety and of an incapacity to make decisions. She reported having had a series of painful, disappointing, and futile affairs with numerous men over the past twelve years. A marriage at 19 to a man much older than herself had ended two years later in a divorce initiated by the patient, and it was the recent news of her former husband's intention to remarry that seemed to the patient to contribute a good deal to the anxiety she presented upon coming into treatment. She described a feeling of desperation that her own life would pass without marriage and motherhood.

The life history that unfolded was eventful. The patient's father died when she was 3, and the patient shortly thereafter began to be shifted about with an infant sister and older brother to half a dozen shelters and foster homes by a mother who, herself, was going through numerous unsuccessful affairs. The mother appeared to have been deeply attached to her children, but this was often expressed by the mother's meddlesome supervision of the various foster homes, so that the patient was mindful of the mother's devotion, yet was deprived by it of an opportunity to get into any long-standing relationships with foster parents. From time to time, the children were reunited with the mother for brief periods but not permanently so until the patient was 12. Throughout childhood the patient's psychosexual development had to accommodate almost incessant sexual traumata involving, among other things, highly erotic bedtime experiences with her siblings and provocations by her mother, whom the patient described on one occasion as an astonishing, seductive beauty. One of the patient's earliest memories, for example, was the mother's bathing one afternoon with the bathroom door open and instructing the patient, who was then 4 or 5, to ask in a delivery man who had just arrived at the apartment with groceries; the patient remembered having stood in the bathroom doorway looking from the delivery man to her smiling mother and overwhelmed with hatred, but subsequently never being able to figure out toward which of the adults in the scene the hatred was directed.

Yet, despite the deprivation, uncertainty, and traumata of the patient's early years, she was able to go on to acquire an education, enjoy a high cultural attainment, and eventually make a gratifying vocational adjustment. At the time she entered treatment, she had been living with and, to a great extent, supporting her younger sister whose emotional adjustment was so marginal as to necessitate continuous out-patient psychiatric care and occasional hospitalization. It might be added that the brother managed to achieve a successful art and university-teaching career; married and the father of three children, he was also to assume financial responsibility for his mother, at times his sister, and he was the family's main confidant and advisor.[1]

Early in the patient's treatment, which was two sessions weekly on the premises of an outpatient psychiatric clinic, a

---

1. It is interesting to note in passing the varying degrees of pathology in the two sisters and the brother that even these bare facts suggest, that is, basic pathology in the younger sister, narcissistic pathology—as will be detailed —in the patient, pathology, if any, at predominantly a more advanced developmental level in the brother. In this family, the degrees of pathology in the children appear to correlate with the degrees of "oedipal deficiency" created by the death of the father when the children were at ages 1, 3, and 7, respectively, and with the degrees of susceptibility to the severity of separation from the mother.

range of symptoms pathognomonic of a severe narcissistic neurosis was elicited. In addition to the anxiety already mentioned, the patient was susceptible to states verging on confusion, which coincided with promiscuous sexual activity. A complex of behavior reactions aimed at reestablishing a sense of identity led to episodes of physical exhaustion with consequences to her physical resistance and health—she would engage in tedious lovers' quarrels long into the night, having to carry out arduous work responsibilities the following day; she would skip lunch-hour meals to attend to some obsessive detail like writing a long, explanatory letter to an out-of-town lover or returning home at midday in the hope of finding an expected letter; and she would, as she described it, "eat herself up alive" with intense, scheming ruminations, often into the night. Her reported use of barbiturates, tranquilizers, and alcohol had numerous characteristics of dependency, though her allusions to drugs and alcohol were invariably prefaced by a denial of any addictive experience. In the sessions, her behavior was histrionic and evasive. She suppressed and falsified material and often left large gaps in her productions by simply forgetting material. Though she did not break appointments, she attempted to change appointments and make emergency appointments. She would seize upon trivia and various "clues" as pretexts for extreme, brooding despair and would as quickly revert to moods of carefree elation. The transference, as a point of any interest, let alone conscious emotional experience, was consistently disavowed by the patient, and any reference to it by the therapist was met for quite some time with either agitated impatience or blank disinterest. (This, of course, is not to say that a transference did not exist or that it was not influential.) With excruciating determination she sought to cast the therapist in the role of the mastermind for her interpersonal resolutions and strategies, and she would describe the behavior and conversation of people with whom she was having conflict, and make all effort to get the therapist to "analyze" their motives and intentions and to predict their behavior. She was characteristically lively and seductive, commanded an easy, winning sense of humor, and very shortly became a "sincere" advocate of "psychoanalysis."

While a number of defensive operations could be demon-strated in this patient's functioning—regression and isolation come readily to mind—it is chiefly the failure of *denial* from which is derived the patient's presenting symptoms both as reported by the patient and evident clinically. The connection between denial, employed as a chief rather than subsidiary defense, and the exuberance, evasiveness, instability, and gen-eral "borderline" quality of this patient is documented in the literature.

It is not simply a theoretical nicety to distinguish denial as a defense from the defense *mechanisms* (e.g., repression, isolation, projection) for, though denial is capable of warding off ideation, unlike the mechanisms of defense, it has no structural compo-nent and cannot transform primary-process energy into second-ary-process energy. It is rather, as Anna Freud (1946) put it, a "preliminary stage of defense," and very early in the ego's development it comes into conflict with the ego's inclination to perceive and take into account reality. Though functionally somewhat different, categorically denial is more similar to *displacement* than are any of the defense mechanisms. (Displace-ment, of course, is also not, strictly speaking, of the category defense mechanism.)

Freud (1927) defined denial as the removal of the precon-scious cathexis from an idea though not from the accompanying affect, and he was, thus, the first to distinguish denial from repression. (It is this distinction that partly accounts for the exuberance that "passes around" this defense. Patients, on the other hand, who chiefly repress are easily agitated, but are affectually dull and withdrawn.) Ostow (1960) has cited the arbitrary and opportunistic relationship between denial and reality, and has elaborated Freud's further idea that denial is an act of aggression turned inward, adding that it holds out the advantage of not depleting the ego of energy, so that its presence in the clinical picture countersuggests suicidal success (though not necessarily suicidal attempts.) Lewin (1950) has discussed the role of denial in mania and related moods. Fenichel has related denial to falsifications of both the intended (lying) and unintended (screen memories, forgetting) kind. According to Fenichel (1954), denial can serve the formula: "If it is possible to make someone believe that untrue things are true, then it is also possible that true things, the memory of which threatens me, are untrue." But, he adds, "only in tendentious forgetting of external events, in 'screen-memories,' and in perversions, does 'denial' seem to be victorious." Its retention, Fenichel goes on, for extensive conscious and near-conscious falsifications of current reality can be severely pathogenic and can lead to psychosis. The prominence of denial in the clinical pictures of narcissistic disorders has been pointed out by Schafer (1954).

Now, it is well known that what the narcissistic character typically denies is the conflict deriving from intensely demanding oral-aggressive and oral-receptive needs. What is at stake in this conflict is a sense, on the one hand, of omnipotence when the patient feels assured of nonending oral supplies and, on the other hand, neediness, helplessness, and abandonment when the supplies are threatened. When this conflict attaches itself to the sexual function, the loved object acquires the unconscious equivalence of food. Moreover, in some significant way, the object must remain unattainable in order that the oral conflict not be laid to rest and with it the opportunity for testing again and again the patient's oral effectuality. The patient being referred to in this chapter, for example, would remark with great chagrin that her whole problem was simply that she could not love men who loved her but had to love men whom she somehow could never really possess. The simplicity, predictability, and repetitiousness of the problematic aspects of the interpersonal relationships of these patients are much like current attempts to abreact a discrete, infantile trauma.

Strongly libidinized and repetitive striving in an adult for mother–infant relationships invariably produces painful anxiety and guilt reactions and leads to psychosexual confusion. The homoeroticism, which this leaves the narcissistic patient susceptible to, is, of course, also denied. However, here the denial is not direct but is rather a denial of ideation that has already been subjected to a particular defensive activity by the patient's ego. The specific defense underlying this denial is *projection*.

The combination of denial and projection in narcissistic

disorders has been discussed by Schafer (1954), and while this defensive combination can also be demonstrated in other conditions (e.g., manic-depression, paranoia, chronic addiction) its presence in the narcissistic conditions of the type being referred to in this chapter is characterized by the stability and relief afforded the patient in the uncovering of projection. In these narcissistic conditions, the removal by treatment of the need to deny amounts to a restoration of a serviceable projective defense mechanism.[2] And it is the serviceability of this defense in narcissistic conditions that imparts a distinctive phase to the treatment of narcissists: There is a sudden relief from symptoms, a pronounced sense of mastery and well-being, and a vigorous determination to break off treatment abruptly. This phase can occur after as brief a period as less than a year of treatment or, as with the patient being presented here, after 3 years of treatment. It has been the writer's experience with several such cases in recent years that this phase of treatment is forecasted by a dream in which the patient experiences a homosexual assault.

Before turning to the patient's dreams depicting the emergence of this well-retained projective defense and to some of the technical problems that arise, an example of its emergence in treatment may be of some interest. It has been mentioned that the patient had been living with a younger sister at the time she entered treatment. At the outset of treatment, the patient was able to regard the sister only as a dependent, helpless child and

---

2. In the frank schizophrenias like manic-depression and paranoia and in frank addictions like alcoholism, projection emerges in a state of decompensation, which makes the course of treatment altogether different from that which occurs in narcissistic conditions. The key to the understanding of the role of projection in "ideational" schizophrenia was given by Freud in the Shreber case. Freud (1911) was quite explicit (though he is notoriously misread) that the quantitative factor is far more significant in schizophrenia than the choice of defense, that is, not projection but *decompensating* projection is the *sine qua non* of paranoia. In manic-depression, denial is the key factor in the mania and is comparatively restitutional; the factor in the depression is the failure of projection, for it is this failure that leaves the punishing introject entrenched. In narcissism as well, the fleeting instability of projection leaves the patient susceptible to manic-depressive reactions (*viz.*, A. Reich 1960), but the comparative strength of this mechanism keeps these reactions diminutive.

as a source of guilt. The patient would defer her comfort and privacy around the apartment to her sister's love affairs and would often dispossess herself entirely in favor of her sister's need for privacy, though she would not request similar consideration for herself. The childhood memories that accompanied these reports had to do with the patient's aggressive and usually successful rivalry with the sister for the attention and affection of the mother, the older brother, and foster parents. These memories of competition with the sister were especially painful when they pertained to periods in which the children had been boarded out, for it was at those times that the mother had charged the patient with the responsibility for looking after the younger sister. The patient's subsequent masochistic renunciation of power for the sister's forgiveness was a feature that could be discerned in most of the patient's significant relationships.

As treatment progressed, it became evident that a large amount of homosexual anxiety and agitation was being generated in the patient by her daily exposure to her sister, whom the patient was growing able to perceive and describe as sexy and immodest. The patient was also able to acknowledge feelings of anger attributable to her sister's immodesty—the sister often lounged around the apartment wearing only panties and would often report her sexual thoughts and activities to the patient at great length. It was not possible for the patient to come to an understanding of the unconscious origins of these feelings of anger, feelings that originated in the patient's early relationship to her mother, certain aspects of which were now being reenacted with the sister as mother. But it was possible for the patient to act on these feelings and to begin to put an end to her sister's provocative behavior. She got her sister to wear more clothes around the apartment, and she made herself less available to her sister's sexual reports. The patient felt licensed to do this in part by an understanding of her history with her sister, for example, the patient's current guilt was for childhood crimes, and in part by a projection of the sexual interests and culpabilities entirely onto the sister. Prior to this capacity to project adequately, the sister's sexual behavior could not be acknowledged by the patient but was simply denied. The projection exonerated the patient sufficiently to come to grips with a significant portion of her everyday reality—the sister was indeed behaving in a distressingly immodest manner. Having done something effectual about the matter, the patient showed a marked relief from anxiety and came into a gratifying sense of control, and while this was the result of functioning on the basis of a profound misperception, it was more satisfactory than the previous vague, passively experienced agitation suffered by the patient *vis-a-vis* her sister. The cement that bound the relationship had not really been cracked; the idea, for example, of taking separate apartments was completely beyond the patient, indeed, veritably unthinkable.

Projection, furthermore, enabled the patient to investigate ideas about and feelings toward the fantasied "other women," the wives and girl friends in the lives of men with whom she became involved. Among other things, jealousy in other women became entirely plausible to her, and she became more effectual in both her fantasies of and actual dealings with women. This effectuality carried over to men as well. In fact, by the end of the third year of treatment the patient had come away from two affairs markedly unwounded and full of decisiveness, and had triumphantly sent both men into psychotherapy.

II

As was said at the outset, in the following dreams from the treatment of this patient, the reader's attention is being invited only to the manifest content and specifically to the presence and nature of ego functioning. Some of the literature in which particular principles appear for observing ego functioning in dreams has been cited above. Sheppard and Saul (1958) are especially helpful in providing a systematic ego-rating scheme based upon considerations of "distancing" between the impulses in the dream and the dreamer's ego. In respect to their system it might be mentioned beforehand that the following dreams taken as a group seem to contain sufficient ego functioning at a high enough level to classify them as dreams of a nonpsychotic ego. (This would lend support to the validity of the diagnostic differentiation insisted upon at the outset between a narcissistic neurosis and a schizophrenia.) The reader does not need to be told, of course, that none of these considerations can lead to the latent meaning of the dream, which is pursued not by an analysis of ego functioning, but by an analysis, through the patient's associations, of the *condensations*, *displacements*, and *symbolizations*—the language at the border of the unconscious.

For the sake of readability, the relationship to the patient of persons appearing in the following dreams will be identified in parentheses. It goes without saying that what these dreams are currently intended to demonstrate to the reader—that is, the development of a stabilizing projective defense—is quite different from what they were intended to demonstrate to the patient. The first dream was reported a month after treatment began:

> Bill (sister's lover) is pulling green vegetable matter out of Barbara's (sister) open mouth. Then my mouth is open with green vegetable matter stuck in my throat. I become nauseous and gag. Then I woke up.

Like most, though by no means all, initial dreams in treatment, this one makes an obvious and straightforward statement of the nature and level of the patient's current conflict. If the expulsion of unwanted oral contents is thought of as the prototype of projection, the status of this defense in the patient's ego functioning is also obvious in this dream—there is an endeavor to mobilize the defense, which is not altogether successful. Though we no longer think of the content of projection as being restricted to unacceptable homosexual wishes, such a wish is much to the point in this dream in that the patient included in her associations her sister's recent suggestion that they switch sexual partners, which is a perversion that employs a heterosexual object to gratify vicariously and yet deny a homosexual wish toward the object's partner.

The following dream is taken from treatment seven months later:

I dreamed I was in a room. It was indoors, or, at least, an indoor kind of room but it had an outdoor feeling about it. There were many people in it, none of whom I knew. I began looking for a way out, though I don't know what I was afraid of. I was opening doors along a corridor. One door I opened I was face-to-face with Ira (a former lover). He wanted me to come in with him. I didn't want to. He insisted. I took off along a street, and after what felt like about five minutes, I decided to go back. On the way back I remember having to stop for a moment because a traffic light was against me.

Here it may be worth pausing briefly to illustrate the difference between viewing this dream for its latent meaning and for its indications of the quality of the dreamer's ego functioning. Upon first hearing the dream, a therapist would very likely entertain two possibilities with regard to the latent meaning: The opening—*I dreamed I was in a room . . . There were many people in it, none of whom I knew*—has a promiscuous inference around which the dream revolves. And there may be an incest wish to which a therapist would be alerted by the *indoor–outdoor* contradiction at the beginning that suggests the importance of opposites in the rest of the dream: Thus, *There were many people, none of whom I knew* becomes *There were few people, all of whom I knew* (family), or, perhaps, *There was one person whom I knew* (mother). *Ira* in the dream is then an incest figure. However, in point of fact, the dreamer's associations carried the interpretation in the direction of a masturbation conflict. A significant association was to *five minutes*—an electric clock that hummed loudly and interfered with the patient's falling asleep. She was aware of being alone in the darkened room. The *five minutes* can rather safely be taken as *five fingers* or *a hand*, and the forbidden wish is to masturbate. *Ira*, as a lover, offers an escape but this would bring the patient into conflict with the therapist (*traffic light*) whose endeavor at the time of the dream was to stop the patient's acting out.

None of this, however, says much about the ego functioning in the dream, which is a matter of the dreamer's resourcefulness, the quality of her participation, her distance in respect to various impulses, the nature of her role assignments, the complication of retained affect, and so on. From the point of view of these things, the dream has a rather weak quality. The patient's ego cannot tolerate the aggression involved in turning down the lover. The urgency of the wish in the dream is so harassing that restriction is assigned to an external agent, the traffic light, which, it should be noted, is a highly distanced feature in being inanimate. Moreover, the patient's responses are exclusively primitive; she registers fear, flight, and passivity.

It was shortly after this dream that the patient began "revising" her "opinion" about other women. They were not as passive and reputable as she had thought. On the contrary, they were greedy and aggressive, disguised by fake respectability. By contrast, the patient described herself as sincere and honest, unwittingly victimized by an enemy she had all along underestimated. In retrospect, it is plausible to regard the traffic light at the end of the dream (*a traffic light was against me* = red light) as a reflection of the patient's fear that she was, her denials and rationalizations aside, promiscuous, whorish, and disreputable.

The following two dreams occurred near the end of the second year of treatment. The first is a nightmare containing a frank homosexual assault. The second is about a married man the patient was involved with at the time of the dream. His wife figured prominently in the patient's fantasies. The second dream contains a successful projection in that the wife is entirely demeaned, her husband is weak and guilty, and the patient is shameless and victorious. Here is the first of the two:

> I am in a hotel room, or rather a hotel. There is a convention going on. I am with this girl whose name I don't remember. It's a salesmen's convention. Suddenly, I have to find the ladies' room, and I begin to go through the corridors in search of it. (I wake up and find I really have to go to the bathroom. The earlier part of the dream has come back to me, I think:) I am riding in a coach car of a railroad train when a woman I have never seen before in reality but apparently with whom I am very friendly makes advances at me. (No, this must have been the end of the dream, because I remember I woke up terrified and went to the bathroom.) Somewhere in the dream I am in my apartment, and Barbara (sister) is standing on the other side of the window on the sidewalk. She is nude. She tells me she has just danced nude before thirty-four people. I am shocked, but also shocked that she did this thing from much the same reason that she began taking Seconol.

While the frankness of the assault and the patient's inability to cope with it in the dream account for the nightmare outcome and speak for a defensive failure, the projection of aggression increases throughout the dream. In respect to the sister, the patient is separate and is able to be critical. Now observe the ego stability in the following dream, despite the latent orality, aggressive rivalry, and homoeroticism:

> Murray (patient's lover) asks me into a cafeteria for coffee, but when I arrive, he's at a table with his maid (=wife) who in the dream is black. When he sees me enter, he tries to brush me off because he is ashamed. I am revolted by his weakness.

The final dream presented here occurred toward the end of the third year of treatment. Its homosexual content originated partly in the fact that the night it was dreamed the patient had slept at the apartment of a new, female acquaintance. The resourcefulness of the patient in the dream is striking. Though the thematic substance remains similar to the preceding dreams and there are indications of an unaltered latent content, projection is well established and the level of ego functioning is comparatively high.

> I am sleeping at Louise's (acquaintance) apartment, in the living room. She is in the bedroom. Her door opens and she comes across the room grinning and determined. She lies down next to me and tries to arouse me. I am terrified. I reach behind me and yank open the drapes, exposing the whole room to the public outside. This stops her all right.

It was shortly after this dream that the patient began to press vigorously to terminate treatment on the grounds of her improved symptom picture. Though an attempt was naturally made to help the patient to comprehend the nature of her current adjustment, she nevertheless broke off treatment. Whether this termination could or could not in fact have been avoided is an interesting question,[3] but what is more relevant

---

3. A discussion of this question would have to be preceded by clarification of what is meant by premature termination in psychotherapy, which, in contrast to

here (and will bear on the question) is an understanding of this typical crisis that can arise in these cases. Suffice it to say, the door to further treatment, perhaps psychoanalysis, was left open to this patient.

III

Though the concept of projection as a defense mechanism is not a simple one, clinicians appear to have a far better facility with it than they appear to have with the concept of denial, about which a number of propositions were cited earlier. In regard to the above dreams and to the accompanying restitution in the patient, two aspects of the concept of projection should be singled out. First: unlike denial, which involves a withdrawal of perception from reality (more precisely, internal representations of reality), projection uses reality. Second: projection involves externalization (of libidinal and/or aggressive id and superego impulses directly or previously subjected to a number of defensive possibilities, such as reversal or displacement). The restitutional effects of projection are based on two advantages that originate in these two aspects of this defense mechanism: The projector "(a) may now flee from . . . or righteously retaliate against the 'external' threat or enemy; (b) by projectively purifying himself, he avoids the especially intense subjective pain that would accompany the intrusion of the objectionable material into his self-concept" (Schafer 1954). These restitutional effects are evident in the above dreams and were quite clear in the behavior of the patient. (Though already suggested, it might be worth repeating that where projection emerges and opposite—that is, decompensating—effects are evident, the patient is schizophrenic, and this can be predicted clinically beforehand from numerous indicators, one of which is the altogether different direction taken by the patient's dream productions.)

The depletion in the patient of motivation to continue treat-

psychoanalysis, is characterized as having limited goals. Though the preparation for a psychoanalysis is often one of the goals of psychotherapy, it is not routinely so, and this would need to be clarified as well.

ment as a result of her experience of comparative competence and comparative loss of suffering has already been observed. But while the technical problem of arousing and sustaining motivation for treatment is quite significant here, it is not as specific as several other problems, for the problem of motivation is basic to all cases at one point or another. The specific problems here seem to relate to certain phases of the countertransference (and it should be said that the writer does not subscribe to the erroneous view that all technical problems can be reduced to a countertransference variable).

To carry a narcissistic patient from a borderline adjustment on the basis of denial to a less shaky adjustment, as temporary and limited as it may be, on the basis of an increased reliance on projection requires the therapist's attention to that anxiety in himself, which can be aroused by the emergence of obvious misperception in his patient. Within our current therapeutic model there is the general postulate that neutrality and abstention are the correct responses when the case before us is showing progress, and intervention and support the correct responses when the case is showing retrogression. The transition in a case from nonperception (denial) to misperception (projection) can easily be confused by the therapist's anxiety for retrogression, and the therapist is then likely to apply a correct principle of technique to a mistaken situation. Few responses on the part of the therapist can arrest the development of this transition in narcissistic patients more assuredly than inappropriate supportive intervention. Indeed, inappropriate support arrests the development of any patient, and it is one of the central theses of this discussion that the transition from denial to projection in narcissistic patients is an inevitable phase of development in their personalities.

Another pitfall exists. These are patients whose transference is almost exclusively at a preoedipal mother–child level, and the countertransference susceptibility is to separation anxiety. In addition, this constellation always searches out in male therapists basic castration vulnerabilities, since the therapist, in these cases, is continuously cast in the role of a woman (mother)– erotic arousal in male therapists by narcissistic patients is often an unconscious countertransference assertion against castration in the transference. While this problem may not be the same for female therapists, the patient's masochistic presentation is very apt to arouse basic vulnerabilities to penis envy.[4] This state of affairs can lead to an enthusiastic anticipation in the therapist of the restitutional effects of projection, which promise relief from the special burdens of the countertransference. As the patient shows signs of retaliation against her previously oppressive environment, the therapist celebrates with inappropriate activity and by so doing can drive the patient into a regression. It may then be seen that the therapist has been caught between a wish to get off a countertransference hook and a fear of separation that only hangs him up again.

Dream material has been presented to demonstrate one source of judgment for the therapist in regard to the course and pace of a typical transition in narcissistic patients. Another source is the patient's actual clinical complaint. Originally, the complaint was of an affective disorder. When the complaint alters and becomes comparatively ideational (nonpsychotic in these cases), the transition can be assumed to have occurred to a substantial enough extent for treatment to direct itself to an analysis of the projective defense. Though ideally we should like the transition to be orderly and treatment to pursue it without interruption, a temporary hiatus may well exist between the affectual and ideational complaints of the patient. In this turn of events, treatment is apt to be interrupted. But if this eventuality is handled properly and with understanding, the patient, more likely than not, will return in the future for further treatment.

---

4. To be sure, these do not exhaust the countertransference possibilities. An abundant variety of other possibilities exist, for example, the patient's promiscuity can arouse resentment in male therapists against an orgiastic, unfaithful, oedipal mother. But the pertinence of these other possibilities varies from therapist to therapist. Separation anxiety, castration anxiety, and penis envy, however, are experiential *donnees* — their pertinence never varies in the countertransference, only their quantities.

REFERENCES

Erikson, E. H. (1954). The dream specimen of psychoanalysis. In *Psychoanalytic Psychiatry and Psychology*, ed. R. P. Knight, pp. 131–170. New York: International Universities Press.

Fenichel, O. (1954). The economics of pseudologia phantastica. In *The Collected Papers, Second Series*, pp. 129–140. New York: Norton.

Freud, A. (1946). *The Ego and the Mechanisms of Defense*, pp. 73–93. New York: International Universities Press.

Freud, S. (1900). The interpretation of dreams. *Standard Edition* 4–5.

_____ (1911). Psycho-analytic notes on an autobiographical account of a case of paranoia (dementia paranoides). *Standard Edition* 12.

_____ (1927). Fetishism. *Standard Edition* 21.

Lewin, B. (1950). The Psychoanalysis of Elation. New York: Norton.

Lewis, H. B. (1959). Organization of the self as reflected in manifest dreams. *Psychoanalysis and the Psychoanalytic Review* 46:21–35.

Ostow, M. (1960). The psychic function of depression. *Psychoanalytic Quarterly* 29:355–394.

Reich, A. (1960). Pathologic forms of self-esteem regulation. *Psychoanalytic Study of the Child* 15:215–232.

Schafer, R. (1954). *Psychoanalytic Interpretation in Rorschach Testing*, pp. 231–55, 251, 279. New York: Grune & Stratton,

Sheppard, E., and Saul, L. (1958). An approach to a systematic study of ego function. *Psychoanalytic Quarterly* 27:237–244.

PART II

Social Realities

12

What is Sublimated in Sublimation?

The whole idea of sublimation has been a vagrant problem for psychoanalysis from the very beginning. This is because sublimation, in one of its meanings, refers to felicitous exercises of mind, while psychoanalysis is suspicious of any such simple creed. Also, since sublimation entails departures from those clinical matters that constitute the suitable subjects of the psychoanalytic method, whatever is sublimated in mental life escapes a certain technical authority of the psychoanalyst. For example, sublimation, in another of its meanings, reduces the significance of personal motive in the outcomes of mental life; that is, sublimation dissolves relations between the psychological origins of social and cultural works and their ultimate self-sustaining validity and import (Whitebook 1990); therefore sublimation deprives the psychoanalytic point of view of some of its investigative and interpretive privilege. Nevertheless, some idea of sublimation remains embedded in psychoanalytic thought, inasmuch as sublimation refers as well to a fundamental concern of psychoanalysis having to do with the ego's involvement with various material, social, and cultural realities.

Freud introduced the term sublimation early on to signify an obverse of neurosogenesis. In the long opening of the Dora case (Freud 1901), where he was summarizing his sexual theory of neurosis, he admitted that the very nature of his theory implicated one and all in perverse deviations from what he called at the time "the standard of normality." However, he went on to give assurances that in normality these deviations constitute only a stage of development in eventual socialization. As provisional stages "in the undifferentiated sexual disposition of the child," perversions are diverted in the course of development "to higher, asexual aims [and] by being 'sublimated' are destined to provide the energy for a great number of cultural achievements" (p. 50). By cultural achievement Freud did not mean necessarily an actual individual origination of symbol and artifact, but merely a symbolic capacity sufficient to enable a participation in various realms of established and available culture.

Then, toward the end of the Dora case, in the famous postscript where he gave an exposition of transference, Freud again employed the term sublimation, this time in connection with the observation that transference exists in degrees of primitivity. Compared to a neurotic transference, a *sublimated* transference is less primitive to the extent that it represents revisions, hence new editions, of the past by virtue of being subject to the moderating influences of the present, for example, "by cleverly taking advantage of some real peculiarity in the physician's person or circumstances . . ." (p. 116). Thus, through an assenting encounter with a piece of reality, a partial liberation from a pathogenic fixation is accomplished.

With these remarks Freud wanted to acknowledge aspects of psychological development that surpassed the constraints of a pathogenesis of conflict, defense, and the return of the repressed. He came back to these issues episodically (e.g., Freud 1905a, 1914, 1921, 1923), but nowhere in his reflections do we get the sense that he succeeded in transforming the idea of sublimation into a theoretically technical concept. He left it rather as a bridging idea that loosely joined, though as often separated, the clinical situation and some other ground seen at a distance. Although a sizeable literature has developed in connection with sublimation, by and large the technical status of the idea has not advanced significantly beyond the point Freud took it (see Boesky 1986, Glover 1931, Kubie 1962, Loewald 1988, Ricoeur 1970). Nevertheless, this is an edifying literature and a crucial one as well, in that it provides an orientation as to where certain boundaries occur between clinical and applied psychoanalysis (Kaplan 1988).

It is here that I want to examine a view of Castoriadis (1989), whose particular concern with the idea of sublimation is an elaboration of Freud's initial view that sublimation entails an assenting response of the personal ego to something presented to it as real and therefore independent of it. The ego's reckoning with an entity beyond itself is what complicates the problem of sublimation as something in addition to an economics of displacement and condensation and of compromise and defense. It is this consideration of reality that underlies a whole psychoanalytic conception of socialization. Castoriadis writes (p. 399), "To put [sublimation] in its proper place, we must recall this banal but evident fact that no one seems to take into account: To speak is already to sublimate."[1] What he means specifically is that to speak is to appropriate a cultural resource, namely, language, which exists in its own right beyond the contrivance of the individual psyche: "The 'subject' of language," Castoriadis goes on, "is not a 'subject' of drives. . . . To speak is a sublimated activity . . . because it is instrumented in and through an extrapsychic creation that goes beyond what the singular psyche is capable of doing by itself, i.e., the institution of language; [therefore] speaking always . . . implies that one is addressing other participants, *real* ones, situated in society. . . ."

We should note that in this view libidinal substitution as an outcome, say, of displacement is not yet sublimation; sublimation begins with the implication of something cultural in the social process of substitution. For example, the boot as a fetish does not yet count as a sublimation; such a fetish may be a preliminary stage of sublimation, but it still lacks a sufficient distinction as an object recognizable by a public larger than the fetishist. That is, a fetish is still too much of a drive-dominated substitution to count as a sublimation.

If sublimations are permeated with actual or virtual social significations that speak for themselves independently as their makers, then transitional objects also do not altogether qualify as sublimations in that a stranger in a nursery will not be able to

---

1. This puts one in mind of Freud's (1893) quoting in English a remark of an unidentified English writer, "The man who first flung a word of abuse at his enemy instead of a spear was the founder of civilization" (p. 36).

discern among the many things lying about which exactly has been turned into a transitional object by the baby who resides there (Kaplan 1972). Even though transitional objects are thought to be more facilitating of development than fetishes (Greenacre 1969), they are not sufficiently in the "public domain" to qualify as fully realized sublimations.

From such comparisons of fetishes, transitional objects, and language we derive the idea that sublimation exists in degrees. The closer analysts get to the "public-domain" component, or what Kuhns (1983) quoting Stokes, calls the "self-sufficient object" (p. 66) in mental life, the less privilege they have in regard to what they encounter (Kaplan 1984, 1990). Psychoanalysts have no technical access, for example, to the "institution of language" as they have to symptoms presented in the clinical situation. Having no clinical approach to "extrapsychic" institutions that socialize behavior, psychoanalysts resort to an applied psychoanalysis (Kaplan 1988).

But then, the subjects of applied psychoanalysis have no direct spokespersons regarding their creation, in the sense that a patient is a spokesperson for the creation of a fetish and the other subjects of clinical psychoanalysis. Hypothetical persons cannot be turned into patients, which is why their cultural achievements do not readily count as psychoanalytic data in the way that perversions, symptoms, and character do. Indeed, this relegation of the better part of sublimation to an applied psychoanalysis is why many psychoanalysts do not find the idea of sublimation particularly urgent or worth holding strong opinions about.

In the case of art we may well have an exception to this state of affairs. Unlike the fetish or the transitional object or the symptom for that matter, the work of art presents itself as first and foremost a recognizable self-sufficient and transpersonal object, and yet it is entirely possible for the psychoanalyst to make a patient of its creator and hope for direct testimony about how the work of art came into being. Whereas fixation and rigidity characterize the outcomes of psychopathology, art is fostered by personal variability even as it submits to the limitations required of an object that aspires to cultural recognition and value (Dervin 1990). Like individual development, art is an outcome of chance and necessity but in optimal measures. This is why knowledge of how its creator creates has always seemed promising for psychoanalytic reflections on socialization and adaptation. What remains to be seen is what direct testimony and observation of artists actually amount to.

Alas, one soon learns that, all things being equal, the successful work of art does not serve as a departure in the clinical situation the way, say, dreams or symptoms do. This fact may be unsettling at first, but one is convinced over time that this fact is not necessarily the result of some shortcoming in analytic technique. If successful by the patient's standards, a particular painting, poem, or any artistic achievement enters what might be called a state of limbo in the patient's reflections, and is thereafter referred to as little more than a marker of chronology or stage in the patient's life story, for example, "It was around the time I was doing those brown paintings." That is, the work of art in its own right becomes what might be called a nonsubject in the analysis. This has always surprised me in view of how otherwise important a work of art is to its artist.

Though my experience on this score has not really changed over the years, 20 years ago I might have reported this seemingly odd lacuna more hesitantly in deference to a certain prevailing arrogance in the literature about issues of analytic technique. Kanzer (1957), for example, in a paper on sublimation, spoke of the analyst's too often "condoning" acting out that looked like sublimation, and he advised invoking a "veto" over sublimations that joined resistances. He reported how he forbade a musician patient at one point in his analysis to give public concerts and at another point to replace a music teacher (pp. 680–681). However, such intrusive activity regarding a patient's creative calling has all but disappeared. I was pleased to come across a recent corroboration of the clinical experience I am reporting by Rose (1987), who writes, "Where the [art] work per se presents no problem, the subject hardly arises for clinical exploration" (p. 139).

Indeed, to force "interpretations" upon the patients' descriptions of their art is to commit what Lewin (1959) called "topographical errors." These are interventions informed by theory but whose actual phenomenological referent is not appropriately situated in the clinical field, as when one interprets, willy-nilly, the purchase of a triangular dinner chime as an enactment of oedipal wishes on an oral level. What is apt to be missing in such interpretive usurpations of the clinical situation is a signification in the patient's material of a fault in representation. Without some prefatory evidence of such a fault, interpretation is apt to be simply gratuitous and therefore to function like a joke that disavows rather than addresses the problem the analysand is engaged in at the moment.

This is not to say that the artist leaves the life of art entirely out of the analysis. On the contrary, an analysis of an artist is largely about rescuing of the life of art from the infiltrations of symptoms in the artist's ordinary life. However, it is the symptoms and their imperfections as representations that motivate a clinical process, not the work of art that analysis liberates from the artist's neurosis.

For example, a poet turning 40, whose published work enjoyed a significant reputation for its technical virtuosity, was distressed to find himself increasingly more involved in academic promotion than in writing poems. Early in his analysis he discovered how he had been constraining his poetic activities and powers to obfuscate and subdue a conflict over an ambition to secede from a younger generation of poets and to identify with an order of older and more established poets. His feelings of both moral anxiety and imposture derived from long-standing apprehensions about his sexual and generational affiliations in his family. He wondered about his sense of being his mother's eternal child, hence a disappointment to his older brothers and his father in respect to maturity and masculinity; also, by virtue of his early verbal gifts and academic achievement, he felt he was his mother's favorite in a household of males, but through means of questionable masculinity. Following a resolution of the immediate conflicts that paralyzed both his writing and his professional advancement, this patient continued analysis of his anxieties over matters in his personal life, which is not, in my experience, usual when an artist is restored to productivity in his or her art. The point is that although I would come across a few poems of his in publications I happened to subscribe to, and did become familiar with various influences on his poetic style, I had only the most general idea about his personal aesthetic project and knew next to nothing about what was going into his next book of poems. Indeed, he was never once moved to recite more than a phrase of something he had written or was currently writing. Nor did it ever seem analytically useful to explore the details of how a successful composition was performed, though there would be plenty of details about what he did mentally and behaviorally when he was having trouble getting into or finishing a poem.

Another patient, a painter also turning 40, presented a severe inhibition in completing work. "In the past three months," he complained, "I have painted 1500 square feet of canvas and have about 200 square feet to show for it." This was a man who had been troubled for years by paranoid fantasies that his success was being maligned behind his back by rival artists, who stole his ideas without giving him credit. Between the lines of reviews of his work, which were highly favorable, the patient construed a taunting and malicious subtext. Always a scrupulous technician, he was now immobilized by compulsive doing and undoing. For weeks on end, he would put paint on canvas and then "erase" it because he could not get any work to look equally good close up and at a distance. A dream, in which he was tormented by a decision whether to choose a knife or an arrow from a tray before him, expressed this problem of succeeding in two points of view simultaneously, that is, close up and at a distance. This dream opened up the current importance in his mental life of a harsh paternal introject that had become the patricidal aim of virtually every brushstroke. To slay his father close up or from a distance was a question that developed into a whole oedipal drama. I am reporting the themes of 15 months of an analysis, which the patient interrupted rather abruptly, inasmuch as he was emancipated from his compulsive doing and undoing and was once again productive and considerably less susceptible to feelings of being put upon and betrayed by colleagues and critics in the art world. As for my knowledge of his actual work, I never developed any clear idea of what exactly he painted, aside from a vague sense that he was influential as a species of "landscape" painter. However, I did learn a great deal about his conflict with temptations to paint easily accessible pictures, this in regard to a maternal muse who requested only sentimental entertainment.

A last vignette of how the work of art escapes the deep clinical attention given to other matters involves another painter. This was a young man who complained of a hysterical symptom consisting of several burning spots on his forehead, such as one would feel from a magnifying glass concentrating sunlight on the skin. Several weeks later, in one of his sessions, he described an afternoon in his studio when he was absorbed in turning out drawings of spots of light, which he now thought of as rendered visualizations of his forehead. In the ensuing months, these drawings went on to become the bases of huge paintings of chandeliers and then of domes, crowns, and other objects dramatized by spots of gathered light. His symptom was a motive for psychotherapy, which embarked upon a crisis of unrequited love and a theme of sexual martyrdom with reminiscences of primal-scene imaginings of his mother, whose outstretched arms he likened to a position of crucifixion. But typically, during his analytic sessions this patient had virtually no interest in the actual paintings he produced across the divide between ordinary life where his symptom resided and the art he produced. He spoke of this stretch of output simply as commodities that figured in his relations with his dealer and his public.

It was easy enough to figure out an etiological version of this patient's conversion symptom and even to see the symptom in his burst of "op art." But to see the pathogenic fantasy in the work is not the same as seeing the work in the fantasy. A psychoanalytic theory of the aptitude for a conversion symptom cannot be stretched to cover as well as aptitude for art. The best artist patients can give is little more than the bare fact of their nimble leap over the boundaries of everyday life.

What I am observing in the case of the artist is the remarkable paradox of so little said about a subject that constitutes an actual other life. Indeed, what could be called the artist's ordinary life—the life of interpersonal matters, including sex, family relations, standing in a social group—holds center stage in the analysis only long enough to be subtracted from the activity of making art. Once the making of art is restored to some optimal level, the conflicts that still may persist in the artist's ordinary life also diminish as motives for analysis. As for the work of art, it has no appeal as a realm of conflict. Only when there is trouble in the execution of the work will the analyst hear about poems that are merely jokes when they were intended to be humor, or brushstrokes that stab the oedipal father, or the actual failure of vision because the painter construes his subject as a maternal phallus. Here we might remind ourselves that it was to interruptions of productivity in the life of art that Freud (1910) addressed his study of Leonardo da Vinci.

The analyst has no business deciding unilaterally that the particular lack of reference to details of art work I am observing constitutes an exemption of resistance. In the course of his review of Loewald's study of sublimation, Fogel (1991) spoke to this clinical problem very prudently:

> Sound technique tells us mostly to act only where we see constraint and mostly to say only what we think we see of the defense and what is defended against. Ideally, only our patients should initiate and make value judgements upon their imagination and creativity, or decide which experiences and behaviors represent a deformation and which a fulfillment of their human potential [pp. 251–252]

So it is ultimately our clinical experience with artists themselves that confirms that works of art, unlike, say, dreams, are subject only to an applied psychoanalysis; for in the case of art there is no working-through; the art that succeeds the cure of the symptom escapes further clinical analysis. That the work of art is something crucially more than a return of the repressed is evident in the clinical fact that its achievement is not experienced by its creator as a fault in representation, which would otherwise be a motive for analysis. In this sense, there is a stage in sublimation that thereafter becomes opaque to the psychoanalytic method. Freud knew this early on. In his "Leonardo" study he noted, "Since artistic talent and capacity are intimately connected with sublimation we must admit that the nature of the artistic function is also inaccessible to us along psychoanalytic lines" (1910, p. 136).

Years later Freud remarked, "It is possible that sublimation arises out of some special process which would be held back by repression" (1919, p. 182). Much of the literature on the psychoanalytic theory of art is speculation about such "special processes" (e.g., Kris 1952, Rose 1987, 1990, Weissman 1967, 1969), and it is important to note that such speculation arises in reconstructions not only of the artist's mental life, but also of the characteristics of art itself and their effects on the viewer. Whereupon some version of an *ideal* reality is attributed to the work of art as an attainment of something optimal in the functions of "special processes." The attribution of something ideal is plausible because, again, psychoanalysis lacks the technical means to give as full an account of the fate of reality in a work of art as it can give of such a fate in neurosis.

Thus we can say for the moment that what is sublimated in sublimation has to do with one of the oldest and most persistent problems of psychoanalysis, namely, the function of the real and, in particular, the claims brought to bear upon this function by ordinary development and neurosis. A point of entry into these matters is Freud's (1911) "Formulations on the Two Principles of Mental Functioning," because this paper contains something crucial about the relation of art to a psychoanalytic version of reality. In this paper, Freud gave a definition of reality in terms of the ego's capacity to restrain an immediacy of drive discharge in the service of forming, as he put it, "a conception of the real circumstances in the external world and to endeavour to make a real alteration in them" (p. 219). In this way, the futility of passive hallucinatory solutions to the problem of desire is superseded by an active reckoning with the actual contingencies of satisfaction. "A new principle of mental functioning was thus introduced [in psychic development]; what was presented to the mind was no longer what was agreeable but what was real, even if it happened to be disagreeable" (Freud, p. 219).

However, with the development of the reality principle a new problem in the economy of pleasure arises. To put it in Freud's terminology, the reality pursued by the ego is a digression from the aims of the sexual instincts. In other words, a wish arising at Time A is no longer the same wish when the contingencies for its satisfaction postpone its fulfillment to Time B. Immediate and delayed pleasures are no longer synonymous experiences. At this juncture in Freud's argument a new quota of pleasure remains to be accounted for that further motivates the ego's delay; for such delay is at the expense of an immediate fulfillment of pleasure. Whereupon Freud gives us a precis of socialization and the compensatory roles of social institutions, such as religion and education, conformities to which introduce narcissistic gratifications as compensations for what is lost in the postponements of libidinal gratification. But, of course, neurosis is the protest to such socialization in a curtailment of the ego's involvement in realities beyond its own memories of satisfaction.

Now it is here that Freud brings in the issue of art as a cultural haven from the inevitable imperfections of the development he has described. "*Art* brings about a reconciliation between the two principles in a peculiar way" (p. 224). Artists, he tells us, are in no less a plight than others, but owing to special gifts, they are able to render "precious reflections of reality" that are free of all the problematic interstices between the two principles of mental functioning. Moreover, artists can achieve this not only because others feel the same dissatisfaction with the renunciation demanded by reality and "the long roundabout path of making real alterations in the external world," but also because "that dissatisfaction, which results from the replacement of the pleasure principle by the reality principle, is itself a part of reality" (p. 224).

Two realities figure in this statement. There is the reality of the libidinal object and its subsequent heirs—the institutions of civilization—in deference to which we suffer dissatisfaction in the form of distressing affects that contend with the ego's hold on reality. Then there is the dissatisfaction itself, not as a provisional psychic state, but as real in its own right—"itself a part of reality"—this when it is objectified as a perception. This unexpendable phenomenon of the reality principle was Freud's point about art. Dissatisfaction as a piece of objectified reality is no longer a motive of defense or action. Thus whenever we encounter the telltale signs of art, as something heard, seen, watched, or read, the affect that arises in the spectator is purified of its instrumental role in mental life and can then be experienced with virtually no purpose beyond itself.

These ideas can be traced back in psychoanalytic thought to Freud's theory of jokes and the comic. Paraphrasing the philosopher Kuno Fischer, Freud (1905b) wrote, "the aesthetic attitude towards an object is characterized by the condition that we do not ask anything of the object, especially no satisfaction of our serious needs" (pp. 10–11). Along these lines of the nonutilitarian function of art, we find these musings of Auden (1968): "The condition of mankind is, and always has been, so miserable and depraved that, if anyone were to say to the poet: 'For God's sake, stop singing and do something useful like putting on the kettle and fetching the bandages,' what just reason could he give for refusing? But nobody says this" (p. 27).

Because they are not functional, affects entailed in the experience of art are not problematic along the lines of the Time A–Time B conflict of the two principles of mental functioning. In states of drive arousal artists have a way of divorcing themselves temporarily from the myriad regulatory devices of ordinary life and becoming involved in certain elemental materials of art—paint, language, musical forms, mimetic behavior—with which they carry on an activity whose solutions to drive arousal result in luxuriant communications. Indeed, art has no other end than communication. In art a scenario is created for a prolongation and complication of affect that is radically different from the fate of affect in ordinary life. (Eissler [1971] coined the term "doxaletheic" to refer to the special communicative power of the artist.) This is why we think of optimal sublimation not as a muting of passion in deference to the reality principle but, on the contrary, as passion expressed, clarified, and, as we shall see, comprehended.

Now, if the artist on the couch conveys little more about the devices of sublimation than the bare fact that an art work is a mysterious leap of some sort from the personal to the cultural, we should not be hasty to make this the end of the ride for psychoanalysis. In addition to this "leap" from mind to culture, psychoanalysis reckons with many discontinuities. In fact, each element that figures in a psychoanalytic account of mental life is, in a crucial sense, discontinuous with regard to every other element—for example, trauma and defense, meaning and force, fantasy and structure, idea and affect. So where the artist's testimony leaves off, the thread may be picked up in the work of art itself and specifically in what the work *does* rather than what one might claim it says.

"In life, the other's otherness is not necessarily our joy and liberation." The analyst knows this well from observations of transference, which is the analysand's protest against the analyst's otherness. However, the remark comes from Goldman's (1975) study of the art of acting. It is prefatory to a passage in which Goldman is making a point about something unusual in the realization of affect in theatrical performance, which is a point that can be extended to all art. Goldman notes that

> in spite of the excitements of performance, we see the people on stage with a relaxed clarity of attention that cannot be paralleled outside the theater, since certain distracting claims that other people inevitably make upon us in ordinary life do not apply. Outside the theater, the need to acknowledge and to be acknowledged by the people we encounter, the pressure of fear, responsibility, and uncertainty that we must feel in any person's presence, assures that time and space themselves are only blurrily felt and possessed by us. [pp. 120–121]

He goes on:

> To put it another way: One difference between actors in a theater and people we see on the street is that, whatever we may mean by the word, we identify more readily with the actors. We identify because we are free to do so; we are not threatened, as in life, by the otherness of other people. It is of course quite possible in our daily affairs to treat people as if they were merely performing for our entertainment; but the moral position and (unless we are lunatics) the experiential quality of such a relation is very different from our relation to actors on a stage. In the theater, the others we watch—frightening, exciting, touching as they are—can do no harm to us, and we can do nothing for them—we are not obligated to save Desdemona from Othello, because we can't. A man, performed by an actor, is so present

that we can respond to his otherness, as we never quite can in real life, with a sense of freedom. In the theater, as perhaps otherwise only in our most intimate or illumined moments, the other's otherness is our joy and liberation. [p. 121]

In an exchange of letters in the *American Psychologist*, Frijda (1989), who has written incisively on the subject of emotion, came up with a virtual paraphrase of this idea of Goldman. Since Frijda's theory of emotion has much to do with assessments of external reality, he was called to account for emotions arising in art, which, as his correspondent argued, puts such reality in abeyance. To this Frijda replied that the assessment of reality always involves a duality: that which is really real is distinguished from that which is only apparently real. (The analyst is familiar with this problem in its various psychopathologies, one of which is the paranoid idea.) About art, Frijda commented, "The play with that duality, of course, is precisely the fun of art. The assessed reality allows us to suffer grief or anxiety; the simultaneously assessed nonreality allows us to enjoy that suffering and that is why we go to the theater" (p. 1547). (Indeed, in an early paper on theater, Freud [1906] spoke about identification with the ordeals of the stage character, an identification that is enhanced by the viewer's knowledge that theater action is ultimately only a game.) In psychoanalytic parlance, we could say that art invites a distressing affect that does not become a motive of defense, but rather survives as a protracted experience that is perceived and examined in a manner fitting reality. Frijda calls this affect promoted by art "aesthetic emotion."

In a cunning discussion of art, Lévi-Strauss (1966) specified a general characteristic of art that both Goldman and Frijda allude to. The art object, Lévi-Strauss argued, works by means of a reduction of the dimensions of life. Thus he described paintings, sculpture, music, indeed all art, as reductions in life's scale and properties, hence as experiments in miniaturization. "This quantitative transposition extends and diversifies our power over a homologue of the thing, and by means of it the latter can be grasped, assessed and apprehended at a glance" (p. 23).

Regarding emotion, such miniaturization fosters amplification because a mere "homologue of the thing" does not necessitate defensive foreclosures. Lévi-Strauss's discussion of a doll as homologue is reminiscent of Goldman's remarks about the actor, who is also a homologue.

> A child's doll is no longer an enemy, a rival or even an interlocutor. . . . In the case of miniatures, in contrast to what happens when we try to understand an object or living creature of real dimensions, knowledge of the whole precedes knowledge of the parts. And even if this is an illusion, the point of the procedure is to create or sustain the illusion, which gratifies the intelligence and gives rise to a sense of pleasure which can already be called aesthetic on these grounds alone. [pp. 23–24]

One of the contributions psychoanalysis makes to the understanding of aesthetic emotion comes from its theory that manifest experience is an outcome—a derivative—of a whole consideration of endopsychic scenarios and functions. Grossman's (1992) extraordinary study of transformation within mental organization is a reminder of the abundant technicalities of the concept of derivative. As a derivative, affect calls attention to much more than itself. As information about other information, affect represents a complex state of affairs, which becomes increasingly evident when affect survives contemplation. A paradigmatic exposition of this psychoanalytic view of affect is Freud's "Mourning and Melancholia" (1917). In this study Freud accounts for a certain depressive affect as an outcome of a fantasized object-relations scenario consisting of an abandonment by an ambivalent object due to the subject's moral unworthiness. Thereafter the subject protests in depressive enactments derived from identifications with the negative traits of the persecutory object. The point is that a psychoanalytic view of affect, including aesthetic emotion, includes as well the possibility of certain experiences of the endopsychic.

A recent paper by Trosman on art and unconscious fantasy provides a bridge from this concern of psychoanalysis with endopsychic processes to art as a scenario for the experience of such processes. One of Trosman's models for the analysis of the

literary expression of the endopsychic is Freud's conclusion to
the Schreber case, where Freud speaks of Schreber's "rays of
God" as "a condensation of the sun's rays, of nerve fibers, and
spermatozoa, [which] are in reality a concrete representation
and projection outward of libidinal cathexes . . . This fantasy [of
the rays of God] . . . is a representation via endopsychic perception of narcissistic regression and the emptying of object
cathexes" (Trosman 1990, p. 51). This is not unheard of in the
testimony of painters. In the brochure accompanying his exhi-
bition at The New York Museum of Modern Art in the summer
of 1990, Francis Bacon is quoted, "I am just trying to make
images of my nervous system as accurately as I can." And here
we might recall the patient I described who painted images of
how his conversion symptom felt. Trosman went on to speak of
poetic forms, tropes, metaphor, alliteration, metonymy, synec-
doche as expressive of endopsychic processes such as merger
and separation.[2]

Aaron (1986), because his view of theater performance is
informed by psychoanalysis, is able to trace a further aspect of
our experience of theater to a correspondence between the
actor's assimilation of a script and the perception by an audience
of a process of internalization (p. 99). This experience of the
script in performance is not, of course, explicitly conceptualized
by the audience; but some sense of internalization is registered
in theater to a higher degree than in life, where it more silently
officiates impulse and desire, leading to more consternation
than wonder. Moreover, the performance of scripts, such as
plays and musical compositions, is an achievement of internalization surpassing mere imitation or a psychopathology of
introjection.

Using one of William Carlos Williams's "empirical" poems as
a talking point, Spencer (1988)[3] showed how the endopsychic in
poetry figures even in the seeming absence of any density of

---

2. For a list of references to the problem of endopsychic perception in Freud's
writings, see Grossman and Simon (1969, p. 93).

3. In "What Would Wordsworth Have Said About the Wolf Man's Dream."
Unpublished.

conflict, thematic figuration, or emotion-laden image. The Williams poem is called "The Red Wheelbarrow":

so much depends
upon

a red wheel
barrow

glazed with rain
water

beside the white
chickens.[4]

In reminding us about Freud's idea of "ultra-clarity" as a sign of the screening activity of screen memories, Spencer shows why the reader experiences more in connection with this poem than is apt at first to meet the eye. In the vividness of trivialities, we detect the uncanny presence of a process of remembering and forgetting, which is an endopsychic vicissitude of repression. This tantalizing presence of "ultra-clarity" in our responses to Williams's several bare lines of verse suggests why the poem is more compelling than it ought to be. "For Tennessee Williams's heroine," Spencer concludes, "so much depended on the kindness of strangers; for William Carlos Williams's poem, given the absence of manifest conflict or psychological density, I think much depends on the clarity of chickens."

In what sense can it be said that the poet knew this? I am not at all sure that he even cared to know this, which brings me back to the clinical experience I reported. I would say that the poet knew when he succeeded in something exceptionally well, but not quite how he succeeded. This lack of interest and perhaps privilege about creative functions can be corroborated abundantly in a perusal of *Artists on Art*, a huge collection compiled

---

4. William Carlos Williams: *Collected Poems 1909–1939, Vol. 1.* Copyright 1938 by New Directions Publishing Corporation. Reprinted by permission of New Directions.

by Goldwater and Treves (1945) of commentaries by Western painters on the making of art over the past six centuries. By and large, technique is what interested these artists rather than the effects and interpretation of art. The epigraph of this volume from John Constable is apt: "I am anxious that the world should be inclined to look to painters for information on painting" (p. 7). Freud (1908) came to a similar conclusion about creative writers. If asked how they manage to make such an impression on us, Freud observed, they give no explanation, or none that is satisfactory (p. 143).

However, before we conclude that such restriction of interest is also a restriction of edification, we should note that the artist's interest in technique is like the analyst's interest in metapsychology. Technique is what transforms the phenomena of nature — for example, vocalizations, noise, color — and of society — for example, vocabulary, canvas, narratives — into art along lines similar to the way that the psyche, instantiated by Freudian metapsychology, transforms the strivings of the body into culture. In this sense, technique is the very "mind" of art, and insofar as all art retains abundant evidence of the technique that brought about the transformations of nature and society that constitute its very existence, art can transport us into ontological reveries that lend an ideal coherence to all the means and ends of our individual humanity. But it is here that psychoanalytic concerns with sublimation trail off into philosophical and other interdisciplinary concerns with the sublime.

CONCLUDING REMARKS

Although the problem of sublimation entered psychoanalysis as a consideration of the effects of transference on reality, the problem was soon referred to the creation of art because, after the facts of skill and talent, sublimation underwrites the success of the artist's whole project. In a record of personal artistic accomplishment, creative failure becomes the clearest evidence of the undermining of sublimation by intrusions of neurosogenesis. This idea, which was explored by Freud (1910) in his study of Leonardo da Vinci, has been repeatedly verified in subsequent clinical experience with artists as patients. However, as magnified as the problem of sublimation promises to be in the case of artists, the concept of sublimation, at least as it refers to ego functions, is still not readily captured by a clinical point of view. One reason for this opacity is that a work of art of an analysand consists of too great a representational composure to motivate an informative clinical interest in the patient.

But inasmuch as the contagion of art extends to a public of ordinary spectators, it could be said that sublimation entails not a special complement of functions, but a special deployment of ordinary functions. Thus the problem of sublimation is encompassed in a general participation in culture, where, for any participant, the question of what is sublimated in sublimation may be answered along lines of alterations in the rate and extent of defenses and other transformations of drive arousal. Such an economics is a means to renovations of experience with the puzzle of one's humanity and the gift of culture, which, like all reality, resides beyond individual contrivance.

REFERENCES

Aaron, S. (1986). *Stage Fright: Its Role in Acting.* Chicago, IL: University of Chicago Press.

Auden, W. H. (1968). *The Dyer's Hand.* New York: Vintage.

Boesky, D. (1986). Questions about sublimation. In *Psychoanalysis: The Science of Mental Conflict,* ed. A. D. Richards and M. S. Willick. Hillsdale, NJ: Analytic Press.

Castoriadis, C. (1989). The state of the subject today. *American Imago* 46:371–412.

Dervin, D. (1990). *Creativity and Culture: A Psychoanalytic Study of the Creative Process in the Arts, Sciences, and Culture.* Rutherford, NJ: Fairleigh Dickinson University Press.

Eissler, K. R. (1971). *Discourse on Hamlet and HAMLET.* New York: International Universities Press.

Fogel, J. (1991). Review of *Sublimation,* by H. W. Loewald. *Journal of the American Psychoanalytic Association* 39:250–257.

Freud, S. (1893). On the psychical mechanism of hysterical phenomena: a lecture. *Standard Edition* 3.

—————— (1901). Fragment of an analysis of a case of hysteria. *Standard Edition* 7.

—————— (1905a). Three essays on the theory of sexuality. *Standard Edition* 7.

_____ (1905b). Jokes and their relation to the unconscious. *Standard Edition* 8.

_____ (1906). Psychopathic characters on the stage. *Standard Edition* 7.

_____ (1908). Creative writers and day-dreaming. *Standard Edition* 9.

_____ (1910). Leonardo da Vinci and a memory of his childhood. *Standard Edition* 11.

_____ (1911). Formulations on the two principles of mental functioning. *Standard Edition* 12.

_____ (1913). The claims of psychoanalysis to scientific interest. *Standard Edition* 13.

_____ (1914). On narcissism: an introduction. *Standard Edition* 14.

_____ (1917). Mourning and melancholia. *Standard Edition* 14.

_____ (1919). Lines of advance in psycho-analytic therapy. *Standard Edition* 17.

_____ (1921). Group psychology and the analysis of the ego. *Standard Edition* 18.

_____ (1923). The ego and the id. *Standard Edition* 19.

Frijda, J. (1989). Aesthetic emotions and reality. *American Psychology* 44:1546–1547.

Glover, E. (1931). Sublimation, substitution, and social anxiety. *International Journal of Psycho-Analysis* 12:263–297.

Goldman, M. (1975). *The Actor's Freedom: Toward a Theory of Drama*. New York: Viking.

Goldwater, R., and Treves, M. (1945). *Artists on Art*. New York: Pantheon.

Greenacre, P. (1969). The fetish and the transitional object. *Psychoanalytic Study of the Child* 24:144–164.

Grossman, W. I. (1992). Hierarchies, boundaries, and representation in the Freudian model of mental organization. *Journal of the American Psychoanalytic Association* 40:27–62.

Grossman, W. I., and Simon, B. (1969). Anthropomorphism: motive, meaning, and causality in psychoanalytic theory. *Psychoanalytic Study of the Child* 24:78–111.

Kanzer, M. (1957). Acting out, sublimation, and reality testing. *Journal of the American Psychoanalytic Association* 5:663–674.

Kaplan, D. M. (1972). Reflections on Eissler's concept of the doxaletheic function. *American Imago* 29:353–376.

_____ (1984). "Thoughts for the times on war and death": a psychoanalytic address on an interdisciplinary problem. *International Review of Psycho-Analysis* 11:131–141.

_____ (1988). The psychoanalysis of art: some ends, some means. *Journal of the American Psychoanalytic Association* 36:259–294.

_____ (1990). Some theoretical and technical aspects of gender and social reality in clinical psychoanalysis. *Psychoanalytic Study of the Child* 45:3–24.

Kris, E. (1952). *Psychoanalytic Explorations in Art*. New York: International Universities Press.

Kubie, L. S. (1962). The fallacious misuse of the concept of sublimation. *Psychoanalytic Quarterly* 31:73–79.

Kuhns, R. (1983). *Psychoanalytic Theory of Art*. New York: Columbia University Press.

Lévi-Strauss, C. (1966). *The Savage Mind*. Chicago, IL: University of Chicago Press.

Lewin, B. D. (1959). The analytic situation: topographic considerations. *Psychoanalytic Quarterly* 28:455–469.

Loewald, H. W. (1988). *Sublimation*. New Haven, CT: Yale University Press.

Ricoeur, P. (1970). *Freud and Philosophy*. New Haven, CT: Yale University Press.

Rose, G. (1987). *Trauma and Mastery in Life and Art*. New Haven, CT: Yale University Press.

—— (1990). From ego-defense to reality enhancement: updating the analytic perspective on art. *American Imago* 47:69–80.

Trosman, H. (1990). Transformations of unconscious fantasy in art. *Journal of the American Psychoanalytic Association* 38:47–66.

Weissman, P. (1967). Theoretical considerations of ego regression and ego functions in creativity. *Psychoanalytic Quarterly* 36:37–50.

—— (1969). Creative fantasies and beyond the reality principle. *Psychoanalytic Quarterly* 38:110–133.

Whitebook, J. (1990). Review of *Freudian Appraisals and Reappraisals*, vol. 3, ed. P. Stepansky. *International Journal of Psycho-Analysis* 71:173–175.

13

Surrealism and Psychoanalysis

If affairs are something more than flirtations, they are also something less than marriages. They begin brightly in those provisional realms between disparate existences where differences have little chance to become reciprocities. Sooner or later conflicts of interest arise that only a dissolution of partnership can relieve. This, I submit, describes the relationship between art and its many academic and political theories (Kaplan 1988), and therefore, specifically, between Surrealism and psychoanalysis.

In one of its more familiar versions, the tale of the passion of the Surrealists for psychoanalysis begins around 1916 with Andre Breton's encounter with the writings of Sigmund Freud. Breton had been serving as a medical aide in the psychiatric center at Saint-Dizier where he was fascinated by the hallucinatory and delusional phenomena of the mental patients evacuated from the front. He tried his hand at interpreting these states of mind along psychoanalytic lines. After the war he transposed certain features of the psychoanalytic method into what came to be known as automatic writing, a technique of literary composition that Breton was to advocate for all the arts. In 1919 Breton began a correspondence with Freud, and two years later he actually paid a visit to Freud (Davis 1973).

By 1924 Breton had become the titular founder of Surrealism, and in his "First Manifesto" (1924/1969) he credited Freud with the discovery of that whole region of the mental life repudiated by the stale realities of social conformity. Moreover, psychoanalysis was the method for restoring one's residence in this forsaken paradise of fancy, sex, and poetry, where each of us, untroubled by necessities of talent, practice and standard, becomes an artist. It was in the "First Manifesto" that Breton defined Surrealism in a way that is immediately suggestive of the psychoanalytic method: "SURREALISM, *n.* Psychic automatism in its pure state, by which one proposes to express . . . the actual functioning of thought . . . in the absence of any control exercised by reason [and] exempt from any aesthetic or moral concern." Breton then gave a philosophic definition: "Surrealism is based on the belief in the superior reality of certain forms of previously neglected associations, in the omnipotence of dream, in the disinterested play of thought." Moreover, this "superior reality" is the solution to "all the principal problems of life" (p. 26). This quote gives us a premonition of the end of the affair.

On his side, Freud was flattered by such benediction. When the sculptor Oscar Nemon asked him in 1931 how he felt about his designation as the Patron Saint of Surrealism, Freud replied, "It is wonderful. The Surrealists send me their newspaper daily with a wonderful dedication on the first page." However, Freud's next remark conveys a rather familiar modesty with regard to certain cultural matters. "I read it every day—but when I am finished with it—I have to admit—I do not find anything in the paper I really understand" (Meng 1956/1973, p. 351). This statement accords with what Freud observed about himself all along. His study of the Moses of Michelangelo (1914) begins: "I may say at once that I am no connoisseur in art, but simply a layman. I am unable rightly to appreciate many of the methods used and the effects obtained in art" (p. 211).

As for modern art, Freud was intolerant. On this score, we have a marvelously playful letter to Karl Abraham in 1922 acknowledging a charcoal drawing of Abraham by the Expressionist artist Tihaniy:

Dear Friend,
I have received the drawing that is supposed to be your portrait.
It is abominable.

> I know what an admirable person you are, which makes it the
> more shattering that such a cruel penalty should have to be
> exacted for such a trivial blot on your character as your tolerance
> or sympathy for modern "art." I hear from Lampl that the artist
> said that that was how he saw you. People like that should be the
> last to have access to analytic circles, because they are all too
> unwanted illustrations of Adler's theory that it is just individuals
> with severe innate defects of vision who become artists and
> draughtsmen. . . . [Freud/Abraham 1907–1926/1965, p. 332]

This attitude toward modern art persisted almost to the end of Freud's life. In connection with a visit by Salvador Dali to Freud's first London home in 1938, Freud wrote to Stefan Zweig, who had arranged the meeting, how he—Freud—had looked upon the Surrealists all along as absolute cranks, despite their having chosen him their patron saint. Any leniency in this attitude was too little and too late: "The young Spaniard, however [Dali was 34 at the time], with his candid fanatical eyes and his undeniable technical mastery, has made me reconsider my opinion. It would in fact be very interesting to investigate analytically how a picture like this came to be painted." Freud goes on to speculate about the ways in which Surrealism tries the limits of art, and to suggest that such considerations constitute "serious psychological problems" (E. Freud 1960, pp. 448–449).

It was not only Freud's doubts about what the Surrealists were up to on the artistic front that made him wary about them. He also had reservations about the Surrealists' grasp and appreciation of psychoanalysis itself. While writing *Les Vases Communicantes* in 1932, which contained some fifty dreams of various Surrealist artists, Breton invited Freud to make a contribution in the way of a few interpretive reactions. Freud responded with the admonition, " . . a mere collection of dreams without the dreamers' associations, without the knowledge of the circumstances in which they occurred, tells me nothing, and I can hardly imagine what it could tell anyone" (Davis 1973, p. 128). However much Breton wanted to give Freud a starring role in this literary venture, Freud was clearly married to psychoanalysis.

Not incidentally, the eventual publication of *The Communi-cating Receptacles* became an occasion for a very painful quarrel between Freud and Breton over some trivial bibliographical matter in "The Interpretation of Dreams," a contretemps that ended on a published note of Breton's renewed devotion to Freud. The larger causes of Freud and Breton were too disparate to enable any real mitigating, let alone lasting, collaboration.

But the implication of psychoanalysis in the Surrealist move-ment involved much more than the direct encounters of its principals and, for that matter, much more than the explicit interests and methods of "The Interpretation of Dreams," which had become a virtual handbook of Surrealism. In the manifes-toes of Breton, which were subscribed to by a whole coterie of painters, poets, and performers, Surrealism was as much a social and political program as a school of art with its own technical definitions. It was, as Blanchot was to call it, "a state of mind" (Waldberg 1965, p. 45). In psychoanalysis, as in Marxism, the Surrealists divined a kindred impiety toward the social order that is most assuredly in Freud, should one have a mind to see it. In the Surrealist movement, however, this spirit is absolute and strives not for a revision of the social order but for an annihilation of all values. It is exemplified in Breton's "Second Manifesto," published in 1930, where Surrealism is equated with a "total revolt, insubordination, of sabotage according to rule." Breton insisted upon a definitive spontaneity and good riddance to all judgment. "The simplest Surrealist act," he hypberbolized, "consists of dashing into the street, pistol in hand and firing blindly, as fast as one can pull the trigger, into the crowd" (p. 125).[1]

---

1. I am indebted to Dr. Martin J. Gliserman for calling my attention to an otherwise bygone publication that construed such exhortations as cultural underpinnings of the rise of fascism in the Europe of the '20s and '30s. In a 1941 paper "Surrealism as Symptom," Efraim Rosenzweig examined certain short-comings of Breton's grasp of psychoanalysis and went on to argue that just as Futurism was the psychic forerunner of Mussolini, the full-blown doctrine of Surrealism corresponded to visions of Hitler's fascism with its suppression of reason and its absolute opposition to political classicism in an effort to establish a "new order." Though Breton was outspoken against the fascism that was taking hold in Europe, Rosenzweig argues that such denunciations were

While nothing so expressly Dionysian can be found in the psychoanalytic literature, something of such subversiveness lurks everywhere. For example, Freud concluded his long reflection on "Civilization and Its Discontents" (1930), which was published the same year as Breton's "Second Manifesto," with a most iconoclastic statement:

> For a wide variety of reasons, it is very far from my intention to express an opinion upon the value of human civilization. I have endeavored to guard myself against the enthusiastic prejudice which holds that our civilization is the most precious thing that we possess or could acquire and that its path will necessarily lead to heights of unimagined perfection. I can at least listen without indignation to the critic who is of the opinion that when one surveys the aims of cultural endeavor and the means it employs, one is bound to come to the conclusion that the whole effort is not worth the trouble. [pp. 144–145]

Indeed, in a letter of June 5, 1910 to the Reverend Pfister, Freud (1963) expressed an analogous impiety at a practical level with therapeutic purpose. Criticizing a clinical paper of Pfister, Freud observed:

> Well, then, I think your *Analysis* suffers from the hereditary vice of–virtue; it is the work of too decent a man, who feels himself bound to discretion . . . [which]is incompatible with an analysis; to provide the latter one would have to be unscrupulous . . . behave like an artist who buys paints with his wife's house-keeping money or uses the furniture as firewood to warm the studio for his model. Without that kind of unscrupulousness the job cannot be done.[p. 38]

Such liquidation of manners and conventions is part of the stuff of modernity (Cuddihy 1974). Epistemologically, psycho-analysis constantly challenges the idea that psychological truth

---

irresponsibly voiced because Breton refused to reflect on the implications of his rhetoric and follow its political ramifications. To be sure, such a political critique of Surrealism was not rare in the '30s and '40s. The rise of Hitler was often portrayed against a background of empty and aimless Bohemian gaiety that was inspired by Surrealist doctrine.

entails stable essences and fixed semiotic structures. Psychoanalysis undermines these structures in the clinical situation showing them to be provisional states of false consciousness (Barratt 1984). The point is that for psychoanalysis knowledge is inseparable from method, and in this regard it joins a vast epistemic self-consciousness that characterizes every aspect of modern culture.

Indeed, the Freudian revolution can be said to have begun with Freud's insight that hysterical symptoms were the outcomes not of fixed lesions in the central nervous system or organic degeneracy, but of dynamic processes entailing psychic trauma, defense, and the return of the repressed. Thereafter, all psychoanalytic concepts are distinguished by their implications of process embodied in outcomes. This is what distinguishes, for example, a psychoanalytic concept of the dream from all other designations of the dream. In psychoanalysis, the very term dream embodies such processes, for example, condensation, displacement, as account for any symptomatic return of the repressed. Hence psychoanalytic interpretation entails the discovery of how outcome is related to process.

In fact, we have here Freud's whole interpretive endeavor with the Moses of Michelangelo. In this study, Freud had nothing to say about the formal achievements of Michelangelo's sculpture. Instead, he set about to reconstruct the prior action that led to the outcome represented by the eternal present of the statue. Thus he gave a historical dimension to a purely spatial entity. Moreover, to advance this purpose, Freud even commissioned a series of drawings of Moses illustrating his reconstruction of the mood and action of Moses that led up to the actual moment embodied by the statue as we see it. These line drawings are printed in the paper itself.

Insofar as Surrealism is also a concern with process in a faith that outcome will take care of itself, it shares with psychoanalysis much that is characteristic of the spirit of modernity in the science, art, and philosophy of our times. Indeed, the whole affair between psychoanalysis and Surrealism achieves one of its finest moments in the analogy that can be drawn between Freud's study of the Moses of Michelangelo and Duchamps's "Nude Descending a Staircase." A comparison of Freud's ap-

proach to the Michelangelo sculpture and Duchamps's ren-
dering of what can be called process might be a point of
departure into a whole account of congruences between Surrealism and psychoanalysis, focusing on their explorations of the
hallucinatory, of the disjunctions of the social and cultural and
the disorientations of modern life, of the universalization of the
plight of being human in so-called primitive and modern
societies, and much else.

Alas, as time wore on, such intimate moments receded; for
the Surrealists never read the fine print of psychoanalysis and
therefore made nothing of certain crucial differences between
their perspectives on a number of things. Among these were the
Freudian view of the ordeal of civilization and a Surrealist view
of a politics of experience. In one of Breton's manifestoes written
with Louis Aragon called "The Quinquagenary of Hysteria"
(Waldberg 1965) we find this concluding remark, "Hysteria is
not a pathological phenomenon but can be considered in every
respect a supreme means of expression" (p. 62). This theme of
disposing of Freud's formulations on the *two* principles of
mental functioning (1911) becomes increasingly prominent in
the Surrealist tradition. In 1934 at the Museum of Modern Art,
Dali, for example, speaks of realism as a mental prison, whereas
"Surrealism attempts to deliver the subconscious from the
principle of reality, thus finding a source of splendid and
delirious images" (Ashton 1973, p. 96).

By the 1960s, it was no longer psychoanalysis but R. D. Laing
and others like him—Wilhelm Reich and Fritz Perls, for example—who were adopted by the heirs of the Surrealist movement. Laing's *The Politics of Experience* (1967) became a handbook
of the counterculture movement as *The Interpretation of Dreams*
had been a handbook of the Surrealist movement in bygone
years. Laing describes schizophrenia as a transcendental experience, while he defines normality as a corruption of repression,
denial, splitting, and so on (p. 27). "In schizophrenia," Laing
writes, "the ego becomes the servant of the divine, no longer its
betrayer" (pp. 144–145).

But if to psychoanalysis normality is not a privileged state,
neither is schizophrenia; for schizophrenia is also a problem of
repression, denial, splitting, and so on, a state purchased at the

expense of the instinctual life. In other words, to psychoanalysis the normal and the abnormal are vicissitudes of each other, and to overlook this is to fail to appreciate one of the most radical consequences of the psychoanalytic point of view, which is its subversion of the very idea of the transcendental, a ruthless revelation of the dynamics of illusion.

Thus for a significant but limited period of time, psychoanalysis and Surrealism came together for purposes of separate advantage. In its traffic with Surrealism, psychoanalysis doubtless saw some chance for greater popularity, especially in France. Nor was Freud indifferent to the possibility of seeing his ideas justified in realms other than the clinical. On its side, art always welcomes new ways to interpret life in culture. With some assurance that an interpretive response exists for certain developments in form and content, the artist develops courage to surpass a present state of art in experiments with the future. Psychoanalysis provided such assurance, which the Surrealists used to the artistic advantage of the whole twentieth century.

REFERENCES

Ashton, D. (1973). *The New York School: A Cultural Reckoning*. New York: Viking.

Barratt, B. (1984). *Psychic Reality and Psychoanalytic Knowing*. Hillsdale, N.J.: Analytic Press.

Breton, Andre (1924/1953). *Manifestoes of Surrealism*. Ann Arbor, MI: University of Michigan Press, 1969.

Cuddihy, J. (1974). *The Ordeal of Civility*. New York: Basic Books.

Davis, F. (1973). Three letters from Sigmund Freud to Andre Breton. *Journal of the American Psychoanalytic Association* 21:127-134.

Freud, E., ed. (1960). *Letters of Sigmund Freud*. New York: Basic Books.

Freud, S. (1911). Formulations on the two principles of mental functioning. *Standard Edition* 12.

_____ (1914). The Moses of Michelangelo. *Standard Edition* 13.

_____ (1930). Civilization and its discontents. *Standard Edition* 21.

_____ (1909-1939). *Psychoanalysis and Faith: Dialogues with the Reverend Oskar Pfister*, ed. H. Meng and E. Freud. New York: Basic Books, 1963.

Freud, S., and K. Abraham. (1909-1926). *The Letters of Sigmund Freud and Karl Abraham*, ed. H. C. Abraham and E. Freud. New York: Basic Books, 1965.

Kaplan, D. M. (1988). The psychoanalysis of art: some ends, some means. *Journal of the American Psychoanalytic Association* 36:259–294.

Laing, R. D. (1967). *The Politics of Experience.* New York: Pantheon.

Meng, H. (1956). Freud and the sculptor. In *Freud As We Knew Him,* ed. H. M. Riutenbeck, pp. 350–352. Detroit, MI: Wayne State University Press, 1973.

Rosenzweig, E. M. (1941). Surrealism as symptom. *American Imago* 2:286–295.

Waldberg, P. (1965). *Surrealism.* New York: Oxford University Press.

14

The Psychoanalysis of Art

Each of us in his or her way appreciates a difference between psychoanalysis strictly speaking and psychoanalysis merely in a manner of speaking. Much that besets that errant activity we call applied psychoanalysis has to do with the various concerns we have about this difference. Whereas clinical psychoanalysis furnishes the technical meaning of the terminology of psychoanalytic discourse, the psychoanalysis of such matters as social institutions, historical events, and literary texts entails a dislocation of such discourse and a trial of its meaning. Freud (1930) recognized this problem and counseled great care in carrying over psychoanalysis to cultural issues. "[W]e should . . . not forget," he wrote, "that, after all, we are only dealing with analogies and that it is dangerous, not only with men but also with concepts, to tear them from the sphere in which they have originated and been evolved" (p. 144). Hence when he likened religion to a collective obsessional neurosis, or allowed that Hamlet suffered unduly from an Oedipus complex, or diagnosed Lady Macbeth a fate-neurotic, he did not broach these observations in the same technical spirit in which he spoke about an actual clinical process. To what avail, then, does the psychoanalyst hazard departures from a systematic process of knowing to undertake a project of applied psychoanalysis? Moreover, what is the process of knowing in applied psychoanalysis? Can we claim for the findings of applied psychoanalysis some characteristic of validity, or are we dealing with matters like pudding for which the proof is simply in the eating? These are the principal questions I shall pursue.

In the way I have already posed the problem of applied

psychoanalysis I have committed my discussion to certain premises about the nature of psychoanalytic practice and thought. For example, I am already suggesting that there is a subject fitted to psychoanalytic practice in a way that other subjects are not. The fit subject is a version of neurosis that differs in crucial, if not all, respects from any other version of abnormal psychology. Compared to this subject, all other subjects are entertained by the analyst in a manner I shall describe further on as analogical.

Consider the subject of religion, which Freud (1927) addressed in "The Future of an Illusion." To certain theologians, for whom religion is an actual practice, transcendental knowledge is as intrinsic to religion as the sexuality of the "Three Essays" (Freud 1905) is to neurosis in the practice of psychoanalysis. Thus a psychoanalytic critique of transcendental knowledge can never fully coincide with the interests of a theologian, inasmuch as psychoanalysis affords no theory of knowledge surpassing experience. It is in the very nature of psychoanalytic thought to reject a distinction between illusion and faith and, in turn, a distinction between God as a transference figure and God as a "wholly other object." To psychoanalysis faith always has motives in longing and functions in regression, and every object of passion has its correspondences to personal history.[1] Begging the question of what is superordinate to what in the order of different kinds of truths, here I simply mean to illustrate the familiar problem of reductionism in applied psychoanalysis and its inevitability in the very transfer of the psychoanalytic point of view from the clinical realm to some other, where psychoanalysis shares an interest of some other methodology.

On this score, we are apt to fancy an ideal analyst who redresses this particular problem by virtue of a capacity to wear two hats, one representing psychoanalysis, the other a different practice, let us say art criticism, because we have the example of Ernst Kris, who produced *Psychoanalytic Explorations in Art*

---

1. Freud's sympathy for these problems is evident in his dialogue over a 30-year period with the Reverend Oskar Pfister, published under the title *Psychoanalysis and Faith* (Meng and Freud, E. 1963).

(1952) while wearing two such hats. (Kris wrote sections of this extraordinary book in close collaboration with E. H. Gombrich, a grand master of art history and aesthetics.) However, whatever these advantages achieve, they do not solve the problem of reductionism. On the contrary, it was precisely because of his remarkable qualifications that Kris's text never aspired to more than an encounter between two subjects, as if a fuller possession of art by psychoanalysis would have resulted in a rudeness to art that Kris was particularly able to appreciate and avoid. Even the title of his book conveys a sense of restraint and reservation. Kris, himself, said as much in his preface, where he acknowledged the many years of thought he had given to a system that would have organized the separate essays he decided at last to bring together as a book, and why such a prospect came to grief. He wrote, "In this volume no psychoanalytic psychology of art is offered." The reason he gave was that he did not feel that "the time for such a systematic presentation of this type has come" (p. 13).

Although this was over 30 years ago, I bring in the example of Kris because I believe there is still something obdurate in the problem of applied psychoanalysis for which the hesitancies of Kris's text continue to be fair trade-offs. This is not to say there have not been advances in applied psychoanalysis. Indeed, I shall be describing some remarkable developments over the past several decades. But the problem of a "systematic psychoanalytic psychology of art," to use Kris's phrase, may be one we should prefer to endure rather than resolve. This is not simply the ordinary problem of reckoning with the discontinuities among different versions of a subject studied from separate points of view. It is also the problem of whether to tolerate the difference between psychoanalytic thought as an outcome of one kind of activity, and art as an outcome of another. What Kris had qualms about was a dissolution of this difference in favor of a common denominator, in what might be called an algorithmic solution. This is a matter not of feasibility, but of decision.

The controversy over Lacan is relevant here because it turns very much on this issue, on his option to radicalize this problem of applied psychoanalysis in an algorithmic solution, which in turn is a radicalization of psychoanalysis, itself. Whether we

regard Lacan's achievement as a lamentably huge conceptual
sacrifice for a negligible methodological innovation or as a bright
new endeavor of edification depends on our professional and
intellectual stakes in the losses and gains. Felman (1980) sum-
marizes Lacan's approach quite faithfully in the course of
examining his "seminar" on Poe's "The Purloined Letter":

> Lacan's approach no longer falls into the category of what has
> been called "applied psychoanalysis," since the concept of "ap-
> plication" implies a relation of *exteriority* between the applied
> science and the field which it is supposed, unilaterally, to inform.
> Since, in Lacan's analysis, Poe's text serves to *reinterpret Freud* just
> as Freud's text serves to interpret Poe; since psychoanalytic
> theory and the literary text mutually inform — and displace — each
> other; since the very position of the interpreter — of the analyst —
> turns out to be not *outside,* but *inside* the text, there is no longer a
> clear-cut opposition or a well-defined border between literature
> and psychoanalysis; psychoanalysis could be intraliterary just as
> much as literature is intrapsychoanalytic. The methodological
> stake is no longer that of the *application* of psychoanalysis *to*
> literature, but rather, of their *interimplication in* each other.
> [p. 145]

I call this approach of Lacan algorithmic because it unifies two
otherwise different categories of text, for example, "The Interpretation of Dreams" and "The Purloined Letter," on the basis of
certain shared literary features, not least their availabilities to
interpretation and their explicit and implicit instruction concerning interpretation.

Clearly this is an altogether different methodological state of
affairs than we find in Kris, and if I admit, in this juxtaposition
with Kris, to being disturbed by Lacan's ambitions, my point, to
repeat it in yet another way, is not that Kris was correct about
things where Lacan was wrong. It is rather that I regard applied
psychoanalysis, haphazard though it is, as a discernible project
with respect to which Lacan has achieved supreme irrelevance.
("Lacan's approach no longer falls into the category of what has
been called 'applied psychoanalysis.' ") Despite the remains of a
psychoanalytic vocabulary in Lacan, he has repaired to some

other endeavor where the problems of technicality and reductionism are no longer vital. Much of our uneasiness over how to respond and what we are responding to in the spectacular displays of Lacan is a matter of believing that we are still pursuing the values of a professional literature when we are experiencing instead the thrills of the exotic. This does not apply to Felman, for whom Lacan's writings are professional literature. Felman's (1977) study of James's *The Turn of the Screw*, an exercise of Lacanian method, is an unforgettable adventure in literary interpretation. Still, it is beside the point of a particular drift of applied psychoanalysis in which the literary text—or whatever the subject to which analysis is applied—retains an authority in its own right that survives any amount of analysis.

Here it will be helpful to introduce a term for the subjects of applied psychoanalysis that distinguishes them from the comprehensive subject of the clinical method. Compared to neuroses as subjects for psychoanalytic investigation, the subjects of applied psychoanalysis could be designated *boundary problems* for psychoanalysis.[2]

During his early practice as a psychiatrist, Freud encountered a rather lively idea at the time that sex and hysteria could be considered in relation to each other. He (1914) quoted Charcot: "But in this sort of case it is always a question of genital issues— always, always, always" (p. 14). Should one then undertake the care of a hysterical patient, this might entail considerations of the patient's sexual behavior. Indeed, in several early publications, Freud, himself, tried his hand at correlations between sexual behavior and neurotic symptoms, distinguishing, for example, anxiety neurosis and neurasthenia along lines of sexual behavior (Freud 1895). However, insofar as the relation was at best correlative, the terms in it—sex and hysteria— belonged to two points of view, that of sexology and that of psychiatry. Since these points of view can be said to have been different not simply by virtue of interests but, more importantly, methodologies (whatever these were at the time), sex remained

---

2. The idea of boundary problems was worked out in collaboration with William I. Grossman, M.D., in a different connection.

a boundary problem for psychiatry, and hysteria a boundary problem for sexology. Like Kris in another connection, Freud, at this stage in his career, wore two hats.

Should one devise a method through which sex and hysteria are joined not in a relationship, but in a unified and single subject matter, a third point of view comes into existence alongside psychiatry and sexology. When Freud devised a way of conceiving of how hysteria was in every respect a particular fate of the sex life of the hysteric, he supplanted a boundary problem with a psychoanalytic point of view. But we should bear in mind that in this turn of events an extant vocabulary for talking about sex and hysteria acquired radically new technical meanings. Indeed, that Freud retained a terminology common to sexology and psychiatry—instinct, libido, narcissism, phobia, perversion, ambivalence—soon resulted in a babble of tongues between him and his colleagues, because in a psychoanalytic perspective the meanings of such a terminology were completely transformed.

This is not to say that had the problem of the technicality of discourse gotten straightened out, Freud's solution to certain boundary problems of sexology and psychiatry would prove irresistible to his colleagues one and all. Whatever the influence of psychoanalysis has amounted to in the course of things, the sexologic and psychiatric points of view that Freud encountered early on have prevailed to the present as separate lines of academic and professional development, whose methods and findings remain boundary problems for the psychoanalyst. Thus, how the analyst makes a particular brand of sexology a provisional interest, for example, Masters and Johnson (1966), to mention one historical line of sexologic research, is a problem of applied psychoanalysis. Why psychoanalysts dropped by only briefly at this particular boundary may not be hard to answer. Masters and Johnson, we recall, appeared in the midst of broad attacks on psychoanalysis for its alleged normative assertions about orgasm in women, and put certain matters to rest on this score by demonstrating that physiologically an orgasm is an orgasm regardless of what facilitates it or how it is experienced. However, the appeal of such research to psychoanalysis can only be of passing interest because the psychoanalytic method is ultimately concerned with the transformations of physiology into motivations in mental life, with the "faculty of representing," to use Loewald's (1971) phrase.

Things are different, we might note, at the boundaries of developmental psychology with its methods of direct child observation. Here the appeal to the genetic, structural, and dynamic points of view of psychoanalysis is so great that we often forget that our commerce with developmental psychology is actually an applied psychoanalysis that entails problems similar to our interests in art. Indeed, if there is a cautionary tale to be told about the encounter of psychoanalysis and art, much the same tale can be told about psychoanalysis and child studies. Brenner has, in fact, done both. With his sometimes penchant for the offhanded *coup de grace*, Brenner (1976) has pronounced virtually everything of the psychoanalysis of art "misdirected," the subject of art being unsuited to psychoanalytic reflection and the findings, therefore, too obvious and simplistic to warrant the effort. He holds a consistent opinion about psychoanalysis and child studies: "To put the matter succinctly," Brenner has stated, "I do not believe that any substantial implication for the psychoanalytic treatment of adults is contained in the recent advances in knowledge about child development." He added that monthly, for a year, he participated in a study group led by E. Galenson and H. Roiphe, but he still missed any pertinence of their findings to the technical work of analysis (Panel 1976).

Now what we have in Brenner is not entirely wrong-headed inasmuch as his views entail an appreciation for what I have been calling boundary problems. It is rather that Brenner's is too extreme a disposition of such problems. What it comes down to for Brenner is that since boundary problems are not imperative to the development of a technical version of psychoanalytic thought—and they are not—they should be eschewed altogether. They run a risk of mischief we do not have to take.

One could reply that urgency itself need not be the only reason to entertain a problem. As I shall show, a significant reason for Freud's first excursions into a psychoanalysis of art was to verify that his clinical interests were representative of a general psychological predicament of being civilized. While one might agree that psychoanalysis can proceed quite nicely without such verifications, mere survival of the technical line of psychoanalytic development seems too austere a restriction on the purposes of curiosity and reflection. Besides, there are many ventures at the boundaries of various disciplines the value of whose outcomes cannot be foreseen until they are tried. Because the relevance of art or child observation or any other would-be subject of applied psychoanalysis is not immediately apparent does not mean that there is none.

To what avail, then, does the analyst depart from the intrinsic business of psychoanalysis in order to address the problem of art? The venture itself can be said to have begun in a letter from Freud to Wilhelm Fliess in 1897. Though prior to this Freud's writing had been laced with references to art and other aspects of culture, such references were merely passingly illustrative of his text, a characteristic of style. But in the letter to Fliess of October 15, which was part of an ongoing report of his self-analysis, Freud (1887–1902) likened in a most unusual way certain of his remembered early emotional aims toward his parents to a set of occurrences in *Oedipus Rex* and *Hamlet*. This moment is auspicious for the psychoanalysis of art because Freud did not simply employ these literary dramas as embroidery for the subject of his personal psychology. For the moment they became the very subjects of his text and the objects of his interpretive activity. "I have found love of the mother and jealousy of the father in my own case too," Freud wrote, comparing himself to his patients, "and now believe it to be a general phenomenon of early childhood," adding that the general allows "individual variations. . . . If that is the case, the gripping power of *Oedipus Rex*, in spite of all the rational objections to the inexorable fate that the story presupposes, becomes intelligible. . . . [T]he Greek myth seizes on a compulsion which everyone recognizes because he has felt traces of it in himself. Every member of the audience was once a budding Oedipus in phantasy." In the next paragraph, Freud continued, "The idea has passed through my head that the same thing may lie at the root of *Hamlet*." Whereupon he addresses a number of questions about Hamlet's aphoristic confession—"use every man after his desert, and who should 'scape whipping," this along lines of the universality in the mental life of the repressed hostilities of the Oedipus complex (pp. 223–224).

That this early exercise of applied psychoanalysis seemed to Freud something more than a casual diversion from concerns more pressingly technical can be gathered from his apprehensive inquiry of Fliess a few weeks later. In November 1897, Freud implored Fliess, "You have said nothing about my interpretation of *Oedipus Rex* and *Hamlet*. As I have not said anything about it to anyone else, because I can imagine in advance the hostile reception it would get, I should be glad to have some short comment on it from you. Last year you turned down a number of my ideas with good reason" (p. 299). (It is not clear from the ensuing letters what Fliess did make of Freud's astonishing ideas about the oedipal appeal of the dramatic action of these plays.)

Leaving aside for the moment the methodological question of how Freud made the interpretation he did, let us pursue what seemed so important to Freud about the correspondence between certain clinical discoveries in himself and his patients and certain turns of plot in Sophocles and Shakespeare, so important, indeed, that he named these particular clinical discoveries by the title of Sophocles' drama. A fact that we should have here is that these letters were written 2 years after the publication of *Studies on Hysteria* (Breuer and Freud 1895), where Freud developed the working idea that the abnormal and the normal, or, more precisely, the clinical and its obverse, were simply vicissitudes of each other, and so he had inklings of producing a vast psychopathology of everyday life and the ordeal of being human, which he went on to do in a succession of extraordinary works (Freud 1900, 1905). In connection with his clinical method, he stated:

> In carrying out his [method] we must of course keep free from the theoretical prejudice that we are dealing with the abnormal brains of "*dégenérés*" and "*déséquilibrés*" [degenerate and unbalanced persons], who are at liberty, owing to a[n] [organic] stigma, to throw overboard the common psychological laws that govern the connection of ideas and in whom one chance idea may become exaggeratedly intense for no motive and another may remain indestructible for no psychological reason. . . . Once we have

discovered the concealed motives [for forming a symptom], which have often remained unconscious, and have taken them into account, nothing that is puzzling or contrary to rule remains in hysterical connections of thought, any more than in normal ones. [Freud 1895, p. 294]

An implication of the principle embodied in this passage is that the psychoanalytic method cannot know directly the difference between neurosis and its obverse, for in order to proceed as it should, the method presupposes there is no difference between the mental processes leading to one and to the other. So, where better than in culture and particularly in art might one contemplate the nonclinical forms of the ordeals of mental life? Many years later, in a long discussion of the therapeutic limitations of the psychoanalytic method, Freud (1937) would call the obverse of neurosis an ideal fiction, this from the point of view of the clinical method. And did he not embark upon his notorious discussion of femininity in his "New Introductory Lectures" (1933) with great hesitancy, because what he would have to say on the subject would seem "unfriendly," inasmuch as he could give only a psychopathology of femininity? "If you want to know more about femininity," he ended, not disingenuously, "enquire from your own experiences, or turn to the poets. . ." (p. 135).

Turn to the poets. What for exactly? For the possibility, I am suggesting, of divining the psychopathology of everyday life, which is the interest of technical psychoanalysis, in outcomes beyond the clinical. Culture, art in particular, reflects such outcomes because its reciprocities with every means and end of the itinerary of mental development entail something more than the compromises of defense and the return of the repressed.

But as something more than these, culture itself cannot be the subject of the clinical method, only of applied psychoanalysis. Therefore what the clinical method assumes about culture is only what it requires in order to maintain a bare account of mind in culture and culture in mind. From the clinical point of view, mind in culture is a vicissitude of object relations while culture in mind is a process of internalization (Kaplan 1984). Thus the clinical concern with culture is a deliberate reduction to a psychopathology of object relations and internalization, a psychopathology of social conformity, in which reduction culture becomes a variable studied, not for its own sake, but only in its manifestations in the transference. (This is why all the privileges and exemptions of any actual priest of culture evaporate on the psychoanalytic couch.) Indeed, this disposition of culture in the clinical point of view was all that seemed to have interested Freud in his treatise on religion, which remained, then, an exposé of the fate of the ordinary imperfectibilities of mind arrested in reciprocities with certain kinds of cultural institutions. The imperfect attainment of the reality principle in respect to the pleasure principle in individual mental life is exploited by the doctrine of salvation in the afterlife for renunciations of pleasure in the present life. Thus the rituals and parables of religion retain a utilitarian function in an ongoing process of socialization, hence Freud's conclusion that religion succeeded in no more than a communalization of neurosis.

But in art Freud glimpsed the Oedipus complex as a structure whose function in a cultural guise excluded any requirement of instinctual renunciation from its audience for the experience of participation in what Freud called "the gripping power" of such masterpieces as *Oedipus Rex* and *Hamlet*. In art, then, there is no problem of the utilitarian, hence of symptom formation and its secondary gains in social advantages. In art the Oedipus complex lends itself entirely to a unity, which is the work of art, and as a fate it acquires a repose it cannot have in life. The discovery of this restless scenario of ordinary life belongs to psychoanalysis, but the view of it as a resolved figuration of existence can only be had in art.

The *Minutes of the Vienna Psychoanalytic Society* (Nunberg and Federn 1962) for the meeting of December 11, 1907 are instructive in this matter of the differences between the clinical and the creative. M. Graf gave a presentation entitled "Methodology of the Psychology of Poets," which redressed certain lapses among the members of the Society (especially I. Sadger and W. Stekel) in their understanding of Freud's view on this score. Graf reminded his colleagues how fashionable it had become in abnormal psychology to examine the psychology of the artist and how in Italy C. Lombroso looked at poets as a variant of

criminals, while the French had coined the term *dégénéré supé-
rieur* to account for poetic power. But "pathographies," as Graf
referred to these approaches, were not Freud's interest. "Professor Freud is interested in the human soul," Graf explained,
"Prof. Freud writes psychological analyses, and everyone who
has an analytic interest in poets must decide whether he wants
to write a case history or a psychoanalytic portrayal" (p. 260). In
his discussion, Freud concurred with Graf. He remarked that
every poet, no more nor less than any other individual, can be
the subject of a pathography, but pathographies reveal nothing
new about the practice of poetry. As regards art, however,
psychoanalysis is ultimately concerned with the creative process
as something distinct from pathological process (p. 265). In fact,
it was several days prior to this Wednesday meeting that Freud
spelled this out in a lecture called "Creative Writers and Daydreaming" (1908), in which he likened creativity to play, dreaming, fantasizing, but only because creativity entails yet a further
process in this series not encountered as such in ordinary life.
Though Freud contributed the term sublimation not very successfully, a terminology for the extended process of creativity is
still lacking in psychoanalysis. We should also note that the
process involves a gift, which is a crucial element leading
beyond ordinary life to the work of art. However, the point is
that psychoanalysis retains a distinction between the life of
mind as a subject of its clinical interests and art as an embodiment of ideal realizations of the potentialities of mind, what
might be called an entelechy of mind in the sense that the
form-giving causes of art can only be suggested but not wholly
described or accounted for in the observational field of psychoanalysis. Thus the Oedipus complex in art is a perfectly stark
realization of what in life can be seen only in its contingencies,
"incomplete and fragmentary," as Freud described his version
of femininity.

In retaining a distinction between art and life, psychoanalysis
does not uphold an exceptional position. Shiff (1979) describes
the distinction plainly enough:

> We know that the identity of art and life is an ideal, not a reality.
> Neither art possessing the immediacy of life's experience nor a

> life having the fixed formal structure of art would seem to belong
> to the world as we know it. . . . If our lives had the form of works
> of art . . . idiosyncracy would seem a flaw. . . . A life perfected in
> art could not be experienced . . . for it would exist in a state of
> absolute knowledge . . . nothing would be in process . . .
> nothing could change. [p. 116]

Harries (1979) has enumerated several consequences that
accrue to the distinction. He speaks of a unity in the work of art
not found in life, a self-sufficiency that led Aristotle to suggest
that art has nothing to do with survival of its public. "But while
art cannot be considered useful," Harries proceeds, "it is precisely this uselessness that gives it a special appeal. Just because
the aesthetic experience justifies itself, because it does not have
an instrumental function and is not a means to some end, it can
give us a sense of being at one with ourselves that we are denied
as long as anticipation binds us to an uncertain future" (p. 74).

We might note that the uncertain future, to which we are
bound in life, is a momentous factor in a psychoanalytic truth
about why we suffer discontent for the sake of submitting to
civilization (Freud 1930). Here an aphorism of Nietzsche
presents itself: "We have art so we may not perish from truth."

We can say, then, if applied psychoanalysis reduces art, it
does so not with respect to the functions of art, which psychoanalysis recognizes as exceeding its own interests. Psychoanalysis reduces art only in a limitation of interests. We know that
art will not reflect more than we are prepared to bring to it, and
we admit that what psychoanalysis brings to it cannot possibly
exhaust its scope and power.

Thus far I have been addressing a prevailing misapprehension about the psychoanalysis of art as an arrogance of reduction. Another misgiving about applied psychoanalysis has to do
with what appears to its critics as a methodological naïveté.
Lacking rules of argument, restraints of evidence, and criteria of
validity, applied psychoanalysis is a pastiche of its proximate
enterprise, which is clinical psychoanalysis.

What is wrong with this view is that it wants to have in one
way what can only be had in another. It assumes that applied
psychoanalysis should be an imitation of clinical psychoanaly-

sis, and since it can only fail in this, applied psychoanalysis cannot be taken seriously. It is true that when we come upon Freud's insight into the plays of Sophocles and Shakespeare in the Fliess correspondence, we are on different grounds than we have been with those insights into sexuality, trauma, repression, and the rest that Freud tirelessly demonstrated before our very eyes in letter after letter. This is not simply because Freud made short shrift of his interpretation of *Oedipus Rex* and *Hamlet*; we have the same experience of a shifting methodology when we pass from his presentation of the case of Paul Lorenz (Freud 1909) to his "analysis" of the memoirs of Shreber (Freud 1911), the former a clinical study, the latter an excursion in applied psychoanalysis. Indeed, the methodological grounds for Freud's reflections on Shreber's autobiography went entirely without saying. All Freud explained about his use of a printed text was that since paranoia did not lend itself to an actual clinical investigation at that stage of the technique, one might just as well have used a subject's written testimony. No methodological issue was argued, raised, or even suggested. So we must now ask by what means does one search a text or any artifact of culture with psychoanalytic concepts.

In *Freud and Philosophy*, Ricoeur (1970) begins a long section called "The Interpretation of Culture" with the passing statement: "In the first place the [psychoanalytic] exegesis of culture is simply an application of psychoanalysis by way of analogy with the interpretation of dreams and of the neurosis. By this . . . we characterize both the validity and the limits of a psychoanalytic interpretation of culture" (p. 153). I think there is no more to the means of applied psychoanalysis than what Ricoeur and many others toss off in passing. When Freud deciphered an oedipal structure in *Oedipus Rex* and *Hamlet*, he simply lucked out on a splendid analogy. Although I have some ideas about stringencies for analogizing, I appreciate that at first blush analogies seem lightweight because their demonstrations are independent of any norms of justification. In this respect analogy is like metaphor, a subject Davidson (1979) introduces in the following manner:

> There are no instructions for devising metaphors . . . ; there is no test for metaphor that does not call for taste. A metaphor implies

a kind and degree of success; there are no unsuccessful metaphors, just as there are no unfunny jokes. There are tasteless
metaphors, but these are turns that nevertheless have brought
something off, even if it were not worth bringing off or could
have been brought off better. [p. 29]

Like good metaphors, good analogies depend not only on
knack, but on critical judgment. We tip our hats to the analyst
who deduces from the passionate obsession of Ahab that Moby
Dick is a mother figure—this from an analogy with the psychoanalytic idea that passion has something to do with a quest for
a libidinal object; but we shake the hand of the analyst who
keeps this deduction to himself—this for reasons I shall come to
further on.

However, I must first make a few observations about analogy, or, at least, clarify the sense in which I am using the term.
One thing should be clear: by analogy I do not mean homology,
which entails correspondences between structures attributable
to common origins. In biology, for example, the bird wing and
the foreleg of an amphibian are homologous. However, among
the similarities of homologies, functions do not figure crucially
as they do in analogies, in which the structures involved in the
analogical comparison are outcomes of different origins however much they may resemble each other in outward appearance. In this respect the wings of birds and of insects are
analogous.[3] So are a camera and an eye, a pump and a heart, an

---

3. Leon Balter, in a discussant of this paper (1986, unpublished) at The New
York Psychoanalytic Institute, agreed to the distinction being made here
between analogy and homology, but took issue with the dismissal of homology
from the method of applied psychoanalysis. In speaking of the power of
homology, Balter put it: "The purpose of all scientific effort may be seen as the
establishing of *homologies*," and he went on to demonstrate Freud's use of
homology in the development of psychoanalytic theory. This is a valuable point
deserving more attention. My sense is that homology may reside in the method
by which boundary problems are resolved into new structures of thought and
concept, while analogy operates in the preservation of boundaries. Thus Lacan's
approach to texts, which I observed earlier, might be called homological in the
same way that Freud employed homology when he combined certain common-
alities of sex and symptom into a psychoanalytic point of view. But to pursue
this would be digressive. Lorenz (1974) had some clarifying things to say on
these matters in his Nobel Lecture "Analogy as a Source of Knowledge," in
which he explored as well the nature and method of homology.

airplane and a bird. Even though the terms in each of these comparisons embody many dissimilar functions, we still think of them as analogous by virtue of the function they have in common. Moreover, in such analogies as these, the second term is clearly the subject for the sake of which the analogy is being made. To liken a pump to a heart, for example, is to want to demonstrate something about a heart. In this sense the subject of an analogy lends only a portion of its features to a totality to which it is being analogized. To liken a pump to a heart is to single out only certain features of a heart, while the pump in the analogy operates more completely in terms of itself. What I am emphasizing in analogy is a disparity in the inclusiveness of the terms that comprise the analogy. A heart is a pump, yet it is something more; a pump is a pump and nothing more—this in the analogy.

I emphasize this about analogy because in the analogy of the psychoanalysis of neurosis to the art object, psychoanalysis is the pump, as it were, creativity the heart. Or, more precisely, the analogies are between such matters as a symptom and a poem, the dream work and creative process, the fate of trauma and the repetition and transformation of a theme of fiction, music, painting, sculpture. The point is that in applied psychoanalysis the art object gives over only a portion of its features to the analogy; psychoanalysis, on the other hand, lends itself entirely. As Burke (1939) put it, "The symbolic act of art, whatever its analogies with the symbolic act of neurosis, also has important divergencies from the symbolic act of neurosis" (p. 436). In this sense, there is no aspect of psychoanalytic thought that cannot be applied to art. To be sure, analogies to art with certain aspects of psychoanalysis come to mind more handily than others depending on the subject one undertakes and one's psychoanalytic interests at the moment. Wolfenstein (1972), for example, gives a list of four "interpretive guidelines," as he calls them, which he has found useful in historical work, for example particular narratives enjoyed by a historical figure are clues to the figure's emotional life (p. 175). But he insists that such guidelines are always personal and arbitrary, hence not given to systematization. More recently, Baudry (1984) compiled a more complex list of approaches from the literature of applied psychoanalysis with critical commentary. Baudry, too, discourages us from expecting a coherent method binding on the practitioner of applied psychoanalysis. Thus, in any undertaking of applied psychoanalysis, there are few matters of principle and plenty of convenience. In a paper on the psychoanalysis of theater architecture (Kaplan 1968), I likened certain abiding structures of theater spaces to R. A. Spitz's concepts of the primal cavity and the primal dialogue in an analogy of functions, and was able to say a few things about what might engross us in theatrical performances. In the bargain, I was able to draw some differences between theatrical performance and the theatricality of everyday life, and to suggest ways in which all the world is not a stage. But inasmuch as these same architectural structures put a performer and an audience into a relationship of high drive arousal, I could have analogized the performance such structures set in motion to much else of psychoanalytic interest. In fact, in a related study of stage fright (Kaplan 1969), I made analogical use of the primal family-romance fantasy as well as some ideas of Rangell (1954) on ego functions that maintain the state of poise, and I was able to draw some distinctions between stage fright as a creative problem for the performer, which contributes something crucial to our experience of performing art, and shyness, which is a symptom in ordinary life.

My point is that depending on one's ingenuity and psychoanalytic interest, there are no limits to what can be analogized. The limits reside in the limitations of psychoanalysis itself. But, as Baudry (1984) comments, "These limitations are not a defect but an inherent property of any theoretical system" (p. 579). This is another way of accounting for the inevitable reduction of all subjects of applied psychoanalysis. If the interpretation of dreams is an analogy to the interpretation of a poem, we shall exhaust the psychoanalytic principles of the formation and interpretation of dreams before we exhaust what can be contemplated of the formation and interpretation of the poem. This must be so because the interpretation of dreams is about a phenomenon of everyday life, and nothing more. A poem is a dream, and something more. Surely no dreamer requires the formal principles and the technique for reckoning with them that the poet employs. The dream process does not include those functions necessary for achieving, for example, the unity of a Pindaric ode.

The problem of the limits of analogy has another aspect that deserves comment. This has to do with what is fair game in the realm of art for psychoanalytic reflection. Typical of controversy about this is the view of Werman (1979), on the one hand, that the art object itself is the appropriate subject for applied psychoanalysis, and the view of S. Weissman (1978), on the other, that a psychoanalysis of the object itself is ultimately "academic, theoretical and thin" compared to "the biographical flesh and bones of the artist" (p. 143). Weissman contends that the art object, like a dream or a symptom, is merely "a mental event in the life of the [artist]" and should be adjunctive to a more genuine interest in the reconstruction of the artist's life. Against this, Werman argues that since a biography obtained apart from an actual psychoanalytic process has no psychoanalytic character, we do better with the art object because it is a completed datum embodying everything it ever will.

We can spare ourselves such controversy if we bear in mind a principle implicit in much that I have been saying, to the effect that there is no one aspect of art that can be singled out over any other as existing, this more than that, for the sake of being more fruitfully analyzed. Since analogy is the procedure, the coherence and resolution that can occur in an actual psychoanalytic process are not to be expected in applied psychoanalysis, which is always, at best, a piecemeal and unresolved affair. Kris (1952) was exemplary with this problem, in respect to which the introductory chapter of his book still bears the closest study because virtually the entire scope of the psychoanalysis of art is set forth there. Indeed, the short paragraph with which the introduction begins contains the whole assignment of art to psychoanalysis. Kris wrote, "What are those things like which, by contemporaries or (under changed conditions) by posterity, tend to be endowed with the specific aura which the word ART conveys? What must the men [and women] have been like who made these things, and what did their work mean to themselves and to their public?" (p. 13). These in a nutshell, are all the elements for consideration of a psychoanalysis of art.

There is the art object itself, namely, the actual achievement of the gifted imagination in which psychoanalysis discerns not only the themes and affects of human existence, but the means as well. In its conscientious display of technique, the art object preserves a record of its very creation. In this regard it coincides with a psychoanalytic concern with the relation between onto-genesis and structure, a concern of the most far-reaching significance to psychoanalytic thought. For example, the whole theory of the ego figures here, for like the ego in psychoanalysis, the art object is a structure of ontogenesis and reflects our psychological passages between beginnings and outcomes.

Another consideration prompts us to try analogies with psychoanalytic accounts of the mental processes by which the ego accommodates culture to the id. Regression in the service of the ego was Kris's concept to account for the artist's analogous accommodations of the raw materials of a medium to ideally consummatory forms. I might remark that if Kris's analogy was good, a later one by P. Weissman (1967, 1969), addressed to similar issues, might have been more incisive. Where Kris spoke of the artist's controlled regression, Weissman added a more unusual combination of dissociation and synthesis. In this he attempted to distinguish more clearly than Kris between ordinary work and creativity, the one leading to "established, useful solutions," the other to "new, original solutions" that surpassed the ordinary attainments of the reality principle. I bring this in order to suggest a progressive characteristic of applied psycho-analysis in the way a good analogy at one stage points to a more informative one at another.

The biography of the artist is a further consideration in Kris's statement, for what the artist must have been like has a bearing on the problems of his or her art in an analogy to the relation among constitution, experience, memory, and destiny. I include constitution because we are apt to think this variable is opaque to psychoanalytic inquiry, when, in fact, psychoanalysis has begun to give a valuable account of what is distinguishably constitutional in the artist. Greenacre's (1957) momentous con-tribution "The Childhood of the Artist" is suggestive of this. If Freud (1927) foreclosed this consideration with his famous disclaimer "Before the problem of the creative artist analysis must, alas, lay down its arms" (p. 177), Greenacre has pried it open with her concept of "collective alternates" and the divided life this describes in the artist. Recently, Nass (1984) has advanced Greenacre's ideas about "libidinal phase development and giftedness" with some remarkable clinical details on the "sensory styles" of twenty American composers. This issue of a constitutional feature of the artist's ego is important if the biographical concerns of psychoanalysis are not to lapse into the mere pathography that Graf and Freud deplored (Nunberg and Federn 1962).

Finally, Kris included the artist's public in a full psychoanalytic consideration of art. Communication is the problem entailed here as reciprocities of pleasure, admiration, gratitude, and allegiance between the artist and the public. Psychoanalytic group psychology is a complex analogy with this aspect of art. The metapsychology of the experience of pleasure is another. Recently, the psychoanalytic process itself has been applied to the problem of communication.

In an appendix to his book on *Hamlet*, Eissler (1971) coined the term "doxalethaic" to refer to the special communicative characteristics of art as distinguished from communication in ordinary life. I went on to make this term the subject of a paper (Kaplan 1972) because Eissler's strategy of neologism seemed to me a further step in applied psychoanalysis toward a vocabulary identifying the ideal nature of our psychological powers, as rendered in art, which we distinguish from the universal fault in the economy of our powers, as we find it in life and in clinical psychoanalysis. Greenacre's term "collective alternates" and Weissman's "beyond the reality principle" are other signifiers of the differences between the life and outcomes of creativity and their analogies with ordinary existence.

I had in mind this ongoing endeavor to exhaust the analogical when I referred earlier to a discernible project in the psychoanalysis of art. A survey of this psychoanalytic activity from the Freud–Fliess correspondence to the present not only shows that every aspect of psychoanalytic thought has been applied at one or another moment to an explication of art, but not surprisingly, what is of current concern in technical psychoanalysis is always poised to be applied to art. For example, over the years since Freud's interpretation of *Oedipus Rex* and *Hamlet* much psychoanalysis has been done on tragedy—tragedy as fate, as expiation of guilt, and so on. Holland (1966) provided what for its time was a definitive survey of psychoanalytic explications of tragedy. More recently, Simon (1983) has produced a psychoanalytic study of the dynamics of tragedy that exceeds what one can find in Holland's study. Simon's study is a departure on Freud's (1900) own further analogy in *The Interpretation of Dreams* between *Oedipus Rex* and now the psychoanalytic process itself, which arrives at the truth of things, in Freud's words, with "cunning delays and ever-mounting excitement" (p. 261). Indeed, these phrases of Freud are part of the title of Simon's remarkable paper, the other part being "Or What Thickens the Plot in Psychoanalysis and Tragedy." Simon (1983) finds in Freud what he describes as an analogy between the process of "becoming" in tragedy and the process of change in psychoanalytic therapy. He proposes that:

> . . . the way tragedy conveys the inevitability of conflict is by means of the interpretations that the characters offer one another about the meaning and import of their actions. I further specify that interpretations within tragedy are misinterpretations, usefully analogized [N.B. analogized] to the *partially correct interpretations* offered within the psychoanalytic and psychotherapeutic process. [Simon makes reference here to Glover's (1931) paper on inexact interpretation.] Further, interpretations within tragedy can also be usefully viewed as "actions" in the sense in which Schafer has introduced that term into discourse about the psychoanalytic process. Interpretations, then, regarded as "actions," help constitute and move the action of the tragedy, that is, action in the ordinary usage of the term. [p. 229]

The appropriation of such current thought as Schafer's to a long-standing interest in the psychoanalysis of art should not escape notice. *Inter alia*, Simon cites Skura's (1981) *The Literary Use of the Psychoanalytic Process*, which is most extensive application of the psychoanalytic process itself to the interpretation of literature, including the transference–countertransference aspect of the process. Simon is quite right in proposing Skura's book as an example of a new set of analogies in applied psychoanalysis.[4]

Skura is also an example of something more for my purposes. Although she is a professor of English, her grasp of the technicality of psychoanalytic thought is astonishingly sophisticated compared to what we used to expect from writers on the other side of the professional boundary. Compared to Skura, much of Lionel Trilling's use of psychoanalysis, alas, dates rather badly—an artifact of a modesty that prevailed in Trilling's day about how much a literary critic should be entitled to know about the technicalities of psychoanalysis.

With this observation of an improved technicality in applied psychoanalysis I come to the first of my last two points. In introducing the subject of analogy, which I insist is central to applied psychoanalysis, I promised a few ideas about criteria for the quality of such analogies. If analogies are like jokes, we should not want to lapse into the Stone Age of comedy by failing to be acquainted with the past. For example, among the developments the field has undergone, the psychoanalytic explanation of the *Ecclesia super cloacam*, of why there is no more suitable place to erect a church than over a sewer, that is, the idea of a relation between what is highest and lowest in instinctual life, has been analogized quite thoroughly at certain levels, so that we can now only groan at the edification that the holes in Henry Moore's sculpture represent infantile cannibalism or that Rodin's "The Thinker" portrays a dialectic of metaphysics and anality. The joke about why the chicken crosses the road may have been brilliantly paradigmatic in its day, but it can no longer be told as entertainment; it can only be told as a datum in a tale of cultural history.

A less obvious problem in the making of analogies has to do with how well one retains what is minimal to a psychoanalytic

---

4. Reed's (1985) "Psychoanalysis, Psychoanalysis Appropriated, Psychoanalysis Applied" must be mentioned in connection with the search for newer analogies. In juxtaposing two poems, one by Marvel, the other by Mallarmé, she explores by analogy the problem of the difference between theoretical and clinical discourse in psychoanalysis and, in turn, how this problem in psychoanalysis is also a problem in the reading of poetry.

explanation of any particular phenomenon. Here the problem is the reduction of psychoanalysis itself, which is not the inevitability that it is for the subject of applied psychoanalysis. We encounter this problem in psychoanalytic statements about art that fall short of a minimal consideration of some enduring relations among conflict, transformation, and structure. What I am saying echoes an important idea presented by Rapaport and Gill (1959) on the points of view of metapsychology. Whatever the fates of those particular points of view have been, there is still merit to the idea that a psychoanalytic reflection on any phenomenon is incisive to the extent that it employs more than one dimension. This is why I suggested that the analogy of Ahab's quest for his mother in the guise of Moby Dick falls short of anything really worth saying psychoanalytically. Certainly it is a psychoanalytic principle that the present object of an obsessional quest is always a representation of a quest for an object of the past, but this alone is too meager an idea to stand as a psychoanalytic version of what is restive in the human spirit.

Lowenfeld's (1941) paper, "Psychic Trauma and Productive Experience in the Artist," is a case in point of such truncation of psychoanalytic explanation. Even assuming that Lowenfeld was correct in his conclusion that the creative personality is particularly prone to neurosis, does he give us a minimally acceptable explanation of this in his statement that "the frequency of neurosis in artists may be explained by their heightened bisexuality"? Although the concept of "heightened bisexuality" is part of a psychoanalytic explanation of neurosis, just as the quest for an aspect of the maternal object is a feature of all motivation in a perspective of object relations, this concept by itself is insufficient. It is but one psychoanalytic element in an explanation that begins with an account of why (motive) and by what means (structure) bisexuality becomes implicated in neurotic process. Fenichel (1946) put it axiomatically: "Bisexuality and ambivalence do not form conflicts in themselves; they do so only when they represent a structural conflict" (p. 297).

Commenting on the fustian that had overtaken British and American poetry in the early years of the present century, T. S. Eliot somewhere quoted Ezra Pound that "Poetry ought to be as well written as prose." My point about the psychoanalytic side of the analogical equation with art is that applied psychoanalysis ought to be as well conceived psychoanalytically as technical psychoanalysis.

I need go no further to encourage the point because it is amply in favor in the current developments of applied psychoanalysis. I have mentioned Skura's refreshingly complicated book. Blatt's (1984) *Continuity and Change in Art* is another recent work of careful conceptualization and technicality. Blatt is also very good on the limits of analogy between psychoanalysis and art; where his interests exceed the interests of psychoanalysis, as they do with certain historical issues of form and representation, he is careful to let us know that he repairs to thought other than psychoanalysis, to Piaget, for example, and developmental psychology. Too many analysts—Otto Rank and Erich Fromm come to mind—would have us believe that simply because they are analysts anything they write on the subject of art is psychoanalytic. This is like a musician who would have us believe that any commotion he makes among us is melodious.

To what avail does the analyst inquire into problems of art? This question extends in two directions: What is the profit to art and to our appreciation of art? What is the profit to psychoanalysis?

The influence of psychoanalysis on art and its appreciation is a huge topic for which I have prepared very little. However, there is one matter lying in this direction that I want to address briefly because it bears on the problem of reduction and on a certain defensiveness among analysts who are apt to be too painfully cognizant of this problem and hence oppressed by it. While it is true, as Freud put it, that art is a precious reflection of reality, it is also true that art itself is a reduction of certain realities of existence. What art reflects is life on a reduced scale. The too much and too little, the too soon and too late that plague us in life (and in clinical psychoanalysis) are perfectly stilled in the moment of art. An actor performing *Hamlet* has precisely the right words and no more nor less of them than he will ever need for that occasion. Moreover, the temporal is reduced entirely. With respect to this Gadamer (1977) referred to Hegel, who saw in art one of the forms of

Absolute Spirit, that is, a form of Spirit's self-knowledge in which nothing alien and unredeemable appeared, a form in which there was no contingency of the actual. . . . In fact, an absolute contemporaneousness exists between the work and its present beholder that persists unhampered despite every intensification of the historical consciousness. . . . It seems instead to belong to the experience of art that the work of art always has its own present. [p. 95]

Gay (1976) has made the same point exactly:

One quality that differentiates art from nature, little commented on but still uncanny, is that art has always enjoyed a factitious immortality. Before the advent of modernism . . . everyone knew the meaning of a crucifix, remembered the attributes of saints, took pleasure in a landscape and found humor in a tavern scene. Yet even in those days art constituted a moment of frozen history, insolently refusing to age while generations who had stood before the same painting had grown old and disappeared from the world. [p. 182]

Lévi-Strauss (1966) spoke of art as "miniaturization." "Even the paintings of the Sistine Chapel," he observed, "are a small-scale model in spite of their imposing dimensions, since the theme which they depict is the End of Time." Nor is there ever a "natural size" in art, since transposition of life into art always involves a sacrifice of dimension: "volume in painting, colour, smell, tactile impressions in sculpture and the temporal dimension in both cases since the whole work represented is apprehended at a single moment in time" (p. 23). Kris (1952) had his way of putting it: "Every line or every stroke of the chisel is a simplification, a reduction of reality," to which he added, "But destruction of the real is fused with construction of its image" (p. 52). There is irony here in that art reflects life so preciously only in its subtractions, indeed its estrangements, from it. Looking back in life on his artistic career, Yeats (1938) conveyed this in the couplet "Players and painted stage took all my love/And not those things that they were emblems of." And he went on to confess the sources in his life for what we, as readers, find in his glorious poetry:

Those masterful images because complete
Grew in pure mind but out of what began?
A mound of refuse or the sweepings of a street,
Old kettles, old bottles, and a broken can,
Old iron, old bones, old rags, that raving slut
Who keeps the till. [p. 347]

Remarking on the trite moralism of an early draft of *Anna Karenina* and the very different version Tolstoy finally achieved, Kundera (1985) attributes this not to a revision of Tolstoy's personal moral ideas, but rather to a shift in attention from moral issues to the problem of writing a novel. Such a preoccupation with the elements of form, with which one can do much better than with certain elements of life, is how Kundera explains why it is that "great novels are always a little more intelligent than their authors" (p. 11).

In connection with this matter of the artist's reduction of interest to issues of form, two passages from Freud's letters to Lou Andreas-Salomé (Pfeiffer 1972) are irresistible. Though Freud was not, strictly speaking, an artist, he was endowed with an exceptional talent. Had one a mind to, one could begin an account of the factitious immortality—to use Gay's term—of Freud's thought with the following observations he made of how he worked. In the letter to Lou Andreas-Salomé of July 30, 1915, Freud wrote: "I so rarely feel the need for synthesis. The unity of this world seems to me so self-evident as not to need emphasis. What interests me is the separation and breaking up into its component parts of what would otherwise revert to an inchoate mass" (p. 32). A year later, in the letter of May 25, 1916, Freud has this to say:

> I am always particularly impressed when I read what you have to say on one of my papers. I know that in writing I have to blind myself artificially in order to focus all the light on one dark spot, renouncing cohesion, harmony, rhetoric and everything which you call symbolic, frightened as I am by the experience that any such claim or expectation involves the danger of distorting the matter under investigation, even though it may embellish it. Then you come along and add what is missing, build upon it, putting what has been isolated back into its proper context. I

cannot always follow you, for my eyes, adapted as they are to the dark, probably can't stand strong light or an extensive range of vision. [p. 45]

Such considerations as these add up not only to a license to interpret art, but to an unavoidable necessity to do so. Lévi-Strauss was very good in this matter. Since art is not a mere projection or passive homologue of an object, but rather constitutes a real experiment with form, that is, with scale and reduction,

the choice of one solution involves a modification of the result to which another solution would have led, and the observer is in effect presented with the general picture of these permutations at the same time as the particular solution is offered. He is thereby transformed into an active participant without even being aware of it. Merely in contemplating it he is, as it were, put in possession of other possible forms of the same work; and in a confused way, he feels himself to be their creator with more right than the creator himself because the latter abandoned them in excluding them from his creation. [p. 24]

This is why the relationship between the artist and the critic is so unsettled; to the critic contemplation is interpretation; to the artist interpretation is desecration. And sensitive to this, analysts may become diffident in their encounter with art. Yet they should not be because in this state of affairs psychoanalysis makes its invaluable contribution to art; it brings to the inevitable act of interpretation a highly special and cunning slant on life as it is lived in its disunities, trivialities, incidentals to which it restores the momentousness lost to defense and compromise. Indeed, what psychoanalysis has added to the possibilities of interpretation has allowed the creative imagination of our century a new liberation. The artist is free to experiment in form only to the extent that the artistic outcome can find an interpretive reciprocity in a contemplative public. Could the art of our age be thinkable in a culture in which psychoanalysis did not exist, it would be a solipsistic art and hence not art at all. Much (though not all, to be sure) that we have in the way of art has been feasible by virtue of what psychoanalysis has prepared us to bring to its interpretation.

But what does its encounter with art enhance in psychoanalysis? In the analogy of clinical psychoanalysis to art I have tried to point out that while psychoanalysis unpacks certain psychological possibilities of art in an exhaustive application of interests and calculations of theory, in the same process art reflects the limitations of this endeavor because art is always something other than the fit subject of clinical psychoanalysis. In the disanalogies, as it were, where art escapes psychoanalysis, psychoanalysis encounters what it can never realize directly but can only suspect in the realm proper to its conduct. Stage fright is not examination anxiety; the "doxaletheic function" is not merely successful communication; "collective alternates" is not an achievement of an imagined longed-for other life; "beyond the reality principle" is not a deliverance from the burdens of necessity and the wariness against chance. These are terms for what is remaindered at the limits of analogy where the ideal still bears a discernible relation to its counterpart in ordinary life. Clarification of what the ideal is an idealization of and, conversely, of what the ordinary aspires to in its optimal possibilities is a kind of knowledge of great orienting value to psychoanalysis.

Burke (1939) spoke of culture as rounding out the drama of existence, a crucial part, but only part, of which drama is given by clinical psychoanalysis. Burke understood as well the concept of the analyst's neutrality in the clinical situation, a neutrality that must sacrifice a concern with the perfectibilities of development—an entelechy of ontogenesis—for a concern with the reparations of development:

> The Freudian procedure is primarily designed to break down a rhythm grown obsessive, to confront the systematic pieties of the patient's misery with systematic impieties of the clinic. But the emphasis here is more upon the breaking of a malign rhythm than upon the upbuilding of a benign one. There is no place in this technique of examining the available resources whereby adoption of total dramatic enactment may lead to correspondingly proper attitude. There is no talk of games, of dance, of manual and physical actions, of historical role, as a "way in" to

> this new upbuilding. . . . The theory of rhythms—work rhythms, dance rhythms, march rhythms—is no explicit part of this scheme. . . . The establishing of a new pace, beyond the smashing of the old puzzle, would involve in the end a rounded philosophy of the drama. Freud, since his subject is conflict, hovers continually about the edges of such a philosophy. [p. 435]

Burke then spoke, poetically one must caution, of idioms, actions, and transitional states that are revealed in art but also pertain to what he calls the "Freudian cure": salvation in the purification of identity, the transformation of neurotic principle into the principles of proverbs, monasticism, and evanescence as parts of one's gesture idiom, and much more in this direction.

If this is vague and fragmentary, and not a little exhilarant, it is better to have it this way than programmatically. Burke's view is not really novel with respect to psychoanalysis. We find a variant of it in Freud's ideas about the superego. Freud believed that the superego enabled life in culture its fullest possibilities beyond neurosis, which Freud regarded as an isolation from culture, an escape to the "monastic seclusion of childhood" (Freud 1927). He was careful to tell us that not all antagonisms of id and ego were by way of superego regulation. But when the superego made its contribution at its optimal level of development, the individual began to act on behalf of culture in himself rather than in mere submission for the sake of avoidance of personal anxiety and shame. Indeed, Freud analogized the superego to Kant's categorical imperative, in which a personal deed is generalized as an ideal for humankind. Freud did not regard the superego, hence culture, wholly as an imposition on autonomy. In fact, he regretted that with conscience "God did an uneven piece of work," for the transpersonal aspect of the superego was, in Freud's view, a liberation of the individual from the tyrannies of personal history. Though it was not in any exclusive consideration of culture that Freud gave us his great second topography of mind, "The Ego and the Id" (1923) begins to emphasize certain matters of mind in culture that figure increasingly in Freud's subsequent writings.

Such matters did not fail to survive as an interest of psychoanalysis. Hartmann comes readily to mind. His essays on ego psychology (1964) reckon constantly with the interface—the boundary—between the clinical and the cultural and with the very difficult concept of sublimation. It is not always possible to sort out in Hartmann's writing a presentation of the yield of a clinical point of view and a teleology of adaptation. Schafer's (1970) comment on this score is apt: "Although in this sphere Hartmann contributed many acute perceptions, thoughtful differentiations and searching questions, he did not always make it clear when he was working *within* the content of psychoanalytic theory and when he was developing *orienting propositions* to analytic theory as a whole" (p. 431). (By "orienting propositions" Schafer meant, in this context, issues such as social causes, biological principles, and child observations, that take on forms of presentation to the mental life as problems of conflict and transformation.)

Whether we call such extraclinical interests as Hartmann's "orienting propositions," as Schafer did, or, in a pejorative spirit, "byzantinism," as Nacht (1952) did, the fact is that the problem of culture in general, and therefore art as one of its instantiations, is a problem for psychoanalysis that cannot be rescinded. Nor should we desire this, for even granting the mischief it has made, applied psychoanalysis has also been fruitful. Compton (1981) reminds us that the theory of narcissism, for example, was given a boost by Freud's contemplations of Leonardo Da Vinci's art and life. Indeed, we may never know how much of Freud's contemplations of art and culture actually pointed him in clinical and theoretical directions. The problem, then, is to analyze how an "orienting proposition" finds its way into the development of psychoanalytic thought, not how to insulate psychoanalysis from the perils of an applied psychoanalysis that creates such a proposition.

To be sure, it is always too soon to say with the clarity we prefer how psychoanalysis might fashion a way of using the findings of applied psychoanalysis in its method, or even representing such findings in its metapsychology. What is abundantly clear is that when Freud, before the turn of the century, took the momentous step of relating a finding in his self-analysis to two dramas of Sophocles and Shakespeare, he brought psychoanalysis into a relationship with culture that remains a principal concern in the development of psychoanalytic thought and a gift to culture as well.

REFERENCES

Baudry, F. (1984). An essay on method in applied psychoanalysis. *Psychoanalytic Quarterly* 53: 551–581.

Blatt, S. (1984). *Continuity and Change in Art: Development and Orders of Representation*. Hillsdale, NJ: Erlbaum.

Brenner, C. (1976). *Psychoanalytic Technique and Psychic Conflict*. New York: International Universities Press.

Breuer, J., and Freud, S. (1895). Studies on hysteria. *Standard Edition* 2.

Burke, K. (1939). Freud and the analysis of poetry. In *Art and Psychoanalysis*, ed. W. Phillips, pp. 412–439. New York: Meridian, 1957.

Compton, A. (1981). On the psychoanalytic theory of instinctual drives: IV. Instinctual drives and the ego-id-superego model. *Psychoanalytic Quarterly* 50:363–392.

Davidson, D. (1979). What metaphors mean. In *On Metaphor*, ed. S. Sacks, pp. 29–46. Chicago IL: University of Chicago Press, 1979,

Eissler, K. R. (1971). *Discourse on Hamlet and HAMLET*. New York: International Universities Press.

Felman, S. (1977). Turning the screw of interpretation. In *Literature and Psychoanalysis, Yale French Studies* 55/56:94–207.

_____ (1980). On reading poetry: reflections on the limits and possibilities of psychoanalytical approaches. In *The Literary Freud: Mechanisms of Defense and the Poetic Will*, ed. J. H. Smith. New Haven CT: Yale University Press.

Fenichel, O. (1946). *The Psychoanalytic Theory of Neurosis*. New York: Norton.

Freud, S. (1887–1902). *The Origins of Psychoanalysis. Letters to Wilhelm Fliess*. New York: Basic Books, 1954.

_____ (1895). On the grounds for detaching a particular syndrome from neurasthenia under the description "anxiety neurosis." *Standard Edition* 7.

_____ (1900). The interpretation of dreams. *Standard Edition* 4 and 5.

_____ (1905). Three essays on the theory of sexuality. *Standard Edition* 7.

_____ (1908). Creative writers and day-dreaming. *Standard Edition* 9.

_____ (1909). Notes upon a case of obsessional neurosis. *Standard Edition* 10.

_____ (1911). Psycho-analytic notes on an autobiographical account of a case of paranoia (dementia paranoides). *Standard Edition* 12.

_____ (1914). On the history of the psycho-analytic movement. *Standard Edition* 14.

_____ (1923). The ego and the id. *Standard Edition* 19.

_____ (1927). The future of an illusion. *Standard Edition* 21.

_____ (1928). Dostoevsky and parricide. *Standard Edition* 21.

_____ (1930). Civilization and its discontents. *Standard Edition* 21.

_____ (1933). New introductory lectures on psycho-analysis. *Standard Edition* 22.

_____ (1937). Analysis terminable and interminable. *Standard Edition* 23.

Gadamer, H. (1977). *Philosophical Hermeneutics*. Berkeley: University of California Press.

Gay, P. (1976). *Art and Act*. New York: Harper & Row.

Glover, E. (1931). The therapeutic effect of inexact interpretation. In *The Technique of Psycho-analysis*, pp. 353–366. New York: International Universities Press, 1955.

Greenacre, P. (1957). The childhood of the artist. *The Psychoanalytic Study of the Child* 12:47–72.

Harries, K. (1979). The many uses of metaphor. In *On Metaphor*, ed. S. Sacks, pp. 71–88. Chicago, IL: University of Chicago Press.

Hartmann, H. (1964) *Essays on Ego Psychology*. New York: International Universities Press.

Holland, N. H. (1966) *Psychoanalysis and Shakespeare*. New York: McGraw-Hill.

Kaplan, D. M. (1968). Theatre architecture: a derivation of the primal cavity. *Drama Review* 12:105–116.

_____ (1969). On stage fright. *Drama Review* 14:60–83.

_____ (1972). Reflections on Eissler's concept of the doxaletheic function. *American Imago* 29:353–376.

_____ (1984). "Thoughts for the times on war and death": a psychoanalytic address on an interdisciplinary problem. *International Review of Psychoanalysis* 11:131–141.

Kris, E. (1952) *Psychoanalytic Explorations in Art*. New York: International Universities Press.

Kundera, M. (1985). Man thinks, God laughs. *New York Review of Books*, 23 (10):11–12.

Lévi-Strauss, C. (1966) *The Savage Mind*. Chicago, IL: University of Chicago Press.

Loewald, H. W. (1971). On motivation and instinct theory. *Psychoanalytic Study of the Child* 26:91–128.

Lorenz, K. Z. (1974). Analogy as a source of knowledge. *Science* 185:229–234.

Lowenfeld, H. (1941). Psychic trauma: a productive experience in the artist. *Psychoanalytic Quarterly* 10:116–129.

Masters, W., and Johnson, V. (1966) *Human Sexual Response*. Boston: Little, Brown.

Meng, H., and Freud, E., eds. (1963) *Psychoanalysis and Faith: The Letters of Sigmund Freud and Oskar Pfister*. New York: Basic Books.

Nacht, S. (1952). Discussion of mutual influences in the development of ego and id. *Psychoanalytic Study of the Child* 7:54–59.

Nass, M. (1984). The development of creative imagination in composers. *International Review of Psychoanalysis* 11:481–492.

Nunberg, H., and Federn, E., eds. (1962). *Minutes of the Vienna Psychoanalytic Society*. Vol. I. New York: International Universities Press.

Panel (1976). The implications of recent advances in the knowledge of child development for the treatment of adults, reporters J. H. Thiel and N. Treurniet. *International Journal of Psycho-Analysis* 57:37–50.

Pfeiffer, E., ed. (1972) *Sigmund Freud & Lou Andreas-Salomé Letters*. New York: Harcourt, Brace & Jovanovich.

Rangell, L. (1954). The psychology of poise, with a special elaboration on the psychic significance of the snout or perioral region. *International Journal of Psycho-Analysis* 35:313–332.

Rapaport, D., and Gill., M. M. (1959). The points of view and assumptions of metapsychology. *International Journal of Psycho-Analysis* 40:153–162.

Reed, G. S. (1985). Psychoanalysis, psychoanalysis appropriated, psychoanalysis applied. *Psychoanalytic Quarterly* 54:234–269.

Ricoeur, P. (1970) *Freud and Philosophy: An Essay on Interpretation*. New Haven, CT: Yale University Press.

Schafer, R. (1970). An overview of Heinz Hartmann's contributions to psychoanalysis. *International Journal of Psycho-Analysis* 51:425–446.

Shiff, R. (1979). Art and life: a metaphoric relationship. In *On Metaphor*, ed. S. Sacks, pp. 105–120. Chicago, IL: University of Chicago Press, 1979.

Skura, M. (1981). *The Literary Use of the Psychoanalytic Process*. New Haven, CT: Yale University Press.

Simon, B. (1983). "With cunning delays and ever-mounting excitement" or what thickens the plot in tragedy and in psychoanalysis. *Hebrew University Studies in Literature & Arts* 11:226–253.

Weissman, P. (1967). Theoretical considerations of ego regression and ego functions in creativity. *Psychoanalytic Quarterly* 36:37–50.

————— (1969). Creative fantasies and beyond the reality principle. *Psychoanalytic Quarterly* 38:110–133.

Weissman, S. (1978). Review of Whitman's journey into chaos. A psychoanalytic study of the creative process. *Psychoanalytic Quarterly* 47:142–144.

Werman, D. (1979). Methodological problem in the psychoanalytic interpretation of literature: a review of studies on Sophocles' *Antigone*. *Journal of the American Psychoanalytic Association* 27:451–478.

Wolfenstein, V. (1972). Some technical aspects of applied psychoanalysis. In *The Psychoanalytic Study of Society*, Vol. V, ed. W. Muensterberger and A. H. Esman, pp. 175–184. New York: International Universities Press.

Yeats, W. B. (1938). The circus animals' desertion. In *The Poems of W. B. Yeats*, pp. 346–348. New York: Macmillan, 1983.

15

"Thoughts for the Times on War and Death"

Each of us owes Nature one death, Freud was given to say, and this being so, one's only heroism in this matter can be to pay the debt as fully on one's own terms as possible. In conveying a sense of a total communalization of sudden death, the present nuclear situation threatens the very possibility of this fundamental heroism Freud perceived in the death of every human being. However, such a line of thought is rather faint and brief. For it is merely an existential consideration in a vast turbulence of political, historical, and technological problems, among which it is not readily apparent how psychoanalysis itself might figure, if at all, in a view the analyst takes of the plight he shares with every other citizen at this most fraught moment in the history of civilization. To suppose that the urgency alone of an issue, regardless of its source or nature, is sufficient to arouse a relevant psychoanalytic commentary is to expect that psychoanalytic discourse can endure any dislocation from the contexts in which its technical meaning is furnished. There is a difference between speaking psychoanalytically and psychoanalysis in a manner of speaking. While the difference is always worth bearing in mind, not all subjects compel us to retain the difference to the same extent. However, to address the problems that have brought us together on this occasion in simply a manner of speaking would amount to irreverence.

To be sure, analogies from the clinical to the social and cultural realms are common in Freud's work. Freud likened religion to a collective obsessional neurosis; he allowed that

Hamlet suffered unduly from an Oedipus complex; he diagnosed Lady Macbeth a fate-neurotic. Indeed such exercises of analogy are what we mean by applied psychoanalysis. On the other hand, there were certain crucial points in his concerns with social, political, and cultural processes where Freud was careful to disanalogize individual and social psychology, insisting that the explanatory principles appropriate to each were different. Toward the end of "Civilization and Its Discontents," for example, where Freud (1930) was drawing similarities and differences between the development of the individual and of society, he had this to say:

> May we not be justified in reaching the diagnosis that, under the influence of cultural urges, some civilizations, or some epochs of civilization—possibly the whole of mankind—have become 'neurotic'? [N.B. "neurotic"] . . . I would not say that an attempt of this kind to carry psychoanalysis over to the cultural community was absurd or doomed to be fruitless. But we should have to be very cautious and not forget that, after all, we are only dealing with analogies and that it is dangerous, not only with men but also with concepts, to tear them from the sphere in which they have originated and been evolved . . . And as regards the therapeutic application of our knowledge, what would be the use of the most correct analysis of social neuroses, since no one possesses authority to impose . . . a therapy upon the group? [p. 144]

Thus from a technically psychoanalytic point of view it is fatuous to speak of society as neurotic or self-destructive or sadistic in the sense in which we speak of such outcomes in the development of individual patients studied in the clinical situation. To describe a particular political state of affairs as a state of insanity is a manner of speaking but it is not an analysis. Nor is the dissemination of information for the well-being or improvement of a community, through whatever tactics this takes place, a particularly edifying analogy to the analyst's attempts by means of interpretation to alter a patient's defensive self-deceptions.

What I mean to suggest in these opening remarks are the cautions I believe one should keep in mind in preparing to advance some lines of Freud's thoughts for the times on war and death. Whoever speaks for psychoanalysis on issues of social and political moment must be prepared to allow psychoanalysis to expire with dignity at the limits of its pertinence and to leave to other callings the huge remainders that exceed psychoanalytic reflection.

Since my discussion, like Freud's own manner of dealing with the issues before us, will not be systematic but rather fugitive, a statement about these limits and remainders should be helpful at the outset. Much that I shall be pursuing in a wide-ranging reading of Freud can be contained in the following thesis: as a psychology, psychoanalysis is concerned with an account of how mind transforms the biological into the social. Psychoanalytic principles and concepts are pertinent essentially to mind and only incidentally, if at all, to biology and society. Though the concepts id and superego, for example, conjure something biological and social, respectively, their technical meanings are limited to psychological circuits of desire and morality. Since psychoanalysis is also a clinical psychology—a psychology of conflict and its outcomes in symptoms and character—the issues of conflict include the biological and social, for these are issues with which mind reckons. But, again, with respect to this, the pertinent principles and concepts answer only to mind as the theatre of conflict. As for society as one of the terms in mental conflict psychoanalysis simply takes what it needs. For the most part, it treats social structure as a received fact and the varieties of social structure as contingencies in a general problem of mental development and adaptation. What psychoanalysis assumes about the social is only what it requires in order to maintain an account of mind in society or society in mind. Thus mind in society is a vicissitude of object relations, while society in mind is a process of internalization. However, such assumptions of psychoanalysis, which are independent of any compelling social accounts of its own, are hardly extensive compared to the interests of sociology, anthropology, political science, and history. This is not to say that psychoanalysis has contributed nothing to an account of social structure itself. Freud's ideas about group psychology embody great explanatory power with respect, for example, to the liberation of individually proscribed behavior by the communalizing processes of social institutions. Nor are Freud's ideas about art and other aspects of culture negligible. However, it is no detraction from such achievements to observe that vast realms of social, political, economic, historical, cultural, and technological processes are opaque to psychoanalytic inquiry.

One of the problems this statement assigns to a reading of Freud on social and cultural matters is the nature of his many excursions into these matters.[1] When was he on business? When was he on pleasure? That is, which commentaries were imperative to the structure of his thought and which were simply the musings of a brilliant spirit worth attending to on virtually any subject? Such questions, I expect, will answer themselves in the course of things. But at the outset I must insist that a significant amount of intellectual traffic Freud conducted at the interface of psychoanalysis and society was imperative. One reason for this was that from a psychoanalytic point of view the civilizing processes of a developing mental life leading to its engagements of social structure inevitably entail conflict. Hence such processes and their outcomes in socialization become considerations in a general psychoanalytic theory of pathogenesis.

In a comprehensive statement on the nonclinical value of psychoanalysis—"The Claims of Psycho-Analysis to Scientific Interest"—Freud (1913b) notes: "It is true that psycho-analysis has taken the individual mind as its subject, but in investigating the individual it could not avoid dealing with the emotional basis of the relationship of the individual to society" (p. 188). If it is the

---

1. This might be a place for some definition of the terms society, civilization, and culture, though more often than not Freud used these terms interchangeably, since what psychoanalysis has to say about them does not require any hard and fast distinctions. By society I shall mean the system of relationships among persons regulated by institutionalizations of facts, manners, rules, and practices. Needless to say, such institutionalizations, particularly in so-called modern societies, are inconsistent and contradictory. Culture might then be thought of as the symbolic accounts in ideas and art that represent the experience of persons in social relationships. Civilization is the utilitarian process, involving the education of behavior and skills, through which society and culture achieve a relationship. For a psychoanalytically more stringent explication of these differences compare Ricoeur 1970, p. 248ff.

emotional basis of the relationship of mind to society that concerns psychoanalysis, then psychoanalysis entertains a psychopathology of conformity precisely as it does a psychopathology of object relations. That is, precisely as we speak of the development from one psychosexual stage to another as an enlargement of the libidinal object in the mental life, so we may speak of the social structure, with which mind interacts developmentally and in connection with narcissistic and anaclitic supplies, as an aspect of the enlarging, libidinal object of mind. In "Mourning and Melancholia" Freud (1917) made the point explicitly:

> Mourning is regularly the reaction to the loss of a loved person, or to the loss of some abstraction which has taken the place of one, such as one's country, liberty, an ideal, and so on. In some people the same influences produce melancholia instead of mourning and we consequently suspect them of a pathological disposition. [p. 243]

A psychopathology of conformity would then consist of the emotional costs and conflicts—the intrapsychic means—with which one maintained the fact of belonging to one or another social order. Indeed Freud spoke of neurosis as a psychopathology of socialization no different from a psychopathology of object relations. He went on in the 1913 passage I have been quoting: "Psycho-analysis has recognized that in general the neuroses are asocial in their nature and that they always aim at driving the individual out of society and at replacing the safe monastic seclusion of earlier days by the isolation of illness" (p 188). It is worth stressing here that Freud is not describing neurosis as a social protest in the political sense, an equation that informs that brand of Soviet psychiatry in which political dissent has become diagnostic of mental illness. Freud simply means that neurosis can be regarded as a psychopathology of the process of socialization.

This is not to say that Freud deemed every social order, each in its own way, hospitable to mind. Since psychoanalysis embodies no predictive power in these matters on the experimental order "if a, then b," Freud's ideas of what is and is not socially salutary are a species of common sense. From the point of view of mental health he held that the simpler the social order the individual deals with the better. When one of his colleagues—Theodor Reik—complained in a letter that Freud had made it seem in his study of Dostoevsky that any dull and unimaginative Philistine was morally superior to Dostoevsky, Freud (1928) replied, "I should not wish to deny the excellent Philistine a certificate of good ethical conduct, even though it has cost him little self-discipline" (p. 196). As for Dostoevsky in life, as against art, Freud was unimpressed by the great writer's complicated arrival at some resolution of his problem with authority, "a position which lesser minds have reached with smaller effort" (p. 177). To the end of his life, Freud regarded social complication sceptically. In his posthumous "Outline," he (1940) continued to insist: "We must not forget to include the influence of civilization among the determinants of neurosis. It is easy, as we can see, for a barbarian to be healthy; for a civilized man the task is hard" (p. 185). Clearly, social structure is a crucial consideration in the psychoanalytic theory of development and adaptation no less than any of the other factors of fate and chance that figured in Freud's account of the etiology of neurosis. Moreover, he believed that a favorable set of social structures could transform a neurosis that various childhood experiences would otherwise lead to, much as certain favorable conditions at any stage of development could transform what was pathogenic at some other stage (Freud 1913b, p. 188). I stress this because there still lingers over Freud's thought a reputation for a peculiar biologism that pre-empted all other determinants in his considerations of the mental life.

However, that society embodies reciprocities, opportunities, and regulations continuous with various conditions for mental development and adaptation, places mind and society in a relationship so intimate that they are apt to be thought of as mirror images of each other inviting conceptualizations by a single set of principles. Yet we know that the principles that govern the environment are not synonymous with the subject's version of those principles. The primal scene of the oedipal child is only a selection of its parents' version of sex. Similarly, society has a way of its own, independent of mind in the psychoanalytic sense, and Freud was careful to keep these accounts straight. I quote at length from "Thoughts for the Times on War and Death" because Freud's point here will be important for much that follows:

> The development of mind shows a peculiarity which is present in no other developmental process. When a village grows into a town or a child into a man, the village and the child become lost in the town and the man . . . the old materials or forms have been got rid of and replaced by new ones. It is otherwise with the development of the mind. Here one can describe the state of affairs, which has nothing to compare with it, only by saying that in this case every earlier stage of development persists alongside the later stage which has arisen from it; here succession also involves co-existence, although it is to the same materials that the whole series of transformations has applied . . . This extraordinary plasticity of mental developments is not unrestricted as regards direction; it may be described as a special capacity for involution—for regression—since it may well happen that a later and higher stage of development, once abandoned, cannot be reached again. But the primitive stages can always be re-established; the primitive mind is, in the fullest meaning of the word, imperishable. [1915b, pp. 285–286]

In this passage, the difference between mind, on the one hand, and cultural and maturational structures, on the other, is a function of the process of regression, which Freud assigns exclusively to mind. I shall not pause over the technicalities of the concept of regression except to note that regression is an access to one's past whose conservation in mind determines what it is in the present that affords a continuity of personal development in thought, action, and experience. Such a conservation of the past does not take the form of replications of original immaturities but rather of restorations in present fantasies of long-standing desires that have become attenuated in successive considerations of reality. It is in a comparison of fantasy with other modes of thought directly implicated in the operational rules of reality that psychoanalysis differentiates primary and secondary process and speaks of the primitive as a function of primary process and as an imperishable characteristic of the mental life. Thus primitiveness is not immaturity. Dreams, for example, do not consist of immature but rather of primitive modes of thought. Nor do dreams represent mind in ruins. The past that survives in the mental life by virtue of regression is merely that which psychologically contradicts certain actualities—perceptions—that constitute the present, in particular actualities that seem, for various reasons, inconsistent with one's version of personal existence. Yet regression also fosters memories of those pleasures of one's past in the broadest sense that match opportunities in the present for their repetitions, which guarantee an experience of personal continuity. If the contradiction of regression with which Freud was concerned in the passage I have just quoted was dire—a contradiction of vast parts of reality in a permanent psychosis—it was because Freud was addressing the most dire political event in his life to that moment—World War I. However, the extreme crises of the mental and the political in this essay were largely associative. Ordinarily regression is an expectable process of mind enabling the plasticity required for problem solving, creativity, recovery from the improbable, and other adjuncts to the maintenance of one's bearings in the odyssey of development. Much that is primitive in mental life is not necessarily pre-emptive or catastrophic.

With society and its institutions things are different. When a village develops into a town, which was Freud's metaphor here for a social process, an earthquake, or, for that matter, an economic depression, does not reinstate anything remotely resembling the village it once was. An accident in the social structure does not set in motion processes representing a reversion to a past useful to a reparation in the present. The burnt-out tenements of the South Bronx do not exist for the sake of those rural expanses that preceded them in the history of that urban region. Nor does an unemployed population exist for the sake of the opportunities it once had as carefree schoolchildren. There is nothing comparable in society to the provisional fantasies of mind, which do exist for the sake of something individually historical; a persecutory delusion, for example, may exist for the sake of some dreadful excitement of once having been the absolute center of parental attention, but we distinguish a persecutory delusion even in a social order of total persecution – a paranoic is no less so because of the fact of an actual plot against him, while the plot, on the other hand, exists only for purposes of the present. And though the plot was assuredly hatched in the past, this past is social history, not the past of primary process; hence it is the purview of the historian, not of the psychoanalyst.

Nor are our collateral ideas about social catastrophe, to the effect that it only happens in the social realms of others, a contradiction of primary process, since protection by social permanence is what society is constructed to assure. In "Civilization and Its Discontents" Freud (1930) singled out three sources of existential danger to the individual: the indifference of nature and its elements to the individual's survival; the limitation to the individual's psychic power; and the disadvantage of that limited power in relation to the power of a collectivity – "the family, the state and society" (p. 86). Because the social order is not a wish-fulfillment but a fact, we give credence to such assurance. Though Freud referred to such credence as illusion, he gave it no diagnostic import; for nothing so reduces our sense of exposure to the dangers Freud enumerated than our participation in our various social orders. Reality-testing requires only that we differentiate wishes and perceptions to the extent that we achieve a sense of reality. It does not require any far-reaching truth value for our perceptions. Even with respect to extreme circumstance, such as the political action of the Nazi regime against its Jewish population, we can understand why the great majority of Jews, whose final fate was as yet unknown to them, behaved in the belief that trust in the social order, as demonstrated by increasing compliance, would guarantee their survival, even as this belief was tried to its limits by the knowledge that Jews *qua* Jews were already beginning to perish. That many Jews had the apparent perspicacity to flee the Nazis cannot serve as a critique of the sense of reality of those who stayed behind. What such flight may represent is a fortunate capacity to exchange one social order for another. However, that the majority of European Jews stood fast by their various social orders only demonstrates that tragedy is one of the outcomes of necessity. For a social order does not exist in relation to any other alternative except that fortuitous alternative of another social order. With respect to mind, a social order is always a present stage of reality whether it is in a state of ruin, stability, or development.

In one of his Norton Lectures, Czeslaw Milosz, the 1980 Nobel Laureate for Literature, recalled the social and cultural disintegration in Poland following the pact concluded by Hitler and Stalin in August 1939. Milosz (1983) observed how very far things had to go in Poland and how many years they had to be that way before the general population responded to a change in perception. "People always live within a certain order," he wrote, "and are unable to visualize a time when that order might cease to exist. The sudden crumbling of all current notions and criteria is a rare occurrence and is characteristic only of the most stormy periods of history" (p. 20). It is amazing how the business of "notions and criteria"—customs and standards of behavior—goes on as usual, while the social order itself has already undergone radical change from top to bottom or is imminently about to. In the midst of the Cuban Missile Crisis, how many Americans fled to the Andes, the Alps, or other localities reputed to be safe from massive radioactive fallout? Indeed, how many Americans interrupted the routine comings and goings of their everyday lives in consideration of the fact that for a week in 1962 their very existences hung by a thread?

Nor does subsequent outcome decide anything about the relative merits of the judgments of those who stay put as against those who do not in social, political, military, or economic crises—asssuming that judgment is being exercised. Here I call upon a piece of academic psychology. One of the more modest conclusions that Kahneman and colleagues (1982) make in *Judgment Under Uncertainty: Heuristics and Biases* is that while acts of human judgment about situations embodying uncertainty are not without systematic features, the quality of such judgment is absolutely no good. Moreover, our suspicions of this limitation in ourselves is why we do not exert ourselves to exercise judgment precisely when uncertainty arises in our prevailing circumstances. The alternative to an exercise of judgment that will be poor anyway is to persist in behavior that is more tried and true, which is our ordinary behavior even in extraordinary situations. This is hardly denial. It is rather a considered risk that a situation that has passed into uncertainty will revert to our favor in good time. Thereafter we relate to the situation as though it were an object in its own right, and we enlist the measures of object relations—submission, compliance, idealization, identification, and so forth—in the service of regulating anxiety. And through these measures combined with personal character and social status we become variously victims, victimizers, isolates, free-loaders, and refugees.

With this we have returned to Freud's idea that the relationship of mind to society is always an emotional one. What psychoanalysis includes in this idea is that the relationship always entails measures of ambivalence. To this extent mind in society is also a plight, and we suffer this by universal necessity. Freud's views on this particular problem involved ideas about the origins of civilization, which I shall return to shortly.

But in our relationship to society we suffer also by universal accident, and this was by far the more alarming to Freud in the long course of his reflections on social problems. The accidental were those problems that followed unpredictably from the very solutions of any immediate social moment. Though Freud might just as well have made reference to urbanization or economic events, for each creates its own forms of accident, he dwelled on the introduction of advanced industrialization into human society and the massive disruptions this application of knowledge inflicted on all members of society. Freud's doubts about the unbridled complications to our lives by industrialization is caught in a passage in "Civilization and Its Discontents" where he (Freud 1930) was praising the telephone and the telegraph for enabling him to speak to his child hundreds of miles away and to be assured of the safe arrival of his friend who had embarked on a long and difficult journey. But he adds:

> If there had been no railway to conquer distances, my child would never have left his native town and I should need no telephone to hear his voice; if travelling across the ocean by ship had not been introduced, my friend would not have embarked on his sea-voyage and I should not need to cable to relieve any anxiety about him. [p. 88]

Though Man has become in Freud's phrase in this passage a "prosthetic God," it is questionable that the attainment has contributed commensurably to his happiness, let alone to his actual survival. And among these issues Freud gave thought to war whose increasing violence was also an accidental factor of the ordinary pursuit of knowledge. Industrialization imbues the inventions of society with violent potential, while their multiplication and their devastating effects on the natural environment follow principles independent of the designs of any mind or institution in society. The airplane was invented for purposes quite irrelevant to military ones, but Freud observed that since its invention the military relevance of the fact that England was an island suddenly came to an end.

If these were partly the musings of Freud in the guise of an aging citizen who lived through the accelerations of social change characteristic of our present century, there was also an analytic principle at work here having to do with the reality principle as the great detour through the contingencies of the "real object of satisfaction" (Freud 1911a). According to Freud's thought, all satisfaction acquires contingencies in the course of development but the difference between the contingent and the accidental is not necessarily clear, so that we are never sure whether our efforts are advancements of our cause, whatever it may be, or departures from it in our assumptions of the digressive assignments of accident. Nor does society furnish any guidelines in the matter. And as for society itself do we not have a sense that the rate at which it works creates problems of an order geometrically greater than the capacities of our existing institutions to solve them? "An unpleasant picture comes to mind," Freud (1933) remarked, "of mills that grind so slowly that people may starve before they get their flour" (p. 213).

On the issues of the origins of civilization, where Freud located the necessity of the plight of mind in society, he spoke with more credentials, though only partially with those of a psychoanalyst. As I have said earlier, the issues concerned him because the problem of socialization was synonomous with the problem of individual development in which society itself becomes a final stage in the construction of the libidinal object. Though Freud's approaches to a history of the process of civilization—and it was only a history of process that concerned him—begin with elements of fancy, they initiate an account that becomes increasingly authoritative inasmuch as it becomes increasingly psychoanalytic. In giving a précis of this aspect of psychoanalytic thought, I shall bring matters to bear on the functions of force and violence, which figure crucially in Freud's theory of the development of society. We shall see that alternatives to these functions as accompaniments to civilization are feeble indeed in Freud's thought and are better sought elsewhere than in psychoanalysis. Though Freud characterized himself a pacifist in his paper "Why War?" (1933), psychoanalysis does have a problem with the change from war to law, which it shares with Hobbes, Spinoza, and Hegel.

In "Totem and Taboo" (1913a), Freud's most extensive departure into social anthropology, he argued that early civilization evolved in connection with the replacement of certain behavior characterizing a stage of human prehistory by certain laws interdicting such behavior. A history of civilization begins when ordinary slaughter and cohabitation among stipulated members of a human group achieve a conceptual status of murder and incest. Thereafter the social order itself takes on the devices of power and the right to exercise them upon its individual members in order to restrain the commission of acts that have acquired a moral quality. In the relations among the father, mother, and sons of Darwin's primal horde, Freud deciphered the birth of society not as an extinction but as a deployment of force and violence at the service of a moral order. Force and violence became the properties of society and were kept in abeyance only to the extent that remorse and obedience regulated social organization. An adjunct to force and violence is the institution of law, which gives external support to less than optimal internal developments of remorse and obedience, among members of the community. In Freud's view law rests on society's power to enforce it. In brief, might makes right.

Indeed, it is through force that the individual first encounters ethics in development. Chapter 7 of "Civilization and Its Discontents" (Freud 1930) is an exegesis of this psychoanalytic principle of development. However, succinct statements of the principle can be found earlier in Freud's writing. In "The

Economic Problem of Masochism" (1924), for example, we come across the following passage:

> One might expect that if a man knows that he is in the habit of avoiding the commission of acts of aggression that are undesirable from a cultural standpoint he will for that reason have a good conscience and will watch over his ego less suspiciously. The situation is usually presented as though ethical requirements were the primary thing and the renunciation of instinct followed from them. This leaves the origin of the ethical sense unexplained. Actually, it seems to be the other way about. The first instinctual renunciation is enforced by external powers, and it is only this which creates the ethical sense, which expresses itself in conscience and demands a further renunciation of instinct. [p. 170]

In other words, to a child the advantage of a set of ideals that will fit him or her for a future social existence is not at once apparent. What is apparent is the superior power of the parents and the succession of other authorities who transmit the ideals that become motives for the restraint on impulse. It is only later in development that mind discovers the value of ideals as a wherewithal to achieve good standing in a community. However, a relationship between force and ethicality is a permanent vicissitude in mind. Indeed, the ironies and paradoxes of the moral life is a principal subject of Freud's thought from its very outset, becoming increasingly explicit from the years of World War I in his elaborations of the superego concept.

Thus force and violence are the very instrumentalities of morality. However, it is also consistent with this principle that the prevalence of a moral order will subdue the necessity of force and violence. This is why Freud (1933) is able to say in his reply to Einstein on the problem of war, "Whatever fosters the growth of civilization works at the same time against war" (p. 215). And since it was possible for Freud to observe in the long course of history certain developments in the general mentality, specifically a strengthening of intellect corresponding to a greater internalization of aggression, Freud is also able to say that pacifism is becoming "a *constitutional* intolerance of war" (p. 215). Freud's evidence for this claim of social development, which he likens to the domestication of certain species of animals, is the fact that "sensations which were pleasurable to our ancestors have become indifferent or even intolerable to ourselves" (p. 214). In line with this he had already noted in "The Future of an Illusion" (1927) that of three former strivings that have acquired moral qualities in civilization—cannibalism, incest, and murder—only murder can still find a socially moral context for its justification (pp. 10–11). He does not mean, of course, that the other two are unheard of but only that they have lost all moral justifications in most human communities. Nor does Freud regard such evolution in communalization without hazard, particularly to the sexual life of mankind in the way of sexual inhibition with consequences to genetic distributions in the population—the least civilized in the population in these respects will become the more represented. Such was Freud's habit not to lose sight of the probability that every silver lining has a cloud. Even so, he means to be sanguine.

It is this line of Freud's thought, as it points specifically to the problem of international violence, that I referred to earlier as feeble. Not that Freud's speculations on social evolution do not hold water. There is, for example, a burgeoning literature relating the incidence of stress diseases to the intellectual and moral complexities created by modern societies that a slower rate of biological evolution has not quite fitted us for. Nor is it far-fetched to regard stress disease as one of the clinical expressions of the discontent in civilization Freud analyzed in his monograph on the subject. However, that mind in modern society reveals a capacity to surpass direct physical conquest as a crucial endeavor of everyday life is an observation that offers too little too late. For the problem of war and the quality of death war incurs is not the problem of mind. It is the problem of society. Actually, in a larger view, this was always Freud's position, which is why psychoanalysis is an iconoclastic and revolutionary critique of society. The difficult inconsistencies of Victorian morality, which have not disappeared by any means, or the martial law that a totalitarian politics imposes on mind were appalling to Freud, and he laid much of our individual woes—our plight of necessity—at such doorsteps.

Still, was Freud not saying in his letter to Einstein that if mind has become more pacifist in its strivings, then civilization must have become less violent in its ideals? For in psychoanalytic theory social ideals are as much motives of mind as superego contents, and social ideals as regards every form of oppression and cruelty have changed quite rapidly since the Enlightenment. Presently most governments are shamed by prevailing values into keeping secret the sanctions they impose on political dissent and the atrocities they carry out on prisoners deemed enemies of the state. I might interject in this connection that psychoanalysis itself has made an extraordinary contribution to the momentum of changing social values that took a new turn since the eighteenth century. In one historical perspective we read Freud as a continuity with Darwin, in another with Nietzsche and also Kant. But in still another, Freud's writings extend from John Locke's (1693) *Some Thoughts Concerning Education*, a fuse that exploded a whole liberal ideology that characterizes our present century, including even the political tracts and manifestos of totalitarian states. In his poem memorializing Freud, W. H. Auden (1939) describes psychoanalysis in the public domain as a "whole climate of opinion," a general threat to political perversity, "the concupiscence of the oppressor," as Auden put it:

> No wonder the ancient cultures of conceit
> in his technique of unsettlement foresaw
> the fall of princes, the collapse of
> their lucrative patterns of frustration:

> If he succeeded, why, the Generalised Life
> would become impossible, the monolith
> of State be broken and prevented
> the co-operation of avengers.
> [p. 216]

However, in the light of Freud's own psychological principles, what he observes of social evolution as it bears on the problem of war does business both ways. Whatever fosters the growth of civilization also makes for a superb military community. The army was one of the social orders Freud used to exemplify the psychoanalytic principles of communalization in his study of group psychology (1921)—the church was another. An internalization of aggression with its concomitant intellectualization of impulses—the constitution of the pacifist Freud later spoke of—is also what fosters a passionate allegiance to group ideals. If the group in question is a military one, these psychological dispositions will make a good soldier. In fact, in so far as neurosis is, as we saw earlier, a psychopathology of socialization, the more mentally healthy a recruit is, the better soldier he will become, all things being equal, including an absence of conflict with the moral order of the state served by the military.

But this line of thought may well be obsolete. Whether or not history or sociology can demonstrate that something like national character was a variable in different qualities of soldiering during World War II, for example, the problem currently is that modern military technology does not require significant differences in soldiering to bring havoc to the entire planet. Military communities of both more and less civilized dispositions are fast becoming able to wage wars of what for all intents and purposes are equally destructive to their enemies. Technology has eliminated the value of communal passion in the waging of the total war we presently dread.

Against such a note one might want to remember that the military is not, of course, synonomous with the state. It is merely a standing instrumentality of the state and does not represent the moral order of the state. No modern nation stockpiles weapons with the claim that militarism is its national purpose. Its national purpose is always of a higher moral order, and military security is only a means of preserving national morality. Viewed this way, the hatred of all things military can signify that one does not believe that one has something moral to defend, that any one moral order is interchangeable with any other. But such a position on the arbitrary interchangeability of moral orders is contrary to the whole process of civilization, which involves the attainment of values and ideals and their codifications in law. There is no human society in which such things are deemed arbitrary, because such things are the very particulars of socialization itself. It is true that national purposes can be defended by alternatives to war, but such alternatives are the equivalents of force. Even the threat of martyrdom, which

was Gandhi's strategy in his radicalization of the national law of
India, is ineffective in advancing a moral order unless it entails
potential violence among the followers of a resistive leader.

Having arrived at such a conception of the problematic
relationship between force and morality, Freud could imagine
no other alternative than the deployment of force to a structure
of law superordinate to separate national entities, a deployment
to yet a higher moral order. He writes: "Here, I believe, we
already have all the essentials: violence overcome by the transference of power to a larger unity, which is held together by
emotional ties between its members. What remains to be said is
no more than an expansion and a repetition of this" (1933, p.
205). And he goes on to say:

> Wars will only be prevented with a certainty if mankind unites in
> setting up a central authority to which the right of giving
> judgment upon all conflicts of interest shall be handed over.
> There are clearly two separate requirements involved in this: the
> creation of a supreme agency and its endowment with the
> necessary power. One without the other would be useless. The
> League of Nations is designed as an agency of this kind, but the
> second condition has not been fulfilled. [p. 207]

To which he adds something quite crucial that rests on a
principle somewhat as follows: once a communalizing moral
order is established, the largest share of the power behind its
maintenance reverts to the family where the moral order of the
community is passed on in child rearing. But in the family,
power need not be violence as a fact, only as a provisional
fantasy in the mind of the child, which fantasy yields to a more
benevolent experience with ideals in the course of development.
This is the principle I surmise in Freud's suggestion that the
value of ideals can gain a sufficient appreciation among nations
to create affinities that become regulating in themselves. That is,
the appreciation and adoption of an already existing moral order
does not entail violence; on the contrary, it leads to restraint.
There is something to be said for this final statement of Freud.
Despite the mutual suspicions among nations poised for combat
at this very moment, history has never seen a greater sharing

among nations of a vocabulary of ideals. To be sure, there are vast hidden realms of hell on earth and terrible events of terrorism and belligerence. But this is not to deny an increasingly common discourse among nations about what constitutes a more salutary and fulfilling social and political order. Nor should we shrug as if such discourse is merely words. Words count heavily in human affairs, and there are more words passed among us now than ever before. As for this, I return to Freud once more. In 1893, in one of his earliest psychoanalytic papers, Freud quoted an unidentified English writer to this effect: The man who first flung a word of abuse at his enemy instead of a spear was the founder of civilization" (p. 36).

It is here that my subject of some of Freud's views on the relationship among mind, civilization, and war leaves off and branches out to a number of questions for political science, history, and psychological theories other than psychoanalysis. However, I should like to repeat a point I was at pains to make near the outset. I had been mindful of yet another allegation against psychoanalysis for a doctrine of reductionism to the aggressive instinct as the *deus ex machina* in the affairs of social life. In separating mind and society, as was Freud's strategy, we can say that while an aggressive instinct is in mind, the instrumentalities of aggression come to reside in society where they exist as facts, not as mental representations, which is how instincts are seen in mind. By this I mean to suggest a line of thought that would unburden psychoanalysis of its alleged position that individuals by their very nature, by some obdurate determinism, are murderous and warlike. Were this so, there would be no repository of the unconscious whose very existence is what enables the common decency, heroism, reformatory commitment, and other virtues that psychoanalysis remarks in the great round of human existence.

But I was about to end with a few questions raised by this reading of Freud that cannot be answered by any further pursuit of psychoanalysis. For example, global communication has increased significantly over the past several decades. What are the ongoing effects of this on a standardization of values and ideals across national boundaries? This bears on Freud's thought about the regulation of aggression in shared values.

Also, what is the actual extent of international regulatory agencies such as the international monetary system, international trade agreements, the international postal system, information exchange programs, and the myriad treaties pertaining to military and extramilitary affairs? This also bears on the problem of increasing affinities among nations inasmuch as such matters are aspects of a superordinate legal system.

Furthermore, why are treaties between hostile nations so often obeyed? The international agreement, for example, to ban atmospheric testing of atomic weapons has not been violated since its inception nearly thirty years ago. This would bear on the problem of the variety of forces short of actual aggression that underlies the compliance with law by independent sovereignties.

Finally, what does a history of warfare reveal of the comparative incidence of war over the past decades? Has a large outline of a unifying moral order been sufficiently established to reduce its further promulgations by war? Was Vietnam a proving ground for the power of an existing moral order to compensate for an inferior military force? In other words, has there been a cultural evolution toward significantly less conflicting moral orders that reduces the justifications for extreme measures of conflict such as war?

I should not be surprised to hear that such questions are not the right ones. Perhaps they lack urgency and put us in mind of Freud's image of "mills that grind so slowly that people may starve before they get their flour." But, then, this would be as it should, because with such questions the psychoanalyst reverts to an ordinary citizen who now listens rather than speaks.

NOTE

The title of this chapter is taken from a 1915 essay by Freud in which he assessed the vast moral plight engendered by World War I, then raging in Europe. Freud deplored this military recourse to international affairs on grounds that warfare had at last become anachronistic in the development of human culture. This essay was one of several over the ensuing years in which

Freud drew lines from his clinical and psychological concerns to political and social problems. His reflections on such issues as the origins of law in the social order and the effect of technology upon the quality of culture constitute no less plausible an outcome of general psychoanalytic principles than his more systematic theory of the development and maintenance of individual mental life. The limits of Freud's political and social thought are also explored.

REFERENCES

Auden, W. H. (1939). *Collected Poems*. New York: Random House, 1976.

Freud, S. (1893). On the psychical mechanism of hysterical phenomena: a lecture. *Standard Edition* 3.

_____ (1911). Formulations on the two principles of mental functioning. *Standard Edition* 12.

_____ (1913a). Totem and taboo. *Standard Edition* 13.

_____ (1913b). The claims of psycho-analysis to scientific interest. *Standard Edition* 13.

_____ (1915). Thoughts for the times on war and death. *Standard Edition* 14.

_____ (1917). Mourning and melancholia. *Standard Edition* 14.

_____ (1921). Group psychology and the analysis of the ego. *Standard Edition* 18.

_____ (1924). The economic problem of masochism. *Standard Edition* 19.

_____ (1927). The future of an illusion. *Standard Edition* 21.

_____ (1928). Dostoevsky and parricide. *Standard Edition* 21.

_____ (1930). Civilization and its discontents. *Standard Edition* 21.

_____ (1933). Why war? *Standard Edition* 22.

_____ (1940). An outline of psycho-analysis. *Standard Edition* 23.

Kahneman, D., Slovic, P., and Tversky. A., eds. (1982). *Judgment Under Uncertainty: Heuristics and Biases*. Cambridge: Cambridge University Press.

Locke, J. (1693). *Some Thoughts Concerning Education*. Cambridge: Cambridge University Press, 1902.

Milosz, C. (1983). Ruins and poetry. *The New York Review of Books*. March 17, 1983: 20–23.

Ricoeur, P. (1970). *Freud and Philosophy*. New Haven, CT: Yale University Press.

16

Freud and the Coming of Age

Although it scarcely needs saying that psychoanalysis has momentously influenced social life in the present century, I believe its influence has been something more than the influence science in general has had on society. Psychoanalysis has directly affected not only our cultural interests and conceptions, but our personal strivings and social relationships as well. In what follows I shall single out one mode of this influence, a vast frontier of social life—the frontier of aging and dying. In referring to an inevitable maturational stage as a recently opened frontier, I have in mind (1) the idea, long familiar to psychoanalysis, that the biological side of human existence finds expression in social and cultural representations and (2) the observation that our expectations of the advanced stages of individual development are presently undergoing elaborations that were previously considered exceptional and unessential. Unless I am greatly mistaken, our language should begin to include the term *gerontologic* movement.

Since the psychoanalytic practitioner perforce discovers within himself the experiences and problems that others reveal because of the analyst's own praxis, the following argument is pertinent to the analyst's own adaptations to aging. I believe that in the analyst's relationship to Freud, a relationship established by the analyst's training, it may be possible to find a paradigm of personal extrication from a social situation that engenders certain desperations in those approaching old age. In other words, the psychoanalyst in the course of practicing and studying Freud's method and thought will learn more appropriate ways of approaching his own aging than those that society offers the general populace.

Let me embark on these themes by quoting a passage from a letter Freud wrote to Marie Bonaparte in which Freud disclosed his reaction to a social visit from Albert Einstein in 1926: " 'The lucky fellow has had a much easier time than I have. He has had the support of a long series of predecessors from Newton onward, while I have had to hack every step of my way through a tangled jungle alone. No wonder that my path is not a very broad one, and that I have not got far on it' " (Jones 1957, p. 139). The distinction between Einstein and himself that Freud makes in this letter corresponds to two kinds of intellectual achievement: one, like Einstein's, which repairs known flaws in our understanding of nature; the other, like Freud's, which creates a new subject matter by calling attention to an aspect of nature hitherto unnoticed. The distinction is a rough one, to be sure; great achievements are always combinations of both. Nevertheless, I believe the distinction has some merit. When Einstein published his early series of papers in 1905, he attained celebrity status virtually overnight because he solved recognizable problems that were of concern to an established intellectual community. Freud's "The Interpretation of Dreams" (1900), on the other hand, sold less than 350 copies in its first 6 years of publication. Its complement, "Three Essays on the Theory of Sexuality" (1905), took four years to sell a small, inexpensive first edition. The vicissitudes in mental life of memory and desire had not yet become a subject of any professional curiosity.

However, achievements such as Freud's do more than merely identify realms for curiosity to flourish in. Eventually such achievements innovate experience in the very realms they identify. One might interject that Freud's was a social science and was, therefore, bound to touch human lives more directly than any physical science. But such a statement obscures a crucial issue in Freud's comparison with Einstein. In Einstein's productions, extraordinary as they were, a professional community could see at once the decisive beginnings of physics' deliverance from the contradictions that had accumulated by the turn of the century. Einstein's achievement enabled an establishment to survive with renewed credibility.[1] Freud's achievement involved something else—a triumph over prevailing authority, a devastation to institutions, a disruption of a whole order of complacency. Unlike Einstein, or perhaps even Pavlov, to mention a behavioral scientist, Freud was no Messiah. He was a prophet, which is to say that while his method was compelling and his vision was clear, his message was alarming and ambiguous.

To extend my claim of the influence of psychoanalysis to the "gerontologic movement," let me begin by documenting this influence on an earlier stage of human development. Philippe Aries (1962) notes in his remarkable history of child rearing that "Our world is obsessed by the physical, moral and sexual problems of childhood" (p. 411), and he attributes this preoccupation largely to the dissemination of psychoanalytic lore in the present century. Now *obsessed* is precisely the word, for obsessions are reactions to a loss of confidence; they attempt a reinstatement of certainty; yet, the lapse of certainty that occurs in the meantime allows new experiences to enter. Freud's influence on child rearing occurred as a result of his discovery of a new world of infantile appetite for which parental reciprocities are not immediately available. Prior to the impact of psychoanalysis, a child's psychological misfortune was lamented as bad luck originating in constitutional defectiveness. The personal guilt and defensiveness in parents of children in trouble today were unheard of in previous eras. The frantic experimentation and misadventures in child rearing and education in this century have been pursued as much to acquit ourselves of those doubts raised by the popularization of psychoanalysis as to avail ourselves of a modern enlightenment suspected to exist somewhere in Freud's canon.

---

1. This particular aspect of Einstein's career can be compared to Alfred Binet's achievement in psychometrics, which has flourished (to put it mildly) since 1905 when Binet first brought out his instrument for measuring the intelligence of school children. Binet was commissioned by an established institution, a school system, to solve a recognized problem, and his ingenious (and, as we now know, portentous) solution was immediately heralded by those authorities whose power Binet enhanced. But however much they have come to regulate our lives, psychological tests and measurements do not directly touch our personal sensibilities.

However, there is no niche in the structure of Freud's thought for prescription or, at least, for the amount of prescription that would compensate for what his thought unsettled. When Freud devised the means for resurrecting the childhood of his patients, he created an opportunity for the life cycle to undergo an experiential revolution. It is cant to say that Freud discovered childhood. Certainly, in a manner of speaking, he did. But what is more to the point of his accomplishment was his casting a shadow of doubt and uncertainty upon the entire enterprise of child rearing. Under this shadow, childhood assimilated an extraordinary increment of sensibility.

I do not intend to convey the notion that authority over the child has lessened. From a psychological point of view such an idea is hardly conceivable, despite the "permissiveness" of the enlightened middle class and the admonitions of its critics. What happened is that authority became inconsistent and equivocal at the same time it became more pervasive because of Freud's discovery of the child's psychosexual potentialities. Such an approach to authority by the parents leads not to a sense of inner freedom in the child but to alterations in the child's narcissistic economy. An increase in the variety of parental reciprocity intensifies the child's sense of uniqueness and entitlement to experience, while parental uncertainty creates an imbalance between the child's aroused expectations and his capacity for developing the means for modifying and fulfilling them. Internal wishes retain a disproportionate priority over external contingency. Carried into adolescence, a narcissistic imbalance will confuse conviction, which is the passionate representation of a sense of reality, and subjectivism, which is sensation devoid of the contingencies of object relations. In the parlance of theoretical psychoanalysis, these trends in personality structure and cognitive style, so typical of the latter decades of the present century, are spoken of as a loss of boundaries between self and object representations.

Since the early 1960s, clinical psychoanalysts have observed a notable increase in the so-called narcissistic disorders among late adolescents and young adults, whose early childhood coincided with a significant moment of Freudian influence in the late 1940s and early 1950s. Not by coincidence, this period was when Riesman (1950, 1952) observed a shift in the character style of parents of the present generation of young adults, a shift from an authoritative certainty (inner direction) to a dependency upon fluctuating external information in a quest for certainty (other direction). Riesman metaphorically speaks of the firm inner gyroscope in these parents giving way to a set of shaky antennae. The narcissistic disorders in the grown offspring of these post–World War II, other-directed parents involve action-oriented symptoms – drug addiction, promiscuity, wrist slashing, delinquency, imposturing, exhibitionism, impulsivity – symptoms that differ from the psychoneuroses in the degree of physical sensation these narcissistic symptoms entail. Such symptoms are desperate measures to ward off a fundamental narcissistic susceptibility, namely, a depression evolving from the frozen rage at a parental imago that arouses expectation but immobilizes its consummation by well-meaning ambivalence. Wrist slashing, for example, is often more sensate than suicidal; in the absence of any other credible sign of consummatory reciprocity, the direct experience of one's own warm blood does give evidence, however bizarre, of a residual vitality.

Since only a marginal population exhibits psychopathology, it is a risky index to the actualities of any society. Those who describe society as a collective mental disorder are stretching the concept of psychopathology beyond clinical intelligibility. However, if the marked prominence of a particular form of psychopathology does not describe actualities of a general population in whose midst it arises, it does reflect the psychological issues that shape the trials of existing institutions and the ideals that institutions are called upon to embody and redeem. Narcissism (for my present purposes the definition does not require the precision it would in a more technical discussion) has become one of the most prominent psychological motives in social change. The libidinization of the self, which is one of the implications of the term *narcissism*, demands that the environment provide not simply material supplies, but narcissistic supplies as well. When the United States Supreme Court struck down the concept of "separate but equal" educational facilities, the basis for its decision was narcissistic: Technological supplies in themselves were no longer qualified to meet the entitlements of individuals; these supplies had to be made available in a way that maintained the self-esteem of the recipients. Beneath the extravagance and mayhem of the 1960s and beyond the din of the "pop" psychologies of charismatic figures like R. D. Laing and Fritz Perls, a politics of experience has been advancing in serious and believable ways since at least the early 1950s and has begun to contend with a politics of power as an irresistible force in contemporary industrial societies. To attribute this force exclusively to the ascendance of psychoanalysis would be far-fetched indeed. Coming from an analyst such an attribution would be grandiose in the bargain. The values and ideals that coalesce in a politics of experience arose in fact much earlier than the late nineteenth century in a variety of intellectual enterprises in Western society. However, it is not far-fetched to say that psychoanalysis has made an enormous contribution to the momentum this force has recently gathered.

I have singled out psychoanalysis's influence upon part of the life cycle in contemporary society in order to extend my claims for this influence to another realm of human existence that has begun to lose its innocence just as childhood lost its innocence in the course of this century. I am referring to the other end of the life cycle, namely, old age. Near the outset of these remarks I suggested the social appearance of a "gerontologic move-ment." Though it is too soon to tell what psychological struc-tures such a movement will promote in those advancing toward old age, certain themes reminiscent of former years of the Freudian influence are already on the agenda. For example, the expectation is that hitherto unnoticed forms of appetite and sensibility are potential in the aged and that appropriate reci-procities will have to be forthcoming. The denials and taboos that have kept old age an undiscovered realm are poised to go under. The apprehensions and uncertainties in the psychosocial domain of aging, which a long-standing conspiracy of silence has deprived of expression, are becoming apparent. The coming of age is upon us at this moment in ways analogous to the coming of childhood earlier in this century.

I particularly want to stress the psychosocial dimension of aging. The type of knowledge we now have regarding old age is what I referred to earlier as the kind that repairs recognizable flaws in the current perceptions of the natural world. The fields of geriatrics, gerontology, actuarial studies, and other technical disciplines have long histories. Geriatrics, for example, can be traced back to Hippocrates, who compiled a rather exact pathology of old age.[2] However, geriatrics relates to the psychosocial events of old age as remotely as pediatrics did to the comparable events of childhood prior to Freud's influence.

Only recently old age has begun to generate not only data, but also publicity. The media are full of news about the aged, which has already had the effect of identifying a new disadvantaged group in our midst. Bevan (1972), in a *Science* editorial, made a distinction between the technological and social responses to old age: " . . the key to the problems of the aged is not national resources or the know-how of the medical and behavioral sciences. It is a fundamental change in national attitude" (p. 839). The basis for such a statement is similar to that which led the United States Supreme Court to strike down the concept of "separate but equal" material facilities. Economic disinterest in the aged has been giving way to economic exploitation of their unique needs, and in the United States such exploitation is a familiar form of social recognition. Homes for the aged are a booming business, opening at the rate of seven a day, largely for profiteering so criminal that a Senate subcommittee has been investigating this particular sign of "fundamental change in national attitude" for several years. Another exponent of social actualization, militancy, is beginning to pick up support among the aged; witness the formation of the Gray Panthers and their subsequent actions. However, militancy among the aged is not confined to those who live in the United States. The *New York Times* (Sept. 16, 1972) carried a front page story about a rally of 15,000 "elderly" Japanese near Tokyo on the Keiro No Hi holiday—the "Day of Respect for the Aged." Protesting the degradation of the aged in all industrialized nations, this group adopted as the theme for their rally, "Change the Day of Respect for the Aged to the Day of Anger of the Aged."

Virtually all appeals regarding the social plight of the aged begin with citations of demographic change. For example,

---

2. Hippocrates noted *inter alia* typical respiratory troubles, urinary difficulties, kidney diseases, arthritis, cataract, vertigo, pruritus, and fatigue.

In this century, the *percentage* of the United States population aged 65 and over has more than doubled (from 4.1% in 1900 to 9.9% in 1970), while the *number* increased more than sixfold (from 3 million to 20 million). To put the same basic fact slightly differently: a child born in 1900 could expect to live to an average age of about 48 years; a child born in 1969 could expect to live 22 years longer, to an average of 70 years. [Bier 1974, p. ix]

Such statistics are asserted as if they, in themselves, account for society acknowledging the problems of old age, as if such figures describe a reality so compelling that to continue denying the social existence of the aged would jeopardize that minimum degree of reality testing we require for our sense of sanity. Such a notion is plain nonsense. The mere extensiveness of human degradation has never been a reason for its undoing. The passion energizing social action arises in the credibility gaps between ideals and their redemption. Where nothing has been promised, infinite degradation is absorbed with infinite resignation and forbearance. The gerontologic movement is not a function of numbers; it arises from a shift of social motive from material welfare to psychological aspiration. Thirty-five years ago Edward Tolman (1941) addressed the American Psychological Association with the thesis that "psychological man" was replacing "economic man" in American society; in other words, material ideals were losing their exclusive priorities to what Tolman called "ego needs" — self-esteem and a sense of purpose beyond mere survival. These ideals, which resulted in informed child rearing, are now finding their way into society's considerations of its older members.

What share in this expansion of ideals can be assigned to psychoanalysis? The psychoanalytic literature on old age is scant indeed compared to that on childhood, which no doubt reflects some limitation in the psychoanalytic curiosity about the aged. Freud himself was skeptical about the value of his method for older patients. Although this view is changing, the influence of psychoanalysis cannot be judged by its practical applications.

The entire psychoanalytic literature on childhood can be read on two levels: one as a contribution to actual developmental processes in the human being; the other as a case in point relating to superordinate issues in the human condition having to do with fantasy, illusion, myth—the myriad representations of the great debate between desire and authority. The psychoanalytic method is therefore two things—a scientific praxis and an iconoclastic activity (Kaplan 1973). The former characteristic is emphasized in the technical literature of psychoanalysis; the latter is what has affected society. The fact that things are not what they seem to be has been the message of psychoanalysis from the beginning. Childhood has been one case in point. However, the whole life cycle is no less the subject of such a message, for there is no stage of life exempt from susceptibility to illusion. It was, in fact, only a matter of time before the unsettlements inspired by such a message occurred in the life cycle beyond childhood.

In Simone de Beauvoir's (1972) eloquent and extensive treatise, *The Coming of Age*, she raises some issues that have special relevance to the present topic—what the psychoanalyst has learned in the course of practicing and studying Freud's method and thought that will help him approach and come to terms with his own aging. Although de Beauvoir enlists history, biology, anthropology, psychology, and philosophy, she sees old age as a class struggle. Since the Industrial Revolution, the process of growing old has gone from bad to worse. The plight of the aged de Beauvoir views as an example of the exploitation and underprivilege created by capitalism. The aged[3] are at the extreme polar end of the disadvantaged classes, the obsolete human material of an economic structure whose ultimate purpose is profit. The development of humanistic values since the turn of the century de Beauvoir regards as mere window dressing.

The Coming of Age, saturated with the details of the everyday existence of the legions of nonproductive old persons, exposes the "convenient illusion" of serenity surrounding old age. De Beauvoir describes the primitive routine and physical environment of typical homes for the aged. She reports interviews with old people. She cites Rorschach findings on the personality of the average old person—the rigidity of response to the ink blots,

---

3. All things being equal, de Beauvoir identifies the "aged" as those who are beyond age 65.

the stereotyped thinking, the intellectual doubts, the distrust, the evasiveness, the inwardness, the low threshold against anxiety and frank terror, the deterioration of certain kinds of memory and its compensation through confabulation. She constructs poignant and familiar narratives of how middle-aged adults manipulate and tyrannize their dependent, aged parents with cold rejection—often as not, rejection coupled with ironic kindness and infantilizing attention.

"Life's parody" is de Beauvoir's felicitous phrase for old age. The physical deterioration that inevitably characterizes old age cannot be reconciled in our present society with any affirmative direction in life. Old persons find it impossible to evoke the genuine responses that formerly gave their lives meaning and pleasure. A parody of reciprocity begins to occur. At best we humor the old. We are stilted and polite. Often we ridicule them. More often we ignore them. The only genuine interactions we can muster are primitive ones: When the old succeed in infuriating us, we rage at them; if they persist, we lock them up.

Do the aged have any alternatives? De Beauvoir searches the memoirs, biographies, and other accounts of the late years of those who were privileged by birth, talent, nerve, or intelligence to escape the fate that the social structure inflicts on the masses. Despite her view that the problems of old age in our society originate largely from underprivilege, de Beauvoir's use of a privileged population—mainly writers and statesmen, who were more likely to be articulate about the tribulations of old age—remains realistic. Although she has more respect for her topic than merely painting the future out of hand and then selecting only that evidence which confirms the vision, she does allow herself to

> . . . dream that in the ideal society . . . old age would be virtually nonexistent. As it does happen in certain privileged cases, the individual, though privately weakened by age but not obviously lessened by it, would one day be attacked by some disease from which he would not recover; he would die without having suffered any degradation. The last age would really comply with the definition given by certain bourgeois ideologists—a period of life different from youth and maturity, but

possessing its own balance and leaving a wide range of possibilities open to the individual. [p. 543]

Yet the range of possibilities de Beauvoir discovers in a variety of lives—Voltaire, Goethe, Gide, Chateaubriand, Lou Andreas-Salome, Winston Churchill, Freud—contains little that is immediately consoling. True, she turns up an occasional instance of what could be construed as an enviable passage toward death. Victor Hugo, for example, survived a stroke when he was 76, but it did not prevent him from continuing his previously active and apparently fulfilling sexual activities—suffering, as nearly as can be told, no feelings of inferiority whatsoever. Furthermore, he persisted in his writing until a few weeks before his death. Goethe, on the other hand, at the age of 72, fell hopelessly in love with the enchanting 17-year-old Ulrike; he courted her for a year with increasing boldness and finally proposed marriage; when she gently and tactfully rejected him, Goethe's confidence drained away; soon he was bedridden and remained embittered until the day he died.[4] Freud, who lived with cancer the last fifteen years of his long life, described his old age in his last letter to Marie Bonaparte as " ' . . . a small island of pain floating on an ocean of indifference' " (Schur 1972, p. 524). Although they cannot be dismissed, material advantages alone cannot account for this privileged population having a more bearable time of it. After all, Goethe was not inured against mortification nor Freud against the anguish of disease.

However, for all the variety she finds among this population,

---

4. De Beauvoir presents only part of the story of Goethe's last years, curiously omitting the part that sustains her thesis that a commitment to culture can rescue the aged from the degradations of aging. It is true that following the Ulrike incident Goethe succumbed to all kinds of physical disabilities and was bedridden. Mann (1948) described Goethe a year after the rejection by Ulrike as " . . in a most critical condition, physically weakened and spiritually apathetic" (p. xxvii). However, Mann goes on to remind us that in the midst of this condition Goethe managed to write the inspiring, if uneven, *Trilogy of Passion*. Goethe also worked on Wilhelm Meister's *Travel Years* and the second part of *Faust*. Mann concludes, "What an old age! With all its dignity, there is nothing of desiccation, of ossification about it. It is full of sensitivity, curiosity, interest in life" (p. xlii).

de Beauvoir is able to distinguish something in these privileged individuals' last years that sets their old age apart from that of the vast majority. Transcending moral opinion and its limits on affective options, the privileged are possessed of passions strong enough to prevent them from turning inward, however much physical change and ailment beckon the mind. De Beauvoir concludes, "There is only one solution if old age is not to be an absurd parody of our former life, and that is to go on pursuing ends that give our existence a meaning—devotion to individuals, to groups or to causes, social, political, intellectual or creative work" (p. 540). Aging is not an activity, a project requiring preparation, a retirement from living, a laying in of hobbies. De Beauvoir counsels, " . . live a fairly committed, fairly justified life so that one may go on in the same path even when all illusions have vanished and one's zeal for life has died away" (p. 541). However, for the average aged person, " . . the meaning of his existence has been stolen from him . ." (p. 542). Industrial society concedes value to a person only if he is gainfully employed and strips him of this tenuous value when he is not; it also enshrines the "here and now" as a tyrannical reign of progress. Indeed, obsolescence has become a positive correlate of progress. "Modern technocratic society thinks that knowledge does not accumulate with the years, but grows out of date. Age brings disqualification with it: age is not an advantage" (p. 210). Lost in all this "progress" is what is commonly called "culture"—the wherewithal to reconstruct and elaborate the value of one's relationship to the environment at every age. Culture affords something different from the hectic seizure of personal value according to what de Beauvoir calls "Lassalle's 'brazen law' of wages" (p. 542).[5]

I have presented this much of de Beauvoir's view of aging not so much for *what* she dichotomizes—that mass of faceless human relics as against a small breed of fortunate personages—

---

5. De Beauvoir submits that an exclusive economic criterion of personal value permits us no more than the right to reproduce ourselves. Ironically, the adoption of this outrageous criterion by large factions of the feminist movement has begun to undermine the value of domesticity and the bearing and caring for children.

as *how* she dichotomizes.[6] The idea can now be advanced that aging takes place under two auspices: the social, where it goes badly, and the cultural, where the opportunity for it to go comparatively better is present. By *social* I mean the everyday, personal interactions and relationships that are structured by habits, fashions, and rules. By *cultural* I mean something less immediate—the traditions, ideas, and values by which social experience acquires and maintains meaning and purpose. This distinction is not always dichotomous, but it has become increasingly so in industrial societies over the past 50 years. A "disjunction of culture and society" is how Bell (1965) labels the special difficulty " . . in finding appropriate symbolic expression for efforts to grasp the meaning of experiences in contemporary society" (p. 208).

By focusing more sharply than de Beauvoir needed to for her particular purposes upon those persons who aged with dignity, privileged by virtue of their vital connection with some form of culture, it is evident that they do not comprise one category but two. In the first category are those who create culture and whose involvements with the process of creation pre-empt the claims of society. This path is not an option; the difference between a penchant for creativity and a talent for it is a matter of genetics, an unusual biological capacity and imperative that achieve representation in cultural innovation. Those in the second category attain what de Beauvoir calls a justification of life through an identification with a creator and his cultural cause—a vicissitude of narcissism. The psychoanalytic profession itself is a paradigm of these processes and relationships. In the first category is Freud who extricated himself from society through his pursuit of innovation, which was psychoanalysis. In the second category is the psychoanalyst, whose relationship to Freud and to Freud's innovation embodies a cultural privilege larger than an ordinary psychiatrist enjoys (a hint that I am

6. The enormous variability found in how ordinary persons deal with old age can be appreciated in Mass and Kuypers's (1974) study, which examines the personalities and life styles of over 140 individual subjects at an average age of 70 from a longitudinal point of view. There are, however, sociological studies (e.g., Riesman 1954) that employ broad categorical strokes similar to de Beauvoir's.

drifting toward sensitive, if not inflammatory, professional issues).

Since Freud's life is well known, the few biographical facts I shall cite will suggest the large and powerful theme in Freud's life of extricating the self from society in a passionate commitment to culture. After a point, a consuming involvement with money and power and the manipulations required for these social achievements disappeared from Freud's life. Though Freud made no secret of his ardent wish for fame, it is abundantly clear, particularly from the personal revelations in his letters, that the fame he was after was Miltonic, divorced from public relations. Indeed, Freud's controversy with Jung centered crucially upon the issue of preserving whatever fame would come to psychoanalysis against the inevitable compromises of public relations.

Freud was never a rich man, not even at the height of his fame. In fact, he often lacked the money for small trips. In the 1920s, following the appearance of cancer and the necessity for a complicated oral prosthesis, he was upset about having to pay a specialist's fee with the money he had earmarked for his small psychoanalytic press. Yet he turned down a huge sum offered by Samuel Goldwyn for a consultation on a film depicting psychoanalysis, and he rejected an offer from William Randolph Hearst of any sum Freud cared to name to cover the Leopold-Loeb trial in Chicago (Hearst threw into the bargain an ocean voyage to America on which Freud would have had a large section of the boat all to himself). Such offers seem not even to have been tempting. They were without any plausibility to Freud. His reasons for casting them aside were that he was too busy or that they were "not in my line," a phrase he used in English.

This indifference to ordinary social advantages, which is all the more extraordinary in a man of Freud's middle-class bearing and habits, predated his fame—an observation worth making in order to dispel any notion that he took a stand of indifference only upon the security of his eventual notoriety and acclaim. Earlier, in the 1890s—he was then in his forties and deeply felt his responsibility for his growing family—the steady erosion of his successful career as a neuropsychiatrist was an unregretted, indeed, almost unnoticed state of affairs as he followed the logic of psychoanalysis, which was clear to no one but himself. During his years of professional isolation, he played cards Saturday nights at the B'nai B'rith in Vienna with nonmedical friends who had no idea about what he was up to the rest of the time. I do not mean to imply that Freud took leave of his senses about the ordinary affairs of his life. A comment in a letter to Fliess in 1902 is typical of Freud's concern: "I myself would still gladly exchange five congratulations for one good case coming for extensive treatment. I have learned that the old world is governed by authority just as the new is governed by the dollar" (1897–1902, p. 344). Although he involved himself in the lives of his family, friends, colleagues, and sometimes strangers, there was something unremittingly aloof about him, a core of social unavailability. The development of psychoanalysis soon replaced all his social aspirations. Later it rescued him from the near annihilation he experienced at the death of his adored grandson, Heinele. Psychoanalysis came to stand for the opportunity to "die in harness," a phrase Freud borrowed from *Macbeth*—the opportunity to die in the midst of creative labor, which, for Freud, combined the play, pleasure, and even risk most others seek in realms outside of work. This aspect of Freud's life reminds me of the proud and daring motto of the Hanseatic League, which Freud (1915) quotes in his essay, "Thoughts for the Times on War and Death": "'*Navigare necesse est, vivere non necesse.*' ('It is necessary to sail the seas, it is not necessary to live')" (p. 291).

Such commitment to cultural innovation also guarantees autonomy from physical claims of aging. In his biography of Freud, Schur (1972) testifies that during those long, painful years of malignancy his patient resorted only to occasional aspirin in order that he not lose his mind to his body through psychotropic palliatives like morphine. Only the most intense attachment to the life of creativity can enable such transformations of primary narcissism. In Freud's instance, there is more than an approximation of de Beauvoir's ideal vision of aging and dying; there is its replication.

When I referred earlier to the kind of love affair with cultural innovation as involving a genetic imperative, I had in mind

Greenacre's (1957, 1958) idea that a "talent" or a "gift" originates in a favorable perceptual anomaly. This fundamental *donnee* of the creative mind, which it would not be too fanciful to think of as an actual mutation, motivates the gifted individual to construct a personalized universe out of what ordinary individuals perceive as the peripheral features of reality. Although the gifted person perceives both the central and peripheral features of reality, he has a sensitivity to the latter—a sensitivity that forces him to look at the world he constructs out of peripheries with as much plausibility as ordinary persons look at the ordinary world. An example from Freud's experience is the idea that "hysterics suffer from reminiscences" or that sex has something to do with neurotic symptoms. In the professional minds of Vienna in the 1890s, these ideas were not missing; however, they were strictly incidental to the reality shared by ordinary doctors. Of such peripheral ideas—ideas that had been simply thrown away by others—Freud constructed a reality equivalent to what was consensually agreed upon; he then found that he needed to look further into the alternative reality he had constructed. This development was not an option for Freud; rather, it was a matter of retaining his sense of reality by engaging a reality that was unique with him yet every bit as urgent as more ordinary reality. Greenacre (1957) has given the name "collective alternates" to the constructed world with which the gifted person begins to have his special love affair. The gifted individual departs the ordinary social realm rather gracefully and comparatively free of those conflicts and desperations found in morbid processes that lead to social estrangement without cultural substenance.

On another occasion, I (1972) elaborated a psychoanalytic view of what is intriguing about the evidence of technique visible in the art, science, or intellectual system it gives rise to, and how a person can identify with the creative process through the perception of its technique. If a person cannot emulate the creative process, he can identify with it to varying degrees, thereby achieving some communion with culture and some distance from the social flux in which meaning and justification for existence are so elusive and hard to retain. By identification with things cultural I do not mean simply the conscious acquisition of an assenting conversance with art, science, or systems of ideas. I mean an internalization of the creator's technical style and strategy that produces a conviction of exactly why a particular innovation has to be precisely what it is and not something else. Freud was well aware that different students of psychoanalysis achieved different levels of comprehension of his thought. Karl Abraham suggested Freud's awareness of these differences in a letter to Max Eitingon in 1908: " 'Freud has come to divide his followers into three grades: those in the lowest have understood no more than *The Psychopathology of Everyday Life*; those in the second the theories on dreams and neuroses; and those in the third follow him into the theory of sexuality and accept his extension of the libido concept' " (Abraham 1974, p. 35). In other words, some issues in Freud's thought can be understood through a study of this or that text, and some issues are accessible only through personal contact and struggle with the entire architecture of Freud's canon, for that is where the soul of his thought resides.

I know of no specialty in the mental health professions other than psychoanalysis that affords a student so much opportunity to attempt the kind of identification I am describing. I am not saying that psychoanalytic institutes require students to avail themselves of all the opportunity; but it is in these institutes that a student should acquire the motivation—a motivation that should increase further on in his career—to cultivate such an identification. The possibility of such personal immersion in the life and work of a single individual, even an individual of Freud's stature, is most unusual in a rite of professional passage. This possibility is disturbing to many who regard it as a danger to the kind of open-mindedness that most people believe education should instill. Although it is not my intention to enter into that controversy here, I shall add more fuel to it by quoting Kohut (1976), who reminds us that the imago of Freud even enters the student's most personal aspect of training, namely, his training analysis. Kohut recognizes the danger that "To end a training analysis on the high-minded note of a shared admiration for Freud. . . . may in some instances tend to close off certain postanalytic potentialities for the future analyst" (p. 390). But he hastens to add another view:

> . . . a (training) analysand's spontaneously arrived at, realistic,
> non-defensive capacity to admire Freud as one of the great minds
> of the Western world, and as a model of scientific rigor and moral
> courage, by no means indicates that the narcissistic sector has not
> been successfully dealt with in the analysis. On the contrary, it
> may at times even be considered to be a sign of analytic success,
> especially in personalities who were formerly unable to mobilize
> any enthusiasm for greatness, whether encountered in the form
> of admirable ideas or of admirable personalities. [p. 391]

Let me be candid. The average psychoanalyst is a middle-
class physician involved in money, status, fashions, appearances, and other social strivings. As far as most forms of culture
are concerned he is (to give him the benefit of the doubt) a
harried spectator. If anything, science is his greatest cultural
potential, and it would be hard to say how much of this
potential had been developed before he encountered psychoanalysis. The psychiatrist enters the social maelstrom as a
fledgling bearing heavy responsibilities; he could well go on to
become a skillful old bird. However, at a certain point in life and
from a position of considerable social attainment—he is now,
after all, a doctor and, what is more, a specialist—he chooses to
embark on the arduous years of psychoanalytic training with its
daily personal analysis, its night classes, its low-paying training
cases, its seemingly endless supervision. He will be 40, more or
less, when it is over. He does not make this choice with the hope
of future financial improvement. Any nonpsychoanalytic psychiatrist with half a brain earns as much or more than a
psychoanalyst since he is not hindered by the peculiar time-
consuming procedures of clinical psychoanalysis. The choice is
a gravitation toward culture.

Although this choice may improve personal sensitivity, it will
not put virtue into the practitioner who has none to begin with,
nor will it elevate basic intelligence. It will no doubt have a
radical effect upon the doctor's work style and his presumptions
of interest—he will see fewer patients, each for longer periods of
time, and he will deal less with social parameters and more with
individual psychology. One gain is certain, and it is usually kept
a shameful secret. The choice leads to a sense of privilege
through the energetic appropriation of an immense cultural

object, namely, psychoanalysis. This acquisition is apt to be the average analyst's only profound cultural opportunity. Pondering Freud's work will transform him as great culture should. He has been socialized enough; this experience will civilize him. And in turn it will affect his ambition for his patients, whose pursuit of social experience the analyst meets with reflection and interpretation. Psychoanalytically informed therapy differs from most other psychotherapies prominent on the current professional scene in its interpretive ambition, in its provisions for reflection upon rather than enlargements of social experience. The psychoanalyst tries to structure a clinical situation in which the patient's attempts at social interaction with the therapist are discouraged in favor of their interpretation. The psychoanalytic contention is that acting out in the social environment is a resistance against understanding the meaning of one's daily behavior.

Here I have arrived full circle at a problem raised earlier in this discussion—the necessity of locating a vantage from which to interpret everyday existence in the social realm, a vantage de Beauvoir (1972) defines as the cultural realm. Employing terms I introduced earlier, I can say that psychoanalytic therapy wants to replace a disjunction of social experience and cultural meaning with a synergism. If I have failed to rid the concept of culture of its elite connotation, so be it; let the familiar accusation—that psychoanalysis embodies an elite point of view counter to the prevailing social current—stand. Only unless the flotsam that swells the social current at this moment in history is forgotten can this allegation be regarded in a negative light. Besides, since when has it not been part of the democratic ethos to encourage a distribution of elite experiences among a population wider than the elite?

I should like to make one further observation along these lines. De Beauvoir points out the relentless obsolescence of all things technical and human in industrial societies, and she laments that the passage of years has become filled not with opportunities for things to last and mature, but rather with the inevitability of decline. Psychoanalysis runs counter to this social process and is, therefore, vehemently attacked. Its slow rate of technical and theoretical change, which could represent the durability of a worthwhile set of ideas, is regarded as a manifestation of professional complacency, pig-headedness, and irrelevance. In a world in which psychological technique and the theory that informs it must advance like the gross national product, the psychoanalyst is seen as someone with his head stuck in the sands of his calling, a figure self-absorbed in an aberration of narcissism, mirroring Freud's social isolation.

This imputation of vanity in the analyst's stand against the social tide has something (not everything, to be sure) to do with an envious fantasy about an option—a privilege, I should say— regarding the problem of aging, of growing old, of dying. The psychoanalyst is not exempt from the problems of aging and dying, but he has chosen a path out of the social realm where aging and dying go badly, even for doctors.[7] I am not suggesting that we wring our hands in sympathy for one of society's most advantaged groups. Doctors, like other prestigious profession-als, age and die better than most. However, since it is common knowledge that hostilities are aroused when a person feels abandoned to his day-to-day social trials by those he imagines have acquired some special privilege, I do not think it out-landish to say that a psychiatrist is not immune to feeling envy for his psychoanalyst colleague, whose actual daily labors and responsibilities are no less onerous. Although the psychiatrist often tries to conceal these envious reactions in scientific and professional controversies, they are expressed so stridently that they betray issues other than substantive ones.

I have juxtaposed a vast social problem, which de Beauvoir calls the "coming of age," and a small and, by comparison, inconsequential sociocultural enclave, the psychoanalytic pro-fession, because they seem to resonate to the same issues critical to our times. Whatever the merit of my initially attributing the current gerontologic movement to the influence of psychoanaly-

---

7. Following the completion of this chapter, my attention was called to an essay I had not seen by Eissler (1975), which may be the only sustained discussion of the advantages and limitations posed by old age for those in the actual practice of psychoanalysis. Eissler makes a convincing case that for the practicing psychoanalyst the advantages of being old outweigh the limitations. Among the advantages, Eissler singles out the enhanced capacity in the aged for empathic involvement with the patient's early childhood experiences.

sis's popularization, it does not follow, of course, that the actual practice of psychoanalysis will supply anything practical to the need for new forms of human reciprocity with aged populations. Solutions must come from transforming society's response to the aged on a large scale.

Ritualization is the only process broad enough to encompass the problem. Rituals are gestures that conserve the meaning of social experience, and it is meaning that the shapeless narcissism making its appearance among the aged is seeking. At this moment there are no credible rituals for this looming population. There are only parodies of ritual—empty gestures. Myth is what generates ritual, but the present century has not been a good one for mythopoesis—the process that ensures credibility for mythic values and ideals by providing their content with new forms. Trilling (1972) remarks that ". . . it is characteristic of the intellectual life of our culture that it fosters a form of assent which does not involve actual credence . . ." (p. 171). He is referring to what happened in the past decade to our ideals of individuality and individual entitlement to self-realization, which were inflated beyond the bounds of credibility: ". . . each one of us a Christ—but with none of the inconveniences of undertaking to intercede, of being a sacrifice, of reasoning with rabbis, of making sermons, of having disciples, of going to weddings and to funerals, of beginning something and at a certain point remarking that it is finished" (p. 172).

Beatification disengaged from responsibility is essence deprived of existence. The motor idles; there is no traction. This state was what Trilling reproved; it was the huge folly of the decade just past, a miscarriage of certain humanistic forces, including psychoanalysis. I speak of it in the past tense because there are signs of its receding. The casualities of the 1960s are beginning to drag back from their ill-fated expeditions in solipsism. But those of us who resisted the monkey business ushered in by the "flower children" of the early 1960s should find something more within ourselves than an inclination to gloat over the failure of "salvation." In a demise there is often a legacy, and the recent excesses of subjectivity may have been an unavoidable phase in a social process leading to a general sense of entitlement that will not soon abate.

This sense of entitlement becomes more urgent when time is short. With the coming of age we grow more desperate, especially about promises made but unredeemed. The narcissistic trends of this century have reached those in their later years, and the privilege they seek has become a problem of the greatest urgency. Freud never tired of cautioning us about the lengths we go to deny urgency, even when our own lives are at stake. Old age and death are in store for us all, yet we treat them as things that happen only to others. Freud also gave us the wherewithal to reduce self-deception. On this score, I can think of no other time when it has been more important to preserve what Freud gave us. The promises we have made earlier in our epoch, perhaps in blindness, we must now take responsibility for in an enlightenment more faithful than ever to the intellectual resources of this century.

REFERENCES

Abraham, H. C. (1974). Karl Abraham: An Unfinished Biography. *The International Review of Psycho-Analysis* 1:17–72,

Aries, P. (1962). *Centuries of Childhood: A Social History of Family Life*, trans. Robert Baldick. New York: Knopf.

Bell, D. (1965). The disjunction of culture and social structure: some notes on the meaning of social reality. *Daedalus* 94(1):208–22.

Bevan, W. (1974). On growing old in America. *Science* 177 (4052):839.

Bier, W. C. (1974). Preface. In *Aging: Its Challenge to the Individual and to Society* (Pastoral Psychology Series, No. 8), ed. W. C. Bier, pp. vii–xi. New York: Fordham University Press.

De Beauvoir, S. (1972). *The Coming of Age*, trans. *Patrick O'Brian*. New York: G. P. Putnam's Sons.

Eissler, K. R. (1975). On possible effects of aging on the practice of psychoanalysis: an essay. *Journal of the Philadelphia Association of Psychoanalysis* 2:138–52.

Freud, S. (1887–1902). *The Origins of Psycho-Analysis: Letters to Wilhelm Fliess, Drafts and Notes: 1887–1902*, trans. E. Mosbacher and J. Strachey, ed. Marie Bonaparte et al. New York: Basic Books, 1954.

_____ (1900). The interpretation of dreams. *Standard Edition* 4/5.

_____ (1905). Three essays on the theory of sexuality. *Standard Edition* 7.

_____ (1915). Thoughts for the times on war and death. *Standard Edition* 14.

Greenacre, P. (1957). The childhood of the artist: libidinal phase development and giftedness. *Psychoanalytic Study of the Child* 12:47–72.

_____ (1958). The family romance of the artist. *Psychoanalytic Study of the Child* 13:9–36.

Jones, E. (1957). *Sigmund Freud: Life and Work*, vol. 3. London: Hogarth.

Kaplan, D. M. (1972). Reflections on Eissler's concept of the doxaletheic function. *American Imago* 29(4):353–76.

———— (1973). A technical device in psychoanalysis and its implications for a scientific psychotherapy. In *Psychoanalysis and Contemporary Science*, vol. 2, ed. B. B. Rubinstein, pp. 25–41. New York: Macmillan.

Kohut, H. (1976). Creativeness, charisma, group psychology: reflections on the self-analysis of Freud. In *Freud: The Fusion of Science and Humanism: The Intellectual History of Psychoanalysis* (Psychological Issues, Vol. 9, Nos. 2/3, Monogr. 34/35), ed. J. E. Gedo and G. H. Pollock, pp. 379–425. New York: International Universities Press.

Maas, H. S., and Kuypers, J. A. (1974). *From Thirty to Seventy: A Forty-Year Longitudinal Study of Adult Life Styles and Personality*. San Francisco, CA: Jossey-Bass.

Mann, T. (1948). *The Permanent Goethe*. New York: Dial.

Riesman, D. (1950). *The Lonely Crowd: A Study of the Changing American Character* (Studies in National Policy #3). New Haven, CT: Yale University Press.

———— (1952). *Faces in the Crowd: Individual Studies in Character and Politics* (Studies in National Policy #4). New Haven, CT: Yale University Press.

———— (1954). Some clinical and cultural aspects of the aging process. In *Individualism Reconsidered and Other Essays*, pp. 484–91. Glencoe, IL: Free Press.

Schur, M. (1972). *Freud: Living and Dying*. New York: International Universities Press.

Tolman, E. C. (1941). Psychological Man. *Journal of Social Psychology* 13(1):205–18.

Trilling, L. (1972). *Sincerity and Authenticity*. Cambridge, MA: Harvard University Press.

17

Preaching Old Virtues
While Practicing Old Vices

The title of this chapter doubtless conjures the bewildering and deplorable events that have been coming to light in our socio-political realms over the past several years. Though the preaching of old virtues while practicing old vices is nothing new in the life of society—consider, for example, the observation of Terence that "there is a demand today for men who can make wrong appear right"—I think we feel at the present moment a greater sense of outrage (more, a greater sense of desperation) than ever before toward the duplicity and hypocrisy that we have always taken for granted in the human comedy. The Watergate Affair cannot go unmentioned. But Mr. Nixon may have been right about one thing. His conduct and the conduct of those who functioned under his authority are not exceptional in the operations of government, or, at least, the Nixonian species of morality is not unknown in human affairs. Indeed, like Nixon himself, such morality is really quite ordinary and unimaginative, which is precisely its shortcoming at this moment in history, for something tells us these are extraordinary times requiring an imaginative response different from the banalities of Nixonian politics. Toward the end of my remarks I shall document the fact that a number of sober minds are no longer anticipating what kind of future we are fashioning but rather are anticipating the unique likelihood of no future at all within two or three human generations. Thus, a morality as ordinary as preaching one thing while practicing another, precisely because it is so ordinary, has become grotesquely irrelevant on the human agenda. The morality of Watergate has become as idiotic as the idea of employing confirmed morphine addicts to staff a terminal cancer ward. The idea is monstrous not because we despise drug addicts but because we would see at once the folly of assuming they would remain levelheaded toward the humane tasks required of them.

Do I mean to say in these opening remarks that I would hold the particular morality of Watergate less impeachable at another time in history? Whether I would or not merely disposes of the question from a personal point of view. However, it is from a psychoanalytic point of view that I want to proceed. In my questioning the adaptive value of a particular kind of morality I am suggesting that morality can be regarded as an aspect of adaptation. In other words, morality is an adjunct of reality-testing and as such has something to do with the quality of individual and group survival.

It is this principle that I want to amplify. However, before I do, let me hasten to add a corollary that follows from such a principle: Just as mental functions that serve reality-testing are susceptible to regression, so is morality susceptible to regression. In Saul Bellow's novel *Mr. Sammler's Planet* (1969) there is a passage in which the scholar, Sammler, in a freezing forest, hounded by anti-Semitic Polish partisans and nearly doomed, finally turns upon one of his pursuers and shoots him twice. "You would call it a dark action?" Bellow questions on Sammler's behalf. "On the contrary, it was also a bright one. . . . When he fired his gun, Sammler, himself nearly a corpse, burst into life. . . . His heart felt lined with brilliant, rapturous satin. . . . When he shot again it was less to make sure of the man than to try again for that bliss" (pp. 140–141). That second shot occurred, I submit, in a temporary state of regression induced by the anxiety of Sammler's having committed an act wholly alien to his established manner of coping with the world. In the triumph of nerve over character represented by the first shot, Sammler lost for the moment a personal moral structure and then fired the second shot. In the bargain, Sammler also lost an expectable inner experience of pity for his victim. It could be said that in this regression, or perhaps dissociation, Sammler's ego temporarily lost the capacity to generate an affectual response to its aggressive inclination—I mention this point because I intend to return to the role of affect in moral life, specifically to the contentions between affects and drives that enrich and sustain the moral quality of human existence.

Less dramatic and more omnipresent regressions in reality-testing and its adjunctive moral structures occur in the processes by which groups and communities are formed—another problem I shall return to further on. The relationship between regression and group formation is the subject of Freud's (1921) monograph on group psychology in which he advanced the thesis that the formation of groups exacted a toll from each member's ego functioning and from his ego ideal. To come back to the Watergate affair as an example, there is abundant evidence in the testimony of many implicated and indicted persons that membership on Nixon's staff liberated them to commit acts that in subsequent solitary reflection they judged both unrealistic and unethical. The "banality of evil," Hannah Arendt's famous phrase for Eichmann's role in the genocidal activities of the Third Reich, derives from the good standing of Eichmann in Hitler's party; Eichmann was loyal, conscientious, one might even say self-effacing in the sense that he placed his personal values secondary to those of the group he served so faithfully. Eichmann, too, at a later time and in another situation lamented his poor judgment and his blunted moral sensibilities. Such recantations were also found among the subjects whom Milgram (1974) enlisted for his famous study of the degradation of personal judgment that may result from adherence to the very virtue of group allegiance. In the words of Zimbardo (1974), " . . evil deeds are rarely the product of evil people acting from evil motives, but are the product of good bureaucrats simply doing their job" (p. 566).

MORALITY AND REALITY-TESTING

Reality-testing may be defined as the capacity to distinguish apperception from perception, fantasy from actuality, or, more

simply, inside from outside.[1] The cognitive situation we reconstruct from the human newborn's point of view is one in which
the infant's appetite is indistinguishable from the appetite-
reducing maternal attention he receives. From the infant's point
of view it is not an independent agent—the mother—who gives
the breast; it is the infant's hunger that creates the breast. In this
earliest stage of existence, the absence of an experience of the
distinction between personal desire and the externality of its
gratifications is an absence of reality-testing, called by some
analysts autistic and presocial. Before long, the infant enters a
social stage marked by the maturation of his capacity to locate
the source of his desired supplies in the mother—in her activities
and her comings and goings—rather than solely in his own
personal desires. The infant begins to construct the momentous
realization that it is not his desires that produce what creates his
good feelings, but something—someone—independent of him.

One can predict the scheme I am pursuing. Compared to his
nearest mammalian kin, the human child's sense of reality-
testing develops over a comparatively long period and involves,
at various stages of maturational crises, a separation between
the experience of drive arousal and the actual external circumstances of permission and restraint in which the drives must
find expression. In psychoanalytic parlance we speak of drives
as having not only aims but objects as well—objects, moreover,
with functional reciprocities that alter with the various stages of
drive development. Functional reciprocities at the oral stage of
drive development, for example, are different from reciprocities
at the oedipal stage. There is evidence in the work of Blos (1972)
and Erikson (1959) among others that the aims of human drive
development undergo new maturational crises now and again
throughout the entire life cycle; thus, the processes of reality-
testing—the capacity to make distinctions between appetite and
forms of external reciprocity—have ongoing opportunities for
enrichment. I might stress here that psychoanalysis does not
describe any particular version of reality but is concerned rather
with the psychological processes by which a *sense* of reality—*any*
sense of reality—is achieved and maintained.

---

1. See Robbins and Sadow (1974) for a recent review and explication of this
definition.

Now what role does morality play in the achievement and maintenance of a sense of reality? It is precisely in the paradigmatic situation of the infant who is discovering a distinction between his desires and the external conditions of their fulfillment that the origins of morality can be identified. The infant must now begin to make a further distinction between the actual supplies that gratify his desires—let us say milk and fondling—and the style and conditions by which the mother makes the supplies available. After a point early in life, the actual supply—milk—is no mystery to an infant, if, indeed, it ever was. Like the less tangible supply of approval at a later stage, milk does what it does with a direct and unfailing reliability. This statement, however, cannot be made of the mother *qua* person. Although the things she supplies are clear, the manner of giving them is not. Thus, the mother's manner becomes every bit as interesting as the direct supplies she possesses. Hereafter we begin to distinguish two categories of feeling states in the infant: appetite, which originates in drive arousal, and affect, which originates in experiences with the person possessing drive-reducing supplies. Before long we can detect in the emotional life of the maturing infant a difference between oral-longing, which is a state of desire, and anxiety, which is an affectual state having to do with an interpersonal situation with the mother. At a subsequent stage of development where the child's bladder and sphincter acquire erogenous possibilities—the anal stage—we can distinguish between eliminative desires and the affect of shame. At yet a further stage of instinctual maturation, we can distinguish phallic-genital appetite and the affect guilt.

Using such a scheme, I would define morality as the regulation of desire by affect. For example, when we observe a person behaving in a manner we take to be crudely appetitive, we ask why the person has no shame. We raise a question of morality when we ask about the seeming absence of anxiety or guilt in acts of violence. But originating as it does in processes that distinguish internal and external, morality is a function contributing to reality-testing and hence to the survival of the individual.

Of course, I am leaving out of this sketch its enormous innards—the structures postulated as repositories of drives and objects and of those functions that represent drives and objects

and that produce affect states of varying degrees of uncon-
sciousness—the id, the superego, the ego, for example, and the
functions of synthesis, memory, defense. But even without such
detail we can still imagine that insofar as one's notions of
psychopathology are informed by a psychoanalytic concept of
reality-testing, one could describe the problems of patients in
terms of a variety of moral conflicts without being moralistic.
One can see what I mean by recalling Freud's (1917) "Mourning
and Melancholia." In this paper, it could be said that Freud
described the plight of the melancholic patient as a form of
moral anguish, as when he wrote of the pathetic intrusions into
the melancholic's behavior of unwitting greed and egocentricity
by virtue of a particular failure of the depressed ego to furnish
narcissistically enhancing signals of shame and guilt in connection with strong drive arousal.

Certain moral exponents of the controversy between drive
arousal and affect can be found in Rapaport's (1959) exegesis of
Bibring's theory of depression. The derivatives of anal drives,
for example, are transformed into defensive needs "(1) not to be
hostile; (2) not to be resentful and defiant; (3) not to be dirty" (p.
765). Among the outcomes of the failure of defensive transformations of such anal inclinations, Rapaport describes self-
accusation in moral terms: "I will never be good, loving, will
always be hateful, hostile, defiant, therefore evil" (p. 765).

On this matter of casting fundamental psychic processes into
moral propositions, Loevinger's (1966) work on the meaning
and measurement of ego development is interesting, for she
describes a schedule of ego development with a vocabulary that
is largely moral. For example, Loevinger labels several developmental stages as "opportunistic," "conformist," "conscientious," and she identifies the emphatic regulating affect at each
of these stages as anxiety, shame, and guilt, respectively. The
interpersonal styles at various stages of ego development Loevinger also describes with moral resonances: The opportunistic
ego leads to an exploitative and manipulative mode; the conformist ego to a reciprocal and superficial mode; the conscientious to an intensive and responsible mode. Each stage adds
something to a developing sense of reality, and each mode has
something to be said for and against it regarding its advantages

and disadvantages for adaptation. The opportunistic mode (and here I depart from Loevinger's specific interests) may contribute to a capacity for taking risks in the pursuit of ego interests or it may contribute to self-destructive relationships with the environment in the form of delinquency, impostures, or counter-phobic misadventures. The conscientious mode is essential to the fulfillment of social contracts but can devolve into self-arresting compulsive fixations, and so on.

I have been saying no more than that the moral life is inextricably involved in the issues of human adjustment and adaptation, including the fundamental issues of pleasure and pain. Morality is not a "higher plane" of existence, though it can be observed in varying degrees of advancement from its original primitive forms and can be assessed in its manifestations according to its adaptive power in the life of the individual. The clinical observation of a defective moral sense is as diagnostic of a defective ego as the observation of, say, an impairment of memory. Indeed, Loewald (1971) has suggested that analytic therapy, in its various aims, is also a reparation of moral life. " . . I think it is an unwarranted limitation, at this stage of our science," Loewald writes, "to maintain that self-knowledge, making the unconscious conscious, transforming id into ego, is a purely 'objective' matter of self-observation and self-understanding, and not a moral phenomenon and activity in and of itself" (p. 63). However, with Loewald's next statement— "In this respect our theory is far behind the best in our practice and technique"—I am not at all sure I can agree, for I have tried to demonstrate that psychoanalytic theory does furnish a basis for the moral quality Loewald locates only in technique.

Moreover, I have been emphasizing certain aspects of personal conflict, notably in connection with reality-testing and the problem of the contingencies of desire. I have been stressing these matters not only because they have always been central to psychoanalytic concerns, but also because I am preparing to say that the deterioration of an experience of uncertainty into complacency is a symptom of a degradation of moral life, which is synonymous with the presence of a maladaptive neurotic process. Maintaining distinctions between wishes and perceptions, between desire and affect, between, if you will, self and object, places incessant stresses upon thought processes and produces a virtually constant imminence of psychopathology seen abundantly in everyday life, not to mention clinical populations. Like reality-testing in general, the moral sense at its most personally experienced level often arrives at unsettling ambiguities, frequently mitigated by extreme psychological measures, by the fanatic certainty of the paranoic, the interminable doing and undoing of the obsessive-compulsive, the naive submissiveness and dependency of the hysteric, the protracted emotional ventilations of the borderline. In everyday life, psychological measures are less extreme, more ordinary, and, perhaps, more detractive from moral vitality precisely because they are less likely to clamor for clinical attention. I have in mind the problem of social grouping, and, in returning to this point, I shall also be returning to a political stance that is fast unwinding in a cultural spiral that turns in an opposite direction.

THE GROUP AND MORAL AMBIGUITY

Earlier I alluded to the formation of groups and communities as yet another measure for mitigating the stresses of reality-testing. It was Winnicott, for one, who explored in detail a common yet significant means of reducing the stresses I have been describing. I am referring to Winnicott's (1953) idea of the transitional object, which evolves along with the trials of maturation and development into mitigating illusions, the sharing of which is one basis of group formation. Freud had a less tolerant view of illusion than Winnicott. From Freud's heroic position, illusion was not much more than the self-deception that avoids the injury truth does to complacency. Winnicott, owing to a milder temperament, was more accepting of the average human spirit and was less disdainful of the relief of tension between inside and outside that illusions afford those who share them. Since illusions are exempt from the basic question of whether they are wishes or perceptions, that is, whether they are inside or outside, those who share illusions are relieved of the burdens of deciding such a question. Groups are havens for the individual psyche, removing it temporarily from the conflicts between appetite and affect that inevitably stem from intrapsychic strivings and generate moral experience. Despite the popularity of Winnicott's theory of transitional objects and phenomena, I nevertheless want to permit Winnicott some of his own words:

> The transitional phenomena are allowable to the infant because of the parents' intuitive recognition of the strain inherent in objective perception, and we do not challenge the infant in regard to subjectivity or objectivity just here where there is the transitional object.
>
> Should an adult make claims on us for our acceptance of the objectivity of his subjective phenomena we discern or diagnose madness. If, however, the adult can manage to enjoy the personal intermediate area without making claims, then we can acknowledge our own corresponding intermediate areas, and are pleased to find overlapping, that is to say common experience between members of a group in art or religion or philosophy. [p. 96]

Nor would Winnicott have objected to our adding to this list politics or science. An important possibility is implied in this passage (one made more explicit in the subsequent literature) to the effect that an "intermediate area" can lose its power to gain acknowledgement and can revert to inflicting a personal subjectivity upon us which we then "discern or diagnose [as] madness." In the wake of such reversions, we often discard our leaders and their claims, a process that coincides with a general experience of moral renewal.

I should note that I am not saying all that much about group process, which is a subject for sociology, a discipline whose relationship to individual psychology is separated by as much a leap as the relationship between mind and body. I am limiting my account only to the fate of certain psychological processes as individuals enter into and function as part of groups. In this respect, Freud's admonitions about groups should not be ignored.

Freud (1921, 1927, 1930) observed that the relief groups afford from the moral stresses and ambiguities that arise in the course of individuation involves us in a shaky bargain with adaptation.

Nothing in the rituals, manners, emblems, ideals—in a word, the illusions—binding us in groups is at the same time constructively responsive to the inevitable alterations in the social, political, technologic, and ecologic environment in which groups exist. This fact is especially true for what I would call megagroups, such as nations, where illusion and bureaucracy virtually are the only brain and muscle with which such enterprises operate. Human history is a graveyard of gigantic sociopolitical entities that prevailed for a time and then lumbered and reeled helplessly in an inexorably altering environment that finally absorbed their distinctive structures.

Illusions in their various forms provide an important means for individuals to adapt to one another. But such adaptation by illusion takes a toll on the intellectual and emotional resources of the individual. Indeed, Winthrop's (1974) view in his paper "The Group as a Surrogate for the Individual" is typical of many social scientists. The loss of individual resources in contemporary forms of "togetherness, conformity, and herd-mindedness" is so lamentable that Winthrop maintains something like desocialization may be as important to society as socialization.

Be this as it may, if morality is a plan of action that arises in a personal controversy between ambition and its objects, between desire and the affects foretelling its manner of consummation, then morality is not a property of groups. By certain actions groups may be judged criminal—genocidal, for example—but I would distinguish criminality and morality as separate realms of human activity. Thus, it is possible to function in a group with a positive moral experience while engaging in a criminal activity. The rituals that determine group action are not equivalent to individual conflict. Rituals of atonement, such as national ceremonies after the death of prominent public figures, are not the equivalent of personal grief, any more than carnivals are personal triumphs over the constraints upon libido and aggression. On the contrary, rituals exist to relieve us of "the strain inherent in objective perception." Like illusion in general, they are codifications of experience. They are simulations of perceptions of events.

I do not mean to say that the codifications and simulations that spare us the individual problem solving preliminary to the execution of more exclusively personal deeds are arbitrary and without relevance to ontogeny. The continuity between social institutions and ontogeny is the subject of Freud's (1913) "Totem and Taboo," whose shortcomings should not eclipse Freud's valuable thesis that social institutions and the conduct they prescribe are informed by the evolutions of family life and child-rearing practices (which is where human ontogeny is most alive and most visible). Indeed, the idea of "childhood and society" has become quite pervasive in our society. Ariès's (1962) *Centuries of Childhood* and Hunt's (1970) *Parents and Children in History* are recent examples of scholarship that continue to refine our ideas of the commerce between social institutions and individual development—ideas advanced in such well-known contributions as those of Erikson (1950, 1964) and Riesman (1950, 1952).

My point is that if social institutions are morally empty, they are not for that reason exempt from the requirement to evolve in some way consistent with the particular moral solutions that enable the members of one generation to separate from another generation. One crisis of inconsistency between "childhood and society" we call the "generation gap." The void in every generation gap is filled with the complaint that existing social institutions no longer furnish the maturing generation opportunities for the relief of moral conflict. In other words, the prevailing social illusions are no longer sufficiently credible to a generation raised on newer illusions. A thwarted expectation is the broken promise that leads to reactive moral outrage, the consequence of which is either institutional tyranny, institutional dissolution, or a change of leadership. At such times we are in the midst of the aroused forces of the moral life, which before long lead to new establishments and to generational encampments.

MORALITY AND SURVIVAL

There is a further way of describing the functions of illusion that will bring us full circle to the bankruptcy of the particular sociopolitical style that I identified at the outset of these excursions. In the writings of Hegel is the idea of a debate between truth and fact. Truth refers to what is enduring and expectable in our existence, to what we can count on and hope to live by. Facts are adventitious. They are, to use another phrase of Hannah Arendt, "disconcerting contingencies." In this sense, illusion is the embodiment of truth and maintains us against the traumatic intrusions of fact upon the coherent versions of reality so necessary to communal order. In this formulation we can recognize a residual of the infant's earliest struggle with personal expectation and external contingency.

The preaching of virtue while practicing vice is one form of the Hegelian debate and is also a residual of one circumstance of human development. To preach virtue while practicing vice is a way of preserving reputation against contradiction. Truth abides by a concealment of fact. In child rearing we have become aware of the pathogenesis of precocious exposures of the child to certain facts of life. Indeed, all good parents employ concealment for the sake of creating a sense of security in the child. As parents, we strive for some balance between disclosures of threatening contingencies in the environment and their concealment. On the one hand, we wish to avoid traumatization; on the other, overprotection. But a certain degree of secrecy must prevail in the very service of allowing a dynamic sense of reality to evolve, as well as its adjunctive morality.

I think it was Lin Yutang who said that patriotism is the good food we ate as children, which is to say that allegiance to institutions and to the leaders who preside over them recapitulates ontogeny. In government we tolerate the preaching of virtue while practicing vice in many guises—in diplomatic discretion, for example, or in what is called *arcana imperii*, the mysteries of government. We expect from presidents, prime ministers, dictators, and their spokesmen disclosures of facts in accordance with the preservation of national images and reputations.

But, unless I am greatly mistaken, I think something has changed considerably both in the lives of our children and in society at large. I think a breakdown in the distinction between disclosures and denials has occurred, with the effect that there are no disclosures to be made. We have moved from the provisional preservations of privacy to the decadent myth that the private and the public are virtually identical. In child rearing we have come to appreciate, for example, a difference between protecting a child from the sexual and aggressive exchanges that occur between his parents and denying that such exchanges exist among adults; the former educates the child's curiosity, the latter dissociates it. As for the spokesmen of social institutions, we can continue to tolerate the statement "I have no comment at this time." But the statement "There is nothing to comment upon" strikes us as ineffectual piety, narcissistic entitlement, or some other perversity. In the accommodations of truth and fact, in the discrepancy between what is professed and what is actually happening, we have come to expect a degree of wit rare in the annals of leadership.

Why this circumstance should exist at this time will carry me to a conclusion. It is a question that goes far beyond the personal antics of former President Nixon, bizarre though these antics may have been. But the social tides that have swept him under have been swelling in the course of the present century and will not too quickly subside.

I submit that the epistemologic fervor that has characterized cultural life from the outset of the present century has at last reached every crevice of our social life. We are obsessed with how things work, far beyond what physical science hoped to tell us. An enormous increase of information is being conveyed throughout burgeoning media about strategies and tactics of daily existence that were previously exempt from public consideration.

A passage in Freud's (1927) "The Future of an Illusion" exemplifies the epistemologic spirit of our age at the cultural level. Freud, arguing for the superiority of the methods of science over the consolations of religious faith in sustaining humanity, addresses himself to the argument that since a scientist uses his mind in the scientific method, he must therefore arrive at a subjective reflection of the organization of the mind itself, "whilst the real nature of things outside ourselves remains inaccessible" (p. 55). Freud answers that not only does the fact of survival confirm that the mental apparatus is capable of reckoning somewhat expeditiously with an external world by forming faithful representations of it, but also that the mind is capable of investigating its own operations in connection with its investigation of the external world. Freud adds that "the problem of the nature of the world without regard to our percipient mental apparatus is an empty abstraction, devoid of practical interest" (p. 56). Thus, he asserts not only the possibility of acquiring knowledge, which is one emphasis on epistemology, but also the conviction that knowledge divorced from epistemology is platitudinous.

Psychoanalysis itself has been a powerful current of epistemology in this century. Nietzsche's idea that no message can be rightly understood without divining the will that fashions it is yet another powerful current. The logical positivism staked out by Russell, Whitehead, Wittgenstein, and other philosophers of the century represents an effort to keep the linguistic and symbolic instrumentalities of knowledge straight. The art of this century has been about the very means of art; it has been concerned with materials and technique—how art works. The sociology of Goffman carries this interest in the instrumentalities of meaning into the most plausible, hitherto unnoticed gestures of everyday social life.

At the social level, the mass media have been increasingly informed by this iconoclastic direction of culture and have finally exempted nothing from scrutiny and communication. Within the past decade not a detail of the actualities of human conduct has remained privileged. There is nothing left of the Other American in the analogous sense that Steven Marcus spoke of the Other Victorian.

Since our elite populations control so much of how things work, our curiosities have naturally invaded the palaces and mansions of the rich and powerful and have revealed the perversities with which the life styles of the elite have always been embroidered. Not a day passes that the *New York Times* does not report on its front page yet another scandal from a judge's chamber, an executive's suite, a vice-president's office. These days the front page photograph of a decade ago of Governor Rockefeller escaping a fire in the governor's mansion during the night by climbing out of the maid's bedroom window would hardly seem dismaying at all.

If the fact-mindedness, which the epistemologic point of view of our century has come down to in the general public, has deprived the public of its innocence, it has also sensitized the public's moral conflicts in unique ways. The facts of life are always an intrusion upon illusion and, thus, a jeopardy to community coherence. The sensitization of morality arises in disenchantment because of the heightened experience of personal self in its "detachment" from groups. Riesman's (1950) designation *The Lonely Crowd* is felicitous, for Riesman was describing in the late 1940s a growing alertness in the American public to new and novel information that was undermining the stabilities evident in the disappearing tradition-directed and inner-directed social character. Along with such terms as *alienation, estrangement,* and *isolation, The Lonely Crowd* has passed into common usage signifying the loss of group coherence occurring in consonance with the deterioration of the binding power of illusion. Though this loss may well generate the desperations of togetherness and herd-mindedness Winthrop (1974) warned us about, it is possible at the same time to observe a renewal of moral experience in the incessant transitions between the undoing and realigning of social groupings.

Thus, the political leader who strives for aloofness from the facts of his own regime or who disavows knowledge of such facts or who isolates himself from those who can provide them strikes us as quaint and complacent. He declares himself disinterested in a major preoccupation of the public, disinterested in salvaging what is viable in institutions that find themselves at this moment in the midst of an extraordinary escalation of unassimilated facts. A plea of simple ignorance by anyone invested with authority has lost whatever moral persuasions such a plea might once have had. Irresponsibility—vice, if I may—has become synonymous with the old conviction that knowledge of certain events can tarnish virtue. Know-nothing politics along with its related laissez-faire economic doctrine, once at the center of the political spectrum, is now at the lunatic fringe of our sociopolitical existence.

Toward the end of 1969 in a single number of *Science* there appeared two sober yet horrendous studies (Crowe 1969, Platt 1969), independently written, both calculating the rate at which social, political, economic, and ecologic problems are currently enlarging as compared with the rate at which existing social and political institutions are solving them. Crowe's article, "The Tragedy of the Commons Revisited," carries the summary subtitle: "Major problems have neither technical nor political solutions; extensions in morality are not likely."[2] Both studies conclude that the rate at which mankind is progressing toward planetary extinction is significantly more rapid than the rate at which existing institutions solve problems.

These calculations are not hysterical by any means. They are made as if in chorus by representatives of a variety of learned professions. S. R. Eyre's (1971) presidential address to the Geography Section of the British Association for the Advancement of Science is entitled, "Man the Pest: The Dim Chance of Survival." Eyre questions, among other recent notions that have afforded us solace, the contribution to survival of even the improbable achievement of holding population growth to zero. In an article entitled "The Human Prospect," Robert L. Heilbroner (1974) makes the observation that a crisis of actual survival of the human species is already a realization in the minds of vast numbers of people not otherwise given to pessimistic or catastrophic visions of the future. And Heilbroner himself is no more sanguine about the human prospect than the others I have cited.

However, if I have been at all clear in my foregoing representations of a psychoanalytic version of the relationship among adaptation, morality, and their inevitable expressions in sociopolitical groupings, then the particular hope that Heilbroner manages to reserve from his grim skepticism comes as no surprise. Heilbroner (and he is not alone in this view) pins his hope on a transformation of political groupings "to the discomfiture of those who would hope that the challenges of the human prospect would finally banish the thralldoms of authority and ideology and foster the 'liberation' of the individual"

---

2. By morality Professor Crowe means institutional values, such as technologic expansion, bureaucratic specialization, and the equation of scarcity with poverty.

(p. 31). More, not less, political structure is Heilbroner's anti-dote, as if it were possible to conceive of politics (and society in general) as existing in greater and lesser degrees. In a psycho-analytic perspective, the alternatives are not between more or less authority and ideology, but always between *kinds* of authority and ideology. Authority and ideology—leadership and illusion, to use terms more familiar to my present discussion—are apodictic in the human condition. True, we speak of individuation and autonomy, of internalization and separation; but ultimately these concepts describe qualities of relationships to groups.

On this score, what, then, can psychoanalysis promulgate in these times of gathering doom? In all candor I must say that I have never been impressed by any positive relationship between psychoanalytic experience and political sagacity. Worse, in the Freudian praxis one is admonished from offering even benedictions.

Still, there may be something to be said in connection with the psychoanalytic concept of morality with which these departures began. The dialectic between passion and affect is an essence of moral experience and accompanies the solutions to the problems of adaptation. When such problems are relatively quiescent, moral concern is also relatively quiescent, and we describe such periods as normal and complacent. In individual psychology, the dialectics of morality have many outcomes. But we should not overlook more advanced forms of moral vitality in certain transformations of conflict and doubt—in paradox, irony, modesty, and wit.

Nor should we overlook the evidence of an aroused moral sensitivity in the styles of leadership, insofar as leaders represent ideal dispositions toward anxiety, shame, guilt, and other affectual responses to the passion for survival. If these are times that call for the fullest play of institutional function, then we must resist our temptations for alliances under those who aspire to leadership by claims of fearlessness, shamelessness, and perfection of foresight—claims that signify an arrogant unre-sponsiveness to moral necessity. Preaching is the rhetorical mode of such claims, and this mode does not accommodate the facts of existence, but rather attempts to exclude them perpetually by an attitude of certainty, an attitude that has become wholly obsolete at this moment in history.

If Freud's own life is any model for contemporary virtue, if his persisting sense of doubt, which attained expression in his style in paradox, irony, modesty, and wit, constitutes the moral stance of a true prophet, then we must conclude that any attitude of certainty is the true measure of a false prophet. And need it be said that false prophets are luxuries we can no longer afford?

REFERENCES

Aries, P. (1962). *Centuries of Childhood: A Social History of Family Life*, trans. R. Baldick. New York: Knopf.

Bellow, S. (1969). *Mr. Sammler's Planet*. New York: Viking.

Blos, P. (1972). The epigenesis of the adult neurosis. *Psychoanalytic Study of the Child* 27:106–35.

Crowe, B. L. (1969). The tragedy of the commons revisited. *Science* 166:1103–1107,

Erikson, E. H. (1950). *Childhood and Society*. New York: Norton.

———— (1959). Growth and crises of the healthy personality. In *Identity and the Life Cycle. Psychological Issues*, Vol. 1, #1, Monogr. 1, pp. 50–100.

———— (1964). *Insight and Responsibility: Lectures on the Ethical Implications of Psychoanalytic Insight*. New York: Norton.

Eyre, S. R. (1971). Man the pest: the dim chance of survival. *New York Review of Books* 17(8):18–27.

Freud, S. (1913). Totem and taboo. *Standard Edition* 13.

———— (1917). Mourning and melancholia. *Standard Edition* 14.

———— (1921). Group psychology and the analysis of the ego. *Standard Edition* 18.

———— (1927). The future of an illusion. *Standard Edition* 21.

———— (1930). Civilization and its discontents. *Standard Edition* 21.

Heilbroner, R. L. (1974). The human prospect? *New York Review of Books* 20(21&22):21–34.

Hunt, D. (1970). *Parents and Children in History: The Psychology of Family Life in Early Modern France*. New York: Basic Books.

Loevinger, J. (1966). The meaning and measurement of ego development. *American Psychologist*. 21:195–206.

Loewald, H. W. (1971). Some considerations on repetition and repetition compulsion. *International Journal of Psycho-Analysis* 52:59–66.

Milgram, S. (1974). *Obedience to Authority: An Experimental View*. New York: Harper & Row.

Platt, J. (1969). What We Must Do. *Science* 166:1115–1121.

Rapaport, D. (1959). Edward Bibring's theory of depression. In *The Collected Papers of David Rapaport*, ed. M. M. Gill, pp. 758–73. New York: Basic Books, 1967.

Riesman, D. et al. (1950). *The Lonely Crowd: A Study of the Changing American Character*. New Haven, CT: Yale University Press.

———— (1952). *Faces in the Crowd: Individual Studies in Character and Politics*. New Haven, CT: Yale University Press.

Robbins, F. P., and Sadow, L. (1974). A developmental hypothesis of reality processing. *Journal of the American Psychoanalytic Association*. 22:344–63.

Winnicott, D. W. (1953). Transitional objects and transitional phenomena: a study of the first not-me possession. *International Journal of Psycho-Analysis* 34:89–97.

Winthrop, H. (1974). The group as a surrogate for the individual. *Bulletin of the Menninger Clinic* 38:239–49.

Zimbardo, P. G. (1974). On "Obedience to Authority." *American Psychologist* 29:566–67.

18

The Psychopathology
of Television Watching*

Since the early 1950s there has been a flourishing number of
studies on the impact of commercial television on American life.
These studies have been largely economic and sociologic: how
television distributes consumer goods, affects leisure, organizes
family activity, transmits manners, fashions, fads, shapes the
experience of children. Yet there have been no clinical studies
on psychopathologic television watching, what I shall call for
the moment "television addiction." The index of the *American
Handbook of Psychiatry* contains no reference to a psychopathology of television watching. Nor are there any studies on the
subject within the past two decades of the standard professional
periodicals like *The Psychoanalytic Quarterly*, the *Journal of the
American Psychoanalytic Association*, and *The Psychoanalytic Study
of the Child*. In case reports there are passing references to
television watching. A brief communication called "Television
Addiction and Apathy" appeared in a 1954 number of *The
Journal of Nervous and Mental Diseases*, but this was a page and a
half comment that said no more than its title suggests. In verbal
case presentations, I have been hearing increasingly about
patients who consume extraordinary numbers of hours
watching television, neglecting their lives the way alcoholics

---

*Editor's Note: Despite the monumental advances in television technology in the last
quarter century and the fact that viewers of 1995 are not sheltered from erotic or
pornographic imagery, the author's 1972 diagnostic distinctions between addictions,
compulsions, passive-submissive disorders, and the psychopathology of TV watching—
passive-impulsive disorder— are still valid.

often do; but these presentations go on to other aspects of the clinical situation, for neurotic television watching is only a manifest part of a larger, unconscious neurotic conflict.

For present purposes, I want to dwell on the psychology of television addiction. Since the study of psychological symptoms sheds light on so-called normal functioning as well, the dynamics of television addiction may tell us something about the relationship of the general public to commercial home television. In the course of things we may also come to see something more about the television medium itself.

The behavior characterizing the symptom is not very exotic. In symptomatic television watching, the patient—usually in solitude—finds himself watching the lit television tube, though no particular programs, for hours on end against his conscious will. His watching overrides his intention to perform even ordinary actions such as answering mail and returning phone calls. It soon overrides his intention to go to sleep at a particular hour. There is no internal motive strong enough to interrupt the behavior. Only external circumstance may interrupt it—a standing appointment, an incoming phone call, and so on. Otherwise the behavior terminates in sleep. On closer study, secondary symptoms can be detected. In some patients, neurotic television watching is accompanied by waves of guilt and attacks of anxiety. In others, the consumption of food, cigarettes, and alcohol goes up; I suspect a high correlation between this symptom and weight gain. Still others have reported stupor, feelings of disorientation and unreality.

As with most addictive behavior, neurotic television watching begins, through withdrawal and neglect, to undermine the patient's adaptations to the environment. A colleague of mine not long ago presented the case of a patient who had gotten into an extremely morbid involvement with the television set. The patient described how he had succumbed to the habit of watching the eleven o'clock news on the living room couch, then, following the news broadcast, lapsing into television watching for hours, while his wife had long since retired. The patient surmised that he fell asleep on the couch somewhere between three and four o'clock in the morning. The next morning his wife would discover him asleep and fully dressed with the television set still on. This happened virtually every night for the better part of two years. The symptom affected his daily schedule, which began later and later and required all sorts of excuses to business associates. His wife finally began divorce proceedings. Doubtless the patient's sexual conflicts were at the bottom of this manifest television behavior (incidentally, the case presentation centered more on the sexual conflicts than on the television symptom). But the intractability of this manifest television behavior can be appreciated in the fact that, much as he resolved, he could not give up his television watching, even in the face of divorce and the threat to his career.

Another patient, a 38-year-old unmarried woman, self-employed in her own editorial service, would turn on the TV set upon awakening each morning and fix on it into the early evening, surrounded by a week's accumulation of empty beer cans and dishes. Through heroic effort, she would tear herself away from the set—without turning it off—and accomplish a minimum of productive work in crisis and desperation. Eventually she would go to sleep in front of the set. Though I don't want to pursue the point, I might add that this patient was structuring the equivalent of a clinical depression, through her repetitive extrication from and reattachment to a primitive object represented by the television set. Again, the programs flashing by are quite irrelevant.

Here it is worth categorizing the symptom itself diagnostically, for we can learn something about the symptom from what is known about its category. Though the behavior exemplified by the two patients I referred to seems to be compulsive, there are significant differences between this behavior and compulsions. For one thing, compulsions are planned and deliberate acts. For another, compulsions facilitate intentions and goals. The inner experience of a person with a hand-washing compulsion, for example, is that he must complete the compulsion in order to proceed to what he intends to do. The compulsive neurotic expects the compulsion to free him for action; the compulsion is preparatory to an intended goal-oriented task.

Nor is the television symptom an addiction. An addiction may begin as the pursuit of a special pleasure, but before long the addict finds that he feels normal only through his addiction, which becomes, like a compulsion, a facilitation of existence. A cigarette smoker, for example, feels normal only if he smokes. Abstention leads to mental and physical symptoms, which the addictive behavior reduces, freeing the addict for goal-oriented tasks. This is true even in the use of amphetamines, alcohol, and heroin: though addictions impair the capacity to accomplish tasks—for many reasons, including impairment of motivation—the conscious hopes of the addict are otherwise. This is not true of the neurotic television watcher, who knows that his behavior is postponing rather than facilitating action.

Symptomatic television watching belongs to a category akin to compulsion and addiction, but with a notable difference. This category is called impulse disorder, and specifically, passive-impulsive as distinguished from passive-submissive. Passive-impulsive behavior involves yielding to inner temptation (rather than external pressure, as in passive-submissive behavior). The yielding is experienced as being against one's opposing will. It should be stressed that it is not the activity that is diagnostic, but the *experience* of the activity. A passive-impulse is performed against one's intentions and is at variance with one's aims and goals. In this experience of failure of will, passive-impulsive behavior can be distinguished from play, entertainment, and relaxation, which are also without goal direction, but which do not involve a conflict in intention. Impulsivity is not abandonment of goals; it is a paralysis of the will to pursue them.

Moreover, impulse of the kind we are examining does not strive for pleasure as much as for relief of tension. Often these motives—pleasure and relief of tension—are mixed, as in impulsive gambling, sexual perversion, and addiction. In passive-impulsive television watching, however, the pleasure motive is inoperative, while the relief of tension is uppermost. No one reports any thrills from impulsive television watching, only tension reduction with occasional pangs of anxiety accompanying the realization of what is happening. Tension resides in the oppressively expectant environment; its relief in the avoidance afforded by watching. It is as if the claims of the environment are postponed by the patient's total unavailability, not simply in a determined solitude but in a complete degradation of conscious mental process induced by the television screen. It is difficult to think of another activity that so nullifies conscious mental process—even staring into space allows, indeed promotes, daydreaming.

Television's suppression of fantasy production can also be observed in schoolchildren and adolescents who habitually do homework in front of the TV. Here the TV set actually facilitates concentration by regulating distracting sexual fantasies and the impulses they give rise to; it functions the way radio used to among youth, as a kind of jamming device against fantasies. Child analysts have observed the dampening effects of television on the fantasy activity of preschool children. They report that over the past ten years the normal fantasy life of children has become increasingly stereotyped and attribute the impoverishment of originality in children's fantasies to the long exposure to television. Imagery is appropriated directly from the visual stimuli into fantasy, without the effortful transformation that is necessary when imagery is received through an auditory or literary mode.

It seems that no other medium can be reacted to with such cognitive blandness as television. This is also evident in the fact that very few images and incidents seen on television turn up in the dreams of analysands. (I am including patients who are not neurotically involved in television and who therefore view programs with more discrimination and alertness than do "television impulsives.") Considering the number of hours spent on television—hours close to and up to bedtime—it is extraordinary that what goes on between the viewer and the TV screen very rarely furnishes day-residues for dreams. Though everyday life is the main source of day-residues, media can provide meaningful unconscious conflicts for dreams. Movies very frequently do; so do books and magazines. Even comic strips are employed in the dream process. But patients rarely associate television content to their dreams. The implication is that the television medium is practically devoid of interpretive demands upon the viewer. The experience of viewing most commercial TV fare rarely coincides with anyone's personal conflicts. This is not to say that television does not meet psychological needs. Obviously it does. The needs, however, have to do with disengagement from structured stimuli, and regression to a prestructured, preconflictual state. Television establishes itself in the nervous system with a bare minimum of active negotiation between the subject and the object.

How television meets these needs better than movies is hard to say. I make the comparison with movies because television is often likened to movies since they are both audiovisual; but psychologically they are quite different media. Certainly the environment in which television is experienced contributes to regressive reactions. Movies still enforce a social occasion. The constant interruption of TV content by commercials generates a rhythm, a predictability, not present in movies. But most significant, I suspect—and this is a point made by Jonathan Miller (*The New York Review of Books*, October 7, 1971)—is television's peculiar technical problem of having to register images on some five hundred electronically excitable lines that make up the tube's surface. This electronic state of affairs imposes severe limitations on what can be projected on the tube. Small objects and objects at a distance are going to be portrayed by very few lines and therefore are going to be unrecognizably indistinct. A movie screen, on the other hand, receives its images from an emulsion process and can faithfully show, for example, a horse and rider moving on the distant horizon, something that can't be shown on a TV tube. Television is limited to large objects and narrow angles, that is, closeups— big heads, broad mugging, overcrowded sets, restrained movements—one false step and the performer is off-camera. It is for this reason that movies lose so much when shown on TV. It is also for this reason that the principal TV forms have always been closeup conversation, stand-up comedy, and indoor-situation melodrama. Pageantry, nature, and dance never succeed on TV.

Short of a technology that could increase those five hundred lines many times over, the TV medium must continue to reduce everything within range of its cameras to the sameness that now prevails. (Technical development was squandered on color, which does not liberate the medium from any of its visual restrictions.) To the caller's question, "What are you doing?" the answer is more apt to be, "I'm watching TV" than "I'm watching 'The Doris Day Show.' " I know that patients on the analytic couch trying to report their comings and goings in detail almost never identify the television programs they have watched the day before. They seem to feel that it is sufficient to remark that they watched TV for a couple of hours, as if that alone identifies the activity and the experience. Whatever else television ratings may measure, they do not measure cognitive activity.

I have been using the word *cognitive* in its ordinary sense, descriptive of that process of knowing that involves awareness and judgment. Not all processes of knowing are cognitive. There are modes of knowing that are visceral, or subliminal, or intuitive—modes of knowing that more or less exclude awareness and judgment. But cognition is the one mode establishing and reaffirming a sense of reality. (I do not mean a grasp of what reality is; this is philosophic. I mean a *sense* of reality, which is psychological.) This is because of the operation of judgment, as we shall see further on. But the point at the moment is that television ranks so highly as a leisure-time activity because it can be related to without very much cognition on the part of the viewer and thus affords the most convenient relaxation of the sense of reality. The alternative to the sense of reality is not always a sense of unreality, but, as I mentioned earlier, there are patients who report disturbances of the sense of reality following long, symptomatic exposure to television.

This peculiar possibility of cognitive deprivation gives television, as no other medium, its suitability for the kind of symptom formation I began to describe in patients "addicted" to TV. Yet there is something more to observe about impulsivity with which television can easily reciprocate. Impulses are unpremeditated, and the lack of premeditation in the impulsive act is what mitigates the guilt over the act and allows impulsive transgression against the dictates of personal conscience. "I am guilty but without premeditation" is a persuasive plea, softening an otherwise strict conscience. To insure a quality of unpremeditation, impulses have to be succumbed to quickly and without conscious decision; they occur in a moment of denying everything "out there." This is a large part of the experience of the impulsive television watcher. However regularly he watches TV, he always describes the inception of the impulsive act in the same way: "I really didn't intend to watch more than the news," "I turned the set on for a minute, and before I knew it . . ." and so on. Offering even less trial to decision making than merchandise to a kleptomaniac, the television set meets the impulse far more than halfway. When the television neurotic begins his incessant channel flipping, we have a case of impulse within impulse. The medium is superb in its convenience and lack of resistance to such impulsivity.

Though different impulsive acts have in common the experiential features I have noted—failure of will, paralysis of intention, absence of premeditation—they also differ from one another in their unconscious significance. Impulsive gambling, for example, expresses unconscious masturbatory impulses, while certain sexual impulses, like fetishism, regulate unconscious fears about body integrity. This television impulse, as near as I can tell, wards off a primitive separation anxiety by re-creating an experience of fusion with an early maternal imago. This I surmise from the behavior's quiescence, its passive hypnotic quality. Compare it to the highly charged risks and thrills of gambling and sex. TV viewing isn't even voyeuristic; the screen never shows anything remotely pornographic. Furthermore, the homogeneity of all TV programs, their merging one into the other, generates an experience of fusion.

Aside from these phenomenologic reasons, there is a theoretical reason why I suggest that the television experience involves regression to a preseparation state. Here I return to the idea of cognition and the sense of reality, and specifically to the psychoanalytic theory of the development of judgment. Judgment begins early in life, in the rudimentary capacity to distinguish what is inside the body from what is outside. Our original experience of existence resides solely in the registrations of sensation and appetite upon the body. Since there is no distinction between inside and outside, there is no possibility of psychological interaction with the environment. The breast is experienced as an extension of the infant's appetite. At this stage, the infant is said to be merged with the breast. There is no cognition, and the experience of existence does not include the idea of awareness.

Judgment begins with the recognition that personal appetites are not continuous with the supplies that gratify them. There is an inside (appetite) and an outside (milk), and these are separate realms. Out of such primitive recognitions dawns a sense of separateness from the environment and a capacity to interact with the environment, both human and nonhuman. Cognition is built upon the ontogenetics of the subject/object split, which begins with psychological separation from the mother, and an appreciation of the mother as a person in her own right.

The maturation of the nervous system itself can be said to proceed parallel to this psychological development. If we think of the functional relationship of the cortex to the subcortex as a relationship between higher interpretive functions (cortex) and arousals requiring interpretation (subcortex), we could conclude that a split requiring ongoing integration is eventually present even in the structure of the nervous system. This division between interpretive and interpreted activity in the brain is not present at birth but matures in the course of childhood. I bring in this anatomical point to stress how important to the sense of reality is a separation of functions and realms: inside and outside, apperception and perception, the interpretive and the interpreted.

Certain circumstances, chemical and otherwise, temporarily can reduce separation and the hazards that separation entails (such hazards as alienation, the drudgery of self-sustenance, and the confrontation with burdensome and traumatic knowledge). Indeed, all cultures provide opportunities for escape from separation, through experiences of remerging with an early oral-maternal imago, often through drugs affecting the ratio of cortical and subcortical activity, and rituals that guarantee belonging and fulfillment without the necessity of problem solving. Such opportunities are usually restricted to special occasions.

In our culture, television affords such an opportunity, but unrestricted. The medium requires so little judgment and interpretation that it never raises the question whether it is inside or outside, whether the eye or ear is a distinct sense organ or simply a variant of the mouth; for this reason, experience with the medium must be placed at the primitive level I suggested earlier. Nor is it difficult to see why watching television could be a godsend to those in whom interpretive activity and the self-awareness it leads to produce anxiety—the experience of the imminence of trauma and personal crisis.

One would think that the omnipresence of such a medium would produce a pandemic of the symptom my small neurotic population complains of. There are a number of good studies that reveal the most reliable variable in addiction epidemics to be simply the availability of the drug. If morphine, for example, were readily available over the counter, as alcohol is, morphine addiction would be pandemic, cutting across all personality types. Has the availability of television with its regressive seductions to a preseparation state produced a pandemic of passive-impulsive symptomotology? There are signs that it has, and I am not so sure that the pandemic is subclinical—that is, present but as yet unfelt.

I am not a behaviorist. As a rule, I do not diagnose from actions but rather from the personal experience that accompanies actions. When I raise a question in connection with television about a slippage from entertainment to an experience of some morbidity or other, I am not referring to the fact, however arresting in itself, that television at this moment consumes—with the possible exception of sleep—more hours than almost any other single activity. I am referring rather to a growing consciousness of guilt and even despair over the waste of it all.

Joyce Maynard, an 18-year-old Yale freshman, wrote some reflections for the Sunday *Times* (April 23, 1972) on growing up over the previous two decades. She recalls television: "If I had spent at the piano the hours I have on television, on all those afternoons when I came home from school, I would be an accomplished pianist now. Or if I'd danced, or read, or painted. . . . But I turned on the set instead, every day, almost every year, and sank into an old green easy chair, smothered in quilts, with a bag of Fritos beside me and a glass of milk to wash them down, facing life and death with Dr. Kildare. . . . Looking back over all those afternoons, I try to convince myself they weren't wasted. . . . Five thousand hours of my life have gone into this box." Notice the phrase "But I turned on the set instead." This is a revelation of passive-impulsiveness. Elsewhere Miss Maynard tells us that all the programs of any given series were the same, and that was why she watched them:

"boring repetition is, itself, a rhythm—a steady pulse of flashing Coca-Cola signs, McDonald's golden arches and Howard Johnson roofs." There was nothing to interpret. Miss Maynard clearly is speaking for a very large population.

Evidence of a vast conscious experience of the television medium is also found in movies. A movie scene involving a television program instantly symbolizes the deadliness of our national TV pastime. Such a scene requires no embellishing comment because the movie audience can be trusted to see at once the pathetic implications for the persons viewing the TV screen. We know in a flash that the characters watching the TV screen are paralyzed cognitively and emotionally, that they have better things to do but can't bring themselves to do them. They are doomed. Contempt, I believe, is also somewhere in our reaction. We despise them for their weakness.

There are other signs of such consciousness. Earlier, I cited an extreme example of a patient whose wife divorced him, partly because of his television habit. But there are countless less extreme examples of domestic disputes about one party's being deprived of interpersonal interaction by the other's television viewing, when no such dispute would arise if solitude involved the printed word or music or even what passes for meditation. Very often such disputes over television have a distinct rescue motif. I am also impressed by a tone of shame in the reports of many people about the dozen hours of television they may watch a week. Often patients will report an increase in television viewing in order to begin to identify some trouble as yet unknown elsewhere in their lives. The degree and amount of morbidity surrounding this medium is truly alarming.

I wish I could conclude with some meliorative recommendations. Alas, I have none. The problem I have been describing is extensive, but unlike many others, it is not yet recognized as significant. Environmental pollution has a better chance of solution, if only because it is clearly identified as a crisis.

Only the aesthetics of commercial TV is an acknowledged national disgrace. Nobody disputes the fact that television is a rippling of homogenous slop. Though it may evoke a grunt or two, television is never the subject of any real conversation. Even the daily press, which can always be counted upon to exaggerate the substance of the most trivial events, has never been able to work up any sustained interest in television; the press leaves this coverage to *TV Guide*, which in its million-some-odd pages has yet to print one memorable paragraph about the medium. And for years the Federal Communications Commission has been reacting with alarm (though with little else) to the wasteland commercial broadcasting has made of the television medium.

Television is not only a waste—it is also a menace. Doubtless an improvement in the aesthetics of television would reduce its emotional toxicity to the public, for the morbid regression induced by television occurs precisely because there is no substance to engage the mind of the viewer. However, unless the problem of television is conceived of in other than aesthetic terms, the medium cannot change: aesthetics is simply not a credible basis for social action. Television is already purely an industry, which means that its major problems have to do with capitalization, profit, and survival. I am not indifferent to the prospect of a more powerful National Educational Television and variations of it. But this would not dent the mental health problem I have been describing. For commercial television would always be there in all its vastness and irresistibility. No industry making the money TV makes voluntarily retreats from or alters the good thing it has going. Only clubbing by government loosens the grip of corporate industry upon the public's flesh, and such clubbing occurs only when the flesh is undeniably torn. The idea that television has finally torn the flesh is not even in the offing. Television is regarded as no more noxious to the population than opium and morphine were regarded in the cough syrups of nineteenth-century England.

I haven't even any doctorly advice. Junk your set? Use it sparingly and in peril? Myself, I have the tiniest Sony buried on the bookshelf of a chairless foyer. That way I stand as I watch the last quarter of a Knicks game. You would be amazed at how little else there is on television worth standing for.

19

Stage Fright

Stage fright is a state of morbid anxiety disturbing the sense of poise. This, at least, is how it makes its appearance at a certain point; for, like all morbid states, stage fright proceeds through various phases. Thus I shall try to describe it longitudinally. Also, since not all anxiety states lay claim to the sense of poise, stage fright is a particular species of anxiety, and a psychological study of stage fright will involve more than an inquiry into the general nature of anxiety. We shall have to look into, for example, a psychology of poise. And as poise depends upon our anticipations of others' receptions of how we are hoping to represent ourselves, we shall have occasion to account for feelings of personal fraudulence and the dread of exposure and to refer to a psychology of imposture. Finally, I shall try to revise the notion that stage fright is simply a deplorable occupational hazard of the performing artist the way blight is of the farmer, and to identify it rather as a creative problem that the performing artist attempts to solve along with other problems of artistic performance. That is, I hope to find a perspective for stage fright beyond the clinical, where the phenomenon mainly resides, and to suggest what it contributes to performance.

Let us begin at the clinical level. I have already alluded to the loss of composure in stage fright arising specifically in connection with ideas of being scrutinized detrimentally by other people. In stage fright there is always the fantasy of an audience, persons with whom one anticipates interacting as an exhibitor to onlookers. Without such a fantasy, you cannot have stage fright. The everyday counterpart of stage fright is shyness, and you cannot be shy in the knowledge of being in absolute solitude. In the shower, painfully shy people are able to sing gloriously. True, they may have an accompanying fantasy of performing before an audience, but the fantasy is free of the sense of imminent actualization associated with stage fright. Such solitary activities, regardless of the skill they employ, are not performances.

All anxiety states tend to invoke defensive activities of mind and behavior. Indeed, defense can be so successful that anxiety is extinguished before it attains the intensity of a conscious experience. Moreover, successful defenses themselves operate below a threshold of conscious experience. What is consciously experienced about a successful defense is something like self-determined *facilitation*–despite the fact that all defenses actually *limit* functioning inasmuch as an engagement with anxiety consumes activity otherwise available for thought or action. When a defense fails, however, the unregulated anxiety goes on to produce a symptom, which is (unlike a defense) a consciously experienced limitation upon behavior. Common examples of symptoms in this sense are inhibitions and phobias, and they serve to ward off the conscious experience of anxiety with a conscious experience of personal limitation. If a shy person avoids social events or restricts himself in their midst, he will experience his avoidance or self-restriction as a regrettable limitation on his functioning—but he will not feel anxious. (Later I shall discuss why anxiety is to be avoided at all cost.) Likewise, a claustrophobic will be free of felt anxiety as long as he avoids crowded spaces, but he will experience his avoidance as a personal quirk. When such symptoms fail, a person comes into the anxiety in an unmitigated form, which is called an anxiety state proper, and if this gets too intense, a new line of symptoms are formed that are very malignant indeed.

One point I want to make is that while stage fright progresses into an anxiety state proper and corresponds to the processes I have just outlined, including the formation of an advanced line of symptoms, it is an *induced* anxiety state by virtue of the fact that the performer, unlike the neurotic, defies the phobic situation in pursuit of some subsequent advantage. Thus if the dynamics of stage fright are identical to certain forms of psychopathology, this is not to say that those awful moments a performer often suffers as he approaches a performance (and which worsen temporarily upon his entering the stage) are identical in purpose and outcome to comparable morbid processes in the neurotic. Psychoanalysis, the psychology that is informing our discussion, has always been at pains to distinguish between morbid and creative processes, however identical it finds the *dynamics* of both processes to be.[1]

Stage fright begins with the materialization of a piece of reality, namely, with the scheduling of a performance.[2] That anxiety is already being generated in connection with the particular performance is often betrayed by the performer's report that momentary pangs of anxiety are released whenever he admits into consciousness the simple fact of the impending performance. Dismissing the fact, he is free of anxiety. This mental sampling of a future danger tests the efficacy of suppression, a conscious mechanism of mastery hardly equal to the conflict.

Other common signs of an underlying conflict in the performer at this point are spells of manic agitation and moods of depression. Sudden disruptions of interpersonal relations are almost inevitable. That such disruptions are experienced by the

---

1. Ernst Kris (1952) introduced the term "regression in the service of the ego" to distinguish from neuroses those submissions to morbid processes leading to psychic reparation and creativity. Citations to this point could be numerous–for example, Lionel Trilling's classic paper, "Art and Neurosis" (1952) and Philip Weissman's "Theoretical Considerations of Ego Regression and Ego Functions in Creativity" (1967). Erik H. Erikson's pathobiographies are pertinent, his study of Freud, for example, "The Dream Specimen of Psychoanalysis" (1954). An excellent paper I shall return to is Phyllis Greenacre's "The Relation of the Impostor to the Artist" (1958).

2. Reality, in the psychoanalytic sense, refers to a part of complex functional principle. Reality is any external circumstance calling for a modification of impulses. The sense of reality is what organizes impulses into effective behavior and guarantees the security of continuity of the self, the experience of predictable efficacy. The loss of a sense of reality, as in schizophrenic episodes, leads to the terror of unpredictable impulsivity. To the performer *qua* performer the performance promises to organize very important expression-seeking impulses into effective behavior and is therefore an indispensable piece of reality, the sense of which stage fright threatens. The idea that his grasp on the performance–the organizing reality–might fail inspires great fear in the performer because then his unspeakable impulses will be revealed.

performer not anxiously but with righteousness is a sign that displacements are operating from reality to more manageable localities in the performer's environment. (Displacement is an unconscious defensive process and affords a sense of facilitation.) It is amazing the subtle accommodations the immediate loved ones of an actor begin to make once he announces an opening night and preliminary rehearsals, so as to defend themselves (also unconsciously) against the displacements that they have learned are certain to come.

Further signs of stage fright at this point in the process are obsessional fantasies, often with hypochondriacal features: "What is the most severe form of cancer I could contract and yet continue to perform?" "If my mother dies the day of opening night, do I or do I not go on?"

Nor are moods uncommon in the initial phase of stage fright. Though moods, especially unpleasant ones, can be connected with the dread reality and do retain something of the emotional value of this reality, they serve to repress the ideational components of the reality. That is, moods are equivalents of fantasies but devoid of imagistic-syntactic properties. Notice in the following segment of an interview with the actor Paul Muni how his wife, a bystander in the interview, recalls Mr. Muni's mood upon signing a contract and then how she goes on to side with the repression of the ideational components of the fantasy represented by the mood, as these components begin to surface under the encouragement of the interview. At the time of this interview Mrs. Muni had been married to her husband forty years. With blind intuition (and some heavy-handedness), she knew where to support her husband's defenses, and where to keep the lid on:

MUNI: I was walking up Sixth Avenue toward Broadway. After all the pictures that I've made, after so many years in the theatre, after never having played a subordinate role either on Broadway or in films–and if you check back you'll find out that I never was anything but the leading man and the so-called star. And yet when I walked up from Sixth Avenue to Broadway and saw "Paul Muni in *Inherit the Wind*," I got sick to my stomach. And I got nervous and unhappy and I thought–I don't know what I thought at the time but I was sick. I was unhappy about the whole thing.

MRS. MUNI: The night that he signed with Herman [Shumlin] to do *Inherit the Wind*, and I think it was my birthday and I had a few people for dinner, and he sat there, he was the most miserable man in the world.

MUNI: Well, it's because . . .

MRS. MUNI: There's no other name for it. It's running scared.

MUNI: No. It's a desire. There's a desire for . . . First of all, if one wants to make a kind of an analysis, a self-analysis, you say for one thing you have a self-respect for yourself. You're afraid to fail.

INTERVIEWER: Maybe it's conceit.

MUNI: I am conceited but in an oblique sort of way.

MRS. MUNI: In a modest way. In other words, he's *meshugeh*–crazy.

MUNI: I think conceit is necessary. I think one should have what we call conceit, or vanity, or whatever you choose to call it. It's allied to self-respect. It's allied to believing in your own worth.

INTERVIEWER: You must be a very nervous man on an opening night.

MRS. MUNI: What do you mean, opening night? He's a nervous man period. . . . You should go up to him and touch his hands before he goes on the stage. Anyway, let me tell you a story which has nothing to do with your tape . . . [Funke and Booth 1961, pp. 189–190].

Whereupon Mrs. Muni elaborates a long anecdote about an angry scene between her and her husband in connection with a performance many years before, an incident in which she was reduced to tears by Mr. Muni's anger. And the interview never returns to the fantasy her husband was almost getting to when he spoke of conceit and vanity.

Moods, pangs of anxiety, interpersonal vicissitudes, and obsessional preoccupations are among the derivatives of incipient stage fright. Evidence of psychic conflict, such reactions nevertheless belong to the wide range of normal-neurotic phenomena and are analogous to the psychopathology abounding in everyday life. If I am neglecting the more serious manifestations of conflict that occur in this phase among performers with markedly disturbed personalities, it is because I am attempting to describe a typical process rather than a clinical population.

But the defensive activity that these reactions suggest cannot mitigate the anxiety of the performance forever. In stage fright the reality enlarges with the passage of time; the defenses cannot alter the fixed moment of the performance. And the failure of these defenses heralds a symptom whose analogy goes beyond the psychopathology of everyday life. The symptom that begins to form days before the performance consists of the well-known irrepressible attack of anxiety accompanied by delusional thinking—delusional because the terror accompanying the thinking is actual, while the content is fantastical. The delusion has it that the audience is convening for an occasion of devastating ridicule and humiliation for the performer. This delusion, grandiose and persecutory, is frankly paranoiac. The neurotic phase of stage fright is progressing toward a psychosis; for in truth no audience motivated by persecutory wrath weathers the elements to attend a performance.[3]

However, all paranoid ideas contain a nucleus of truth, and I submit that the performer's delusion at this point in the process is fashioned out of a real and truly momentous possibility: the audience's indifference to the performance. Delusions of persecution are very often constructed out of a confusion between indifference and hostility. To the paranoiac, who desperately craves the contact of human attention and interaction, a world of strangers and events irrelevant to him is equivalent to a thwarting of his needs for contact. His fantasy of collective persecution with himself as referent establishes human relationships where none otherwise exist. The paranoiac's frenzied disappearance into a doorway to avoid being photographed by the airplane overhead is one of the behavioral exponents that classifies his fantasy a delusion, just as the performer's physical symptoms impart delusional characteristics to his fantasies about the convening audience. But in these matters the paranoiac has the advantage over the performer; for the paranoiac can regulate his anxiety by behaving with deference to the delusional dangers. Ducking into a doorway, he does feel safe. The performer, on the other hand, cannot take comparable precautions, which would require flight from the theater or

---

3. Philip Weissman (1969) has coined the term "creative psychosis" for the transient delusional and other morbid phenomena involved in certain creative activity. He states, moreover, that "the 'creative psychosis' of the creative artist is independent of his usual mental state which may be normal, neurotic or psychotic."

concert hall.[4] (We shall have something to say later about the crime for which the performer anticipates persecution.)

The performer goes on to a final phase of extreme symptomatology: blocking and depersonalization. Familiar to all performers at one time or another and to some always, these reactions occur in the agonizingly protracted moments just before and after appearing onstage in front of the hushed audience. Blocking is the momentary experience of complete loss of perception and rehearsed function. Not to be confused with inhibition (which has a volitional element and constrains only certain but not all functioning), blocking erases all sense of control and aims at a total extinction of impulse by disconnecting the self from all avenues of functioning, including speech. Once onstage, blocking gives way to depersonalization. This reaction is most often experienced as a split between a functioning and an observing self, with pronounced spatial disorientation. The observing self perceives the functioning self as off at a distance, operating mechanically before an audience that is also perceived as quite distant. Otherwise preconscious aspects of the body image and physiologic functions come into consciousness and feel overwhelmingly close; the performer is conscious of his limbs, face, and posture and loses a sense of trustworthiness about their coordination; the heartbeat intrudes upon consciousness, often audibly, sometimes deafeningly. Color perception is lost, and the visual components of the experience resemble a black-and-white dream.

Such disorientation, including as it does destruction of the prevailing body image, is pathognomic of an advanced psychosis. This is the terminal point of the stage-fright reaction. Full recovery from it is usually rapid in the performer, though some performers report a series of recoveries and relapses during the first minutes of a performance before recovery is permanently established.

I might add that the clinical process I have just described—the

---

4. This is not to say that certain measures are not attempted, such as ritualistic actions, verbal litanies, hand wringing—behavior I shall go into. But short of revising the entire persecutory fantasy of the audience, which is not feasible, these measures are merely straws in the wind.

progression from comparatively mild to severe reaction–does not vary with kinds of performance. I mention this because, regarding stage fright, performers are given to envying advantages imputed to different kinds of performance. Actors, for example, express envy of musicians, whose skills seem more bona fide, more confirmable, as if this removes a major cause of stage fright. Musicians are correspondingly mistaken about the advantages of actors, who are thought to be blessed by the opportunity for initial flexibility in their performance; actors, they think, can improvise their way around their nervousness until they gain their composure and no one need be the wiser, whereas for the musician one false note is a glaring calamity. I have not been able to discern significant differences in the dynamics of stage fright among actors, musicians, dancers, singers, or even public speakers. Though many problems of performance vary with the specific performing art, stage fright originates in the mere act of performance itself.

We have been tracing the fate of the anxiety generated by the anticipation of a performance before an audience. What is there about such anticipation that creates anxiety? And what allows a performer to persevere against the increasing quantities of anxiety in stage fright (when clearly perseverance is not entirely a conscious option)?

How we shall answer these questions will depend upon our concept of anxiety, a set of propositions *explaining* our shared and familiar experience of this most unpleasant of affects.[5] The concept I shall concern us with is the one derived from psychoanalysis, because the Freudian concept includes a developmental point of view. I am hoping here to advance the view that among the varied pleasures of theater (and art in general) is the celebration of a host of developmental stages in the growth of the individual from birth to maturity. (see Chapter 20.) In theater, our individual historical trials acquire a dynamic sense of triumph. That is, the performer's exposure to and conquest of

---

5. One of the criticisms of psychological explanation is that it needlessly complicates phenomena already well understood. For an excellent discussion of this matter, which includes clarification of certain methodologic problems in relating psychology to art, see Eissler 1968.

stage fright (a process intrinsic, if not to every performance, then certainly to his long-range career) is a creative solution, the *essence* of a solution, to specific developmental issues universally arrested at one point or another in the individuals comprising an audience. Stage fright and its vicissitudes can be regarded as a revitalization of a universal developmental plight settled by the audience with residual discontents; the audience now participates in this revitalization as if in a renewed opportunity.

Let us approach a concept of anxiety through a definition that we will then go on to account for: Anxiety is a signal of the violation of the *conditions* guaranteeing life-sustaining supplies. A key idea here is that anxiety has to do with a cognizance that survival is conditional. Moreover, this cognizance undergoes an evolution. Anxiety may, then, refer to one or several stages of this evolution retained in the functioning of the adult individual. Thus we may label anxiety according to the developmental conflicts it signals; the more archaic conflicts arousing *primal anxiety* (actually a presignal anxiety), the more advanced *guilt* (which is a rarefaction of anxiety), and the grades in between. As we shall see, when stage fright reaches the point of threatening the sense of poise, a regression from issues involving guilt to earlier forms of anxiety has occurred in the performer, a circumstance that evokes the direct and intense reciprocity with an audience that so distinguishes the performing arts. Let us begin to account for these assertions.

Anxiety evolves in the human being from an extraordinary perception that dawns during the first year of life. Over a period of months following birth, the human infant becomes aware that food and handling appear through the cooperating presence of an agent—the mother—external to the infant. Prior to this perception, there is only the sensation of appetite and its reduction in a boundless continuity with the environment. Following this perception, there is a shift in interest from the supplies themselves—food and handling—to the cooperating agent. And so begins the infant's first human relationship. If your actual survival depends upon the reliability and interest of another person, you will soon become engrossed in this person even more than you will in the supplies she provides, whose reliability is already well known. Milk unfailingly quenches thirst and without delay; the problem is the comings and goings of the person who provides it.

Henceforth displeasure is complicated by a division: appetite for food and handling leads to one kind of tension; the temporary loss of collaboration with the attentive presence of the mother leads to another. Primal anxiety is the displeasure over the latter and begins a development of its own, related to but distinct from the displeasures of appetite.

Now primal anxiety will arise only, of course, in connection with what a newborn employs in his collaboration with the mother. Needless to say, speech, values, morals, and such are not as yet the collaborative instrumentalities. Certain muscular kinestheses are. Also available are coordinations in the oral region and the respiratory apparatus. Successful coordination of the lips, chin, the musculature of the throat, the nose, and the respiratory apparatus permits sucking, swallowing, and breathing during physical contact with the mother. But such coordination depends upon the mother's providing much more than milk. The nursing conditions are as crucial to survival as the milk. An infant will not feed properly unless a kinesthetic reciprocity is established with the mother. For example, the mother's cradling the infant in a nursing position must preclude the sensation in the infant of imminently falling, a sensation that arises if the infant's head is not firmly supported—at birth and for some time after, the infant's neck muscles are capable of revolving the head toward the nipple but not of supporting the head. There is also an empathetic kinesthesis involving the mother's own breathing tempo. The presentation of the mother's face is crucial because of an inborn readiness to recognize a gestalt of the human face—during feeding and handling the infant's visual fixation is upon the mother's *face,* not the breast. (For a long period, the face gestalt is the only one there is an inborn readiness to recognize. Primal anxiety attends the disruption of these and other coordinating features of the earliest infant–mother relationship. Rage reactions, loss of appetite, apathy, and failure to establish diurnal rhythms are concomitants of primal anxiety.)

Here we can introduce a momentous observation having to do with the human hand. The first step toward psychological autonomy of the infant–diminishing his complete dependence upon the mother for salvation from primal anxiety–originates in his hand-mouth explorations and their eventual coordination (Hoffer 1949). The hand is the first object in connection with which certain experiences of facility with the mother can be reproduced without the mother's collaborating presence. Thumb-sucking, for example, is pursued for much more than oral-erotic pleasure in a narrow sense. Thumb-sucking reunites the child with earlier states of integration in the feeding position, and the entire hand in its contact with the perioral region, including the nasal area, is as important to the experience as the thumb in the mouth. Indeed, hand-mouth contact seems to precede the mother–child relationship in affording rudimentary security *in utero*. Attempts to regain poise in later life activate the hand significantly. In everyday life, unpoise is a disintegration of a favorable anticipation of collaboration with other people, and the hand is used to provide the sense of coordinating facilitation deemed absent in the external environment.

The state of poise as a derivative of the early period of infancy is the subject of an extensive study by Leo Rangell (1954), an exceptionally able psychoanalytic worker. On the hand-mouth element in the state of unpoise, Dr. Rangell refers to Hoffer's classic paper and then goes on:

> When there is a disequilibrium, a state of unpoise, the hand, as much as any other organ, seems suspended, or in the way, or as if groping and looking for the object. "What to do with the hand?" is an uppermost question during states of discomfiture.
>
> The unity of mouth and hand is brought out here as it has been described by Willie Hoffer in relation to ego function. Hoffer points out that already in intrauterine life the hand becomes closely allied to the mouth for the sake of relieving tension and that within this alliance is the first achievement of the primitive ego. Owing to the posture of the foetus within the uterus, the hand or fist is nearest to the chin and mouth. Neurophysiological confirmation of this alliance is provided by the palmomental reflex which is accentuated when separated from the higher centres by pyramidal tract disease. . . . In earliest life both mouth and hand seek to grasp the mother object. From the twelfth week the hand helps in the feeding process by being placed half open

on the breast or bottle. In the absence of the latter, they also find
and explore each other, leading to the first self-discovery, which
is enlarged later into an oral-tactile concept of the body and the
world around. . . . In later life there results an abundance of
derivative activities, all types of mannerisms, in which the hand
or fingers "play around" the mouth or chin or nose or face. It is
the hand as well as the lips, which is steadied and reassured by
the poised cocktail glass. Of similar effect is the cigarette. . . .
[p.329]

In addition to the hand, Rangell cites the general musculo-
skeletal postural system as a mediator of poise and finds much
in postural mannerisms seeking to establish an experience of
support and facilitation that is reminiscent of being cradled in
the original feeding situation. All sorts of postures are struck in
an effort to protect oneself from being "put down," dropped, as
it were, by another person or persons. Even "casual" postures
aim to enhance autonomy from the danger of noncollaboration,
this by a disqualification of the potential collaborator. In contrast
to muscle tensing, "an attempt to deny any dependence on the
outside is seen in the way in which an adolescent, or adolescent-
like adult, will lie sprawled out on the floor or on a chair in a
position designed to give the impression of utmost poise. This
position, a kind of opposite of erectness or muscle tone, is as if
to say, "I don't need any muscle tone, you affect me or threaten
me so little–I am so self-sufficient!" [p. 328] Hysterical fainting,
a complete crumbling of posture, represents a fantasy of absolute collaborative failure by the environment to meet the hysteric's state of absolute dependence.[6]

_____

6. I am reminded of a patient, a female hysteric, who described how she
would swoon and often faint during sexual relations when things didn't go as
she anticipated they should. Her specifications were so precise that things very
rarely went as they should, and the outcome struck terror, as well it might, in
her various lovers, who naturally believed she was dying or was dead. Her
behavior was a resurrection of issues of primal anxiety, her fainting warding off,
for example, a rage reaction. In addition, her comatose state was a histrionic
indictment of her lover's incompetence, aimed really at an early mother
image–the patient as a child actually played dead to such a degree that she
scared the wits out of her mother. Also, the patient was a poor collaborator. Her
tenseness and frigidity parodied her image of her mother and deprived the lover

It is the perioral region, or snout, which the activities of the postural system and the hand seek to coordinate with, for this is the passive and vulnerable region when poise is at stake. Rangell's study is brilliant for its microscopic attention to the snout, which he delineates anatomically:

> Rather than solely the mouth, I would widen the circle to have it include what is commonly called the snout. The region would now correspond to a circle with its center in the philtrum of the upper lip or at the center of the mouth. Its lateral margins would be the two nasolabial folds; its upper margin the ventral surface of the nose; its lower margin through the middle of the chin. On closer thought, it is this larger area, rather than the mouth alone, which is buried in and is contiguous to the surface of the maternal breast during the earliest interpersonal contact. It is in the tissues of this area, its skin, fasciae, and muscles, through which the first proprioceptive sensations of being steadied and attached and anchored are mediated. Correspondingly, in later life this is a focal area which, when one feels unanchored in any more complex social or interpersonal situation, feels unsteady and shaky and has to be supported. [p. 320]

There are other reasons, converging with this ontogenetic role, which enhance the snout's centrality in states of poise and unpoise:

> Among these is first an anatomic–embryologic consideration, namely that this oral snout area is, both phylogenetically and from the standpoint of embryological development, the true rostral tip of the organism, a fact which in quadrupeds is still anatomically visible. As the most cephalad and forward point, this area psychologically and biologically is the pseudopod which projects furthest into the outer world and is therefore invested with the function of making the first tentative contacts with objects of the environment to determine which to accept or reject. [p. 320]

---

of what he anticipated. Of course, there were more advanced issues involved in her fainting behavior–guilt, for example.

Indeed, in man this is the only anatomical region that must remain in contact with the world for individual life to continue.

The amount of effector response to emotion that is concentrated in the perioral region is also very pertinent. Rangell calls this region "the window to the emotions," where the mimetic expressive system is most active, more active than the eyes, for example. It is in this region, therefore, that we most fear betrayals of our inner emotional states, for "the neurological mechanisms for mimetic expression are mediated in pathways separate from those for voluntary facial activity. A voluntary or forced smile can be differentiated from a genuine and involuntary one. Organic lesions can affect one and spare the other. Voluntary facial paralysis can exist while mimetic expression is normal, and *vice versa*." (p. 323). Thus concealment is not always reliable around the snout. Blushing, an involuntary confession of feeling, begins in the snout and radiates outward. Also, it is a region connected intimately to the viscera, organs regulated by the autonomic system. Indeed, the snout is an extremity of the viscera, the naso-oral cavities being continuous with the gastrointestinal tract. (The other extremity is the anus, with which the snout acquires associations. Nasal mucous, for example, is considered "dirty" in a fecal sense, as are saliva and oral odors.) The snout registers very personal feelings and appetites. Though Rangell mentions stage fright only in passing as an example of poiselessness, he observes one of its most common accompaniments, dry mouth, which is the first appetitive state of the newborn, following the loss of constant lubrication by the amniotic fluid. (Hunger is secondarily differentiated from thirst long after birth.) The snout vitalizes very archaic experiences.

To take stock: Poiselessness is a disequilibrium between appetitive arousal (for narcissistic supplies including recognition and approval) and executive facilitation, which is anticipated as absent in the environment. The personal executive musculature, the hand and postural system, is enlisted to substitute for the collaboration anticipated as absent in the environment. This enlistment is exemplified by the activities of the hand directed protectively to the perioral region, and by shifts of posture, in an effort to restore poise. In varying degrees, such activity is constant in everyday social life.[7]

Here we can appreciate a staggering element in stage fright. *The performance deprives the performer of recourse to the hand and postural system.* This is what leads to the grisly feeling of being fully exposed onstage. In performance a concert pianist has no option about what he does with his hands. Nor can he assume a comforting defensive posture at the piano. This is an extraordinary thing, having no counterpart in everyday life. Fear quickly leads to motility. Onstage motility appropriate to the danger (the existence of which we have yet to account for) is disallowed. Indeed, this state of affairs may be another of those elementary criteria for defining the difference between a performance and a social event. *A performance would be an activity where poise is achieved through behavior alien to the performer's personal style of achieving it.* That his personal style of achieving poise is disallowed by the requirements of the performance is what elevates a performer onstage beyond the realm of everyday life.

Also, I think this distinguishes the performer as performer from the "show biz" personality. I have in mind, for example, the hours upon hours of nonperformance television shows like the "Tonight Show" on which Johnny Carson so ably holds forth. His incessant nose scratching and wiping his finger across his forehead are gestures reminding us–*insisting*–that he is not giving a performance but simply exercising his personality. (If Mr. Carson's nose actually itched to the extent that he scratches it, it would be diagnostic of a serious, chronic dermatitis.) Performers who appear on that show do much the same thing to indicate that they are not performing. This is not theater but show business, and we enjoy it because we participate as onlookers in what we believe is the performer's relief from the

---

7. This formulation of a collaboration between an executive neuromuscular apparatus and a visceral system originating out of an early oral situation is consistent with René A. Spitz's studies on the "primal cavity" (see Chapter 20). Rangell (1963), in his contribution to a *festschrift* for Spitz, observes the independent agreement between his and Spitz's idea of the "primal cavity."

stringencies of performance. These occasions are sort of casual limbos, neither everyday life nor performances.

Along these lines I might interject that personal props tend to distinguish pure performances from what could be called acts. The fuming cigar that George Burns cannot do without, Sinatra's cigarettes (before he gave up smoking), marked speech mannerisms such as Peter Lorre cultivated–these are remnants of poise-establishing activities from everyday life and prevent a final dissolution of the personal self into performance. I think Bert Lahr's retention of his famous near-lisp spoiled something in his celebrated participation in *Godot*. Ideally, I believe performance requires an ultimate elimination of all personal security-seeking mannerisms, and I should think that training must include education in how to do this–onstage, not in everyday life. Of course, this ability to gain poise solely through performance does not guarantee a memorable performance or even a good one.

Knowing what the performance is going to deprive him of in the way of establishing composure, the performer, prior to going onstage, will heighten certain behavior (including thoughts and fantasies). This behavior bears directly on what I have been describing. Backstage, when things get bad, many actresses knit; Rangell includes knitting with cocktail-glass and cigarette-holding as a notable poise-maintaining activity. The constant squeezing of a rubber ball has been reported by several performers. Hand-wringing is very common, as is pacing, which increases the experience of the neuromuscular system and diminishes visceral signals, the latter being able to be received only in a state of some passivity. Cigarette smoking is also common, the kind where one cigarette after another is put out. This is different from smoking to accompany contemplation; backstage smoking is a repetition of hand-mouth coordination, the oral-respiratory supply–the smoke–being secondary. The kind of speech in which verbal communication is incidental to primal contact is common. Jim Hall, a jazz guitarist of awesome talent, describes how he will try to control occasional episodes of stage fright by voluntarily assuming a posture he knows he has when he is feeling very confident about his playing. "I carry myself as if I am confident. It doesn't really help. But I always think it will. You just can't wait around like a sitting duck." A list of physical behavior in these circumstances could be very extensive.

Behavior and thoughts expressive of more fully formed fantasies take us into other issues. Many performers go through a business-as-usual charade backstage that expresses an indifference to the imminent danger of going onstage. They joke and laugh with friends and continue social relationships up to the very moment of walking out on the stage. Or they read a book in a spirit of deep engrossment. Some performers go through the motions of napping. Others stand around blank and noncommunicative. These activities are like that sprawling posture Rangell observed. Here there is a direct reference, largely preconscious, to the audience, a defensive contempt, a retraction of the authority that stage fright invests in the audience. Stanislavski's advice about overcoming nervousness belongs to this category of defense. He counseled that the actor begin the performance with all his attention concentrated on an object on the stage, a cup on a table, for example. Then the circle of attention can widen to include larger aspects of the scene, but must not wander beyond the other actors onstage. This is what imbues Stanislavskian performances with their typical self-centered, defiant quality. The audience feels both impressed and demeaned, which is either good or bad depending upon your aesthetic biases. (I rather admire it in occasional doses.) Unlike hand-wringing, which attempts to repair a *fait accompli*, this kind of behavior attempts to ward off stage fright before it happens, by addressing itself to the dynamics prerequisite to stage fright.

Certain thoughts and inner dialogues are also resorted to. Pep talks muttered half aloud are invariable. Previous achievements and awards are mentally conjured. By these tactics reassurance is secured, not through diminishing the audience but through enhancing the self, part of the comfort being the sense of continuity of the self, which reference to the past can convey, and part the mitigation of the power struggle with the audience so close to consciousness in the previous category of behavior.

Power is even borrowed from the audience to enhance the

self, as when the performer dwells upon prestigious characteristics of the audience, bolstering himself with the idea that he
can't be all that bad if such a group is willing to turn out for the
performance. This is obviously different from the defiance
contained in thoughts that denigrate the audience, such as
performers often have in summer stock, where they believe they
are playing to tourists rather than knowledgeable theatergoers,
or late in a long-run production when the more earnest and
critical theatergoers have long since disappeared from the
audiences. The attempt at identification with an audience conceived as qualified and aggressive represses, rather than expresses, aggression. Such a defense rests on the hope that the
enemy won't turn against its own kind.

Thus we are able to observe three strategies for coping with
stage fright in its poise–threatening phase: variations of primal
hand-mouth behavior, pre-emptive defiance, and identification.
Backstage, these strategies are going on to greater or lesser
degrees all the time and alternate with each other in the same
performer.

If primal anxiety motivates hand-mouth activity and its
variations, chronologically more advanced infantile-anxiety situations motivate the performer's other backstage behavior,
including those thoughts through which he attempts to reassure
himself. In turning to these more advanced childhood situations
and continuing our narrative of anxiety development, we shall
be able to account also for the origins of the performer's
anticipations of punitive humiliation by the audience.[8]

In primal anxiety, perception–educated, organized sensation–

---

8. The psychoanalytic idea that current behavior derives from specific infantile stages of development leads to an error, common even among analysts, that
the more chronologically archaic the source, the more "sick" the behavioral
derivative. If this were true, then a mild depression, which derives from oral
dynamics, would be more pathologic than a severe jealousy having a chronologically more advanced oedipal stamp. Actually, intensity–psychic economy
rather than dynamics–is the diagnostic criterion. I say this on the outside chance
that misformulations incidental to our discussion will be constructed, such as
the mistaken idea that it is "healthier" to be defiant than fidgety, or some such
normative scheme. I should emphasize that there are no normative recommendations in our discussion, no prescriptions for a fictitious state of mental health.

is comparatively weak. The interpersonal situation that originally gives rise to primal anxiety is overwhelmingly physical, and the infant's reaction is immediate and literally thoughtless. Equilibrium is established if the infant's impulsive discharge induces suitably caring responses in the mother.

Primal anxiety evolves into signal anxiety during the second year of life. Signal anxiety arises in connection with thought processes that can already anticipate a dangerous situation before it occurs in all its ramifications. With signal anxiety, mental life has developed sufficiently for situations to be sampled in thought and for an anxiety signal or the lack of it to represent the verdict to act or not. The curtailment of action by anxiety requires a repression of the impulse that was sampled. Thought is experimental action, and anxiety is one of the crucial tests in the experiment.

At this point in life such thought still centers on the mothering person, but it includes much more than direct physical contact in the feeding-handling situation. The child is developing perceptions that the mother attaches conditions to her ongoing availability. There are now purposeful actions beyond impulsive discharge that the child can take to guarantee the mother's loyalty, which remains the essential of survival. Even in the mother's absence the child can carry out acts of obedience. Indeed signal anxiety has reference to a mental representation of the mother and signals a loss of love with regard to a maternal introject.

If anxiety represents an imminent violation of some condition or other of a supervising introject, it is not hard to see how pleasure can confirm the fact that conditions have been fulfilled, that an act of obedience has occurred. For if pleasure cannot be had outside of a behavioral program that allows it, then the experience of pleasure can confirm adherence. Thus pleasure is as much a signal of compliance as anxiety is of imminent transgression. Indeed, addiction to pleasure, as in drug addictions, is a complete capitulation to maternal stipulations, lip service to the contrary by the loved ones of addicts notwithstanding. I bring in this idea to nip in the bud the simplistic notion that if anxiety defines the limits of pleasurable freedom, autonomy resides in the dogged pursuit of pleasure. It is quite possible–indeed it is very frequent–that a triumph over a restrictive anxiety lands one in the maternal net nevertheless. When a mother who surrounds herself with fearful conditions teaches at the same time that submission to fear is unfitting and ungainly, she is creating a project out of fear. In the child, anxiety will become a challenge as much as a restriction. Commonly this comes about when a mother constantly denigrates those around her, notably the father, for weakness and lack of achievement. A lack of courage is not to be emulated, while the mother's power to command obedience–to a standard everyone around her is failing–is increased by her obvious tyranny over those around her. A child will then be forced into a bravery surpassing his or her father's, but will be motivated by submissive fear of the mother, so that the persistence against anxiety will be an act, not of autonomy, but of capitulation. Not bravery, but *bravado* is the subsequent life experience of those counterphobic daredevils who are driven compulsively to perform the very acts they most fear.

Certainly performance is a species of counterphobia and stage fright an anxiety that invites, rather than restricts, action. The successful outcome of this action (the performance) brings the relief afforded by some compliance or other with an internal agent that had something to do with the anxiety in the first place.[9] The performer's triumph over the particular anxiety we are investigating removes him from one hook but hangs him on another, which is why he is never entirely done with stage fright the way other people get over the anxieties, much like stage fright, with which certain public acts are undertaken. The medical novitiate, for example, is apt to be anxious and quite shaken at his first examination of a live patient. A stage fright reaction is also likely in the lawyer trying his first few cases in a real courtroom. But with experience such anxiety disappears. A lively counterphobic dynamic, which calls for a repetition of dread and deliverance, is not a requirement of good medical or legal practice. This is not so with performance. Whatever else

---

9. Otto Fenichel (1954) makes a similar point several times in his extensive writing. He goes into it in detail in two places: "The Counter-Phobic Attitude" (pp. 163–173) and "On Acting" (pp. 349–361).

may *force* the performer to go on–loyalty to the performing group, for example–a fascination with the counterphobic possibilities of the occasion *allows* him to go on and, furthermore, to expose himself repeatedly to the anxiety. Nor is all this an option, but rather a piece of unwitting life style.

More than simply a tolerated unpleasantness, counterphobic anxiety is the isthmus joining two continents of the soul, both of which need experiencing.

I have suggested that a counterphobic dynamic is often set in motion by a possessive and challenging mother who represents the child's father to the child as impaired and ineffectual. (Fate often assists by removing the father through death or divorce, which the mother represents as cowardly desertion.) Tempted as I am to claim that close approximations to this family constellation are routinely found in the population that gravitates toward theater stages, I think such a claim would be misleading. Patients other than performers reveal such a history, so that it does not distinguish between the counterphobic in everyday life and the counterphobic on stage whose appearance has a significantly different value as behavior. But there exist more general, less risky explanations for the counterphobic element in stage fright.

I have in mind several observations made by Phyllis Greenacre in a group of interrelated papers on the childhood of the artist.[10] Her observations have always struck me as exceedingly relevant to the performing artist, though most of her reference is to the literary artist. To grasp Greenacre's meaning we shortly shall have to resume our developmental scheme of anxiety.

Talent is one of those qualities easier to recognize than to define. In the adult, the presence of talent is self-evident, even if degrees of it are disputable, and what precisely it is is really less important than what it accomplishes. Greenacre's concern is not with the essences of talent, but with the effects of talent upon the childhood of those who are born with it. Several of her generalizations about the gifted child are of considerable interest

---

10. The most pertinent are "The Relation of the Impostor to the Artist" (1958a), "The Impostor" (1958b), and "The Family Romance and the Artist" (1958c).

for our present purposes. Greenacre makes the observation, not in itself startling, that from early infancy onward the artistically gifted child responds to the environment with greater range of sensitivity than the less gifted child, with the consequence that objects in the environment–including persons and the child's own body–take on increased symbolic possibilities. The perceptual enlargements of the gifted child elevate ordinary peripheral properties of objects to perceptual ranks of significant import. The gifted child not only sees things differently (as does the disturbed child), he sees the extraordinary *in addition* to the ordinary, and he perceives it not fleetingly and vaguely, as less exceptional children do, but steadily and vividly, so that the extraordinary becomes a familiar and organized set of perceptions. Greenacre (1958a) has coined the term "collective alternates" for those perceptions of nonhuman objects evolved from the extended responsiveness of the gifted child. She suggests several effects of "collective alternates" on the development of the gifted child.

> It is my belief . . . that because the collective outer world does offer alternates for the specific objects of the human object relationships and frequently is invested to a greater extent with fantasy, it may furnish a retreat from the exigencies of personal pressures, and permit a less decisive dealing with their problems. This together with the fact that the gifted child is, in his very nature, subject to possible overstimulation may conceivably predispose to an earlier stimulation of the developing libidinal phases, resulting in a less clear hierarchy in the phase progression. This is particularly obvious in the fate of the oedipal conflict *which is rarely solved as well as in the less gifted individual*. [Italics added, p. 527]

Elsewhere Greenacre implies that the exceptional responsiveness of the gifted child also amplifies peripheral versions of human objects, for which outcome I would suggest the term "phantoms," a term borrowed from Wittels (1939),[11] which

---

11. A definitive study of identifications, "phantoms," the whole variety of "inner presences" appears in Schafer 1968.

Fenichel (1954) uses in his paper on acting. "Phantoms" would be special cases of Greenacre's idea of "collective alternates," particularly noticeable in the young potential performer. Fenichel writes, "The 'phantoms' are developed under the influence of real experiences and represent earlier identifications, *not necessarily identifications with real objects* but also with objects as the child saw them, or as the child would have liked them to be." (italics added, "On Acting," pp. 353–354.) Fenichel adds that compared with true identifications (which are unconscious) "phantoms" derive from imitations; they are pseudo-identifications and never afford the experience of authenticity of identifications. If a child *imitates* his father, a child who can't yet read might sit in a club chair with a newspaper spread in front of his face. But if a child has *identified* with his father, the child has learned to read the newspaper, in which case he is like his father, even if the child goes on to read books rather than newspapers and reads them at the kitchen table rather than in club chairs. Imitative actions, however well learned and spontaneous, always retain a lively element of pretense. The illiterate child with the newspaper is really an *impostor* who at any moment could be exposed and shamed by his parents were they of so cruel a mind to accuse him of the sham–"You little liar, you may look like a grownup, but you *really* can't read." Similarly, in later life, actions involving "collective alternates" and "phantoms" are aways subject to humiliating exposure if the onlooker's complicity is not maintained. The punishment of such exposure is for aggressive pretense; the directive is banishment to a world of joyless mediocrity.

Most of us have learned to banish ourselves. "The master beats the horse," goes a Kafka parable, "then the horse takes the whip and beats himself, so that he can be the master." But the gifted have more at stake. The "collective alternates" and "phantoms" of the gifted child emerge as an organized world *demanding* attention and commitment comparable to the more ordinary world fashioned from more ordinary relationships to the human and nonhuman environment. Though pseudo-identifications are inevitable in the development of all human beings, in the gifted child they attain a marked psychic palpability, virtually an additional existence. Greenacre (1958a) describes the process:

> It has already been noted that every artist is at least two people, the personally oriented self and the artistic one. The relationship between these two (or more) people in one body varies enormously. Sometimes they are on good speaking terms with each other; sometimes the identities are relatively separate and in extreme cases may be quite dissociated one from the other. How much the personally oriented self resembles the "ordinary citizen" must depend largely on the nature of the pressures, personal attachments and especially the identifications of early childhood. In the matter of identification both the character of the person(s) who furnish the models for identification and the mechanisms through which it is achieved are important. Even where a fairly secure beginning of ordinary-citizenship development is established early, one finds then the creative pressures asserting themselves in rebellious attacks against ordinary order in the blind search for liberation. Quite as frequently the creative pressure achieves early some room for itself, whether or not its nature is recognized and appreciated. It then may still infiltrate and upset the ordinary course of development, producing seemingly unreliable or even chaotic behavior which is likely to be regarded only as perverse or psychopathic until the strength of the artistic demands have brought about some definite fruitions.
>
> As the capacity for artistic creation emerges, develops and is accepted into the individual's life, it is not unusual for some kind of pattern of rhythm in the creative work to become established. The interplay between the aggression of creative activity and compulsive controls would be a subject worthy of a study. . . . [pp. 528–529]

We already have seen that anxiety has to do with a sense of loss of collaboration with a ministerial agent. Using Greenacre's formulation, we might say that stage fright signals a separation from this agent as it resides in the performer's "ordinary" world, where he can avail himself of those means for achieving security through behavior that are consistent with the "ordinary" world. Recall, for example, those incessant poise-establishing mannerisms of everyday life that are precluded by performance. Ordinary mortals heed anxiety, repudiate action, and retain their "collective alternates" and "phantoms" in fantasies; the artist is encouraged to action by the unique palpability of his other world.

In the first passage quoted from Greenacre, I underscored a concluding statement about the gifted child being deprived of an opportunity to close the door on childhood with the finality of the less gifted. The gifted child, Greenacre says, very rarely resolves the final oedipal phase of childhood. What does this mean? And what are the consequences? With these questions we shall finally be trudging out of developmental psychology and back into theater and performance.

Anxiety regulates impulse and participates in the evolution of a format for gratifying appetite, which diversifies with physical maturation. We have already noted that at birth appetitive impulses center in the perioral region, which early in life is the most reliable part of the anatomy, and we have analyzed a phase of stage fright as a derivative of primal anxiety.

Other aspects of the developmental scheme also figure in stage fright. For example, somewhat later when the anal sphincter undergoes a spurt of maturation and acquires reliability, retentive and eliminative impulses become prominent and subject to the regulation of anxiety. There is an element in stage fright having to do with a dread of loss of control over such impulses, now represented by fantasies of performing one's part chaotically, creating a laughable mess. Toward the end of the second year of life, the maturation of the skeletal-muscular system takes the limelight and so-called phallic impulses arise–an erect posture with pleasure in locomotion. Exhibitionism–pride in physical integrity and wherewithal–becomes a source of pleasure, with attendent impulsivity; irresponsibility toward the physical environment becomes a contention between mother and child. The genital area including the perineum–the crotch–matures in its capacity to register erotic sensations (so much so that the perineum becomes a locality of extraordinary interest–tactile, olfactory, visual–which interest results in a lingering confusion between the genitalia and the anus and the harrowing bewilderment that the world is populated by creatures possessing two kinds of genitals). The relationship between exhibitionism and performance is common lore, and I shall not pause to examine the amalgam of truth and error that has accumulated around it. But we could attribute to stage fright anxious fantasies that the audience will not take seriously what the performer claims to have: adult sexual power. In other words, stage fright retains apprehensions at all levels of psychosexual development.

Now this series of maturational crises is not endless. Within the sixth year of life, crises subside, at which point the child is physically a miniature adult, and his maturation proceeds on all fronts at an equal rate. It had been a spurt here, then a spurt there. Now he expands like a balloon, which is far less conducive to new anxiety–inducing interactions with the environment. Respite lasts until puberty, when the next maturational jolt occurs. In the meantime he consolidates his past.[12] This so-called latency period is a time of fantasy elaboration. It is during this period that the gifted child reveals his talent by crossing into his world of "collective alternates." Experienced teachers of art and performance can begin to recognize whether they have a future artist in their care.

But what conspires with biology to insure this period of relative quiescence for the normal child and budding, restless creativity for the gifted child is the glimmering in the fifth and sixth years that however well the family's lessons of survival are learned, the maturing appetites of the child cannot in the end find definitive gratification with those who laid down the myriad conditions he has so diligently incorporated. The oedipal crisis is like a lens that focuses the past on the future, because the present is suddenly unsuitable for the longings and ambitions the child is finally capable of entertaining. It all culminates in a bit of a swindle. The parent has supplied the child the means but is unavailable for the ends. Schooling, which begins significantly during this last period of childhood, is the first formal step in the exodus from the family into the

---

12. The psychosexual schedule I am alluding to here, which is cross-cultural, has appalled the general public and nonanalytic intellectuals alike since Freud first proposed it over sixty years ago in his notorious "Three Essays on the Theory of Sexuality" (1905). For a recent discussion of extra-analytic confirmations of Freud's theory, see Yazmajian 1967.

larger social world and in the long quest of other persons and opportunities for the fulfillment of desires aroused in the family. The normal child accepts his fate, more or less (the neurotic child less). The gifted child tends to protest vigorously.

Two possibilities about this protest are of interest in respect to the performer. One has to do with the capacity to experience guilt; the other with a residual fantasy technically named "the family romance."

First, guilt: It is during this last phase of childhood that quantities of anxiety are transformed into guilt. (There is some evidence that anxiety is a transformation of early olfactory sensations.) Like anxiety, guilt is also a signal of transgression; but the transgression in guilt is against a highly formed conscience, a well-established, uncontested, internalized agency perpetuating the family style. Though anxiety and guilt are often indistinguishable clinically, anxiety continues to have an external referent—the subjective feeling is of some violation of security "out there"; with guilt one feels on bad terms with one's self. Guilt is consistent with a resolution of the oedipal crisis, because an advanced conscience is based on final identification with the family, removing temptation to continue to do battle with the inexorable taboos against oedipal supplies (e.g., getting from the mother what the father does) and frees the child to direct his efforts toward the world. (If the family itself has participated in the world, the transition is facilitated.)

But too much guilt correlates with the sense that a person is finally what he is, lamentably. Protest is minimal, except insofar as too much guilt indicates a final coercion through meticulous compliance. The scant comfort is in at least knowing what you are, however limiting what you are may be. Also, anxiety is diminished—the family is firmly inside.

Too little guilt—the artist's plight—correlates with the sense that bold alternatives of selfhood are still possible, if only one had the nerve in the face of anxiety. Life is a round of hopes and trepidations, and what often substitutes for guilt as an effectual symbol are gambles taken and lost. At his worst, the guiltless person has a tendency to play to lose, at his best a flair for adventure. The performer belongs to this category of relative guiltlessness, especially the actor. I have rarely seen an established painter or creative writer, artists who also navigate through more anxiety than guilt, as reckless with their talent as so many actors are. In no other art is the term "making a comeback" so current as in the performing arts.

In this matter of guilt, it is the audience that is potentially the guiltier party to a performance than the performer. The audience is a collection of "ordinary citizens," spiritually dullards, separated from the stage as much by spiritual restraint as by architecture, incapable of performance. On the other hand, the actor, as Fenichel (1954) puts it, "is privileged, but he remains somewhat beyond the pale of 'honest' society. He sins publicly and thereby exculpates the others. Like the whore, he is held in contempt, but secretly envied." ["On Acting," p. 358] Fenichel adds the reminder that for long periods actors roamed in acting companies like gypsies.

There is a suggestion of exile. But it should be carefully noted that it is not really clear who it is who *feels* ostracized, the audience or the performer. I submit that it is both. The performer feels ostracized by virtue of his psychological criminality, his original refusal to form a conscience, to relinquish his childhood love objects, and join the world as a "citizen" among "citizens." But to the audience, the performer is one who has never lost the original paradise from which the audience feels exiled. (In no other walk of public life but the arts can a person maintain an esteemed position whose sexual exploits are fully known to the community and known to be perverse in the bargain, as they often are. The public not only allows the artist such liberty, it expects it.) The relationship between performer and audience is a confusion of shifting forces, especially during the period of convening before the performance. There is enmity and wariness, but the latent feelings of one are the manifest feelings of the other. It is like a preparation for a consorting of enemies.

Earlier I called attention to several categories of backstage behavior among performers combating stage fright. We can now appreciate the value of those mannerisms that symbolically denigrate the audience, the blasé lounging about of anxious performers, their sometimes napping. Also, the attempts to identify with the audience by dwelling upon the audience's prestigious characteristics, thereby elevating one's own stature--these attempts originate in the identificatory opportunities taken in preoedipal crises but rejected where they are now felt to have really counted: in those several years of late childhood. But the performer is too far into the game of life for this identificatory effort to be anything more than an ineffectual imitative charade. Though anxiety looms larger in stage fright, regret is also very much a part of it. The performer has the sense that it is too late to turn back and envies the road taken by the audience long ago to its present role of spectator, a more comfortable, if less promising, role. (With the performance under way, all this changes.)

If stage fright signals the jeopardy of one set of internalized objects, performance represents the possibility of recovering yet another set, and this possibility accounts for the counterphobic behavior of the performer. The idea of *recovering* something implies, of course, an idea of original loss. Indeed, all behavior that results in emotional triumph has succeeded in rediscovering a lost object in the guise of the object's current representability. "Money alone," Freud once said, "does not guarantee happiness, because money was not an infantile wish." Relying on his own theory, Freud might have added that since money is so versatile in what it can represent, it is rare that it doesn't bring happiness to some extent.

Lost objects are retained in fantasies that employ what can currently be represented. The loss of a benevolent mother in the first year of life, who by anxious, forbidding conduct the following year banishes the tolerant, giving object she once was–this loss will not be remembered through images of gentle lifting, sweet odors, nipples, carefree vomiting, and urination. It will be remembered through age-specific ideas. One universal fantasy evolved in late childhood attempts to retain the possibility of restoring the benevolence of an earlier period of childhood: "the family romance." I have never studied an adult who did not recover whole pieces of this fantasy. Nor have I ever seen a child who was not moved by this fantasy in its many variations in familiar fairy tales. Greenacre finds this fantasy unusually lively and compelling among artists and impostors, to the point of their actually taking steps to redeem the fantasy in action. I find this fantasy also notable among the shy and embarrassed, who are, however, inhibited against acting it out.

The family romance is any elaboration of the nuclear idea of being a foundling reared by foster-parent substitutes for the absent biological parents. The elaboration usually has it that the absent parents are of a higher cultural station than the foster parents, and therefore the fantasizer is living an existence in a fallen state. His destiny is to rejoin his real parents and to recover his original privileges. In the meantime he is an unacknowledged aristocrat in an ordinary world. As the fantasy proceeds, there is usually a theme of pardoning the foster parents for ill-treatments during their lapses in realizing that the child on their hands was really of noble birth, and of rewarding them for the survival they insured. In the words of Greenacre (1958c), "The germ of the family romance is ubiquitous in the hankering of growing children for a return to the real or fancied conditions at or before the dawn of conscious memory when adults were Olympians and the child shared their special privileges and unconditional love without special efforts being demanded. Family romance fantasies of a well-organized nature seem to emerge most clearly in the early latency period" (p. 10).

Cinderella is an example. The comic-strip character Superman, whose foster parents were markedly ordinary folk, is another variation. *The Prince and the Pauper* incorporates the frequent detail of a sibling in the family. The Oedipus myth is one of many myths involving a hero who returns to reclaim his realm. The biblical Moses is based on a reversal, a "secondary revision," as it is called psychoanalytically. Even *The Importance of Being Earnest* draws on the family romance, Mr. Worthing having been a foundling abandoned in a handbag in Victoria Station, who is in the end rejoined with his true mother.[13]

It is not hard to imagine how aggressive a fantasy the family romance is in the everyday life of the child. More than protesting the exile from childhood, it denigrates the actual parents (principally the father). It is constructed out of the shameful

---

13. In her paper "The Family Romance of the Artist," Greenacre describes the fantasy in detail in the lives of five men of genius: St. Francis of Assisi, Thomas Chatterton, Nikolai Gogol, Henry M. Stanley, and Rainer Maria Rilke.

wish that one had different, better parents. We sooner retain in conscious memory all sorts of play from childhood with violent and sadistic themes than we do the family-romance fantasies, which are routinely repressed.

In the adult, repressed family-romance ideation returns as feelings and notions of being an exception, an outsider with respect to all groups in the environment. A common exponent of this is shyness and an inability to engage in "small talk"–a person whose destiny is to extemporize aristocratic utterances, whose speech ought to be exclusively brilliant verse can hardly settle for conversational exchanges of ordinary pleasantries. Often there is a hunger for romantic love that is forever unrequited and a sense of doom to forced mediocrity and a pallid existence, as if a noble soul is being condemned to a life among ordinary mortals and affairs.[14]

With this, we have come full circle. Near the outset we saw that shyness–an inhibition protecting poise–arises in connection with a potentially rejecting audience. We can now appreciate that the expectation of rejection in shyness is largely a projection of the shy person, whose high standards for himself are based upon his low estimation of those ordinary souls he is condemned to deal with. Humiliating exposure is the anticipated retaliation for such contempt. Shyness preserves these issues in the momentousness of displeasure and wards off the retaliation by inhibition (the shyness itself), which allows no inkling of the aristocratic pretense. The pretense is routinely found in the daydreams of stupendous glory that the clinically shy indulge in in solitude. These daydreams are variations of the family romance. So again we encounter the controversy between the ordinary and the noble, this time in the neurotic symptom having analogies to stage fright.

---

14. I recall a patient, a young lady, who spent years in compulsive leisure, postponing an apprenticeship prerequisite to the profession she had studied for. In late spring one year she finally contracted a nine-to-five position for the fall. The intervening summer she very nearly spent in Europe with an aging lecher, a European, whose advances she was surprised she was about to yield to. Her would-be lover proved to be qualified by virtue of his claim to a title and a castle. Though barely 25, the patient regarded the summer as a "last fling" before her descent into the quotidian.

Terrified at the prospect of being accused of fraud for his shameful pretense, the shy person enjoys neither the ordinary nor the noble world. Withdrawn from both, he has only his fantasies. In the impostor, on the other hand, the family romance is acted out through the assumption of a false (imitative) identity. All impostures, according to Greenacre, are variations of the family romance. The acting out insures sanity; for the ordinary world of the impostor is impaired beyond any possibility of surviving in it. Greenacre has observed a complete disparity between the stupidity and ineptness of the impostor in the ordinary world and his adroit handling of details and simulation of emotional nuances in his imposturous one.

But is the impostor, like the performer, anxious? That he is not is what makes his imposture something other than a performance, however akin to a performance it may be. An imposture is a symptom, not an instance of art, despite resemblances not the least of which is the necessity of an audience. "For the typical impostor," writes Greenacre (1958b), "an audience is absolutely essential. It is from the confirming reaction of his audience that the impostor gets a 'realistic' sense of self, a value greater than anything he can otherwise achieve" (p. 367). The significance of phallic exhibitionism in imposturous behavior, the gratification in exercising competence and physical integrity, is also like performance. "The impostor seems to be repeatedly seeking confirmation of his assumed identity to overcome his sense of helplessness or incompleteness. It is my impression that this is the secret of his appeal to others, and that often especially conscientious people are 'taken in' and other impostors as well attracted because of the longing to return to that happy state of omnipotence which adults have had to relinquish" (p. 370).

But the impostor does not have stage fright. For one thing, his audience does not convene consciously as an audience. As in shyness, the "audience" is in the dark about its most potent characteristic–that it is an audience with conscious options about complicity. For another, the impostor is free to regulate his "public appearances," when he will and will not continue his "performance" and for how long; he is not dominated by an impending, inevitable moment. Foremost, however, he is *both* spectator and performer. A part of him is a super-audience. Though he requires complicity, he gives nothing for it in return—nothing. Audiences at a bad performance show displeasure of varying sorts, sometimes anger, rarely outrage approaching the homicidal. But a discovered imposture frequently produces raging panic in the victims. There is a difference between duplicity and an aesthetic illusion.

Unlike the neurotic and the impostor, the performer redeems his family romance out in the open. He is an honest man. His suffering, which is stage fright, testifies to that and to the courage of his convictions about the possibilities of redeeming dreams and wishes extrapolated from common human experience. His triumph is ours, and if he must repeat it time and again, so must the audience; for there is no performance without an audience and no audience without a performance. This differs from everyday life, where performance is inhibited or unacknowledged and audiences imputed or coerced.

Several points remain to be made. I mentioned at the outset that stage fright is ultimately a creative problem the performer must solve along with other problems of performance. That is, as a phenomenon of theater it contributes to the aesthetic complex of theater and shapes the artistic career of a performer. (But solution in this case does not mean dissolution.) By now it must be amply clear that I regard any given moment as far more pregnant than meets the eye. I have at some length suggested how certain historical trials in our lives are compressed and retained in an affect like stage fright. To suggest how an audience perceives and appreciates the performer's pre-performance apprehensions is the subject of another discussion. But an audience does not sense these things through trembling hands and unsteady posture, which are very rarely evident in a trained performer. It is quite the reverse. The audience experiences the performer's stage fright through the perceptual reciprocity between performer and audience, which is what banishes stage fright as the performance gets under way. That reciprocity, which quickly replaces stage fright, acquires its felt significance for the audience from the desperation with which it is solicited. We have seen how collaborative reciprocity is antidotal to anxiety. Part of a good performance is the result of a performer's succeeding in obtaining this antidote from the audience, who gives it "knowing" somewhere what succor it affords. And, incidently, the availability of such antidotal reciprocity describes an audience–I think there are such things as good audiences and bad ones.

A final point has to do with the relationship of stage fright to a performer's career. The intensity of stage fright tends to diminish when a performer is resting on his laurels or consolidating his artistic development at one or another phase in his career. Each creative advance, however, is ushered in by intensified anxiety, until the pretense felt in the advance is confirmed as a creditable activity by the audience. This is only to say that anxiety is part of the phenomenology of taking risks.

But stage fright can also revolutionize careers. The comedian is an example. He makes light of the pretenses he harbors along with all other performers. If the recovery of childhood nobility is the issue in performance and exposure the risk, the comedian makes a career of causing us to doubt his commitment to his pretensions. Victor Borge is said to have started as a serious concert pianist, or with ambitions to be one, but stage fright turned him into a piano-playing comedian. There is more than a grain of truth to the saying that all comedians want to play Shakespeare.

Stage fright can drive would-be performers out of performing altogether. My experience leads me to suspect that a person who begins to perform at some point in life miraculously free of stage fright will sooner or later leave the stage. Complete freedom from stage fright occurs in those with a modicum of talent who repress completely the issues delineated in this essay and whose fantasies are involved elsewhere. Denigrations of the audiences go beyond fleeting backstage fantasies. Usually the audiences such people play to are of one particular sort having no status with the performer. When a professional step forward is attempted, the anxiety appropriate to what is happening drives them away, invariably with far-fetched rationalizations.

As for those who persist, I hope I have established that stage fright is no disease of the psyche, unless all powerful apprehensions about significant and worthwhile enterprises are likewise pathologic. Despite its resemblance to human neurosis, stage fright goes on with other means to other ends, and this makes all the difference.

REFERENCES

Eissler, K. R. (1968). The relation of explaining and understanding in psycho-analysis: demonstrated by one aspect of Freud's approach to literature. *Psychoanalytic Study of the Child* 23:141-177.

Erikson, E. H. (1954). The dream specimen of psychoanalysis. *Journal of the American Psychoanalytic Association*, no. 2.

Fenichel, O. (1954a). The counter-phobic attitude. In *The Collected Papers of Otto Fenichel*, 2nd series, pp. 163-173. New York: Norton.

_____ (1954b). On acting. In *The Collected Papers of Otto Fenichel*, 2nd series, pp. 349-361. New York: Norton.

Freud, S. (1905). Three essays on the theory of sexuality. *Standard Edition* 7.

Funke, L., and Booth, J. E., eds. (1961). *Actors Talk about Acting*, vol. 2, pp. 189-190. New York: Avon.

Greenacre, P. (1958a). The relation of the impostor to the artist. *Psychoanalytic Study of the Child* 13:521-540.

_____ (1958b). The impostor. *Psychoanalytic Quarterly* 27:359-382.

_____ (1958c). The family romance and the artist. *Psychoanalytic Study of the Child* 13:2-36.

Hoffer, W. (1949). Mouth, hand. and ego integration. *Psychoanalytic Study of the Child* 3/4:49-55.

Kris, E. (1952). *Psychoanalytic Explorations in Art*. New York: International Universities Press.

Rangell, L. (1954). The psychology of poise, with special elaboration on the psychic significance of the snout or perioral region. *International Journal of Psycho-Analysis* 35:313-332.

_____ (1963). *Counterpoint, Libidinal Object and Subject*, ed. H. S. Gaskill. New York: International Universities Press.

Schafer, R. (1968). *Aspects of Internalization*. New York: International Universities Press.

Trilling, L. (1952). Art and neurosis. In *The Liberal Imagination*. New York: Viking.

Weissman, P. (1967). Theoretical considerations of ego regression and ego functions in creativity. *Psychoanalytic Quarterly*, no. 1.

_____ (1969). Creative fantasies and beyond the reality principle. *Psychoanalytic Quarterly*, no. 1:110-123.

Wittels, F. (1939). Unconscious phantoms in neurotics. *Psychoanalytic Quarterly* 8:141-163.

Yazmajian, R. V. (1967). Biological aspects of infantile sexuality and the latency period. *Psychoanalytic Quarterly* 36:203-229.

20

Theatre Architecture and the Primal Cavity[1]

Among the cultural odds and ends that supply the architectural imagination are prevailing conceptions of the human body – its functions, perfectibility, and possibilities for pleasure and pain. Though architects of various periods have employed ideal proportions of the human body in conscious decisions about the structural proportions of monuments and buildings, this is not the only way, nor the most interesting way, in which the human body informs architecture. What is also meant by the body's relationship to architecture is the memory of body states that architecture evokes in the observer. These body states are recalled in the form of their psychological derivatives: moods, affects, and emotions. These derivatives initiate and qualify our aesthetic judgments about architecture.

1. The psychoanalytic concepts that will be employed further on in this chapter have been developed by René A. Spitz and summarized in his book *The First Year of Life: A Psychoanalytic Study of Normal and Deviant Development of Object Relations* (1966). A number of papers by Spitz that I have found especially useful are: "Diacritic and Coenesthetic Organizations" (1945), "The Primal Cavity: A Contribution to the Genesis of Perception and Its Role for Psychoanalytic Theory" (1955), *No and Yes: On the Genesis of Human Communication* (1957), "Life and the Dialogue" (1963), and "The Derailment of Dialogue: Stimulus Overload, Action Cycles, and the Completion Gradient" (1964).

Also, I should like to acknowledge my gratitude to Mr. William Herman of The City College and to Professor Richard Schechner. Mr. Herman placed at my disposal his personal collection of technical materials and photographs of theatres. Professor Schechner has always been generous with the details of the rationale for his experimental activities in theatre, lately having to do with his revisions of traditional theatre spaces for play production.

Architecture is able to evoke moods, affects, and emotions because perceived forms vitalize an observer's kinesthetic sense, a sense exemplified by a bowler's listing empathetically to one side or another as he follows a bowling ball visually down an alley toward the pins at the far end. Like the bowling ball, but with far more subtlety and variety, architectural forms are capable of arousing and organizing our neuromuscular inclinations and playing upon them with rhythms of tension and release. The appeal to our kinesthetic system accords with idealizations of body attitudes, which are experienced as psychological epiphenomena. The transition, for example, from the square and circular forms of Renaissance design to the rectangular and oval of the baroque produced a changing kinesthesis, as a cultural mood of implacability gave way to a mood of greater leniency.

The interaction between architecture and mnemonic kinesthesis is by no means a novel idea. It can be found in Geoffrey Scott's well-known study *The Architecture of Humanism* (1914). "A spire, when well designed, appears—as common language testifies—to soar," Scott writes. "We identify ourselves not with its downward pressure, but its apparent upward impulse. So, too, by the same excellent—because unconscious—testimony of speech, arches 'spring,' vistas 'stretch,' domes 'swell,' Greek temples are 'calm,' and baroque facades 'restless.' The whole of architecture is in fact invested by us with human movement and human moods" (p. 213). Scott acknowledges his debt for this approach to Theodor Lipps, whose work along these lines at the turn of the century influenced many discussions. More recently—Scott's book on architecture came out in 1914—Lipps has been integrated into Rudolf Arnheim's brilliant analysis *Art and Visual Perception*. However, the idea of art and body states seems to have always been current. Vasari talked of it. So did Michelangelo. And it crops up in the writings of Bernard Berenson.

But were the idea really to come to roost, I think it would do so within contemporary psychoanalysis, where for the past 20 or so years there has been considerable interest in locating the origin of perception in early body states and functions. René A. Spitz is a luminary of this phase of psychoanalytic development. At any rate, I should like to place theatre architecture—the stage-auditorium unit—in the context of these issues, in hopes of glimpsing yet another detail of the complex experience of theatre. If "arches 'spring,' vistas 'stretch,' domes 'swell,' " what does a theatre do?

There is a sense in which it could be said that theatre architecture has persisted virtually unchanged since antiquity. (This is to leave aside for the moment certain radical alterations of theatre space and structure, like John Cage's Black Mountain Theatre of 1952.) New York City's ANTA Playhouse and Vivian Beaumont Theatre, for example, are much more similar to the theatres at Epidaurus and Priene than they are different. While it is true that the intervening centuries produced notable developments in the structure, position, and function of the proscenium and in the compartmentalization of the auditorium into boxes and balconies, no development has gone so far as to destroy the integrity of the fundamental unit of two segregated spaces, one for action (the orchestra/stage/*skene*), the other for the formation of an inactive group (the auditorium).

Indeed, whenever a development has threatened the integrity of this fundamental unit, that development has tended to recede. The compartmentalization of the auditorium, which reached prominence in eighteenth-century England and fostered interactions among different classes of the audience, has subsequently declined in theatre design. On the other hand, when the house lights were snuffed out in the English playhouses of the 1830s, they were not to be turned on again; for a darkened auditorium and brightened stage further clarified an important kinesthetic function of the stage-auditorium unit. With the advent of the electric light, the stage curtain is now merely vestigial and is disappearing—light is an actual architectural material, curtains are not. It is almost as if theatre architecture has a life of its own that not only outlasts the immediate social wear and tear it submits to, but goes on to acquire technical sustenance for its own perpetuation. I have the idea that the kinesthesis evoked by theatre architecture, a least to this moment in history, has been too gratifying, fascinating, fundamental, and continuously valid to be outdone and disposed of in the wake of social-psychological developments.

Consider a prospective member of a theatre audience entering a theatre. He is about to occupy one of the two major spaces inside the theatre, and he is joining others who will share this space with him. The repetition of geometric forms in the auditorium—the rows and files of the seats, for example, with the likeness of one seating space to the next—induces a crowd to become a group. As you enter a theatre, your perceptions of those people still finding their way to seats discriminate individuals, mostly unknown individuals, but individuals nevertheless. "Who is that?" is the perceptual inquiry. As the audience finds its seats, the perceptual inquiry shifts to what kind of a *group* you are getting involved with.

With this fading of discriminatory perception, the unlighted, unoccupied stage begins to function quite powerfully. Though a circumscribed space, a stage does not consist of a repetitious geometry, as the auditorium does. The stage space, however conventional, is suited for activity in a way that the auditorium is not. A stage furthers a regression in those occupying the auditorium, because it reminds them that they are not present to sustain an activity, as the group about to appear on the stage assuredly is. The audience is devoid of a work mentality.

Consider an actor entering the theatre. The group he joins inside the theatre is a work group and requires, for continued membership in good standing, a performance of highly specified skills. In contrast to the audience, the actor must rise to the occasion of a populated auditorium. Prior to going on stage, he experiences the audience as a unified, demanding force, entirely free of obligations to think or act—a kind of thoughtless hunger emanates from the auditorium. This contrast between actor and audience is a source of very notable enmity in the actor toward the audience. Anxiety in the actor, manifested as tension and "stage fright," is a signal of the presence in the situation of aggression mixed with solicitous impulses. The actor despises his own eagerness, which is a very confusing state of mind. (His internal order is restored only after he begins performing onstage, for he thereby experiences command over the mindless force created by the auditorium.) These processes reach an apogee during the long moment when the stage is just about to be occupied, a moment enhanced in modern theatres by a marked alteration in the lighting of the entire theatre.

Thus, as the theatre fills up and the performers prepare to go on, a voracity in the auditorium is about to be shaped and regulated from the stage by an active exercise of some kind of prescribed skill. At this point, we can begin to answer the question of what a theatre does kinesthetically by observing that its geometries and functions favor a juxtaposition of a *visceral* and *executive* experience.

Though we might suppose this to be more or less true of any space that relates a spectator and an object, only a theatre makes an extensive use of such a juxtaposition. The spectator space in museums and galleries, for example, is comparatively weak in regressive, visceral inducements. Indeed, mobility by the spectator is encouraged. One reason for this is that painting and sculpture are static entities in the sense that their essence does not unfold in time. Museums and galleries mount objects, not performances. Occasionally, as on planned tours, a group of spectators is formed, in which case the art objects become props for the performance of a guide. However, there is no architectural tradition for such performances, which use elements of theatre for nontheatrical ends.[2]

A movie house is closely derived from a theatre. It consists of an auditorium, and its screen may be likened to a stage—except that a screen is not exactly a stage. The flatness of a screen promises only an illusion of action and of agents responsible for the immediate occasion on which the movie is viewed. However, the real occasion of the movie is over long before the audience assembles. Actually, the visceral position induced in the audience by the geometry and lighting of the movie auditorium finds its executive counterpart in the projectionist, an absented agent, whose shaping and regulatory skills are not

---

2. Erving Goffman has produced a series of studies on the theatricality of everyday life. Theatre occurs just about everywhere, from around bridge tables to hospital operating tables. But where all the world's a stage, Goffman uses the term "setting" for the space in which the action occurs. Architecturally, these settings are not theatres. Even an operating room that contains a special spectator space does not function as a theatre, because there is no stage. The space in which the operating team performs is a technologic area that does not induce regression in the spectators. An audience of medical students witnessing an operation possesses a didactic tension not discernible in a theatre audience.

relevant anyway, inasmuch as they are concerned entirely with a machine and not with the audience's appetitive vicissitudes. Compared to a theatre, an empty movie house is merely a machine that has been clicked off, which is why the emotions that arise with the impending use of the premises are relatively bland. A movie house is at most a phantom theatre. It lacks a stage with a tangibility equivalent to the auditorium.

But let us return to the theatre and our quest for its architectural kinesthesis. I have emphasized the importance of two spaces segregating two groups with different, yet reciprocal, agendas. If we assign the terms *anticipatory* and *appetitive* to the experience a theatre induces in the audience and the term *consummatory* to the reciprocating executive task of the acting company, we are talking about what psychoanalysis, following Spitz, calls an *action cycle*. Whether or not, or to what degree, the consummatory end of the action cycle will bring the cycle to a successful completion depends upon the actual performance and its relationship to the audience on a given occasion, an obviously important matter but not bearing on this discussion. What is relevant is that a theatre is a place where an action cycle is not only feasible but inescapable. The *essential* elements of a theatre—those that seem to want to persist—have no other purpose.

Now, an anticipation-appetite-consummation series can be completed autonomously. Indeed, certain action cycles must be completed autonomously—for example, nobody can urinate for us. However, action cycles are also completed in connection with partners, and such reciprocities have been called by Spitz *primal dialogues* (to distinguish them from verbal dialogues). A theatre, then, structures an opportunity for a primal dialogue between the audience and the actors. Psychoanalytic findings about the primal dialogue may have interesting implications for theatre design, and I shall suggest several. However, I want now to stress the powerful forces at work in a primal dialogue: there is a myth that the passivity (what I have called a *visceral* state) that a theatre induces in an audience is equivalent to emotional inertia and nonparticipation; this myth, which is based on an assumption that physical activity and vigorous sensual stimulation guarantee involvement, can (and, in fact, does) misguide experimentation in theatre design and in the arts in general.

I recall a theatre production in a small cabaret in Greenwich Village, during which the actors circulated among the audience and spoke lines directly to individual members of the audience, staring into their eyes and stroking their faces. The aesthetic motivation here was painfully apparent: this was the way to "reach" the audience, to involve the audience, as if more physicality is equivalent to more involvement. Another production I recall sent actual odors out into the audience to enhance the experience of the *mise-en-scène*. However, the arousal and engaging of the motor apparatus of the audience—the activation of *behavior* in the audience—is not *ipso facto* more desirable than the evocation of perception, which is always shut off when external stimuli provoke motor apparatus to respond, that is, to behave. The notion that a passive motor apparatus leads to a lack of experience is an enormous myth. The provocation of behavior suppresses the possibility of perception, and, as I shall show later, it is perception, not behavior, that shapes experience.

I mentioned earlier this business of the actor's aggression toward the audience, and I want to return to it because its source can be traced to the primal-dialogue situation in the theatre; moreover, this aggression that so troubles the actor in states like stage fright resides, I think, in the audience, but is taken on by the actor as part of his general responsibility for the occasion.

In the rather casual yet outstanding paper "Life and the Dialogue," Spitz (1963) undertakes a discussion of how we distinguish between the living and the inanimate, suggesting that the discriminatory sense we use in this regard permeates more of our existence than we are aware. This sense achieves such cunning that we can distinguish, unfailingly, a child from a very lifelike doll in a photograph. There was such a photograph used for an advertisement for a doll, in which a little girl was kissing a doll that in all respects resembled the little girl. The caption read, "Which one is the toy dolly?" "The photograph fools nobody," Spitz writes, "Even though absence of color, lack of motion, and two-dimensionality handicap photography in conveying meaning, we 'know' the child from the doll immediately." The "we" means we adults. In neonates this highly specialized sense of discrimination is not present. Longitudinal studies of child development indicate that this sense begins to appear (within normally expected variations) around the sixth month of life. Before the sixth month, an infant will not discriminate between a human face and an inanimate artifact, such as a balloon with painted facial features. But it is not until the eighth month that this discriminatory sense is established with some reliability. The maturation of this sense coincides with a prolonged phase of infancy called 8-month anxiety, in which the infant, also for the first time, discriminates reliably between the mother and strangers. Anxiety is an important concomitant of this stage of development.

The 8-month-old infant's fear of strangers is a common observation of all those who rear children with reasonable watchfulness. Though equally reliable as a response, fear of the inanimate is not as commonly noticed. Spitz has filmed "doll anxiety." In a typical film "the child, 11 months and 26 days old, looks searchingly at a baby-sized doll, cocks her head as if to look at it from a different angle, then looks at the doll straight on and considers it. She is unable to come to a decision. After a few seconds she approaches the doll, pokes her head at it, touches it with her face and then retreats, watching the motionless doll all the time. After a few moments of contemplation the child begins to show unpleasure, becomes restless and cries." Other filmed incidents eventuate in the child's retreating, in panic, screaming, kicking, and beating the doll.

I might add—and this has always astonished me—that the inanimate produces anxiety in other species as well. A sudden and tremendous furor goes up in a cage of monkeys when laboratory personnel happen to carry a dead monkey past the cage. The experimental psychologist D. O. Hobb discovered that a plaster model of a monkey's head brings forth similar reactions. (He called this a "ghost reaction.") Konrad Lorenz, the celebrated ethologist, tells how he was attacked by a flock of rooks who perceived his black swimming trunks, dangling from his hand after a swim, as a dead rook. (Spitz suggests that "seemingly unmotivated attacks on unsuspecting persons by

birds, reported from time to time, may have a similar explanation.")

Among the several credible explanations advanced for all
these phenomena is the absence in the inanimate of a capacity
for partnership in a primal dialogue. In the mother–infant
relationship, physical handling of the infant, especially in connection with feeding, is the principal activity of the dialogue.
Good mothering consists of the mother's skillful partnership in
a dialogue, her ability to complete an action cycle by adminis-
tering the consummatory phase to the infant's anticipatory and
appetitive arousals. Food, in and of itself, is not sufficient for
infant survival (nor for survival among other species of mam-
mals). Anaclitic depression ("hospitalism") is a pediatric condition, the etiology of which is the absence of a dialogue. It was
studied during World War II on the wards where orphaned
infants were provided with the elements for survival but by
hospital personnel unable to offer these elements through the
medium of a dialogue. Beyond a certain point, anaclitic depression is irreversible and terminates in death. The cause of death,
to put it simply, is the aggression in the infant that is unregulated by a dialogue. Efforts at contact with an infant wasting
away in a terminal anaclitic depression succeed ultimately in
eliciting only one response: a horrifying scream. There is no way
left to begin to shape and regulate the aggression manifested in
that scream, for the infant has lost its capacity to engage in a
dialogue. Short of the scream, the anaclitically depressed infant
is, to all appearances, passive—an inert nonparticipant. But the
aggression at work within such intense passivity is mortal.

Infantile anaclitic depression is the model for all subsequent
depressions and depressive states. Depressions in adults result
from the loss not only of symbolic oral supplies but of their
symbolic provider. The suicides that sometimes terminate psychotic depressions are indications of the extraordinary unregulated aggression involved in seemingly inert states. In
mourning, a so-called normal reaction modeled after the anaclitic depression, the deceased had been a partner in some sort
of primal dialogue with the mourner. The aggression that was
bound by the dialogue comes loose and appears as mourning.
Bereavement at the death of a beloved person is not simply an

emotional collapse into inertia. On the contrary, it is a very powerfully energized state.

There are myriad variations on these dynamics. The shock at the sight of a corpse, for example, or even a dead member of another species, is not unlike "doll anxiety." During the last century, the wax museum was a favorite place to visit; the fascination resided to a large degree in the challenge of the highly naturalistic wax figures to our discriminatory sense of the animate and inanimate and in the "spooky" effect—the flirtatious aggression—that occurs when this sense falls victim to dissemblance.

Aggressive insurgence by audiences is a lively chapter in the history of theatre. Audiences have been reported to have pommelled actors with all manner of debris, to have stamped their feet and hurled obscenities, rioted, even rushed onstage and stripped the costumes from the actors' backs. No other social occasion of comparably expected decorum ends up in such manifest aggression. When a run of bad food is served in a restaurant, customers have not been known to assail the waiters and the chef, despite the fact that food seems to be a more concrete consummatory item than art. Nor is this simply a matter of restaurant diners not feeling identified with a group. Where diners do form a group, as in institutional mess halls, bad fare evokes measly expressions of aggression, like grumbling and complaining, which is not the straightforward aggression of a theatre audience. But stage a meal in a theatre; have the diners enter an auditorium, the chef cook onstage with the house personnel standing by to serve the food to the audience. Imagine the reaction to a bad culinary performance. It would not be hunger that is thwarted, but a primal dialogue—the *medium* through which the food is served.

In speaking of such matters as the phases of an action cycle, aggression, the dialogue and the complex sense perception through which the phenomena of these concepts come to life, I have been speaking about a particular kind of psychology. And I have been suggesting that this psychology is useful in inquiring about the experience of being in the midst of a theatre. Now all the phenomena of psychology originate in the organism's physical processes, which include, very importantly, maturational processes—the maturational schedule of a species influences the psychology of a species every bit as much as its particular physiological structures. (The psychosexuality of human beings is determined much more by the maturational schedule of the human being than by the ultimate functional structure of the genital apparatus.) Psychology is the study of the epiphenomena of an organism's present and past (maturational) biology. Though it is not always pertinent—or possible—to relate psychology to its biologic matrix, the relationship is pertinent for our present discussion, because we are trying to reach the kinesthetic level that a theatre appeals to and that gives rise to the epiphenomena I have been describing. The feelings, motivations, and sense perceptions I have been describing and interrelating are, after all, the reminiscences of certain body states.

But which body states? The kinesthesis of a theatre is not as simple as that of, say, an architectural spire or tower, which celebrates the momentous maturational achievement in man's upright posture by calling forth a kinesthetic response of the muscles and balancing mechanism involved in the upright posture. Here the epiphenomena include feelings of striving, reaching, soaring, achieving. (The notorious "phallic" property imputed to such structures by psychoanalysis derives not so much from the paradigm of an erect penis as from the erect posture of the child, a maturational event that ushers in the so-called phallic stage of childhood, in which muscular striving and locomotion are libidinized.)

With a theatre, the kinesthesis will involve the physiology of that sense perception of the living that is so central to the primal dialogue and its sequels. The maturation of this particular sense perception would seem to depend exclusively on the maturation of the visual apparatus. However, the maturation of the visual apparatus, while an essential factor in any type of visual perception, is never the exclusive factor. Visual perception of any but the grossest kind (like the perception of an indistinct mass in motion) is always matured in concert with other perceptions. If you fit an experimental subject with lenses that turn the visual world upside-down, the subject will begin to rely on his hands to assist his vision in making his way through the environment. He will grope as well as look. But over several days, this groping will have educated his visual perception, and the subject will begin to get about again solely on the basis of visual perception. The upside-down world will have lost its awkwardness. Removing the lenses will necessitate another period of falling back upon the assistance of manual-tactile perception.

For the dialogue, the perceptions that assist vision originate in the organs used for sucking and swallowing: the tongue, lips, cheeks, and throat. To this group of co-ordinating muscles, Spitz has assigned a special term: the primal cavity.

The characteristics of the primal cavity are very interesting. For one thing, the primal cavity has an immediate postnatal responsive reliability that is very high. I have never failed to experience astonishment at the sight of the coordination of these muscles in the otherwise completely uncoordinated newborn creature. The responsiveness of the primal cavity insures survival, and it is through this group of organs that the primal dialogue first takes place. Again, if a dialogue does not get established, the reliability of the primal cavity diminishes; sucking and swallowing lose their vigor and coordination, and nutritional failure begins to occur. Also, the primal cavity has a tactile sensitivity. It can register touch, taste, temperature, smell, pain, and the deep sensibility of deglutition. It is an organ of perception, originally far exceeding visual perception in variety and organization. I might add that the primal cavity is later employed for the first social communication, which carries the dialogue to a higher level: the smiling response.

But more interesting for our purposes is the fact that the primal cavity is the active end of the viscera. Being continuous with the viscera, yet directly in contact with the external world, the primal cavity is the first mediator between the internal and external circumstance of the organism. *The primal cavity is both visceral and executive*. Thus the seed of the action cycle is planted there; for the primal cavity is attached to the anticipatory and appetitive end of the cycle that originates in the viscera and, in addition, is capable of executing a consummatory completion of the cycle.

Much as groping behavior informs the visual sensations of

the subject wearing upside-down lenses, the frequent and complex operations of the primal cavity will inform the sensations of the maturing visual apparatus and educate them into *perceptions*. By the eighth month of life, the activity of the primal cavity will have established a visual perception that discriminates the living from the nonliving. Though we *see* with our eyes, what we actually *perceive* depends upon the memory of numerous senses other than vision.

We should finally observe that the primal cavity remains, through unconscious memory, an ultimate referent in the maturation and later performance of the body. Maturation dichotomizes the original intimate unity of visceral and executive musculature within the primal cavity. As the executive muscles of the face, hands, arms, neck, legs, shoulders, and abdomen mature, they *oppose*, as well as foster, consummation of appeals from the visceral system. The articulation of these muscular systems have an enormous perceptual concomitant. The original simple connection of the primal cavity to the inside of the body and to the external world is elaborated into perceptions of body definition—where the body boundary leaves off and the external world begins, what is me and not-me, what is inside and outside. Yet the effectuality we gain in all this is never sufficiently compensatory. If the joy of civilization is the sense of triumph over the dichotomies of maturation, the malaise is the memory of our lost competence at drawing the world's milk into our parched throats. For every Ninth Symphony, we also produce a Book of Genesis.

It is my sense that a theatre enlivens the executive and visceral musculature in a kinesthesis of separation and interaction. The interface of stage and auditorium is not a celebration of a maturational achievement, as certain other architectural forms are. A theatre reminds us of a dynamic condition. It beguiles us into postures of hope and trepidation.

Western society has proceeded through the development of executive competence in the external world, at the expense of visceral experience. We often glamorize Eastern society, because it seems to us more concerned with visceral matters. If architecture reflects idealized body states, we should find in the history of Western theatre design an emphasis on the executive aspect of the auditorium-stage unit. I think we do. The executive space of the theatre—the stage—has acquired in the course of time an extraordinary technologic complexity, while the stark geometry of the auditorium has been gilded out of all proportion. This situation has culminated in the large Broadway-type theatres, which architecturally tend to institutionalize executive functions. Such theatres evoke a dynamic kinesthesis, but, at the same moment, overwhelm us with a reassuring complacency. Moreover, the technology of the Western stage has invited a naturalism in set design that rigidifies the dichotomy between actor and audience and suppresses the dynamic possibility of theatre architecture. Mercifully, we are beginning to see an end to this eighteenth-century architectural tradition, as newer theatres crop up.

Wrapping the auditorium around the stage, as is done in theatres-in-the-round, seems a very significant evolution in theatre design. This preserves the basic kinesthesis I have been describing. But by abolishing the proscenium—a derivative of an original sacred structure—round theatres tend to divest the kinesthesis of extra-institutional valences. A purer kinesthesis occurs. Moreover, the continuities of space—a full circle encircling a full circle—intensify certain qualities of the dialogue between actors and audience and weaken others. For example, the collaborative elements of the dialogue gain in prominence, while the oppositional elements subside somewhat. The theatre-in-the-round is thus an architecture of intimacy, and though intimacy is merely one aspect of a primal dialogue, it is certainly an important enough aspect to warrant its own architectural counterpart. These theatres are testimonies to the possibility of transforming theatre architecture through experimental activity.

Like all architecture, theatre architecture embodies an institution, and institutions are always conflicted agencies, combining advantages and dangers. Institutions accumulate wisdom and preserve it against the superficial immediacies of daily social flux. An institution wants to be a cultural, rather than social, entity. On the other hand, this conservative function sets constraints on the freedom of imagination and activity of those who participate within the confines of the institution. Though the basic architectural configuration of theatre accommodates a great range of creative activity, it also places limits on this activity, however unspecific they may be. Indeed, one of the functions of art is to find the limits of its institutional forms. The kinesthesis I have been describing and its ramifications constitute a segment of the limits of theatre, which the artist explores and specifies.

Of late there has been a notable experimental activity in theatre that can be located somewhere beyond the limits of theatre because the context of this activity is noninstitutionalized space. I am thinking of happenings, events, environments, and performances of various sorts in anonymous, nondescript spaces, like experimental studios and random localities in the community. The homogenization of theatre space in this recent activity indicates an interim resignation from theatre, at least as defined by the stage-auditorium situation. I say interim because no such resignation continues indefinitely without acquiring institutional auspices, either its own or some other. It does this or comes to grief like last year's best-sellers. More than likely, the vast theatrical establishment will put out a pseudopod, absorb from these activities what is nutritious, and discard the rest.

Whatever, I think "new" theatre does not outstrip the concepts I have been urging in this discussion. Architecture is one application for these concepts. However, the absolute definition of theatre does not depend upon architecture. Architecture happens to be a very powerful context for theatre. But the dialogue is at the heart of theatre. In nontheatre everyone assembled is a performer. The dialogue is intramural—confined within the group. In theatre, the dialogue is between groups, those who perform and those who witness. The nature of the performance and the physical arrangements for the occasion define only the variety of theatre but not theatre as a generic.

As for "new" theatre, my familiarity with it inclines me to several observations, which take us beyond architecture but return us to the issues of the primal dialogue, the action cycle, the distinction between sensation and perception.

One of the leading questions about the exercise of imagination is whether it transforms social experience or merely serves as an advertisement for the social moment. We live in a social moment when industrialization and urbanization are the dominant social processes. Electricity, especially in the form of communication systems, is omnipresent. The population explosion is a prime factor in the urbanization process. A duplication of some of these features of the social moment in colonies of laboratory animals leads to behavior remarkably similar to behavior appearing in large numbers of our human population. Overpopulated rats, for example, become sexually perverse, occasionally homosexual, even delinquent in that they carouse in packs. Some become withdrawn into a passive daze. Others engage in numerous sexual incidents but without apparent consummation. In short, the appetitive branch of the action cycle is activated, while the consummatory branch is crippled. The loss of competence with a primal dialogue leads to a very high mortality rate among litters and eventually to the dying off of the colony. The outstanding experimental variable is increased interaction.

The social processes I have mentioned are beginning to revolutionize human child rearing, literally interrupting the dialogue between mother and child and creating partners unsuitable for any kind of meaningful dialogue. As never before, dialogues tend to be illusory—two-person monologues, which increase interactional sensations and decrease interpersonal perceptions.

The reiterated aspects of the program of the "new" theatre (and not insignificantly its most advertised aspects) include the desegregation of audience-performer space, increased physical interaction not only between the audience and the performer but also between the audience and technologic props of the performance, randomness of events, and unintelligibility ("absurdity"). This program is quite close to the effects of our present social process and to the forms of a derailed dialogue.

The quest of such experimental activity for more profound and varied experiences in the audience is really gratuitous. I am put in mind of the experiments many years ago in psychoanalytic technique by Sandor Ferenczi. Ferenczi (who should have known better) reasoned that if the trouble with the adult patient was the sick child in the patient, he, Ferenczi, would simply treat the child directly. He ended up placing his adult patients on his lap, and nursing them with baby bottles. The program of the "new" theatre involves a similar issue of the dynamics of emotional directness. Deep experiences can be reached not by by-passing intervening defensive perceptions—all perceptions have a defensive function—but only by finding the means for addressing perceptions and transforming them. For perceptions are the medium of experience.

Gyorgy Kepes (1965) speaks of the infatuation with the isolated kinesthetic act, the acceptance of "the autobiographical note of an accidental moment at the expense of the rest of life" (p. 118). This is always a peril of art. Yet a succession of accidents can yield a design—an aesthetic—and in this is the vindication of the artist's infatuation with fortune. If I have been normative, perhaps even prescriptive, I acknowledge this as one of the perils of criticism, especially of psychological criticism. However, I hope I have succeeded in demonstrating also that psychoanalysis, which has offered the arts so much interpretive material in the past, is continuing to produce concepts service-able for the future. It may be that in the social moment theatre will find a new kinesthesis, a new architectural context with perceptual strivings other than those of our present theatre. I cannot imagine that current psychoanalytic approaches to the problem of perception will be without interest.

REFERENCES

Kepes, G. (1965). The visual arts and sciences. *Daedalus*, Winter.

Scott, G. (1914). *The Architecture of Humanism: A Study in the History of Taste.* Boston and New York: Houghton Mifflin.

Spitz, R. A. (1945). Diacritic and coenesthetic organizations. *Psychoanalytic Review* 32:146–162.

_____ (1955). The primal cavity: a contribution to the genesis of perception and its role for psychoanalytic theory. *Psychoanalytic Study of the Child* 10:215–240.

_____ (1957). *No and Yes: On the Genesis of Human Communication.* New York: International Universities Press.

_____ (1963). Life and the dialogue. In *Counterpoint,* ed. H. Gaskill. New York: International Universities Press.

_____ (1964). The derailmant of dialogue: stimulus overload, action cycles, and the completion gradient. *Journal of the American Psychoanalytic Association* 12:752–775.

Spitz, R. A., and Cobliner, W. G. (1966). *The First Year of Life: A Psychoanalytic Study of Normal and Deviant Development of Object Relations.* New York: International Universities Press.

21

Character and Theatre

One of the persisting functions of art, even of iconoclastic art, is the restoration of morality. Art continues to find eloquence for our suffering, heraldry for our strife, lyricism for our passion. And one of its ways of doing this is by reminding us that while we exist in society, we are also participants in culture. Beyond the immediacies of our everyday lives, we have a kinship with generations.

If it can be said that certain times are better and others worse for art, then these times seem very bad indeed. Cultural exponents of contemporary society have been especially scarce.[1] I have in mind the past twenty years. Picasso's *Guernica*, a bit of fiction, and some poetry by Randall Jarrell are among the last works of art which managed to salvage any dignity from society's military impulses. Dachau and Hiroshima thrust us into a vast limbo of amorality: then there were the megaton bursts of the '50s. These events continue to embarrass the imagination and for the time being can exist only factually, or, at most, journalistically. I can think of no other time in history when the most significant occurrences of an age were such as to still the artistic response. You cannot even complain of the futility of art in the context of genocide and nuclear politics, as I am now doing, without sounding bizarre.

---

1. Daniel Bell (1965) speaks of a "Disjunction of Culture and Social Structure": "By social structure I mean the system of social relationships between persons institutionalized in norms and rules. By culture I mean the symbolic expressions . . . of the experience of individuals in those relationships. The disjunction arises because of difficulties involved in finding appropriate symbolic expression for efforts to grasp the meaning of experiences in contemporary society . . ." (p. 208).

Yet in the end, however senseless, these are discrete catastrophes. Life, as we say, goes on.

But the normalcy of the past twenty years has also been difficult for art, though for other reasons. Through electrical industrialization, socialization has become so efficient that the integrity of society and culture is fractured at each of its junctures. Daniel Bell (1965) cites *the eclipse of distance* as the underlying reality of contemporary industrial process, "an effort to annihilate the contemplative mode of experience by emphasizing *immediacy, impact, simultaneity,* and *sensation"* (p. 220). We used to speak of the ambivalence of the artist toward society; we now speak of his ambivalence toward art. This shift is the theme of a flourishing literature on "mass culture" and the impossibility of artistic excellence, a literature foreshadowed by De Tocqueville, established by Ortega y Gasset, and painstakingly cultivated in more recent years by numerous critics. The consensus, *ad nauseam* but true, is that artistic activity, avant-garde included, pours forth socialized products. The growth of electricity has been insidious. If you turned America upside-down at this moment, its underneath would resemble nothing so much as the innards of a transistor radio. Formerly there was an underground for artistic activity that provided, at least for the while, sheltered enclaves; private weddings of culture and society would take place. Currently the underground is a news network, transmitting Orwellian "prolefeed."

Theatre is especially vulnerable to these difficulties. As a performing art, theatre has direct access to the senses and to the possibilities of *immediacy, impact, simultaneity,* and *sensation.* The eclipse of distance is always an ominous possibility. And it is not difficult to predict in which ways this possibility might be used by people who have come to regard it as an exclusive aesthetic aim. Alas, contemporary theatre abounds in such people who, under the noble guise of creative advancement, are producing theatre as sociologic as James Bond, group therapy, and Broadway. Transcendence is never achieved by trying to go society one better. Though so-called random theatre with its projectors, auditory devices, and actors-as-props tells us something of what is going on *inside* the society, it generates practically no cultural information.

More's the pity, for we seem to be at the brink of a reaction against certain consequences of the socialization process of the past twenty years. I am thinking of the cult of experience. The obliteration of privacy by our surfeit of communication has forced upon us a new standard for achievement. It is no longer enough to want what the other fellow has. In fact, it is often irrelevant. Now we must *feel* what we are informed the other fellow feels. An instance of this is how competitive drug users are about their experiences. LSD users are notorious in this respect—they are always talking it up, reading each other's accounts, and comparing notes. The general population does quite the same with sexual experience. There is an extraordinary preoccupation with feeling enough of the right things, as if normality resides somewhere beyond the frontiers of our personal sensual limits. Surely this is tyranny, the public-opinion kind for which democracy is so often noted. On another occasion—in "Homosexuality and American Theatre: A Psychoanalytic Comment" (1965)—I went to some lengths to show how commercial theatre collaborates in this tyranny.

In the meantime, certain alternatives to commercial theatre have been rather disappointing. I have studied Michael Kirby's (1965) lucid scanning of Happenings, Environments, and Events, and was appalled at the immodest assertion that what he was explicating was The New Theatre. For example, Kirby describes Events:

> A piano is destroyed. The orchestra conductor walks on stage, bows to the audience, raises his baton, and the curtain falls. A formally dressed man appears with a french horn under his arm; when he bows, ball bearings pour from the bell of the horn in a noisy cascade. The form demonstrates a type of performing that is widely used in the new theatre [Kirby calls it "non-matrixed" performance] and is one of its most important contributions. [p. 27]

While all this can be quite wonderful (and I mean this seriously), this is The New Theatre only if you have never seen or heard of vaudeville and burlesque—staple forms for centuries. However, New is the slight necessity in The New Theatre for the harsh and sustained labor of creativity. It seems all inspiration with no elaboration—not even the elaboration we remember in the Marx brothers, who were masters at nonmatrixed Events—and thus The New Theatre parodies a society of fun and ease. The grueling business of choice is referred to higher authorities— Chance, which is Kirby's Welfare State of the mind.

New York City's increasingly active Off Off-Broadway theatre is a somewhat different matter. This is also a serious group of people, and its mistakes can be quite edifying. Since I have an interest in the problems of the actor, my concern is for the actor's plight, a plight that represents larger issues.

Last year, Michael Smith, a theatre critic for New York's *Village Voice*, which is Off Off-Broadway's trade paper, directed Sam Shepard's one-act play, *Icarus's Mother*. The play was done at the Caffe Cino in Greenwich Village. In a piece written for the *Voice*, Smith (1965) called himself to task for the failure of the production "to terrify and shock its audiences." Among the problems he failed to solve, Smith includes the actors:

> Shepard's writing is difficult for actors trained in naturalism (all American actors are). Shepard's characters are certainly alive. But they are not "motivated" in a conventional way. The actors had trouble. When, for example, the two men were called upon to make smoke-signals, they wanted to know exactly what they were doing and why they were doing it; and it was insufficient to tell them, although true, that all they were doing was making smoke signals, and the reason was Shepard's (and the play's) rather than theirs. My first fault was failing to make this clear. [p. 24]

In a similar vein, Joseph Chaikin, an important leader of New York's avant-garde theatre, puts down the "kitchen realism" of "method" acting. Chaikin told Elenore Lester (1966) of the *New York Times*, "In the new theatre [the actor] keeps up his awareness that he's an actor on a stage. Instead of portraying an individual, he's a universal man" (p.D3).

This is precisely the wrong thing to go after. What Smith and Chaikin are talking about, though they nowhere give evidence of knowing it, is their interest in allegorical theatre and therefore allegorical acting. However loud their protests, Brecht is their modern mentor (though they fail to pursue him far enough), and the morality play is their tradition. In this respect, they are right to want their actors to play roles rather than characters. But if that is *all* they want their actors to do, they must use children. Called upon to make smoke-signals onstage, children would never ask exactly what they were doing. They would simply make smoke-signals. You can verify this by attending any assembly-day play at your local elementary school. But trained, adult actors just can't do this. Not any more they can't, unless you drive them crazy.[2] The actor is too much a palimpset upon whom accumulate the cognitive styles available in any given society, and individuality, represented in the cognition of character – as I shall go into before long – is as uneradicable from the actor's present sense of craft as universality, represented by roles.

But the point at the moment is that even if the Smiths and Chaikins succeed, they fail, as any theatre of pure allegory must fail. And this is what is so disappointing: the opposition to commercial theatre has aspired to a theatre of *pure* allegory. Despising the neurasthenia that uptown passes for "method" acting, the Smiths and Chaikins are throwing out the baby with the bath water. Allegory continues to be art only in an alloy with theatre's continuing, leading aesthetic problem: modern realism and its counterpart in character acting. Brechtian theatre is always such an alloy.

But pure allegory in these times is begging for virtue from spiritual paupers. The audience (if it still counts for something more than scapegoating) doesn't possess the reliable alternatives that allegory, in its depiction of moral failure, wants to

---

2. In reading Smith's account of his difficulties with his poor actors, I was reminded of a passage from Stanislavski's stage ethics. "Since time immemorial, the office, taking advantage of the peculiarity of our nature, has been persecuting the actors. Always immersed in their creative dreams, over-worked, their nerves constantly on edge, highly sensitive, unbalanced, and easily depressed, the actors are often quite helpless. They seem to have been created to be exploited, particularly as, giving everything they possess to the stage, they have no strength left for the defence of their human rights." Now add, to the office, the director.

remind it of; further, the acting company also seems impoverished of the sort of vested leadership—call it for the moment cultural wisdom—without which allegory is mere presumption. Given this state of affairs, allegory can purvey only the angry hope that you can repair existence by tinkering with roles, which, unlike character, are social entities. In these times, allegory is morally simplistic and rhetorically preachy, alien to moral eloquence and conducive to puritanism.

I am aware that theatres of allegory and theatres that attempt an aesthetic parody of the electrical *Zeitgeist* are reactions, after all, against larger and more influential theatres of sentimentality and gentility, theatres of decadent grief and experiential mythology. However, in the fervor of reaction there is often a defeating disregard for the distinction between a tradition and a tradition gone wrong. A reaction withers when it neglects to reclaim for itself the tradition it has set out to disabuse. In the '20s, Hemingway had Mark Twain. Tristan Tzara had no one. And that has turned out to be a considerable difference.[3]

Which brings me to my thesis, an argument for the preservation of a piece of modernity. Character as a concept and its histrionic translation by the actor have yet to be exhausted by any aesthetic development of contemporary theatre. And I am thinking of character in connection with theater in an unsurprising, indeed, rather ordinary sense; its expression by, for example, Pirandello and Stanislavski. Moreover, the various "experiments" that ignore or "try to go beyond" this aesthetic centrality are not only wasted spirit, but worse, perpetrate that propagandistic mode of communication consistent with a technologic society.[4] Finally, commerce with the histrionic characterology that has been available since the earlier decades of the

---

3. Tristan Tzara and the post-World War I Dadaists are Michael Kirby's avowed tradition. This is like claiming assets on the basis of bonds issued by the continent of Atlantis.

4. I am using the term propaganda in the broad sense of Jacques Ellul. (Compare his *Propaganda: The Formation of Men's Attitudes*, 1965.) In this sense, propaganda is the environment of instant information, a solvent of ideology, morality, and art. In an age of total electric circuitry, propagandistic communication is omnipresent and imperceptible.

century is indispensible for a theater that aspires to art—and therefore to a presentation of alternatives to the despair and absurdity of our age.

Let me begin with character as a concept. If I speak for the moment as a psychoanalytic clinician, I do so because sooner or later it is character that analytic therapy has to struggle with, and therefore psychoanalysis may well have acquired a view of the concept that is applicable to the aesthetic sense of character.

Consider a patient who comes to an analyst for help. Motivated by one or several conscious, though often vague, complaints called symptoms, the patient consults the analyst in hopes of gaining relief. The method, the patient discovers, is in a sense disarmingly simple. He is to appear for regular appointments of an unvarying length of time, to recline on a couch, and try to say what is on his mind with complete candor. The invitation rests on the guarantee that, on his side, the analyst will not hold the patient accountable for what he says. The analyst promises that he will try to understand the patient rather than punish or praise him. Given this guarantee, the patient has no ostensible reason for not speaking freely.

Yet the patient soon has inklings that in all good faith he is unable to avail himself fully of this freedom. Something unpredictable is operating in the patient, against his intentions. Try as he will, the patient cannot accept some aspect of the guarantee and therefore modifies his speech accordingly.

When the analyst points out how the patient is giving a tempered, if not preordained, report of what he is thinking, the patient's inklings gel into a realization he had not bargained for; namely, that his character is as much at issue as his symptoms. Indeed, the patient will go on to see that his *style* of executing the fundamental rule to speak freely—*his character*—has an important relationship to his original symptoms.

It should be emphasized that the analyst has at no time suggested that anyone can achieve a faultless freedom of speech. All the analyst has been asking is that the patient try; for the analyst knows beforehand that success is precluded by the very nature of the psychic apparatus, which does not tolerate a willy-nilly impulsivity. Of course, what the analyst does not know and what he is prepared to find out are the patient's unique and typical safeguards—resistances—against the impulsivity that the analytic situation invites.

Now, taken together, these safeguards constitute an intervening variable between impulse and behavior. Thus, we can speak of character as *a personal program for converting wishes into deeds.*

To observe that this "personal program" is one of the conservative aspects of the psyche is to distinguish character from those volitional roles we execute in our daily living when we are the "customer," the "host," the "stranger-in-the-elevator," the "doctor," the "celebrity," or whatever, and are performing the gestures and dialogue consistent with these roles. Character is not immediately susceptible to volition or to self-observation. In the analytic situation, for example, the patient's role *qua* role is volitional; however, his character is not. As such, character belongs to the unconscious. "All the world is not, of course, a stage," says Goffman (1959) when examining the myriad roles of everyday life, "but the crucial ways in which it isn't are not easy to specify" (p. 72). One crucial way it isn't is where character is concerned. Character is not a pose but a confirmed plan of action, where "theatricality" (role-playing) leaves off and "authenticity" (identity) begins. It is—if I may be allowed the metaphor—the director behind the self as actor. "Be an analysand," the analyst implores the patient, and when the act begins, the analyst uncovers the director.

Roles are social and embody the forms and rules of our immediate factitious collectivity, while character wants to oppose wholesale submission. It is in this sense a good thing that the patient "resists" the role of patient; for character resistance is precisely where the patient is found to "own" himself, and it is not to remove his character that we analyze it, but to put the patient on better terms with it—to allow his character a wider expressiveness and adaptability by demonstrating, first, its existence, then, its unique viability, where the patient has only been able to dread and doubt his personal selfhood. In Hannah Arendt's work on Eichmann, she warns us of the total theft of personal character that collectivity is capable of. Eichmann's genocidal activities and subsequent legal defense were based on the total submission to his role. The collectivity of the Third Reich succeeded in extinguishing the expression of personal character in all significant respects. Eichmann's personal deeds as a Nazi official were trivialities compared to his social acts, which is why Arendt finds it ironic that he stood trial as an individual for acts performed as a social automaton. I might add that the civil rights movement may be seen as an opposition to the total collectivity of the African-American, who hitherto has been allowed to play only a role in the white American society. Freedom means the opportunity to experience and evolve personal character.

One further distinction: roles are contemporary. Character is familial and historical. Character is acquired in the child's psychological strivings to maintain "oneness" with a parental universe that the child begins to perceive as separate from himself. The child's perception of the dichotomy between himself and his parents begins in the dim awareness that someone other than himself regulates his pain–pleasure cycle. Beyond his immediate wishes, there is a "reality"—a separate being whose cooperation is required for the fulfillment of wishes, a parent with a unique manner of cooperation. This realization is a stunning shock to the infant's sense of unity and omnipotence. However, if the child can adopt the parental style of regulating pleasure and administer it himself—internalize the style—he will succeed in the illusion of "oneness" with his otherwise disembodied universe.

The paradox here is that in pursuing a communion with the family, the laying down of character structure throughout childhood actually guarantees the individual's subsequent separation from the family. What was undertaken for communion leads to individuality. It is no wonder that the analyst's invitation to the patient to put aside the regulatory operation of character is met with resistance; for the invitation threatens this double aspect of character—the sense character affords us of a protective communion with conscience as the representative of the original family, and the sense of separateness, the sense of being a self-determined agent.

The condemnation of conscience as an institution of mind (which is something like condemning dentition because the teeth of civilized man are prey to such disrepair) imparts to character its undesirable connotations of a mask upon the spirit, a corruption of the heart. However, I hope I have suggested that psychoanalysis regards character more dynamically, as an ongoing trial, not between vitality and its suppression, but between two states of vitality: wishes seeking expression and wishes finding expression. And the tension between these two states, the urgency for a conversion of one state to the other in a revision of character, imbues personal existence with purpose. Character evolves, and in this we speak of will and integrity and the effort to survive on one's own terms against the oppressions and temptations of the social world, the resistance against the dissolution of the cultural self in the melting pot of society. Character is not in contest with the heart, but rather with collectivity and personal neurosis.

If this hurried account has done little more than indicate the nature of the subject, this would be quite enough; for what I have been meaning to go on to say is how extraordinary that these considerations should exist at all, that character can be inquired into like this, not simply as a resource, a gift for heroism, as in Prometheus, a *donne* in man's strife with circumstance, but rather as circumstance itself.

Just as in physical science experimental design and instrumentation have become inseparable from the truths discovered, so in psychology the perception of the social world, and hence the experience of reality, is inseparable from the intrusions of character that impart to perception and experience an inextinguishable ambiguity: though we function in the "real" world among consensual realities, we do so on the basis of a personal program originating elsewhere.

Henry James has stated this ambiguity in terms of "reality" and "romance," "the things we cannot possibly not know" and "the things that, with all the facilities in the world, all the wealth and all the courage and all the wit and all the adventure, we never *can* directly know: the things that can reach us only through the beautiful circuit of thought and desire." And James (1950/1907) observes that "of the men of largest resounding imagination . . . we feel . . . that the reflexion toward either quarter has never taken place" (pp. 267–268). This ambiguity is one of the significant aesthetic counterparts of the broad philosophic drift defining the modern age, and the maintenance and exploration of this ambiguity have been central to those achievements that are both modern and art.

In theatre, *Hamlet* predicts this epistemologic tradition and fore-shadows much of the writing and staging of Western theater since its social glory in the Restoration and Romantic doldrums in the early nineteenth century.

In *Hamlet*, the execution of a deed steadily loses way to a search for the personal modality of the deed—a search for Hamlet's character within the various mandates of his social position. Indeed, so important is this search that the outcome of the play in the narrow sense of "plot" is the play's least engaging element: after Ophelia's death, the mounting carnage seems to matter less and less, until the death of Claudius occurs almost as a feeble afterthought of the playwright. The conflict within Hamlet is not a conflict of equal and contending social proprieties, the outcome of which would possess some sort of ultimate instruction for the audience. Scripture fades in *Hamlet* against the incandescence of its hero's characterologic vitality. In no other play of Shakespeare, not even in *The Tempest* with its crypto-commentary on the playwright's own theatrical career, is there such abounding prepossession with the ambiguities of personal histrionics and social action. The problem was not to be treated again quite so nakedly until Pirandello. "In our time," observes Francis Fergusson (1949), "Pirandello's desperate theatricality is seen as having been anticipated by Hamlet the *improvisateur*" (p. 160). The problems of Hamlet are the problems of modern realism: What are the consequences to existence when truth depends upon the strategies for establishing it? What are the moralities of self-consciousness?

As for staging, the theatre of modern realism thrusts the actor into the very center of the theatrical event. Like Paganini, Shakespeare, in the writing of *Hamlet*, casts the performer as virtuoso, a role elusively part of, yet apart from, the play's central personage. This treachery plagues every staging of *Hamlet* and exemplifies the leading aesthetic problem of the actor in modern theater—the interpretation of action through characterologic nuance and rarefaction.[5]

Steadily increasing concern with internal process is a well-known feature of the history of Western acting. The expositions of Cicero and Quintilian on acting are early codifications of oratory, rhetoric, declamation. By the mid-eighteenth century, Diderot was urging the actor to adopt "naturalism" —that sheltered valley between classicism and realism. Stanislavski developed the idea that the stage role should be a revelation of a uniquely fashioned style of action, an idea that has always haunted theatre, to be sure, but that Stanislavsky deserves credit for, because he articulated it into methodology.

The personal revision this methodology emphasizes is so "psychological" that the director has become an institution within which the actor can find the emotional permission for an otherwise internally restricted adventure in personal character revision. The director is a relatively recent development in theatre. He appeared in the latter part of the nineteenth century, but acquired his powerful function only with the proliferation of modern realism. A temporary externalization of a restricting piece of the actor's psyche (a piece largely of conscience), the

---

5. Whether this should or should not obtain is not a new dispute. Francis Fergusson, on the subject of modern realism, which he sees as our present phase of theatrical evolution, notes a difference in opinion between Henry James and T. S. Eliot on the matter of the histrionic property of modern realism, "its close dependence upon acting," which "Henry James regarded as a sure sign of its vitality, and Eliot regard [ed] as a weakness." Fergusson sides with James, holding that "in their direct histrionic awareness the masters of modern realism are most closely akin to the intentions and the modes of awareness of Shakespeare and Sophocles" (1949, p. 160). the latter representing a harbinger of the shift in vision from anagogic to intrapsychic regulation. There is a lesson here. While Eliot's ideologic need to postpone coming to terms with the issues of modern realism may account for the impressive, though slight, successes of Eliot's early attempts at theater, it also accounts for the excesses of his middle career. *Murder in the Cathedral,* a lamentable failure (as Eliot himself attested), suffers from Eliot's almost stubborn refusal to respond to Shakespeare and Chekhov at the time he wrote the play. *The Cocktail Party,* though of a lesser magnitude than *Murder in the Cathedral,* is nevertheless a more viable piece of dramaturgy, for, by this time, Eliot was more hospitable to modern realism. However, it must be said that ultimately Eliot, like James, seemed to have lacked a certain indispensible quality of temperament for genuine playwriting.

director cooperates in the actor's character revision. The ideas arising in the relationship between director and actor are among the most important the actor deals with onstage. A paradigm of the child–authority relationship, the director–actor relationship is also paradigmatic of the universal process of acquiring character structure and autonomy.

If artistic techniques are solutions to the problem of finding meaning and value for the materials generated by the activities of society, that is, of establishing ideology for social happenstance, then character-acting can be regarded as a celebration of the continuity of the self within the flux of social roles.

But with this have we come to the end of something?

The question is heuristic and suggests the further question: what makes us think so?

I have alluded earlier to Joseph Chaikin's dissatisfaction with "kitchen realism." Chaikin is not alone, of course. He reflects a neither small nor esoteric uprising of opinion against those melodramatic eccentricities to which character-acting has deteriorated in American theatre. But he is also not alone in wanting to go on to reject the underlying technical model that "kitchen realism" misrepresents. Robert Brustein (1965), a more conservative voice, gives utterance to the same wish. Comparing the Moscow Art Theatre, during its last visit to New York, with American companies, Brustein praised the Russian company for their ability to "attain a high level of emotion without ever spilling over into hysteria." The actors, he observed, "change personality radically from role to role instead of repeating personal mannerisms; and although they are closely identified with their characters, they are not lost in them." And Brustein attributed this superiority to the Russians' firm grasp of the Stanislavski system, which bears as much relation to American method acting "as caviar does to hot dogs." However, in the end, Brustein found the Moscow Art Theatre "old-fashioned," and he concluded that "it is always a difficult thing to reject a father, especially a powerful and brilliant one, but until the American theatre can break the bonds of naturalistic truth and psychological reality, there will be no real advance" (p. 26).

But why exactly do we have to reject a father, especially a powerful and brilliant one? Here it seems entirely arbitrary, a bit of sheer oppositionalism. In art, progress-for-the-sake-of-progress is fatuous radicalism, which is of course no stranger to the artistic community; it is usually with the passage of time that we are able to distinguish novelty and juvenilia from "real" advance. But these days are especially rife with notions of progress, such thoughtless notions that the idea of experimentation (that patient and contemplative procedure) has become practically synonymous with public announcements of a theater company's day-to-day metabolism. Progress-for-the-sake-of-progress is why we want to go to the moon. As an aegis for theater, this is a doubtful doctrine. Though full of lip-service to the contrary, it leads directly to socialization.

The line from *Hamlet* to Chekhov to Pirandello to Brecht, Genet, and Beckett, however, is our "real" advance, the line having been extended by an *unavoidable* necessity, if the maelstrom of social process was to be accommodated symbolically. The anagogue falls away; the cherry orchard is destroyed; imagination loses its moorings and drifts with the freedom of exile; society is about to be wholly shaped by the contention between human beings and a totally efficient industrialization, urbanization, and bureaucratization. The profoundest revelation of this epic controversy is achieved in the intricate reciprocities of role and character by which the work of Brecht, Genet, and Beckett is most typified. To urge going beyond their formal and ideologic accomplishments only encourages, it seems to me, a fragmentation of the past several decades of theatrical advance. Specialization in one or another part of an otherwise complicated whole is one of the meanings of decadence. Such promptings as are now articulated, especially among the current avant-garde, do not promise even decadent theatre, which can be interesting (as John Osborne is, for example), but merely fragmented theatre: an unconstrained mischief done with the forms and ideologies of a maturing tradition.

Here theatre reveals itself as part of a more general state of affairs having to do with what Leslie Fiedler (1965) has called the new mutantism, "the relationship of the young to what we have defined as the tradition, the world we have made for them." The new mutants, Fiedler complains, want to be "drop-outs from history," to obliterate "the notion of cultural continuity," and "it is not merely a matter of their rejecting what happens to have happened just before them, as the young do, after all, in every age; but of their attempting to disavow the *very idea of the past*, of their seeking to avoid recapitulating it step by step" (p. 509, italics mine).

This new mutantism is an adolescence from which there is no exodus, because the leaders embody no rules for membership requiring an *active* and *sustained* psychological effort. (Fiedler notes the unremitting passivity of this social movement.) Characteristic of adolescence is the hope that you can *be* something without having to *become* it, and with the waning of this myth, a new maturity arises in the life cycle and experience produces not only pleasure but wisdom as well. But to persist in the hope of being without having to become is to remain an *amateur* in a perpetual state of rehearsal for a life still waiting to be lived.

To return to theatre: though it is true that "the world we have made for them" is not one that easily invites notions of continuity and recapitulation in our youth, it is not true that only two choices exist: either drop out or dance to the piper—The New Theatre or Broadway Commercialism.

Again, I am thinking of the actor, whose predicament in theater is always the most naked, if not the most crucial. Never before in the history of Western theatre has the actor confronted the opportunity for such diversity of performance. It is not possible to find in any other period of acting the necessities for complex skill that modern realism generates. The interaction in modern theatre of so many human stances—the postures, rhetoric, masks, movements of social roles, and the deep emotional themes of a continuing self—demands an unusual breed of actor, with a histrionic cunning large enough to encompass the muralistic formalities of classic theatre and the awesome ambiguities of characterologic experience. This is theatre's third choice—the intelligence to seize and develop this opportunity.

"The power of the amateur," to use another of Joseph Chaikin's phrases, will not do, nor will Maryat Lee's "drama in the streets and at the crossroads: the next step."[6] The anti-institutionalized, grassroots, hit-and-miss mentality professionalizes no one, and professionalism is what the actor above all is most in need of. Among Stanislavski's most important contributions to the art of training actors was his perception of this very need in the actor. *An Actor Prepares* remains a living masterpiece if for no other reason than that it conveys that indispensible atmosphere of a studio-school, an *enduring* institution through which a trainee proceeds toward professionalism. There are no accidents in the history of ideas. Stanislavski's idea of the "studio" comes forth with the compensatory security for those courageous trials of transformation that theatre was about to require of the actor.

Beyond adolescence a labile and tenuous character structure is a kind of sickness, the common symptom of which is a sense of fraudulence, as if whatever we do lacks authenticity and amounts only to a con game. To the actor, however, this sickness is his stock-in-trade. He is free of it only onstage when he is performing and ultimately when he achieves an identity as a professional actor, which is more than a role, but a way of life, something he has *become*. Since he enters theatre precisely because he has never become anything, he is asking for the opportunity to instrument his being, to cure his sickness. It is no favor to the actor to ease his apprenticeship with lenient short-cuts and assurances that what he is to begin with is little less than what he has to be. The self-conscious and cumbersome routines that the advanced professional can go on to discard must first be acquired before discarding them makes any sense. That a certain actor of acknowledged excellence can tell a joke to a stage-hand in one moment and in the very next moment appear onstage "in character" is no lesson at all. Nor is the ideology of breaking bonds with an old-fashioned father (as if a teacher were *really* a father) a humane one for the actor. An actor needs a long and difficult condition of servitude. If we can distinguish authority from authoritarianism—so poorly distin-

---

6. Course 1416 of The New School's Department of Theatre and Cinematic Arts.

guished at this moment—we can meet this need in good conscience. This is exactly what Stanislavski understood so well.

With this, we have arrived at the epitome of the general issues explored by modern theater in the twentieth century: implementation of myriad roles by a single personal selfhood. Any retreat from, or short-cut in, the confrontation of this problem is a resignation from culture and a submission to collectivity, which, in these times, has become a less than moral direction. If our recent history has taught us anything, surely it has taught us this.

Though many of us would hold that any specific expectation of art is ultimately a matter of faith, I like to think that the moral expectation continues to be a matter of good faith. Among the meanings of morality is the interpretation of immediate experience in accordance with a vision less tentative than such experience ever allows. In this sense, the artist continues to be an exemplary moralist. Indeed, if he is not this to begin with, I cannot see how anything he does will stand a chance against the terrible gamble he faces in the contest between his personal talent and the materials at hand.

REFERENCES

Bell, D. (1965). The disjunction of culture and social structure. *Daedalus*, Winter, pp. 208–222.

Brustein, R. (1965). Russian evenings. *The New Republic*, February 27, pp. 26–28.

Ellul, J. (1965). *Propaganda: The Formation of Men's Attitudes*. New York: Knopf.

Fergusson, F. (1949). *The Idea of a Theatre*. New York: Doubleday.

Fiedler, L. (1965). The new mutants. *Partisan Review*, Fall.

Goffman, E. (1959). *The Presentation of Self in Everyday Life*. New York: Doubleday.

James, H. (1907). Preface to *The American*. In L. Trilling, *The Liberal Imagination*, pp. 267–268. New York: Viking, 1950.

Kaplan, D. M. (1965). Homosexuality and American theatre: a psychoanalytic comment. *Tulane Drama Review* 9(3):25–55.

Kirby, M. (1965). The new theatre. *Tulane Drama Review* 10(2):23–43.

Lester, E. (1966). He doesn't aim to please. *New York Times*, December 25, D1–D3.

Smith, M. (1965). *Village Voice*, December 2, pp. 19–24.

22

The Future of Classical Psychoanalysis

The term classical psychoanalysis conjures up—I think it is safe to say in every clinician—certain inevitable images and thoughts: the reclining patient with the analyst seated behind him—in the zealous quiet, the patient is talkative and not too agitated; the analyst is very attentive, yet inclined to do as little as possible; and the dialogue between them is searching and, at any random moment, probably inconclusive—the session seems to be filled with great concern about what the patient is saying and going through; yet, peculiarly, the ending of the session is not momentous—or, at least, neither person does anything to indicate that it is, for they appear to have learned that this session is one faint unit in a process that is measured by seasons and years—the sessions will go on and on. . . .

. . . At which point in our imaginings we begin to find ourselves gravitating toward one or another side of a controversy. We begin to feel a necessity to defend the scene or modify it, if not attack it. A battleline is drawn between familiar ideologic categories—progressive and reactionary, for example, liberal and orthodox. And try as we may, it is often difficult to remain uninvolved in the controversy, since the controversy finds expression in the actual affairs and politics of our analytic groups and associations. Those of us who identify with the psychoanalytic movement have been, at one time or another, in those situations where, for the moment, the most important information about a colleague has been his reputed position on classical psychoanalysis. (I say reputed, because with greater familiarity it always turns out that the other fellow is never quite enough of what we are.) In such situations we are convinced that this information alone can sustain our colleague's entire claim for good or for evil. Also, what we think our analytic orientation to be is very often a guide to how we make referrals, to how we respond to professional literature, to what conferences and symposiums we attend and do not attend, and in what spirit.

I could go on to much more that the term classical psychoanalysis conjures up—a certain attitude toward Freud, for example, and the history of the psychoanalytic movement—but whatever more the term suggests would, in any event, lead us on to the controversy I suggest here, and it is the controversy I want to say some things about: principally, that the controversy regarding classical psychoanalysis is a matter ultimately of values, and for this reason the controversy cannot be resolved by appeals to impartial procedures, such as the collection of so-called facts about so-called cures. Indeed, I think the controversy is so much a matter of values that I suspect you have the values first, or acquire them somehow, and then you go on as a clinician to choose among the available psychological therapies and theories. It is for this reason that classical psychoanalysis can be congenial even to those professionals who are not therapists, or even clinicians. I know several psychologists who are not therapists but whose values deeply commit them to a psychoanalytic conceptualization of the psychological problems they encounter in testing and experimentation. As for nonclinicians, there is something different in the values of Freudians such as Stanley Edgar Hyman and Lionel Trilling, on the one hand, and non-Freudians such as Alan Watts and Norman Mailer, on the other. Thus I should not think it strange that a classical analyst need not be doing psychoanalysis exclusively in his practice, or doing it even at all in his clinic affiliation. He need only maintain a commitment to it as an ideal; this will influence his practical decisions and actions as a therapist, a supervisor, an administrator, or whatever. The ideal sets his entire professional tone; for the ideal is really an election of values.

Moreover—and here I shall tip my hand completely—it is my

sense that the values underlying the election of a classical psychoanalytic orientation have never been so crucial as they are today for the profession as well as for our patients. Nor can I imagine any future where I should not want to see these values operating.

But let us enter the matter through certain specifics of the controversy over classical psychoanalysis as therapists are familiar with them.

We have all heard the general alarm that times have changed and that those who continue with a classic model of psychoanalytic procedure are doomed to obsolescence. The argument runs that psychopathology and social character have changed, and our procedures must change accordingly. Also, patients have surrendered much of their previous opacity to the psychoanalytic movement; that is, we know much more about them than formerly, and they, on their side, are less guarded; consequently, we can be more active and direct in our approach—treatment can be speeded up. Then we hear that philosophically our patients have arrived at a different set of conditions from those within which earlier analytic patients functioned; this also poses a challenge to our conduct with patients. Finally, the population explosion, an increasing sense of personal welfare among vast numbers of individuals, a greater distribution of wealth, and other social factors create a taxing demand for psychotherapeutic service; and this makes painfully clear what was true all along—the folly of inexpedience that is psychoanalysis, like sending into a disaster area one chauffer-driven Rolls-Royce, when for the same money you can have an excellent fleet of secondhand buses.

Though I believe that the observations leading to these various recommendations are often shallow, I have not presented these contentions in order to argue with them. I have presented them simply to call attention to a commonality among them: In each contention the rationale for modifying or rejecting the classic model is supplied by certain imputed characteristics of the patient. Here we are reminded that the surest step to a repudiation of classical psychoanalysis is the adoption of a patient-orientation.

The alternative is the proposition of classical psychoanalysis that practice and research are identical operations. This does not mean that the classical analyst cares less about his patients than other therapists. What this means is that therapy is a function of arriving at an explicit comprehension of the way in which a particular psychology—psychoanalysis—finds expression in an individual patient.

Now those who are of the belief that the classical point of view tends to subordinate the patient's individuality to a pre-conceived system should notice that within this proposition the most lively variable is the patient. The technique and theory, though complex, are nevertheless stable, or, at least, tend toward a stability. It is the patient who possesses all the distinction and variation. It is the patient's own personal version of psychoanalytic theory that the analyst is so attentive to. Indeed, the extent of the emergence of the patient's unique version of psychoanalysis—which, because it is unique, cannot be coerced—is the extent of his cure.

This identity between practice and research has an important effect upon the analyst's concern with matters of immediate social style and social technique in his patients: his concern with these matters is traditionally secondary. Again, this does not mean that the analyst is insensitive and naive with respect to his patients' vocabulary, conventions, social ideals, contending value systems, vocational problems, role availabilities, dating and sexual formalities, familial patterns, and dynamics. On the contrary, in the course of his practice, the analyst acquires an astonishing knowledge of the form and content of numerous levels and enclaves of society. However, these are not the ultimate factors with which he aims to come to terms, for the analyst is essentially a psychologist. Thus, for example, where others are primarily interested in the theatricality of everyday life, the analyst's interest goes on to a psychology of the imposture and, further, to a theory of identification; where others are interested in the epidemiology of sexual promiscuity, the analyst is interested in the defensive and adaptive properties of acting out; where others are interested in social roles, the analyst is interested in character; and so on. These distinctions in interest are quite clear in a comparison of professional journals, a comparison of, say, *The Journal of the American*

Sociological Association, The Journal of the American Orthopsychiatric Association, and any of the several strictly psychoanalytic journals.

What is of primary concern to the analyst are not the instrumentalities of social adjustment but a theory of mind. Consider the manner by which the repetition-compulsion was originally isolated and formulated as a concept. This aspect of an evolving instinct theory—a still controversial aspect—was conceivable because the identity between practice and research insures the analyst a certain amount of resistance against technical modifications by the phenomena he observes and works with. Thus it happened that psychoanalytic technique failed as a variable with respect to a certain kind of data being generated by the patient; that is, interpretations (a term I shall return to shortly) had no discernible influence on the repetition of reports of certain kinds of behavior; this behavior, moreover, appeared to lack an expected relevancy to pleasure. Withal, there was a conviction that the analytic technique was generally sound—not complete in all respects—nothing in psychoanalysis is—but generally sound. Therefore this seeming impasse in the progress of analyzing the patient's mind was imputed to the patient's psychology, not to the analyst's ineptness, or to a changing social climate. I needn't remind you that the repetition-compulsion was postulated in a period of striking social transition; however, a review of the analytic literature around World War I does not reveal any marked increase in references to social events and changes—where reference is made, it is usually in support of an already existing feature of analytic theory, not a clarion call for a revision of the theory or practice. To a technique-oriented mentality, on the other hand, any challenging aspect of the patient's psychology is a signal, not for studious consideration and conference, but for a technical somersault.

I can see where many professionals would be impatient with, or opposed to, the position being described here and would prefer to pursue activities other than the research psychology implicit in psychoanalytic practice. As I have said, this is a question of values, and some of them I think are already evident: For example, the analyst wants to remain more distant from current centers of social change and action than most of his colleagues. The analyst is not an activist. He is less responsive to the actual systems of social and class relationships than he is to the long-range symbolic expressions of these relationships; this is to say, he is more responsive to cultural than societal data and is generally skeptical of the enthusiasms of the immediate present. He views his patient historically in the context of a life cycle related to a past, present, and future generation rather than in the context of a social present. As a psychologist, he is interested in modern ideas, not current ideas, and as a practitioner, he is committed to modern techniques, not current techniques. To him psychoanalysis happened only yesterday; the debris of that explosive revolution in psychology has yet to settle, let alone be collected and sorted. In short, the analyst's dissent combines the virtues of both the conservative and the radical.

However, I must say in passing that I cannot see how it follows from these values that the classically oriented psychoanalyst is inevitably a rigid intellectual—a cold fish; unless this prevelant notion is informed by the misconception that different kinds of knowledge possess different temperatures. Thus, precisely how a split occurs and functions in a patient's superego is comparatively cold knowledge, while what the best strategy is to encourage one patient in a therapy group to emote toward another patient is comparatively warm knowledge. . . .

But I do not want to be carried away into the vendetta with those who measure the superiority of their emotional capacities by the distance they have traveled from Freud—or, rather, their misreading of Freud. Such would-be celebrities are at any rate lost causes, for they break covenant with a fundamental ethic of the psychoanalytic movement: This ethic has it that analytic careers should not be based on differences and dissatisfactions with Freud. We are entitled, of course, to differences and dissatisfactions—Freud is not God. But we are supposed to do something less narcissistic with our differences and dissatisfactions than to enshrine them and establish coteries and discipleships. . . .

I have used the term interpretation, a term whose complex referent I want to avoid getting into too deeply at the moment.

Whatever more an interpretation is, suffice it to say it is at least thoughtful and verbal. It is also declarative, as against, say, hortatory, inspirational, or parabolic.

Now it is another proposition of the classical point of view that a psychoanalysis proceeds by interpretations. Though numerous noninterpretive interventions may be used more frequently than interpretation—probing, clarification, and silence, for example—interpretation is the only intervention that actually produces an analytic experience in the patient.

Here, I should like to amplify this by specifying what psychoanalysis has centered upon as a least but necessary component of the analytic experience—and I should like to proceed with a minimum of that expository caution that this subject customarily inspires—I am defining policy, not trying to sell an idea. For this I shall have to allude to the ideas of transference and resistance, the interpretation of which—that is, the declarative reference to which—produces the analytic experience in the patient.[1] But I shall first have to remind you of a justly celebrated shift in Freud's thinking about anxiety, an incident in the development of the psychoanalytic psychology of mind that dealt the final blow to any remaining "cathartic" conception of analytic therapy.

While it is an oversimplification of an earlier period of Freud's writing to say that he believed that anxiety and its equivalents resulted exclusively from "damned-up libido," the heavy interest in the instincts in Freud's earlier writing did invite such a limited conception of symptomatology in the everyday practice

---

1. We shall never be allowed to forget that Freud once said that if you work with transference and resistance, you are doing psychoanalysis. For we are often told this by practitioners who quote Freud's remark but in the mode of children who have to defy authority by complying with the letter of the rule to the discredit of its spirit, which in this instance is to be gleaned from the larger context of Freud's general canon. It is not the work itself with transference and resistance that defines the analytic point of view, but the *goal* of the work. Otherwise psychoanalysis is anything anybody does who has been alerted to the existence of a set of reactions that are bound to accrue to a relationship in which one person seeks help from another. I can see the advantage of wanting definitions of comparable breadth for generics like psychology and psychotherapy. But I cannot see the point of wanting definitions of such breadth for a specific like psychoanalysis.

of psychoanalysis, a limited conception of not only the etiology of anxiety, but of its phenomenology as well. The point of analytic therapy was to free the libido, which was poorly regulated by the patient's faulty psychogenetic habits of perception. With this accomplished, the "symptoms" should vanish, as well they might under the endorsement of the analyst as liberator. Trauma and its consequent frustrations were the therapist's principal challenges. "Catharsis" was enjoying a prolonged twilight in the procedures of clinical psychoanalysis.

Freud gave utterance to his dissatisfaction with this merely partially tenable scheme when he turned his attention upon the details of the regulatory function of the ego. Frustration of libido lost its centrality in the theory of neurosis. In Freud's somewhat later view, frustration itself does not give rise to neurotic suffering; it is rather the circumstances that frustration reminds us of that give rise to neurotic suffering. The unattended appetite of the infant may be singularly painful at first. But with the maturation of the psychic apparatus, frustration guides the infant to a cognizance of the *circumstances* of the frustration. Frustration alerts the maturing infant to a realization that the mothering activity in the environment is autonomous from the infant's wishes. Henceforth, frustration reminds the child of the disturbed communion between himself and the world and motivates his regulatory activity in the direction of repairing the communion. Freud speaks of separation-anxiety and the defenses that it motivates.

The paradox of ego-activity is that its efforts at reestablishing communion only assure a further separation. Identification, which seeks a "oneness" with parental power, also guarantees individualization. Thus, to the growing child, objects are "gained" and "lost" by the same defensive processes. With analytic ego-psychology, the ambiguities of selfhood—the losses in the gains—have replaced the biologistic preoccupations of former analytic practice, preoccupations that are now subsidiary in the larger scheme of treatment. The ego—the patient's personal program for converting wishes into deeds—is now the subject of analytic therapy. Insofar as the wishes and the deeds can be distinguished from the intervening program, they are subsidiary.

Consistent with the ambiguities of ego-psychology, we can

speak of resistance in terms of how the patient endeavors to maintain *both* a communion with and a separation from the analyst in one and the same moment of interaction with the analyst. To put it another way, resistance is an effort to ward off an ambiguity by maintaining an ambivalence. Resistance—the patient's actual, active endeavor—originates in the patient's transference, which is an inclination to construe that the analyst requires the same style of expressiveness from the patient as the patient's original environment. Now if the analyst can maintain the courage of his conviction that a conscious ambiguity is more adaptive than an unconscious ambivalence, he will resist the inclination on his side to indicate by word or deed that the patient's transference situation is a viable substitute for the perception of its alternative in the current "reality" of the analytic situation. The analyst will remain, as we say, neutral and will allude in a declarative manner to the patient's unsolicited ambivalence.

The preparation for such an allusion, its timing, its actual articulation, the cogency of evidence to support it, the unyielding conviction in the allusion in the aftermath of its effect upon the patient—these, alas, are matters of individual talent and experience, which vary greatly from analyst to analyst. However, the point here is that the allusion aims to produce an ambiguous effect: liberation (=separation) coupled with sadness (=mourning). Whatever else the allusion produces, the presence of this dual effect in the patient's experience indicates the achievement of an analytic experience and verifies that the intervention producing it was an interpretation.

This dual effect is a far cry from the comparatively simplistic effect of "catharsis," wherein the analyst replaces neutrality with permissiveness; and, of course, the effect differs from a supportive intervention by which there is an attempt to stress the viability of this or that aspect of the patient's transference—every transference contains viable features that the analyst can sponsor by replacing neutrality with collusion. But if it is psychoanalysis that we want to do, I think it is right to suspect ourselves of not doing it when, in response to our calculated efforts, the patient fails to experience this double aspect of relief and depression, this *sine qua non* of the analytic intervention.

But, again, whether or not it is desirable for an analytic

experience to occur is a matter of values. There are indeed many worthwhile "non-analytic" experiences, and there are many ways of approaching patients other than psychoanalytically. Moreover, all psychotherapies affect psychological states in ways that could be called "healing." (So do drugs heal, as well as faith, time, luck, money, and electric shock.) Thus, object lessons by means of certain staged behavior on the part of the therapist can be a powerful therapeutic strategy. Also, a well-timed exhortation can have a profound influence upon the morale of a patient, as can a well-told anecdote, a display of affection, generosity, favoritism, or sacrifice. Patients can also respond in a manner called "positive" to teasing and derision. Nor can it be denied that the conversion of a character disorder into a psychopathy or a neurosis into a perversion is, after all, a new lease on life. It is futile to argue for or against a therapy on the basis of the therapy's sheer effectuation.

Moreover, I do not think that professional and public consensus is much to the point in deciding among psychotherapies. That four-and-a-half billion man-hours were spent by Americans last year watching television does not mean that the novel is dead or obsolete, or that the study of higher mathematics is an unprofitable pursuit. Similarly, that the preponderance of patient hours is nonanalytic, where it very well could be, means nothing with regard to the obsolescence of psychoanalysis.

What we sometimes forget is the distinction between obsolescence and uncommonness. In a frantically expanding mental-health profession, the "third-ear" is bound to be a rare instrumentality of treatment, for it is the antithesis of the time-conserving formulas of psychotherapeutic mill-work, and that style of attention that we call "listening with the third-ear" is an essential prerequisite for making an interpretation. Every interpretation is custom-fashioned for the individual patient; it is a unique hypothesis about a unique sequence of data. This is why an interpretation is difficult to arrive at and to render, and also why its achievement imparts a freshness and vitality to the patient–therapist interaction, which no amount of tricks, provocation, or high-spirited running-off-at-the-mouth can ever duplicate. Indeed, I should go so far as to say that any patient of any amount of sophistication who is being subjected to the grab-bag stunts and homilies of a therapist who himself has never really learned to listen knows with the anxiety and bitterness of secret envy that somewhere there are patients blessed with the fortune of being listened to with a shrewd and practiced attention. It is unthinkable that our social style has so changed—jet-set included—that sheer personal attention, our loveliest of courtesies, is no longer wanted or needed.

The idea of treating the person rather than merely his symptoms is the psychological counterpart of the long-standing clinical view that a symptom originates in some underlying disease process, and if you neglect the process, you cannot really cure the symptoms. With the advent of psychoanalysis and the attendant rise of so-called dynamic psychiatry, psychological symptoms were attributed to underlying conflicts in the person himself, or, as it is put, in the personality, and these conflicts should be treated rather than the symptoms. Psychoanalysis and its various psychotherapeutic derivatives aimed to treat the morbid process in the personality, the process that was giving rise to the patient's presenting symptoms. Today we are so used to this thinking that we lose sight of how daring an idea this originally was when Freud first elaborated it around the turn of the century.

Alas, I wonder whether we are so used to this thinking that it has begun to fail as a guiding principle of psychotherapy. Much of the current talk of brief psychotherapy, for example, has begun to sound like a relapse into a symptom-orientation and a remerging with that large section of psychiatry that has never quite gotten out of the nineteenth century.

Here the classical psychoanalytic position distinguishes itself from this regressive trend by the proposition that treatment should have a beginning, a middle, and an end; it should consist of stages; it should be a plan, a format for its own development and progress—there are first things first, second things second, and so on. Since symptoms are relatively immediate phenomena of a vaster psychological process, they cannot dominate a procedure geared to a program that is earnestly inhospitable to the immediate. Though psychoanalysis begins with final products—symptoms—it proceeds on much more.

If I have couched these assertions in a way that conveys an

idea of formalism in classical psychoanalysis, I have done so purposely. I do not think formalism is avoidable by any approach, the claims of Existentialists and other intellectual anti-intellectuals to the contrary. Whatever our school of thought we share a common responsibility of stating the policies of our procedures and the values related to them.

Since we are not spared the necessity of making procedural choices, the choices at least should be clear. If we live in an age where identification is an especially tenuous process in our patients, do we want to address this problem by a strategy of multiple roles in the therapist and arbitrary treatment arrangements, or by an attempt to present one prevailing identity in the therapist and a rather consistent set of arrangements? If the population and communication explosions have created an ambience of interrupted privacy and frenetic togetherness, do we want to treat our patients in groups with other patients, or do we want to provide a situation for solitary contemplation? If the tempo of our age is quick, do we want to respond with quick therapy, or the slower-paced inquiry of psychoanalysis? If estrangement and alienation are thought to be frequent affect and ideational states in contemporary patients, do we take cognizance of this state of affairs with a simplified program for thoughtlessness and sensation, or with a complex and difficult program for comprehension and insight? In short, do we codify society or treat individual patients?

My point has been that the alternatives are both viable. But you can choose only one; that is, you can be Freudian or something else; I cannot see how you can really be both. And while it is true that in our everyday practices a classical psychoanalysis is more an idea than an actual event (if, indeed, it is ever more than an idea), the values underlying the idea influence the therapist's style of conduct with patients no matter what difficulties his patients present. It should come as no surprise by this point that I would feel better about an analyst not doing psychoanalysis with a patient than I would about a nonanalyst not doing psychoanalysis.

A word about the future: naturally, concern about the future of psychoanalysis varies with a person's point of view.

To the orthodox person, psychoanalysis has always been ruined by newcomers—it will never be again what it once was and ought to be—only a Messianic event, possibly a second Freud, will restore the lost glory. But, of course, orthodoxy is perpetually prepared to begrudge recognition to the very Messiah it so devoutly longs for. In orthodoxy, then, psychoanalysis possesses only a past, and a sheltered present is the guarantee of this past in the future. We should rue the position of the orthodox analyst, were it not that he refers no longer to psychoanalysis but rather to a set of postures having reference only to proprieties and improprieties. Concerned with manners more than science, he is no analyst but a dandy, and what he says of the future of psychoanalysis, though sometimes amusing, is largely irrelevant.

To the liberal, psychoanalysis has a future on the basis of the liberal's infallible faith in the adaptability of any idea. Since psychoanalysis is, to the liberal, a rather immense idea, it possesses an unfathomable adaptability. We should take heart in this optimistic projection, were it not that the liberal is bereft of those criteria for determining when in the course of unraveling a sock he has finally lost the garment and is in possession instead of a tangle of wool.

To the progressive, the future of psychoanalysis really doesn't matter. An avowed pragmatist, the progressive analyst is in more truth an archcynic. To him, psychoanalysis is merely one more arbitrary cosmology in a vast world containing many. The progressive is the mental-health worker *par excellence*. Making his daily way, he has nothing left for the future.

In answer to all of which I should say that I am not without moments of admiration for the work being done in the present, which at times compares quite favorably with the past and even exceeds the past in confronting detail and employing precision. This augurs well for the future. Nor do I feel hopeless about continuing to define psychoanalysis as a distinct theoretical program and methodology. And while it is true that psychoanalysis is only one of numerous possibilities for a human psychology, it is at least one of the better ones, so that only in the event of some kind of Neanderthal future can it find no necessity or purpose.

As for the very distant future, psychoanalysis is after all a limited thing. But there, too, though it is bound to perish, it will also survive.

PUBLICATIONS OF DONALD M. KAPLAN

BOOKS

The Domesday Dictionary: An Inventory of the Artifacts and Conceits of a New Civilization (co-authored with Armand Schwerner and Louise J. Kaplan). New York: Simon & Schuster, 1963 (McGraw-Hill Paperback, 1964).

Editor. *Language and Communication*. A special issue of *Psychoanalytic Review*, vol. 51, no. 1, 1964.

Assistant Editor. *Psychoanalysis in America*. Springfield, IL: Charles C Thomas, 1966.

PAPERS

The emergence of projection in a series of dreams. *Psychoanalytic Review*, vol. 49, no. 1, 1962, pp. 37–52.

Homosexuality and American theatre: a psychoanalytic comment. *Tulane Drama Review*, vol. 9, no. 3, 1965, pp. 25–55.

Classical psychoanalysis: policies, values and the future. *Psychoanalytic Review*, vol. 53, no. 1, 1966, pp. 99–111.

Character and theatre: psychoanalytic notes on modern realism. *Tulane Drama Review*, vol. 10, no. 4, 1966, pp. 93–108.

The vanishing art of psychoanalysis. *Harper's*, February 1967.

Freud and his own patients. *Harper's*, December 1967.

Theodor Reik: a student's memoir. *American Imago*, vol. 25, no. 1, 1968, pp. 52–58.

Theatre architecture: a derivation of the primal cavity. *Tulane Drama Review*, vol. 12, no. 3, 1968, pp. 105–116.

Psychoanalysis since Freud. *Harper's*, December 1967.

Psychoanalytic psychotherapies. *Professional Digest of the New York Society of Clinical Psychologists*, vol. 3, no. 3, 1968.

On the dialogue in classical psychoanalysis. An address to the faculty and fellows of the Menninger School of Psychiatry, October 30, 1967. In *Use of Interpretation in Treatment*, ed. E. Hammer, pp. 129–140. Grune & Stratton, 1968,

On stage fright. *The Drama Review*, vol. 14, no. 1, 1969, pp. 60–83.

A rejoinder to Ackerman on the language of psychotherapy. In *Language in America*, ed. N. Postman et al., pp. 149–154. Indianapolis, IN: Pegasus, 1969.

Comments on the screening function of a "technical affect," with reference to depression and jealousy. *International Journal of Psycho-Analysis*, vol. 51, no. 4, 1970, pp. 489–502.

Gestures, sensibilities, scripts. *Performance*, vol. 1, no. 1, 1971, pp. 31–47.

On transference love and generativity. *Psychoanalytic Review*, vol. 58, no. 4, 1972, pp. 573–580.

On shyness. *International Journal of Psycho-Analysis*, vol. 53, no. 3, 1972, pp. 439–453.

The psychopathology of television watching. *Performance*, vol. 1, no. 3, 1972, pp. 21–29.

Reflections on Eissler's concept of the doxaletheic function. *American Imago*, vol. 29, no. 4, 1972, pp. 353–376.

A technical device in psychoanalysis and its implications for a scientific psychotherapy. *Psychoanalysis and Contemporary Science*, vol. II, ed. Benjamin Rubinstein, pp. 25–41. Macmillan (and The Research Center, New York University), 1973.

On preaching old virtues while practicing old vices: a psychoanalytic perspective on morality. *Bulletin of the Menninger Clinic*, vol. 39, no. 2, 1975, pp. 113–130.

Freud and the coming of age. *Bulletin of the Menninger Clinic*, vol. 40, no. 4, 1976, pp. 335–356.

Differences in the clinical and academic points of view on metapsychology. (Invitational George S. Klein Memorial Address, American Psychological Association, 1976.) *Bulletin of the Menninger Clinic*, vol. 41, no. 3, 1977, pp. 207–228.

Harry Slochower's *Mythopoesis*: some personal and social reflections. *American Imago*, vol. 35, nos. 1/2, 1978, pp. 11–15.

The sexual revolution: psychoanalytic perspectives. *Bulletin of the Association for Psychoanalytic Medicine*, vol. 18, no. 2, 1979.

Some conceptual and technical aspects of the actual neurosis. *International Journal of Psycho-Analysis*, vol. 65, no. 2, 1984, pp. 295–305.

"Thoughts for the Times on War and Death": a psychoanalytic address on an interdisciplinary problem. *International Review of Psycho-Analysis*, vol. 11, no. 2, 1984, pp. 131–141.

Reflections on the Idea of Personal Fate and Its psychopathology: Helene's Deutsch's "Hysterical Fate Neurosis" revisited. *Psychoanalytic Quarterly*, vol. 53, no. 2, 1984, pp. 240–266.

The training analysis from a classical point of view (Summary of Division 39, Section I Symposium on the Training Analysis: American Psychological Association Convention, Washington, DC, August, 1986). *Round Robin*, December 1986.

Three commentaries on female sexuality in Freud's thought: a prologue to the psychoanalytic theory of sexuality. (William I. Grossman, M.D., co-author). In *Fantasy, Myth, and Reality*: Essays in Honor of Jacob A. Arlow, ed. Harold Blum et al., pp. 339–370. Madison, CT: International Universities Press, 1988.

The psychoanalysis of art: some ends, some means. *Journal of the American Psychoanalytic Association*, vol. 36, no. 2, 1988, pp. 259–294.

The place of the dream in psychotherapy. *Bulletin of the Menninger Clinic*, vol. 53, no. 1, 1989, pp. 1–17.

An introduction to Reik's "The Characteristics of Masochism." *American Imago* (50th Anniversary Issue), vol. 46, 1989.

Surrealism and psychoanalysis: notes on a cultural affair. *American Imago*, vol. 46, 1989.

Some theoretical and technical aspects of gender and social reality in clinical psychoanalysis. *Psychoanalytic Study of the Child*, vol. 45, 1990, pp. 3–24.

What is sublimated in sublimation? *Journal of the American Psychoanalytic Association*, vol. 41, no. 2, 1993, pp. 549–570.

Theory as practice. *Psyochoanalytic Inquiry*, vol. 14, 1994, pp. 185–200.

The unfinished manuscript in the drawer. *International Journal of Psycho-Analysis*, vol. 76, no. 2, 1995, pp. 283–298.

BOOK REVIEWS

Szasz, T. (1957). Pain and pleasure. *Psychoanalysis*, vol. 5, no. 4.

Feigl, H., Scriven, M., and Maxwell, G., eds. (1958). Concepts, theories and the mind-body problem. Vol. II, Minnesota Studies in the Philosophy of Science. *Psychoanalytic Review*, vol. 45, nos. 1/2.

Masserman, J. H., ed. (1958). Progress in Psychotherapy, vol. II: Anxiety and Therapy. *Psychoanalytic Review*, vol. 45, nos. 1/2.

Nelson, B., ed. (1959). Freud and the twentieth century; Sigmund Freud: on creativity and the unconscious. *Psychoanalytic Review*, vol. 46, no. 1.

Atkinson, J., ed. (1959). Motives in fantasy, action and society. *Psychoanalytic Review*, vol. 46, no. 2.

Inhelder, B., and Piaget, J. (1960). The growth of logical thinking from childhood to adolescence. *Psychoanalytic Review*, vol. 47, no. 2.

Stein, M. R. (1961). The eclipse of community; J. Grotjahn, psychoanalysis and the family neurosis. *Psychoanalytic Review*, vol. 48, no. 1.

Sherman, M., ed. (1962). A Rorschach reader. *Psychoanalytic Review*, vol. 49, no. 3.

Westwood, G. (1962). A minority. *Psychoanalytic Review*, vol. 49, no. 4.

Deutsch, F. (1963). Body, mind and the sensory gateways. *Psychoanalytic Review*, vol. 50, no. 4.

Shakow, D., and Rapaport, D. (1964). The influence of Freud on American psychology. *Psychoanalytic Review*, vol. 51, no. 4.

Ernst, M. L., and Schwartz, A. (1964). Censorship. *Psychoanalytic Review*, vol. 51, no. 4.

Erikson, E. H. (1965). Insight and responsibility. *Psychoanalytic Review*, vol. 52, no. 1.

Leavy, S. A. (Tr.) (1965). The Freud journal of Lou Andreas-Salome. *Psychoanalytic Review*, vol. 52, no. 3.

Bernays, E. L. (1966). Biography of an idea. *Psychoanalytic Review*, vol. 53, No. 4.

Reiff, P. (1966). The triumph of the therapeutic. *The Village Voice*, September 15.

Shapiro, D. (1967). Neurotic styles. *Psychoanalytic Review*, vol. 54, no. 1.

Abt, L., and Weissman, S. (1967). Acting out: theoretical and clinical aspects. *Psychoanalytic Review*, vol. 54, no. 4.

Wheelis, A. (1967). The illusionless man. *The Village Voice*, February 23.

Manheim, E., and Manheim, L. (1968). Hidden patterns. *Psychiatry & Social Science Review*, vol. 2, no. 2.

Laing, R. D. (1968). The Politics of Experience. *The Village Voice*, March 7.

Brome, V. (1968). Freud and his early circle. *The New Republic*, June 15.

Rosen, R. (1968). Madness in society; W. Sargent, the unquiet mind. *The New York Times Sunday Book Review*, July 21.

Luria, A. R. (1968). The Mind of a Mnemonist. *The New Leader*, August 26.

Schutz, W. (1968). Joy. *Psychiatry & Social Science Review*, vol. 2, no. 9.

Flescher, J. (1969). Dural therapy and genetic psychoanalysis. *Psychoanalytic Review*, vol. 56, no. 3.

Seely, J. (1969). The Americanization of the unconscious. *American Imago*, vol. 26, no. 1.

Blanck, G., and Blanck, R. (1969). Marriage and personal development; W. Lederer and D. Jackson, the mirages of marriage. *Psychiatry & Social Science Review*, vol. 3, no. 3.

Schafer, R. (1969). Aspects of internalization. *Psychiatry & Social Science Review*, vol. 3, no. 6.

Moss, N. (1969). Men who play God. *The Village Voice*, June 5.

Malko, G. (1970). Scientology: the now religion. *The Village Voice*, December 17.

Baker, E. (1970). Man in the trap; F. Robinson, the Freudian left. *Psychiatry & Social Science Review*, vol. 4, no. 6.

Abrahamsen, D. (1970). Our violent society; R. Rose, violence in

America; D. Demaris, America the violent. *The Village Voice*, June 11.

Ekstein, R., and Motto, R. (1970). From learning for love to love of learning. *Contemporary Psychology*, vol. 15, no. 9.

Slochower, H. (1970). Mythopesis. *Psychiatry & Social Science Review*, vol. 4, no. 13.

Millett, K. (1971). Sexual politics. *Psychiatry & Social Science Review*, vol. 5, no. 5.

Schutz, W. (1971). Here comes everybody. *The New York Times Sunday Book Review*, July 4.

Kohut, H. (1972). The analysis of the self. *Psychiatry & Social Science Review*, vol. 6, no. 2.

Holt, R. (1972). New horizons for psychotherapy. *Psychiatry & Social Science Review*, vol. 6, no. 14.

Kanzer, M. (1972). The unconscious today. *Contemporary Psychology*, vol. 17, no. 2.

Chesler, P. (1973). Women and madness. *The Village Voice*, October 11.

Foucault, M. (1973). The birth of the clinic. *The Village Voice*, November 22.

Reich, W. (1974). The Cancer Biopathy. *The Village Voice*, Jan. 24.

Levenson, E. (1974). The fallacy of understanding. *Bulletin of the Menninger Clinic*, vol. 38, no. 1.

Schechner, R. (1974). Environmental theater. *The Village Voice*, March 13.

Blanck, G., and Blanck, R. (1975). Ego psychology: theory and practice. *Bulletin of the Menninger Clinic*, vol. 39, no. 5.

Kramer, R. (1976). Maria Montessori. *The Village Voice*, August 16.

Giovacchini, P. (1976). Psychoanalysis and character disorders. *Contemporary Psychology*, November.

Waelder, R. (1977). Psychoanalysis: observation, theory, application. Selected papers. *Contemporary Psychology*, March.

Fromm, E. (1977). To have to to be. *Contemporary Psychology*, July.

Sulloway, F. (1979). Freud: biologist of the mind. *The Village Voice*, November 5.

Langs, R. ed. (1980). International Journal of Psychoanalytic

Psychotherapy, vol. 7, 1979. *Contemporary Psychology*, January.

Stolorow, R., and Atwood, G. (1980). Faces in a cloud. *Psychiatry*, vol. 43, no. 2.

Epstein, L., and Feiner, A., eds. (1981). Countertransference. *Contemporary Psychology*, January.

Clark, R. W. (1981). Freud: the man and the movement. *American Journal of Orthopsychiatry*, January.

Gedo, J. (1981). Beyond interpretation. *Psychoanalytic Review*, vol. 68, No. 2.

Thomas, D. M. (1982). The white hotel. *American Journal of Orthopsychiatry*, vol. 52, No. 1.

Leavy, S. A. (1982). The psychoanalytic dialogue. *Contemporary Psychology*, February.

Schafer, R. (1983). The analytic attitude. *The Village Voice*, September 3.

Kurtzweil, E., and Phillips, W., eds. (1984). Psychoanalysis and literature. *Contemporary Psychology*, September.

Pruyser, P. W. (1985). The play of imagination: toward a psychoanalysis of culture. *Contemporary Psychology*, April.

Richards, A., and Willick, M., eds. (1986). The science of mental conflict: essays in honor of Charles Brenner. *PANY Bulletin*, vol. 24, nos. 3/4.

Bromberg, N., and Small, V. V. (1987). Hitler's psychopathology. *Journal of the American Psychoanalytic Association*, no. 3.

Bergmann, M. S. (1988). The anatomy of loving. *Readings*, vol. 3, no. 3.

The Menninger Clinic's training video on dreams. *Bulletin of the Menninger Clinic*, July.

Simon, B. (1990). Tragic drama and the family: psychoanalytic studies from Aeschylus to Beckett. *International Review of Psycho-Analysis*, no. 1.

Limentani, A. (1991). Between Freud and Klein: the psychoanalytic quest for knowledge and truth. *Contemporary Psychology*, October.

Lindemann, C., ed. (1992). Handbook of phobia therapy. *Psychoanalytic Quarterly*, 51, No. 2.

Middlebrook, D. W. (1992). Anne Sexton, A biography. *Read-*

ings: A Journal of Reviews and Commentary in Mental Health, March.

Schafer, R. (1992). Retelling a life: narration and dialogue in psychoanalysis. *Psychologist-Psychoanalyst* (APA, Div. 39 Newsletter), Fall.

Dowling, S., ed. (1992). Conflict and compromise: therapeutic implications. *Contemporary Psychology*, December 1992.

Young-Bruehl, E. (1992). Creative characters. *International Review of Psycho-Analysis*, vol. 19, no. 4.

Friedman, R. C. (1993). Male homosexuality: a contemporary psychoanalytic perspective. *Journal of the American Psychoanalytic Association*, vol. 41, no. 1.

Nemeroff, R. A. et al., eds. (1994). On loving, hating and living well: the public psychoanalytic lectures of Ralph R. Greenson, M. D. *Contemporary Psychology*, January.

Sandler, J. et al., eds. (1994). Freud's "On Narcissism: An Introduction." *Journal of the American Psychoanalytic Association*, vol. 42, no. 3.

CREDITS

The editor gratefully acknowledges permission to reprint the following:

Chapter 1: Originally published as "The Unfinished Manuscript in the Drawer" in *The International Journal of Psycho-Analysis*, vol. 76, no. 2, 1995. Copyright © 1995 by The Institute of Psycho-Analysis.

Chapter 2: Originally published as "Some Theoretical and Technical Aspects of Gender and Social Reality in Clinical Psychoanalysis" in *Psychoanalytic Study of the Child*, vol. 45, 1990. Copyright © 1990 by Yale University Press.

Chapter 3: Originally published as "The Place of the Dream in Psychotherapy" in *Bulletin of the Menninger Clinic*, vol. 53, no. 1, 1989. Copyright © 1989 by The Menninger Foundation.

Chapter 4: Originally published as "Reflections on the Idea of Personal Fate and Its Psychopathology: Helene Deutsch's 'Hysterical Fate Neurosis' Revisited" in *Psychoanalytic Quarterly*, vol. 53, no. 2, 1984. Copyright © 1984 by *The Psychoanalytic Quarterly*.

Chapter 5: Originally published as "Some Conceptual and Technical Aspects of the Actual Neurosis" in *The International Journal of Psycho-Analysis*, vol. 65, no. 2, 1984. Copyright © 1984 by The Institute of Psycho-Analysis.

Chapter 6: Originally published as "On Shyness" in *The International Journal of Psycho-Analysis*, vol. 53, no. 3, 1972. Copyright © 1972 by The Institute of Psycho-Analysis.

Chapter 7: Originally published as "On Transference-Love and Generativity" in *Psychoanalytic Review*, vol. 58, no. 4, 1972. Copyright © 1972 by *Psychoanalytic Review*.

Chapter 8: Originally published as "Comments on the Screening Function of a 'Technical Affect,' with Reference to Depression and Jealousy" in *The International Journal of Psycho-Analysis*, vol. 51, no. 4, 1970. Copyright © 1970 by The Institute of Psycho-Analysis.

Chapter 9: Originally published as "On the Dialogue in Classical Psychoanalysis. An Address to the Faculty and Fellows of the Menninger School of Psychiatry, October 30, 1967" in *Use of Interpretation in Treatment*, ed. E. F. Hammer, published by Grune & Stratton, 1968. Copyright © 1968 by Emanuel F. Hammer.

Chapter 10: Originally published as "Freud and His Own Patients" in *Harper's*, December, 1967. Copyright © 1967 by *Harper's*.

Chapter 11: Originally published as "The Emergence of Projection in a Series of Dreams" in *Psychoanalytic Review*, vol. 49, no. 1, 1962. Copyright © 1962 by *Psychoanalytic Review*.

Chapter 12: Originally published as "What is Sublimated in Sublimation?" in *Journal of the American Psychoanalytic Association*, vol. 41, no. 2, 1993. Copyright © 1993 by International Universities Press.

Chapter 13: Originally published as "Surrealism and Psychoanalysis: Notes on a Cultural Affair" in *American Imago*, vol. 46, 1989. Copyright © 1989 by The Johns Hopkins University Press.

Chapter 14: Originally published as "The Psychoanalysis of Art: Some Ends, Some Means" in *Journal of the American Psychoanalytic Association*, vol. 36, no. 2, 1988. Copyright © 1988 by International Universities Press.

Chapter 15: Originally published as " 'Thoughts for the Times on War and Death': A Psychoanalytic Address on an Interdisciplinary Problem" in *The International Review of Psycho-Analysis*, vol. 11, no. 2, 1984. Copyright © 1984 by Donald M. Kaplan.

Chapter 16: Originally published as "Freud and the Coming of Age" in *Bulletin of the Menninger Clinic*, vol. 40, no. 4, 1976. Copyright © 1976 by The Menninger Foundation.

Chapter 17: Originally published as "On Preaching Old Virtues While Practicing Old Vices: A Psychoanalytic Perspective on Morality" in *Bulletin of the Menninger Clinic*, vol. 39, no. 2, 1975. Copyright © 1975 by The Menninger Foundation.

Chapter 18: Originally published as "The Psychopathology of Television Watching" in *Performance*, vol. 1, no. 3, 1972. Copyright © 1972 by The New York Shakespeare Festival Public Theatre.

Chapter 19: Originally published as "On Stage Fright" in *The Drama Review*, vol. 14, no. 1, 1969. Copyright © 1969 by *The Drama Review*.

Chapter 20: Originally published as "Theatre Architecture: A Derivation of the Primal Cavity" in *The Drama Review*, vol. 12, no. 3, 1968. Copyright © 1968 by *The Drama Review*.

Chapter 21: Originally published as "Character and Theatre: Psychoanalytic Notes on Modern Realism" in *Tulane Drama Review*, vol. 10, no. 4, 1966. Copyright © 1966 by *Tulane Drama Review*.

Chapter 22: Originally published as "Classical Psychoanalysis: Policies, Values and the Future" in *Psychoanalytic Review*, vol. 53, no. 1, 1966. Copyright © 1966 by *Psychoanalytic Review*.

INDEX